Trade Strategies for a New Era

Trade Strategies for a New Era

Ensuring U.S. Leadership in a Global Economy

Edited by Geza Feketekuty
with Bruce Stokes

A COUNCIL ON FOREIGN RELATIONS BOOK
Published with the Monterey Institute of International Studies

COUNCIL ON FOREIGN RELATIONS BOOKS

THE MONTEREY INSTITUTE OF INTERNATIONAL STUDIES

The Monterey Institute is an internationally recognized academic institution which has developed a broad range of training and graduate degree programs. The Center for Trade and Commercial Diplomacy at the Monterey Institute was established in 1995 to train the next generation of trade negotiators and commercial diplomats. It is a global center of trade education and research with a broad range of experts in business and trade in residence. The globalization of the world economy has created a growing demand for professionals equipped with the analytical and practical skills required for effective commercial diplomacy. The Monterey Institute provides hands-on, comprehensive training for trade professionals in business and government.

Council on Foreign Relations Books are distributed by Brookings Institution Press (1-800-275-1447). For further information on Council programs and activities, please write the Council on Foreign Relations, 58 East 68th Street, New York, NY 10021, or call the Director of Communications at (212) 434-9400.

Library of Congress Cataloging-in-Publication Data
Trade strategies for a new era : ensuring U.S. leadership in a global economy. / edited by Geza Feketekuty with Bruce Stokes.
     p.   cm.
Includes bibliographical references and index.
ISBN 0-87609-209-1
1. United States—Commercial policy. I. Feketekuty, Geza.
II. Stokes, Bruce.
HF 1455.T658   1997
382'.3'0973—dc21   97-50081
                                  CIP

CONTENTS

FOREWORD

As America approaches the end of the century, it stands astride the global economy. Over the last two generations the United States has taken the lead in liberalizing its own economy and in prodding other nations to lower their trade and investment barriers. No country has benefited more from the "magic of the global market" than the United States. But to maintain its leadership and to continue to enjoy these benefits, the United States needs to reshape its trade policies to reflect the changing nature of the world economy. The recent crisis in the Asian financial markets underscores this need.

With possible new multilateral trade negotiations looming early in the next century, with ongoing regional trade discussions in Latin America and Asia, and with continuing bilateral trade issues on the trade agenda, the United States needs a new vision for the new millennium. To meet that challenge and provide that vision, the Council on Foreign Relations is pleased to publish *Trade Strategies for a New Era: Ensuring U.S. Leadership in a Global Economy*, edited by Geza Feketekuty with Bruce Stokes.

The Council is deeply indebted to Geza Feketekuty, director of the Center for Trade and Commercial Diplomacy of the Monterrey Institute of International Studies, for conceiving this project, assembling the authors, and shepherding them to a final product. For years Geza was the visionary policy planner at the U.S. Trade Representative office in Washington. This book testifies to the continuing vitality of his insights.

Bruce Stokes, a Council Senior Fellow and one of the nation's foremost commentators on trade policy, not only contributed a chapter to the book but also edited much of the volume and coordinated the Council's participation in the project.

Les Gelb, the Council's president, has brought a new sense of purpose to all that we do here. His support for serious analytical work in the area of economic foreign policy has charted a new course for the Council. And his admonition that the Council's work make a difference has helped shape this book in many ways.

The Council's production family pitched in with enthusiasm to ensure that the book was both professional in content and published in a timely fashion. Early on, David Kellogg recognized the importance of this work, helped shape its presentation, and was a constant source of innovative ideas. Patricia Dorff and Sarah Thomas ushered the book through several edits, managed the production process, and contributed many helpful editorial suggestions.

Trade Strategies for a New Era: Ensuring U.S. Leadership in a Global Economy is just one of many books that will be published by the Council's Studies Department on America's deepening engagement in the world.

Gary C. Hufbauer
Director of Studies
Council on Foreign Relations

PREFACE

Two years ago, when I retired after 21 years of service with the Office of the United States Trade Representative (USTR), I decided to commission a comprehensive forward look at U.S. trade policy. My last several years at USTR convinced me of the need for such a volume. With the conclusion of the Uruguay Round of multilateral trade talks, the United States entered a new era of trade policymaking. In the face of widespread skepticism about the merits of the globalization of the American economy, the United States needs new policies to maintain its leadership on international trade issues, to ensure that its business continues to have the opportunity to compete in world markets, and to secure for its people a broad distribution of the benefits of global economic growth. The introduction of fast-track legislation by the Clinton administration presented the country a new opportunity to begin debate on a comprehensive trade strategy for the 21st century. It is my hope that this volume will help guide the vital national discussion ahead.

This volume would not have been possible without the contributions of numerous individuals. First and foremost, the authors of the various chapters need to be recognized. It was truly rewarding to bring together such a knowledgeable group. Indeed, as part of the book project, we held an authors' conference at the Monterey Institute of International Studies in October 1996. The discussions at that conference were particularly rich and thought provoking, reflecting the participants' level of expertise. This group has done an enormous amount of thinking about the various aspects of U.S. trade policy that will need to be addressed in the coming decade. It is my honor to be able to present this thinking in a cohesive package.

One of the authors deserves special mention. In addition to writing a chapter, Bruce Stokes contributed significantly to the actual publication of the book. Bruce spent long hours reading and improving on authors' drafts. He also arranged several Council on Foreign Relations–sponsored events that highlighted the book's findings and recommendations.

I also want to extend my thanks to Congressmen Jim Kolbe and Robert Matsui for contributing a chapter. Much of the public trade policy debate will take place on Capitol Hill. Accordingly, their insights are particularly valuable to a volume such as this one. My sincere thanks to the congressmen as well as to Cynthia Johnson of Congressman Matsui's staff and Everett Eissenstat of Congressman Kolbe's staff.

The three sponsors of the book project need to be recognized. First, the Council on Foreign Relations deserves thanks for publishing the book. Through the Council's sponsorship, the book will reach a wide audience. The Council's Publications Department deserves special recognition for combining speed with quality. David Kellogg, Vice President of Communications and Corporate Affairs, used his extensive experience to guide the process, and Patricia Dorff and Sarah Thomas organized it all. Gary Hufbauer, the Council's Director of Studies, gave the project his wholehearted support, ensuring the book's timely publication. Eric Drabiuk, a Council research associate, spent long hours helping to coordinate matters from the Council's end. A special thanks to the Ford Foundation for its financial support of the Council's participation in the project.

The Center for Strategic and International Studies (CSIS) is the second project sponsor. I want to recognize with special thanks CSIS Senior Advisor Peter Watson, who helped organize activities associated with the book in Washington, D.C., and Sinclair Dunlop for his assistance in organizing these events.

Finally, the Monterey Institute of International Studies needs to be recognized and thanked for housing the project. The Institute bore the major costs associated with putting this book together. The president of the institute, Dr. Robert Gard, consistently supported the project, and several members of my staff here at the Center for Trade and Commercial Diplomacy made important contributions. Bill Keller was crucial to getting the project off the ground and also contributed many hours of editing. Sarah Givens not only made significant editing contributions but also spent long hours working on the myriad details associated with the editing of the book and keeping all the authors happy. Sue Karman and Jill Rainbow provided necessary administrative and secretarial support.

Geza Feketekuty
Director, Center for Trade and Commercial Diplomacy
Monterey Institute of International Studies

Chapter 1

An American Trade Strategy
for the 21st Century

Geza Feketekuty

This book weaves together the threads of a new vision for U.S. trade policy and a strategy for pursuing it. That vision must integrate a comprehensive program of multilateral, regional, and bilateral negotiations with a domestic policy agenda that will equip the American people to meet the challenges of global competition.

Since World War II, the United States has played a leading role in global trade negotiations, both for its own domestic economic reasons and for global strategic purposes. The results have been impressive on both fronts. Trade remains the major engine of growth for the economy, with exports expanding more than twice as rapidly as domestic gross national product (GNP) between 1970 and 1994. The economic prosperity of countries that took advantage of global trade liberalization hastened the end of the Cold War. This outcome has validated the bold economic vision set forward after World War II by great American leaders such as George Marshall and Cordell Hull: The expansion of trade based on market principles has created a more prosperous and peaceful world.

Today the United States and the world need a new vision and a new game plan. The globalization of the world economy, the technological revolution that is transforming the workplace, and demographic changes that are straining social welfare systems are creating new challenges and opportunities for trade policy. Unprecedented consensus exists among governments around the globe on the economic advantages of market competition and trade liberalization. At the same time, domestic dislocations are creating new political resistance to competition and trade-enhancing reforms. This situation calls for bold leadership by the president and other world leaders to pursue trade liberalization opportunities and to address the economic and social adjustment problems that most of the world has in common.

In pursuing a proactive trade strategy, the United States should have four strategic objectives:

• A level playing field with respect to all public policies that impede the global contestability of national markets, including domestic regulatory policies, investment policies, competition policies, and policies on bribery and corruption.

• Gradual elimination of tariff barriers to trade by means of regional free trade agreements, global sectoral free trade agreements, and more comprehensive multilateral negotiations at some future date.

• Domestic and international consensus on the best means of strengthening international cooperation on labor and environmental issues.

• Deeper economic, political, and social ties in the three regions bordering the United States—the Americas, the Pacific Basin, and the North Atlantic—established through the negotiation of regional and bilateral agreements appropriate to each region.

Guided by these strategic objectives, the United States should concentrate its near-term effort on dismantling trade and investment barriers that impede foreign market access for the most promising U.S. industries. In general, those tend to be high-value manufactured and agricultural products and infrastructure equipment and services.

The U.S. government will need the support of the American people to implement trade liberalization measures. Many Americans are being asked to change their jobs and even their occupations as a result of recent historic shifts in the world economy. Americans, like people elsewhere, do not like disruption in their lives, the uncertainty it creates for their families, and the loss of income for those least able to afford it.

In order to persuade the American people to support a forward-looking trade agenda, the U.S. government must make it easier for Americans to change their jobs through improved manpower training and education programs and the greater portability of job-related pension and health insurance benefits. The government also should adopt domestic macroeconomic policies and international monetary policies that reduce the adjustment burdens imposed by misaligned exchange rates.

Above all, the president must persuade the American people that the United States must lead international efforts to tear down barriers to trade and investment, both in its own economic self-interest and in the interest of greater world peace and stability. The nation's adjustment problems must be put in perspective. After all, the United States is in better economic shape than most countries in the world, and its adjustment problems pale in comparison with those in most developing countries and formerly communist countries. In view of the military and economic costs imposed by the Cold War, the United States has a tremendous stake in making sure that these countries are smoothly integrated into the world economy.

This book provides insight into these issues, which are at the heart of the current debate over U.S. trade policy, and suggests how the United States could respond to the challenges ahead. Each of the authors has put forward personal ideas that offer policy-makers a number of possible options in the face of future trade challenges.

This chapter seeks to weave together the various issues addressed by the individual authors and to indicate how they could fit into an overarching trade strategy. There is a great deal of consensus among this group of experts on the general directions that U.S. trade policy should take. But the views expressed in this chapter are those of the editor.

THE DOMESTIC ECONOMIC CASE FOR TRADE LIBERALIZATION

Trade has benefited the U.S. economy by stimulating growth, by expanding output in the most productive sectors of the economy, and by creating new jobs that pay above-average wages. Labor productivity in plants producing for export has been 40 percent higher than in equivalent plants producing only for the home market, and salaries for workers employed in export-related jobs have been 15 percent higher than average wages in manufacturing. Employment in exporting plants rose by 9 percent between 1992 and 1997, while employment in nonexporting plants declined by 14 percent. Imports have pushed American firms producing competive products to be more productive. Imports also have raised the standard of living by providing a wider range of goods at competitive prices to American consumers.

Exports and imports together are now equivalent to 24 percent of domestic GNP, compared to 11 percent in 1970. There is every reason to believe that in the future trade will be even more important to the American economy than it is currently. To ensure that trade remains an engine that fuels economic growth, the United States will need to pursue policies that expand access in the most promising markets and sectors.

The United States is currently in an excellent position to take advantage of a proactive trade negotiating strategy. After a period when it had lost its competitive edge in many industries, the country has regained a strong competitive position in world markets. Surveys of the relative competitiveness of various countries have placed U.S. industries on top or close to the top. As Chapter 3 shows, many industries that suffered a deterioration in productivity in the 1970s and 1980s have made major productivity gains in the 1990s. These improvements have enabled U.S. producers to regain foreign markets in key niches of major industries, such as textiles, steel, and glassware—industries previously thought to have been lost to American producers.

The American economy has demonstrated an unparalleled capacity to generate new jobs and new businesses, and has outperformed most other developed countries in the last few years. This makes the American economy appear strong and vigorous to many other countries, even though Americans themselves do not necessarily see their economy in the same light.

GEOPOLITICAL AND GEOECONOMIC OBJECTIVES

For the past 50 years, the United States pursued the global liberalization of trade barriers and the development of global, multilateral trade rules based on market principles for security as well as economic reasons. In fact, during the earlier postwar period, the United States frequently overrode its narrow commercial interests for security reasons. As other countries gained a competitive edge and became more equal trading partners, the United States became less willing to sacrifice its commercial interests for security objectives. Nevertheless, trade agreements still play an important role in achieving broad strategic goals.

Trade agreements now are the principal mechanism for establishing stable relationships among countries. More than at any time since the end of World War II, the overwhelming majority of countries have come to recognize the critical importance of market-oriented policies and trade for achieving economic growth and the concomitant improvement of living standards. An expansion of international trade and investment stimulates growth by exposing industries to international competition and creating new market opportunities. Increased international economic ties have the added benefit of making armed conflict between and among nations less likely.

Trade agreements thus have become perhaps the most important vehicle for pursuing national aspirations in the post–Cold War world. They are effective not only in removing barriers to international trade and investment but also in dealing with a wide range of related topics. Remarkably, countries have proven willing to negotiate on a range of sensitive subjects as part of comprehensive regional economic integration agreements. Both in Europe and in the Americas, many countries have seen regional trade agreements as a convenient vehicle for embedding domestic economic and political reforms, based on market principles and democratic values, in international accords, thus giving the reforms greater permanence. Moreover, regional agreements have proven to be particularly useful for liberalizing trade and investment because often they are easier to negotiate and more flexible, and thus able to address a wider range of issues more quickly.

Regional trade agreements, however, can themselves become a source of international friction to the extent they are preferential and therefore discriminate against nonmembers. Therein lies a dilemma. The challenge for policymakers is to establish some balance between the pragmatic pursuit of regional agreements and efforts to strengthen the multilateral system as a whole. While some degree of discrimination may be necessary both to achieve domestic political support for regional agreements and to create incentives for other countries to engage in negotiations, there should be a conscious effort to use regional agreements to enhance the multilateral system wherever possible. As Bruce Stokes points out in Chapter 9, "the regional aspect of a new strategic vision is already largely in place. . . . [A] new geoeconomic vision requires a renewed American commitment to multilateralism."

ESTABLISHING A LEVEL PLAYING FIELD IN A GLOBALIZED WORLD

The overall objective of a U.S. trade negotiating strategy over the coming years should be what it has been over the past 50 years, namely to remove barriers to international trade and investment and to establish rules for a level playing field. The United States has pursued these objectives in the belief that they are consistent with the American commitment to market competition as the most efficient means both for allocating economic resources and for creating the incentives necessary to spur innovation and entrepreneurship.

The range of issues that need to be addressed by trade negotiations has expanded. Reductions in trade barriers at the border have exposed less visible barriers embedded in domestic regulations. Globalization of production and markets has eroded the boundary between trade and investment and between trade policy and domestic policy. It therefore is necessary to redefine the goal of open trade and a level playing field to encompass not only the absence of trade barriers but also the absence of entry barriers created by domestic regulatory policy or shortcomings in competition policy. This expanded view of the trade liberalization process is embraced by all the authors in this volume and is discussed at greater length in a number of chapters, particularly Chapters 10, 11, 14, 17, and 18.

The United States should firmly embrace this new, broader view of the scope of trade negotiations. It provides a solid conceptual foundation for what the nation has sought in practice through bilateral, regional, and multilateral negotiations and through actions taken under Section 301 of the U.S. trade law. Explicit recognition of this goal will permit more rigorous analysis of the policy requirements for global market competition and provide broader public support for negotiating objectives that otherwise are seen purely as efforts by individual companies to advance their parochial commercial interests.

A foundation for an international consensus on this expanded view of trade liberalization has been built among the relatively developed countries belonging to the Organization for Economic Cooperation and Development (OECD). OECD ministers endorsed this broader view in their 1995 ministerial declaration by stating that future multilateral trade negotiations should seek to assure that national economies are open to global competition or, to use economic jargon, to assure the global contestability of national markets.

OPENING NATIONAL MARKETS TO GLOBAL COMPETITION

A negotiating strategy that seeks to open national markets to global competition must deal with a number of issues beyond the traditional trade barriers at the border. To the extent that they hamper or distort international competition, investment policies, regulatory policies, sectoral or industrial policies, competition policies, and policies concerning bribery and corruption must all be addressed.

The authors in this volume support this expanded scope of future trade negotiations, although they may differ with respect to specific tactics or particular negotiating solutions. Chapters 11, 14, and 17 provide the most detailed discussion of the rationale and dimensions of this expanded scope of trade negotiations, and Chapter 10 discusses its particular relevance with respect to the American bilateral trade relationships with Japan and China.

The United States should declare that it intends to address each of these policy areas in all of its negotiations—bilateral, regional, and multilateral—where that is necessary to assure a level playing field. The emphasis and the nature of specific commitments sought in individual negotiations will inevitably vary in accordance with U.S. commercial interests and with what is achievable in light of the diversity or homogeneity of the countries involved in the negotiations.

Foreign Investment

Foreign investment traditionally was seen as an alternative to trade, and governments pursued agreements on investment independently of trade agreements. It has become increasingly clear, however, that in the case of certain high-value or highly complex and customized products, investment in local distribution, research, customizing, and service facilities is a prerequisite for effective market access. This relationship was considered central in the negotiations that led to the General Agreement on Trade in Services (GATS) during the Uruguay Round. Commitments on investment were made a key component of GATS because it was quite obvious that the freedom to trade a service would be of limited economic value if firms did not have the right to establish themselves in foreign markets. In the new global economy, production, trade, and investment are generally not substitutes but complementary means for achieving the most efficient production and distribution of goods and services.

In light of these new realities, the United States should seek to incorporate investment issues in all future trade agreements, with the aim of allowing firms to choose the most efficient location of production and distribution facilities. Chapters 11 and 17 probe the content of multilateral agreements on investment, whether in the OECD or in the World Trade Organization (WTO). They argue for rules that give foreign firms fundamental rights: transparency of laws and regulations, due process in the administration of such laws and regulations, national treatment of foreign firms, and market contestability (assurance that national markets are open to competitive entry).

Regulatory Policies

Economic regulations that seek to control production, distribution, pricing, employment, and/or investment decisions can significantly impede access to national markets and preclude a level playing field. Legally established monopolies amount to a total ban on trade and international competition. Overregulation at the sectoral level inevitably limits competition and also is likely to provide fertile ground for private anticompetitive practices. Where regulations give bureaucrats extensive discretionary powers and the political process gives affected enterprises the ability to buy influence, bribery and corruption can further impede nondiscriminatory access to markets and limit international competition.

Past trade negotiations have focused on two very important areas of regulation: the establishment of technical standards and sanitary and phytosanitary standards. The relevant agreements negotiated during the Uruguay Round are the Agreement on Technical Barriers to Trade (which deals with technical and regulatory standards) and the Agreement on the Application of Sanitary and Phytosanitary Measures (which deals with measures designed to protect against harm to plants or animals or to humans consuming products made from such plants or animals). Both seek to minimize the deliberate use of standards as barriers to trade and the creation of barriers in the course of establishing legitimate national standards.

Regulatory issues also have been at the core of sectoral negotiations in services organized under the aegis of the General Agreement on Trade in Services in the WTO. The WTO agreement on international competition in telecommunication services (1997) wonderfully illustrates a recent example of such an agreement. Regulatory issues will be at the heart of all serious future efforts to liberalize trade in services, since most barriers to trade in services are embedded in sectoral regulations covering most infrastructure and professional services.

In light of the growing importance of regulatory issues in international trade, the OECD has embarked on an analysis of the relationship between regulatory reform and trade liberalization, with the objective of crystallizing principles and concepts that might aid future trade negotiations. This effort could prove particularly valuable in the area of international competition in services. Chapter 13 describes in some detail the rationale for international cooperation in the regulatory arena and some of the principles that might provide the basis for such cooperation. The subject also is explored in Chapters 10 and 17.

Competition Policies

Private anticompetitive practices can impede international trade and distort international competition as effectively as government barriers, particularly where the government delegates standards making or regulatory enforcement activities to private entities. Governments even may condone anticompetitive activities as a matter of industrial policy. Investment restrictions can prevent foreign firms from gaining access to restricted distribution systems or other essential facilities.

It is generally recognized that competition policy is a difficult area for achieving international agreement, due to sharp differences in policy among OECD countries and the absence of competition laws in many developing economies. Tackling the practices that most distort trade and international competition, however, does not require across-the-board harmonization of antitrust laws. Since the most egregious anticompetitive practices tend to be concentrated in certain industries and types of practices, a focused approach addressing those practices and industries should prove more feasible. Moreover, since government regulation and policy often are at the source of private restraint of trade, a focused effort to reform the regulations involved or to remove unnecessary restraints on the ability of new entrants to invest in distribution systems or essential facilities could prove adequate in many cases. Chapters 10, 11, and 17 provide a range of possible approaches for tackling trade distorting anticompetitive practices at an international level.

Bribery and Corruption

Bribery and corruption can effectively impede international competition where laws prohibiting such practices are weak and government officials have extensive discretionary authority to make purchasing decisions or to issue licenses for regulated activities. The United States has vital interests in this area because bribery and corruption have a particularly important restrictive effect on foreign purchases of infrastructure and construction equipment, areas where the nation has significant competitive strengths. U.S. trade strategy therefore should give priority to international efforts designed to curb corrupt practices in procurement and licensing decisions affecting international trade and investment. Curbing corruption is bound to have major benefits by reducing waste and economic inefficiencies and by contributing to political legitimacy. Few governments can afford to defend such practices.

OECD countries, in response to a U.S. initiative, have negotiated a convention that will criminalize overseas commercial bribery. WTO ministers in Singapore also agreed to conduct a study on transparency in government procurement, which could lead to a strengthening of provisions in the government procurement code providing for transparency and objective bidding procedures. Work that has been launched in the OECD on regulatory reform and trade liberalization ultimately could lead to the adoption of more objective and transparent regulations. These and other initiatives are explored in detail in Chapter 12.

Institutional Issues

U.S. trade negotiating objectives in many areas are intimately related to the development of open institutional processes and modes of governance at both the national and international levels. A market-based system and the ability of U.S. products and producers to compete effectively abroad depend on the transparency of regulations and the activities of rule-making bodies, the observance of due process in both the development of new rules and their implementation, and access to objective, arm's-length dispute settlement processes. Transparency and due process do not eliminate trade barriers automatically, but they are a prerequisite for addressing them in a forthright manner. Moreover, many patently biased and potentially corrupt regulatory or procurement decisions cannot stand the light of day.

As Stokes points out in Chapter 9, "In the future, the pursuit of U.S. economic self-interest necessitates a reaffirmation of American commitment to true democratization. This course is required, not out of any philosophical commitment to one particular form of governance or as part of some new global ideological conflict but because American business functions best in a democratic environment characterized by due process, the rule of law, and transparency in decision making."

In light of the growing economic interdependence among nations and the expanding number of domestic policies affected by international rule making, there is a growing need to establish public access and accountability with respect to the activities of international economic organizations, including the World Trade Organization. Public acceptance of the new compulsory dispute settlement system in the WTO, for example, will hinge on wide agreement by affected interest groups that the process is fair, objective, and gives full consideration to all views and interests. Some progress has been made in shedding greater light on the internal proceedings of the WTO, but more will need to be done to establish the necessary conditions of democratic process.

Dealing with the Social Dimension of International Trade

Trade-related issues affecting the environment and core labor standards often are lumped together as social issues on the trade agenda. These concerns have proven to be highly controversial, both domestically in the United States and internationally. The debate in the United States has tended to divide the broad political coalition that historically has supported trade liberalization. The absence of a compromise on this issue could block political support for future trade negotiations.

The most ardent advocates propose using trade measures to induce foreign governments to adopt higher standards in environmental policies and labor standards. They hope to achieve higher international standards in these areas and to prevent downward pressures on domestic standards that result from international competition. Opponents argue that the inclusion of these topics in trade agreements is an inappropriate intrusion of nongermane and controversial issues into an overloaded trade agenda. They argue that countries should have a right to choose their own levels of performance in these areas, in accordance with a nation's income level and social preferences. Both advocates and opponents make valid points, and there is a need for a pragmatic compromise on these issues.

Environmental Policies

Developing an international consensus on the appropriate ground rules for the use of trade measures for environmental purposes will be very difficult. At the same time, the subject cannot be avoided, because national legislatures, including the U.S. Congress, have passed laws imposing trade sanctions for environmental practices. Moreover, many international environmental agreements contain trade provisions inconsistent with international trade rules under the WTO. And the economic activity spurred by greater international trade can have a negative impact on the environment. A compromise approach would be to allow trade measures where cross-border pollution directly harms the importing country or where a large number of countries agree that certain practices harm the global environment.

In Chapter 15 Robert Morris analyzes the issues under discussion in trade forums that link trade and environment questions and puts forward a number of creative solutions for advancing international consensus.

Labor Standards

Workers in the United States and other developed countries are concerned that open international competition will undermine what they have achieved domestically in labor standards. However, studies carried out in the OECD and elsewhere have failed to find any consistent impact of trade on labor standards, although anecdotal evidence would suggest degradation of work life attributable to trade in particular cases.

This issue sparked a great deal of debate among the authors of this volume. Some, including Michael Hart, believe that dispassionate dialogue within a trade context ultimately could lead to a consensus view on how the WTO and other trade organizations could play a nonprotectionist role in the promotion of labor standards, bolstering political support for open trade policies. Other authors believe that this subject should be kept out of trade negotiations, although they are prepared to suggest alternative means for addressing the issue, such as development of international standards for labeling by the International Standards Organization (ISO 25000) and a new, more vigorous effort in the International Labor Organization (ILO). In principle, a majority of countries have agreed to abide by core labor standards in the framework of the ILO, but there is widespread dissatisfaction with that organization's effectiveness. One possible solution would be to give the WTO a supporting role in enhancing the work of the ILO, by including labor issues in the Trade Policy Review Mechanism or by creating new trade benefits tied to a good record on labor standards. Moreover, discussion of the labor issue in the WTO and other trade fora could spark the political will necessary to reform the ILO to make it a more effective body.

THE MULTITRACK STRATEGY

Since the mid-1980s, the United States has followed a strategy employing bilateral, regional, and multilateral trade negotiations. The nation rightly believed that a range of negotiating options would make it possible to get around countries that do not want to negotiate on particular issues and address more effectively the challenges and opportunities facing the country in particular bilateral, regional, or multilateral contexts. Under the multitrack strategy, the United States negotiated bilateral agreements with Japan and other individual nations, negotiated a regional free trade agreement with Mexico and Canada (North American Free Trade Agreement [NAFTA]), and set long-term targets for free trade around the Pacific rim (Asia Pacific Economic Cooperation forum [APEC]) and in the Americas (Free Trade Area of the Americas [FTAA]). Multilateral negotiations were used to enhance global trade rules and create the World Trade Organization.

All chapters by authors who address negotiating strategy issues in this book—Chapters 7, 8, 10, 17, and 18—support the multitrack approach of bilateral, regional, and multilateral trade negotiations. The authors differ in their degree of enthusiasm for specific bilateral or regional arrangements, but all agree that the United States should continue to place emphasis on strengthening the World Trade Organization as the foundation of the global, multilateral trading system.

The various authors also differ on tactical issues, in particular with respect to the optimal means of advancing specific regional initiatives and future multilateral negotiations in the WTO. These tactical differences provide a varied set of options for implementing a multitrack strategy.

The United States should establish long-term strategic goals that it intends to pursue in all of its trade negotiations. Experience shows that the nation is most successful in obtaining its objectives when it uses all the available negotiating tools—bilateral, regional, multilateral, and unilateral—to pursue clear, overarching objectives. This was a key to the Uruguay Round successes in the areas of trade in services and intellectual property protection. It also might be key to achieving progress on the new generation of issues, such as the elimination of discriminatory investment restrictions, regulatory reform, and the reduction of business practices that restrict trade.

Multilateral Trade Negotiations

The United States should champion comprehensive multilateral negotiations in the future. As Chapter 7 observes, "multilateral negotiations give the biggest bang for the buck. . . . Regional pacts may produce deeper liberalization in specific areas, but none matches the comprehensive coverage of national trade practices contained in multilateral accords that have been negotiated in GATT [the General Agreement on Tariffs and Trade]." Also, as Alan Wolff observes in Chapter 18, "given the openness of the U.S. economy, and a trading system based on the most-favored-nation (MFN) principle, there is no other practical way to spread as far as possible the area of reciprocal openness."

While other countries are now as prosperous as the United States and have a large stake in international trade, the United States remains the country in the best position to provide international leadership for trade liberalization.

Launching comprehensive negotiations across a broad range of issues is likely to be difficult in view of the increasing complexity of the issues and the increasing number and heterogeneity of the WTO membership. Nevertheless, the rest of the world is likely to gauge the U.S. commitment to the multilateral system by its effort to push for comprehensive multilateral negotiations. This is particularly the case if, in the near future, the United States intends to devote considerable energy to regional free trade negotiations. America's trading partners likely would interpret the absence of a forward-looking agenda for the WTO as a decline in U.S. support for the multilateral trading system and a signal that America is unprepared to exercise bold leadership.

The creation of the World Trade Organization and the introduction of biennial meetings of trade ministers has changed the dynamic of negotiations and opened up the possibility of tackling priority issues as they arise. The successful negotiation of agreements at the 1996 trade ministerial meeting in Singapore to eliminate trade barriers in information technology products and to provide competition in basic telecommunication services (the Information Technology Agreement and the Agreement on Basic Telecommunications) set a welcome new precedent for the negotiation of major agreements outside of massive rounds.

Nevertheless, major progress in liberalizing trade across a broad front is still likely to require the periodic initiation of comprehensive negotiations designed to address a range of issues simultaneously. This is necessary, in part, to give enough countries a stake in agreements being negotiated and to raise the political stakes in what is being negotiated high enough to warrant the involvement and support of the top levels in government and business. As former U.S. Trade Representative Robert Strauss used to say, you need a large enough pile of chips on the table to make either a game of poker or a trade negotiation interesting.

The negotiating results of the Uruguay Round included a number of commitments with respect to follow-up negotiations in areas such as services and agriculture and analytical work that could prepare the ground for possible future negotiations in areas such as investment, environment, and restrictive business practices. This unfinished business has come to be dubbed the built-in agenda of the World Trade Organization. At the first regular, biennial ministerial meeting of the WTO in the autumn of 1996 in Singapore, ministers confirmed and expanded this work program, which covers most of the key issues discussed in this book. The work program is likely to constitute the core of comprehensive negotiations that might be launched around the year 2000. It includes issues such as investment, competition policy, sectoral regulations in services, and bribery associated with government procurement. Ministers in Singapore debated but were not able to decide whether and how the WTO should address environment and labor issues; nevertheless, the trade dimensions of these issues will not disappear and a consensus will have to be developed on how best to address them.

A key issue, one not resolved at the Singapore Ministerial, is the future approach to tariff negotiations. This issue is crucial because much of the debate over regional free trade agreements is over the question of nondiscriminatory global cuts in tariffs as opposed to preferential regional tariff reductions. Tariff cuts negotiated within the WTO have to be applied on a so-called MFN basis, which means that they have to be applied to imports from all member countries equally. Tariff reductions negotiated on a preferential basis within a regional free trade agreement are applied only to imports from other countries in the region.

Leaders in the Americas have committed themselves to complete negotiations on the elimination of tariffs by 2005, and leaders from the Pacific region have committed themselves to eliminate tariffs by 2010 with respect to the developed countries and 2020 with respect to the developing countries. A number of opinion leaders, including Fred Bergsten, director of the Institute for International Economics, and Martin Wolf, an editorial writer for the *Financial Times,* have proposed that WTO ministers follow the lead of regional leaders in the Americas and APEC and commit themselves to the complete elimination of tariffs by a certain date.

As an alternative to a commitment to abolish all tariffs by a certain date, the WTO might consider focusing future tariff negotiations on the time period over which individual tariffs are to be phased out completely rather than on the percentages by which tariffs are to be reduced over a fixed period of time (as has been the case in past negotiations). The periods might vary from immediately upon completion of the negotiations to 30 years into the future. Such an approach could be combined with an expanded application of the so-called zero-for-zero or sectoral free trade approach employed in the Uruguay Round and in the more recent Information Technology Agreement. Under the zero-for-zero approach, all major exporting countries agree to phase out their tariffs in particular industry sectors. A third approach would be to convert regional commitments to cut tariffs into global commitments, where trade covered by regional free trade commitments in FTAA, APEC, and a possible Transatlantic Free Trade Area (TAFTA) constituted say 80 percent of global trade.

Any approach to tariff negotiations also will have to address the issue of agricultural products. The liberalization of trade in agricultural products is likely to remain the most difficult area in any effort to dismantle trade barriers. The agricultural agreements reached in the Uruguay Round, which provided for the coordinated reduction of tariffs and of trade-distorting domestic support programs in agriculture, provide a ready-made blueprint for future negotiations in this area. The most promising approach would be to continue, on an accelerated basis, the percentage reductions built into the Uruguay Round agreement.

SECTORAL PRIORITIES

In choosing sectors for particular emphasis in market-opening negotiations, the United States should be guided by the international competitive strength of its industries and the likelihood that producers will be able to take advantage of reduced trade barriers abroad. To a large extent, the identification of such sectors has to result from consultations with the firms involved, as indeed was the case in the Uruguay Round in the selection of sectors for the elimination of tariffs under the zero-for-zero approach.

Chapter 3 provides a detailed analysis of relative U.S. competitive strength through the computation of "revealed comparative advantage" (RCA) indices. The computation of such an index vis-à-vis major trading regions indicates that the United States remains highly competitive in agricultural and other primary products and in chemicals. Analysis of more detailed RCA indices based on more detailed product groupings shows that the United States remains competitive in high-value, technology-intensive products such as pharmaceuticals; manufacturing, construction, and agricultural machinery; professional, scientific, controlling, and medical instruments; power-generating and telecommunications equipment; and aircraft.

The United States needs to give particular attention to its competitive strength in infrastructure equipment and services, covering areas such as telecommunications and data processing, broadcasting, air transportation, and power generation. Forecasts show that many countries will make major investments in these areas in the years ahead. Estimates put the demand for such equipment at $1 trillion over ten years for the Pacific area alone. Since such equipment typically is purchased by government-owned or regulated monopolies, issues concerning government procurement, measures designed to curb bribery and corruption, and regulatory reform take on increased importance.

REGIONAL PRIORITIES

Chapter 3 analyzes recent regional trade patterns. It confirms the growing importance of U.S. trade with its two neighbors and with the Pacific region and the slower expansion of trade with Europe. Trade with South America is gaining rapidly, albeit from a relatively small base. This regional pattern highlights the importance of NAFTA for the United States and the potential benefits of pursuing regional free trade negotiations in the context of the FTAA and APEC.

The highest priority should go to the negotiation of the proposed Free Trade Area of the Americas, for a variety of reasons: geographic proximity; the apparent willingness of the countries involved to tackle the tough issues; and the economic, foreign policy, and security benefits of embedding recent economic and political reforms in an international agreement. Chapter 8 provides a detailed assessment and set of recommendations for negotiating an FTAA.

APEC also presents many potential benefits to the United States, but progress toward the goal of free trade is likely to be slower in light of the greater economic, political, and cultural heterogeneity of the countries involved. In Chapter 8, Ernest Preeg expresses skepticism about the viability of the free trade targets set by APEC leaders, although he and other authors agree that APEC can play a useful role in facilitating the removal of barriers. Trade and economic output within the Pacific region is likely to increase faster than in other regions of the world, and APEC can help assure nondiscriminatory access to these markets for U.S. firms. Moreover, since the greatest bottleneck to continued growth in the region is inadequate investment in infrastructure services, appropriate economic reforms, spurred by APEC, could give the United States improved market access for both infrastructure equipment and services.

Despite the slower growth in transatlantic trade, the U.S. economic relationship with Europe remains crucial for both economic and political reasons. While U.S. firms face few significant barriers to trade and investment in Europe (with the exception of agriculture and some highly regulated services sectors), they do face an increasing number of issues in the area of standards and regulation. In recognition of this fact, the United States and Europe will pursue bilateral agreements in these areas both through a bilateral business dialogue and through negotiations in the context of the so-called Transatlantic Partnership. As Claude Barfield points out in Chapter 13, the United States and Europe face roughly similar regulatory challenges, and their ability to negotiate agreements providing for wider competition in regulated industries, and for mutual recognition of standards and professional licensing, could provide a foundation for broader international cooperation in such areas.

American and European officials have informally explored the possibility of negotiating a Transatlantic Free Trade Area (TAFTA) but decided to set that idea aside. One reason for the reluctance to pursue the idea is the obvious difficulty of removing barriers to trade in agriculture. Another reason was a concern that the negotiation of a preferential free trade agreement between the two principal members of the WTO would have a negative impact on the multilateral system.

Preeg nevertheless believes that the negotiation of a TAFTA would be the key to integrating the regional and global trade negotiating strategies. He also observes that U.S. tariffs are already very low and argues that "the trade and investment effects of a TAFTA should be relatively small, on balance, for all members, and should not provoke the kind of protectionist reaction that occurred, for example, in the United States over NAFTA, based on the fear of job losses to cheap Mexican labor."

This author, along with Preeg and Stokes, takes the view that the establishment of a free trade vision by countries on both sides of the Atlantic ultimately would have a positive impact on the global liberalization of trade by establishing a new dynamic. If a commitment to free trade by the North Atlantic countries was added to the free trade commitments in the Americas and within the APEC region, the advantages of global tariff cuts would become all the more apparent. To reduce concerns that a commitment by North Atlantic countries to eliminate tariffs would undermine the multilateral trading system, the United States could reserve judgment on whether such cuts would be made on an MFN or preferential basis, pending the outcome of free trade negotiations in the FTAA and APEC, and the willingness of enough countries to eliminate tariffs globally.

Other policy analysts have proposed alternative approaches to building regional cooperation across the Atlantic, which would exclude the preferential elimination of duties within the North Atlantic area a priori. Elsewhere, Ellen Frost has argued for the creation of a North Atlantic Economic Space.

BILATERAL PRIORITIES

The United States' bilateral trade relationships with Japan and China deserve special attention. The trade flows involved are large, and the factors influencing them are unique with respect to each country. In the case of Japan, most formal barriers that count have been dismantled, but the domestic regulatory system and the lack of a vigorous competition policy create many internal barriers to trade. In the case of China, its economy is in a transition from a state-run economy to a more market-oriented economy, and at the moment is not quite either. This situation creates a triple challenge—the need to devise a negotiating approach that will address on a pragmatic basis whatever practices or measures most restrict trade at any given point in time, while pushing China toward long-term, market-oriented, domestic economic reforms and market-based trade policy commitments.

The importance and unique aspects of the Japanese and Chinese trade regimes create the need for bilateral negotiating approaches tailored specifically for each country. It would be a mistake, however, for the United States to divorce its bilateral negotiations from regional and multilateral objectives, as it has done so often in the past. By separating its bilateral problem-solving discussions from regional and multilateral discussions and disciplines, the United States at best risks isolating itself from its other trading partners in solving the problems it faces; at worst it risks having other countries undercut the moral authority of its market-oriented negotiating objectives. As Wolff points out in Chapter 18, the United States has to find a way to exploit every source of leverage available to it beyond the leverage inherent in access to its large market, including the use of international dispute settlement procedures and the mobilization of allied commercial interests and public opinion abroad.

Chapter 10 provides a detailed review of the history of U.S. bilateral trade negotiations with both Japan and China. It recommends a coordinated use of bilateral, regional, and multilateral negotiations to tackle the full panoply of government measures and private business practices that impedes access by U.S. firms to these markets. Chapter 18 provides other insights into both the nature of the problem underlying the U.S. bilateral relationship with Japan and China and the nature of the solutions that should be pursued.

The most promising approach to opening up the Japanese economy over the medium term is likely to be a consistent push, in bilateral, regional, and multilateral negotiations, for the establishment of a more vigorous competition policy and the reform of domestic regulations, making them less pervasive, less discretionary, more closely tied to objective performance criteria directly linked to transparent regulatory objectives, and more insulated from the domestic political process, which is tied to personal relationships and mutual favors. The Japanese government and many opinion leaders agree that such reforms are desirable, and the United States should help them overcome the domestic forces of inertia that now hinder the adoption of the needed reforms. This will not solve all ongoing trade problems but will establish a common reference point for more targeted bilateral negotiations aimed at removing specific regulatory obstacles to trade on a case-by-case basis. As Wolff points out in Chapter 18, the United States has no alternative but to seek full market access, however difficult, remote, and friction-laden the pursuit of that objective might be.

The best the United States can do now with respect to China is what it is seeking to do, namely to negotiate a workable set of commitments as part of Chinese accession to the WTO. Such commitments should recognize that China is going through a transition process and establish target dates by which the country will implement commitments consistent with planned domestic reforms. A modestly ambitious schedule of reform commitments could include provisions for the periodic review and renegotiation of Chinese commitments, as China faces bumps in the road to reform and its trading partners discover unanticipated new trade barriers in the evolving Chinese economic system. The key is to establish an ongoing process for balancing rights and obligations between China and the rest of the world as the country proceeds on its road to economic reform.

REMEDIES FOR DEALING WITH PRIVATE TRADE BARRIERS

As Tom Howell contends in Chapter 16, the United States does not have an effective means for dealing with trade barriers resulting from foreign anticompetitive activities. The use of U.S. antitrust statutes under the foreign effects doctrine is one possible tool,[1] but without cooperation by foreign authorities, the Justice Department lacks the means to discover the facts with sufficient rigor to meet the high standards of evidence built into the U.S. legal system. Section 301 of the Trade Act of 1974 provides an instrument that is more adaptable to a foreign trade environment, but the United States lacks an effective and internationally legal remedy. Howell offers suggestions for how such a remedy might be fashioned. The United States needs to explore alternative approaches, including bilateral ones.

The antidumping statutes are a substitute, albeit an imperfect one, for the removal of trade distortions created by private anticompetitive activities. Supporters of current antidumping rules argue that these rules constitute the most effective defense against anticompetitive business practices that are tolerated, and in some cases encouraged, by protectionist foreign governments. Opponents, however, focus on how antidumping laws are used as a competitive weapon against foreign competitors engaged in normal business practices (such as the use of temporary below-cost sales to build markets or to purge excess inventories). An objective analysis of these mutual concerns could provide a way forward.

Antidumping is an extremely controversial area. No other issue was the focus of as much debate and disagreement among the authors of this volume. This disagreement reflects the wide divergence of views among trade policy analysts more generally. A key problem, as Howell points out in Chapter 16, is the absence of credible research by either governments or private research institutions on global market structures and on the impact of private anticompetitive practices and various forms of government intervention on the operation of global markets. The U.S. government should undertake such analyses as a first step toward developing a domestic consensus on how the country could deal effectively with foreign anticompetitive activities and industrial policies.

DOMESTIC ECONOMIC POLICY CONDITIONS

In order to reap the advantages of open international trade and investment and to maintain domestic political support for an open trade policy, the United States has to get its domestic policies right. Decisions regarding crucial domestic economic policies should be closely coordinated with trade policy decisions and made explicit components of the country's trade strategy. This should be the principal role of the National Economic Council in the White House.

Further, the administration should avoid macroeconomic policies that lead to wide swings of the exchange rate, creating uncertainty for international transactions and eroding the credibility of trade liberalization efforts. As Wolff points out in Chapter 18, trade policy is discredited by a 45 percent swing in the yen/dollar relationship over a relatively short time, or a 50 percent devaluation of the Mexican peso overnight.

In Chapter 6, Marina Whitman explains how the increased share of exports and imports in the economy coupled with the internationalization of financial markets has reduced the ability of the United States to conduct its macroeconomic policies without regard to their cross-border consequences. Lapses of fiscal discipline combined with tight monetary policy, for example, are prone to create large swings in the exchange rate, as higher interest rates in the United States attract foreign funds. While this can successfully reduce inflationary pressures in the United States by increasing imports and reducing exports, it does so at a high price for sectors producing goods and services that are exported or that compete with imports. It does not necessarily prevent inflationary price rises in sectors producing goods or services that cannot be traded. The worst part, from a trade policy point of view, is that this leaves both export interests and import-competing interests disgruntled, creating political pressures for protection that are difficult to resist. Whitman points out that "the major guideline for domestic macroeconomic policy that emerges from these lessons of history is to avoid combinations of monetary and fiscal policy leading to sustained currency misalignments, which have in the past exacerbated pressures for trade protection."

A viable trade strategy also has to include supportive labor market and manpower training policies. Trade liberalization, like technological innovation, creates job losses among those who can least afford it, namely low-skilled workers with relatively low incomes. Social acceptance of trade liberalization is affected by the ability of such workers to acquire training in new skills and to move their pensions and health care benefits to new jobs. Chapters 5 and 6 provide many detailed suggestions on how the government could help workers move to new jobs by giving them the training and counseling they need to upgrade their skills and by making their pensions and health care benefits more portable.

During the first term of the Clinton administration, an interagency task force on workforce retraining considered many creative ideas but never pushed them to adoption. One of the most interesting ideas was to use part of the Unemployment Insurance Fund to finance training vouchers for permanently displaced workers. The government also should help local communities to modernize their adult education programs and link them to business-supported counseling services for the long-term unemployed. The country needs to make the adoption of improved manpower training programs a high priority.

GETTING NEGOTIATING AUTHORITY FROM CONGRESS

In order for the United States to pursue its trade objectives around the world, it will need fast-track trade negotiating authority or, as it is currently referred to, Trade Agreements Implementing Authority. Other countries are extremely reluctant to negotiate in earnest with the United States if the president does not have sufficient authority to negotiate international trade agreements without Congress revisiting the details during the ratification process. In granting fast-track negotiating authority, Congress gives up the right to amend the implementing legislation and agrees to limit the use of procedural delays before taking a simple up-or-down vote on the agreement. This leaves Congress with the constitutional role of approving commitments undertaken by the United States in trade agreements, but it also ensures that congressional views are inserted in the negotiations before, not after, agreements are concluded.

Congressional passage of Trade Agreements Implementing Authority will require considerable political skill and a willingness to find common ground on politically charged issues, such as the role of environment and labor issues in trade negotiations. Partisan divisions and lingering distrust over the environment and labor issues have frayed the bipartisan coalition of moderate Democrats and Republicans who traditionally have passed trade legislation and have given U.S. trade policy a great deal of stability since World War II. As Representatives Jim Kolbe and Robert Matsui point out in Chapter 2, "trade initiatives will require strong support on both sides of the aisle in order to become law. Without a strong coalition of protrade moderates in both parties, no trade legislation can pass the Congress."

Obtaining passage of new trade legislation also will require a major effort to reach out beyond the bureaucrats, politicians, and lobbyists in Washington. More than before, trade and trade negotiations are affecting the everyday lives of Americans, a fact that has made trade negotiations a subject of public debate across the country, from radio talk shows to living rooms. The somewhat emotional debate over NAFTA has left the public ambivalent on trade issues in general and somewhat hostile with respect to NAFTA itself. Overcoming these negative views will require a public outreach strategy.

U.S. TRADE POLICY AND THE AMERICAN PEOPLE

The American public deserves a full explanation of the challenges and opportunities posed by an outward-looking, competition-oriented trade strategy. As Ellen Frost points out in Chapter 4, the number of Americans who have a substantive understanding of trade issues is rather small, and many are misinformed about vital facts. This leads to a paradox. At a time when the American economy is performing extremely well and U.S. industries have regained international competitiveness, many people continue to have deep anxieties about global competition, and public opinion on trade is subject to large swings in sentiment. Frost attributes this incongruity to the restructuring of the American job market in the late 1980s and early 1990s, the downsizing of large corporations, the stagnation of real wages, and the increasing wage gap between skilled and unskilled workers. As a result, a large number of working people, along with labor and environmental activists, see corporations as abdicating their responsibility to the community.

All this points to the need to better educate the public regarding the relatively small number of jobs directly affected by imports from low-wage developing countries; the higher wages derived from exports; the domestic nature of many of the problems that cause the public anxiety; and what the government is doing domestically to address those problems. Frost reports that there is strong evidence that people change their views on trade if they have access to a full range of information about the long- and short-term benefits and costs of integrating the American economy with the global marketplace. At the same time, she warns against putting too much emphasis on job gains from trade liberalization, which may well be spurious, and in any event are easily upset by changes in macroeconomic circumstances.

In order to build deeper understanding and support in the American public for U.S. trade policy, the government needs to reach out and communicate with stakeholders who have not, traditionally, been included in the trade policy process. The message needs to be targeted, in particular, at small export-oriented businesses, state and local officials, schoolchildren, and the public at large through the use of mass-circulation magazines and radio talk shows.

CONCLUSION

The success of U.S. domestic economic policies and foreign policy may well depend on the vision and political skill the government brings to bear in managing U.S. trade relations with the rest of the world. In light of the historic shifts in policies in most of the developing countries and formerly communist states toward market-oriented economic policies, the world stands on the threshold of a prolonged economic boom. As countries such as China have already demonstrated, once artificial constraints on individual initiative are removed and enterprises are given the ability to compete on a global basis, countries can experience tremendous bursts of economic growth.

The U.S. economy is well positioned to supply these economies with the capital equipment, infrastructure equipment, and services they need to sustain their growth. As they grow richer, they will want to import more American high-value-added agricultural products, consumer goods, and entertainment products. To capture these markets for its exports, the United States must negotiate the further reduction of trade barriers and restrictive regulations that now block access to many foreign markets.

The negotiation of trade agreements in the post–Cold War world provides not only for new trade and investment opportunities but also can serve as a basis for strengthening political ties with countries and reducing the risk of armed conflicts. Geoeconomics thus will provide the foundation for peace and stability in the future.

Domestically, the U.S. economy has benefited enormously by leaving its economy exposed to the forces of international competition. By doing so the United States is in a stronger competitive position today than any other country. But the ability of the United States to exercise its leadership role effectively will depend on the wisdom with which it designs and implements its trade strategy.

NOTE

1. Under the foreign effects doctrine, U.S. antitrust authorities have asserted the right to take antitrust actions against anticompetitive practices abroad where such practices affect adversely competition in the United States.

Chapter 2

Forging a New Bipartisan Consensus for Free Trade

Jim Kolbe and Robert Matsui

International trade has benefited the United States greatly. Over the past five years, growth in exports has accounted for about 30 percent of total U.S. economic growth. The jobs of over 11 million workers in the country depend on U.S. exports, and these jobs generally pay higher wages than non–trade-related jobs. Approximately 27 percent of the nation's economy is directly associated with trade, and an estimate by the United States Trade Representative's office projects that proportion will reach 36 percent by 2010. For the immediate future, roughly a third of U.S. wealth will depend on doing business with other nations.

Deepening global economic integration, the spread of free market philosophies, and the rapid economic expansion of developing countries are leading to new patterns of international trade and investment. First, the composition of international trade is changing from its traditional emphasis on manufactured goods produced in a single country. Many companies source goods and services internationally in order to remain competitive in the new global economy. Second, geographic patterns of trade and investment are shifting with the economic development of countries in Latin America, East Asia, Eastern Europe, and the former Soviet Union. Finally, the acceleration of worldwide foreign direct investment (FDI) is amplifying these trends.

At the same time public discourse and distrust regarding international trade and globalization has intensified. A number of issues have resonated with many people, including concerns about U.S. sovereignty, the trade deficit, "runaway plants," and wage depreciation. Many of these issues were first given national attention during the 1993 debate over the North American Free Trade Agreement (NAFTA). They are, however, likely to continue to surface in different contexts, ranging from the extension of most-favored-nation (MFN) trading status for the People's Republic of China to the extension of fast-track trade negotiating authority to the executive branch.

These issues have spilled out of the sometimes arcane world of trade policy onto the editorial pages and into the stump speeches of politicians. The opportunities presented by economic globalization often are not reflected in these messages. One of the most fundamental tasks before the nation is to create a more informed public dialogue about these important matters—one that builds on the economic realities and opportunities of the 21st-century American economy yet fully acknowledges and tries to accommodate the burden a more global economy places on low-income, less-skilled workers and their communities.

EVOLUTION OF THE U.S. ECONOMY

The U.S. economy is emerging from a period of fundamental change that leaves U.S. firms in a highly competitive position vis-à-vis their trading partners. After years of restructuring and defense downsizing, the U.S. economy has gone through a transformation that is widely acknowledged but not well understood. On the technology side, revolutions in communications, information processing, and automated production have radically altered the way Americans provide goods and services in the economy. On the management side, U.S. companies have made dramatic changes to reduce labor costs, increase productivity, and improve product quality. While propelled in part by international competition, these changes are, and continue to be, driven largely by internal economic factors. For the past three years the World Economic Forum has found the United States to be the most competitive major economy in the world. The nation is the world's largest exporter of manufactured goods, high-technology goods, services, and agricultural products.

Americans need markets in which to sell the tremendous work product of this economy. The United States accounts for barely 4 percent of the world's population. That means over 96 percent of the potential customers for American products live in other countries. Put another way, 20 years ago the U.S. economy represented 40 percent of global production; today that figure is about 20 percent. By the year 2010 it is likely to be closer to 10 percent. The economic standing of the United States at the close of the 21st century will be determined by how well Americans position themselves today in Asia and Latin America.

As the center of the world's economic gravity shifts, the challenge facing Americans will be to provide the vision and the policies that will maintain U.S. economic preeminence. The nation's economic well-being has become inextricably linked with its ability to trade. The ability to deliver a better way of life for future generations of Americans will be a function of how well today's Americans pursue economic opportunities abroad.

THE CHALLENGE OF THE NEW GLOBAL ECONOMY

The era when national firms either exported finished manufactured goods or produced the equivalent goods in foreign subsidiaries is largely gone. Firms now assemble goods from components and service inputs produced in many different countries, and sell these goods around the world. International trade increasingly takes the form of trade in parts, components, semifinished goods, and inputs of business services such as software programming, design, research and development, market research, engineering, advertising, and consulting services. Globalization of production and investment has resulted in countries specializing in different phases of the production process.

The challenge posed by global production is compounded by other changes in the world economy, including a shortening of product life cycles, faster changes in the development of both process and product technologies, and more rapid shifts in consumer tastes driven by increasingly global trends. While the dynamics behind this transformation of the global marketplace vary by industry and by country, it has profound implications for both U.S. domestic and international trade policies.

Domestically, more than ever, U.S. policies have to support the development of a highly educated and flexible workforce that can seize the opportunities presented by rapidly changing technologies, markets, and customer tastes. The United States is well positioned to provide high-value products in this dynamic global marketplace—products that incorporate cutting-edge technologies and designs—and use the most up-to-date information technologies. The jobs associated with these products typically demand high-level skills and offer correspondingly high wages. But high-value products are subject to rapid changes in technologies and tastes, and demand a high level of adaptability by both businesses and workers. Accordingly, domestic reforms concerning the portability of pensions and health insurance and the availability of training and adult education programs have an important role to play in equipping Americans with the flexibility to change careers and move from job to job.

The nation's ability to compete in global markets requires a much higher level of integration between trade and investment decisions and opportunities. Often the most troublesome barriers to U.S. exports today are foreign regulatory measures that prevent U.S. firms from investing in distribution and local support or infrastructure facilities in other countries. Private restraints also can block access to existing facilities, and rampant bribery or other forms of corruption can disadvantage U.S. firms that must operate under the U.S. Foreign Bribery and Corrupt Practices Act. Decisions made at the Singapore ministerial meeting of the World Trade Organization (WTO) have opened the door for a global dialogue on these issues. The United States now needs to decide what kind of leadership role it wants to play in these discussions.

Economic integration on a global scale presents important opportunities and challenges for the United States in the area of infrastructure equipment and services. Because of its strong competitive position in digital technologies, the United States is highly competitive in a range of information industries, such as semiconductors and telecommunications. Since these infrastructure services are the driving force behind the ability of countries to take advantage of the growth opportunities, the market for them abroad is strong. In Asia alone, the demand for infrastructure equipment may be as much as $1 trillion over the next 10 years. America's ability to provide the equipment and services other countries need, however, is hampered by a large array of foreign regulatory and investment restrictions. Additionally, bribery and corruption pervade government transactions in these sectors. The United States needs an effective strategy for breaking down these barriers.

THE TRADE POLICY CHALLENGE FACING
THE UNITED STATES

To assure the continued growth of trade, the United States must aggressively pursue the negotiation of trade agreements with other countries. While very considerable progress has been made in past negotiations to knock down barriers to trade and investment, many U.S. exports are still blocked by a variety of tariff and nontariff barriers, regulatory barriers, investment restrictions, and corrupt and anticompetitive private practices. To achieve a system of trade rules that provide a level playing field for U.S. business, U.S. trade negotiators need authority and a full range of negotiating tools and approaches to reduce these barriers. This means pursuing bilateral negotiations, such as those with Japan, the European Union, and China; regional negotiations such as NAFTA, the Free Trade Area of the Americas (FTAA), and the Asia Pacific Economic Cooperation forum (APEC); and broader multilateral negotiations in fora such as the WTO and the Organization for Economic Cooperation and Development (OECD).

It makes a great deal of sense for the United States to give particular attention to opportunities for reducing trade and investment barriers in Latin America and Asia, two regions that are likely to outperform the rest of the world in economic growth yet still also maintain high barriers to trade and investment. Regional initiatives such as the proposed FTAA and APEC thus represent crucial opportunities for the United States.

It would be a serious mistake, however, to neglect the global, multilateral trading system, in particular the WTO. The WTO has much to chew on in completing unfinished business from the Uruguay Round and in negotiating the accession of a large number of developing and former socialist economies, especially China and Russia. The United States must continue to lead that organization to face future challenges and to prepare the ground for broader, global trade liberalization efforts. The recently concluded WTO ministerial meeting in Singapore has established a modest foundation for future work in that organization in areas such as investment, environmental issues, competition policy, and bribery. The United States now needs to sort out its interests in these areas and develop the forward-looking proposals needed to move the organization into the 21st century.

NEED FOR NEW FAST-TRACK AUTHORITY

To accomplish these ends, the Clinton administration and future administrations will need new fast-track trade negotiating authority from Congress. Without such authority, the United States is severely limited in the agreements it can negotiate effectively. Foreign negotiators need to know that the U.S. Congress will give prompt consideration to any trade agreements that are negotiated, without reopening negotiations to accommodate changes made by Congress.

Fast-track negotiating authority essentially means that Congress must act on trade agreements as a package—no amendments, no partial approval. Congress informally works through nonofficial proceedings with the president to draft implementing legislation so that congressional input is possible before the president submits the agreement to Capitol Hill for formal consideration. As this process implies, granting this authority to a president requires a strong degree of mutual respect and common purpose between the president and Congress. Since 1974 there has been significant bipartisan support for giving the president broad authority to negotiate international trade agreements using this method. Since that coalition has frayed at the edges, the Clinton administration will have to work hard to obtain fast-track authority. A large number of the current members of Congress have had limited involvement with trade issues in the past. Approximately 150 freshman and sophomore legislators, or approximately one-third of the House, have never cast a major trade vote on the scale of NAFTA or the Uruguay Round. Many of these new members have not fully developed a position on trade issues and are open to influence by antitrade rhetoric and lobbying. New opposition from people such as former presidential candidates Ross Perot and Patrick Buchanan reinforced recent opposition to free trade by many labor and some environmental groups.

A POLITICAL STRATEGY FOR WINNING CONGRESSIONAL SUPPORT

At its most fundamental level, a successful congressional free trade strategy will rest on the development of a positive and clear agenda in support of open markets and a set of good answers to the legitimate and pressing questions that greater globalization and increased trade present. Equally important is providing cogent and compelling answers to those questions concerning threats to U.S. sovereignty, the trade deficit, job losses, and so-called runaway plants and wage stagnation.

Although these issues arise from unique facts and circumstances, they seem to be converging into a kind of threatening specter that, in recent years, has given rise to economic nationalism and protectionist populism. Strains of both of these responses are increasingly evident in the congressional debate over trade issues. These stepped-up and increasingly coordinated attacks from the left and the right have eroded traditional, bipartisan middle-ground support for trade.

The responses from those who support continued trade expansion also seem to fall into two broad categories. The first are the free trade purists who support the goodness of free trade as an ideological tenet. The second acknowledge only the benefits of trade: increased economic growth, higher-wage and higher-skilled jobs, and exports. The weakness of both these positions is that neither adequately addresses either potential or actual negative effects of increased trade; and therefore, both cede most of the discussion of these issues to those who are opponents of trade expansion. It is time to rethink the way trade expansion is discussed and to rework efforts to broaden the coalition of those who support the continued expansion of trade.

As was true in past Congresses, trade initiatives will require strong support on both sides of the aisle in order to become law. Without a strong coalition of protrade moderates in both parties, no trade legislation can pass Congress. There is no magic formula for assuring success in Congress, but some suggestions might help the administration and protrade groups in mapping out a strategy that may have a good chance of succeeding.

Provide Strong Presidential Leadership. A successful strategy for obtaining political support and congressional passage of fast-track negotiating authority has to be based on strong presidential leadership. No one else in the country can provide the leadership necessary to forge a national consensus on an issue as complex as trade. Only the president can give the case for trade the national focus it requires and successfully pull together the diverse perspectives of individual Americans on the basis of national interest. U.S. history is replete with successes and failures in the trade policy area, and presidential leadership is a feature common to all successes.

Define American Global and Regional Goals. A U.S. trade strategy request for new fast-track authority has to be based on a clear and focused explanation of U.S. goals for future trade negotiations. The administration must explain how the proposed negotiations relate to other bilateral, regional, or multilateral trade initiatives and how they relate to other issues that concern the American people, including bilateral problems in various parts of the world. These goals and initiatives need to be expressed in a way that is understandable to the population at large.

Establish Concrete Negotiating Objectives. The administration will need to mobilize protrade groups to educate new members of Congress before groups opposed to trade seek them out and obtain their commitment to protectionist positions. Such efforts will happen only if the administration has given free trade supporters a reason to do so by spelling out both concrete U.S. negotiating objectives and what various segments of industry and society could hope to gain from achieving those objectives.

Recognize the Strategic Importance of Trade. It is widely argued that in the post–Cold War world, trade agreements have important strategic security benefits because they embed economic reforms in trade agreements and establish strong, mutually beneficial ties between countries. By making this argument clearly, the administration could help highlight the idea that such agreements are in the broad national interest of the United States. The benefits of trade agreements often transcend simple direct economic interests. To bring this argument home, the administration needs to mobilize senior representatives of the national security establishment to argue the case for trade in public speeches and in testimony before Congress.

Combine Tough Enforcement with Tough Bargaining Positions. Americans feel better about new trade negotiations when they believe that the government is prepared to be tough-minded in enforcing previously negotiated trade agreements. U.S. Trade Representatives Carla Hills, Mickey Kantor, and Charlene Barshefsky earned their trust in this regard in recent years, and the administration needs to build on that trust in the future.

Develop a Deeper, Stronger National Consensus. Trade is having a deeper impact on the lives of individual Americans than ever before. As a result, the debate over NAFTA became a national debate, drawing far more citizen interest and participation than other recent trade issues. In future public dialogue about trade, Congress, as the representative of all the people, will come under a much broader set of influences than in the past. In order for Congress to go along with new U.S. trade initiatives, the benefits of those initiatives will need to be sold first to the vast majority of the American public that lives beyond the Washington Beltway. If the trade debate remains an insider's game, then the forces of free trade will draw a losing hand.

Rebuild a Bipartisan Approach. American leadership on trade issues over the past 50 years was built on bipartisan support in Congress. In view of opposition to trade on both the political right and left, there is no alternative to a bipartisan coalition at the center. Over the past few years this bipartisan coalition has been frayed by partisan debate over the role of social, human rights, environmental, and foreign policy issues. In order to reestablish strong support for trade at the center, leaders at both ends of Pennsylvania Avenue and on both sides of the aisle in Congress need to avoid seeking partisan advantage on trade issues. They need to find new common ground on issues that divide the two parties.

Find Common Ground on Divisive Issues. Rhetoric on the role social and human rights issues should play in trade negotiations has tended to widen the gap on trade issues between the two parties. But we both believe that the United States needs to base its goals in these areas in the context of what Americans can broadly agree on and on what can be appropriately achieved in trade negotiations. We agree that there needs to be consistency between U.S. trade negotiating goals and the ground rules Congress writes on individual issues, such as what to do about dolphins caught in tuna nets or child labor. Above all, we agree that any administration needs to craft a balance between trade and social-environmental-human rights goals that will be acceptable on both sides of the congressional aisle.

Involve Small Business and Nonbusiness Groups. Many Americans have become suspicious of large multinational corporations, as indicated by polls cited in Chapter 4. Many Americans at the grass-roots level seem to feel that large corporations have abandoned their responsibilities to American communities in their pursuit of profit and that further free trade negotiations will only make it easier for them to transfer jobs abroad. U.S. negotiating objectives therefore must be seen as serving American interests beyond those articulated by representatives of large business. As Chapter 3 shows, trade negotiations are very much in the interests of a broad cross-section of Americans, small businesses as well as large, workers as well as shareholders. To make this point, the administration needs to mobilize state governors as well as city mayors and representatives of community groups who are prepared to make the case for the economic benefits from expanded trade. This effort should include labor, environmental, and religious groups as well.

Address the Problems of Americans Who Find It Difficult to Adjust. Globalization, corporate downsizing, and the continuing adoption of automated production processes in both manufacturing and services have created a great deal of economic insecurity and lost income for Americans who find it difficult to change jobs. The administration needs to address these concerns with legislative proposals that will be acceptable to both Democrats and Republicans in areas such as worker training, health care, and the portability of pensions.

Improve the Analytical Base. Dealing with the increasingly complex problems faced by American companies and workers in international trade requires better information. At this time the government is not well organized to give sufficient study to the competitive factors and obstacles to trade that account for anomalies in current trade patterns. The International Trade Commission, the Department of Commerce, educational institutions, and think tanks ought to be harnessed to provide a much more sophisticated analytical base highlighting these factors. Currently most of the work being done in academia is theoretical. What trade negotiators and businesses need are empirical studies about the factors that actually shape world trade so that distortions and barriers can be removed through the process of negotiation.

Reinvigorate Congressional Participation. A successful trade strategy will also require Congress to consider how it can more effectively discharge its responsibilities in the trade area. Congressional involvement in trade policy formulation has increasingly been relegated to adopting fast-track procedures and later approving large, complicated agreements with a single up-or-down vote. This is a practical and necessary way of handling the authorization and approval of trade agreements. More congressional participation is needed, however, to ensure that America's trade laws, policies, and negotiating positions meet changing national needs. This might be accomplished through oversight of the operation of trade agreements and the functioning of the WTO; monitoring of the implementation of U.S. trade laws; more frequent and intensive hearings on new problems in international trade such as bribery and private restraints of trade; better coordination and organization of trade-supporting institutions, including the Export-Import Bank and the Overseas Private Investment Corporation; and more congressional interactions with U.S. negotiators and site visits to negotiating venues.

CONCLUSION

For the last half century, America's natural resources, population growth, and entrepreneurial spirit sustained U.S. economic growth and gave it the strength to win the Cold War. Trade and economic cooperation with Europe and Japan certainly helped, but the drive fueling the nation's greatness came from within its shores. The next century, however, will see a different formula for national economic success. America's course for the future must be navigated through the turbulent waters of the rapidly changing global economy. If the nation is to retain its position of preeminence in the world, the United States must combine sound domestic policies of deficit reduction, education, health care, and welfare reform with a visionary trade and foreign policy.

These, then, are the challenges to U.S. domestic and international economic policies: to boost productivity and national income; to stimulate high-wage, high-skilled job opportunities; and, at the same time, to maintain a healthy employment environment for the nation's competitive manufacturing industries.

Rebuilding bipartisan trust in executive branch trade policy on Capitol Hill will be, at best, a difficult assignment. When national economic priorities and foreign policy credibility are at stake—and they most certainly will be in the coming debate—free traders, whether Democrats or Republicans, must rise to the challenge.

Chapter 3

U.S. Performance and Trade Strategy in a Shifting Global Economy

*J. David Richardson, Geza Feketekuty,
Chi Zhang, and A. E. Rodriguez*

Trade has become increasingly important to the American economy, both in terms of the overall proportion of national output and consumption that is tied to it, and in terms of its critical role in stimulating growth and improvements in the standard of living. The proportion of trade to domestic output, a measure of the openness of the economy, more than doubled between 1970 and 1995, from 10 percent to 24 percent, the largest such increase for any developed economy in that period.

More than at any time before in American history, trade is having a measurable impact on the performance and income not only of the very largest American firms but also of medium-size and small firms. Not surprisingly, given the large growth in trade, firms tied to exports have been doing very well. Empirical data shows that firms connected with exports, their workers, and the communities in which they live are enjoying greater income growth and stability than firms, workers, or communities with no stake in exports. Conversely, firms and workers tied to import-competing industries have had to make significant economic and social adjustments.

As a result of the market-driven adjustments the American economy has gone through, the United States is extremely well-positioned to take advantage of expanded global trade and investment opportunities. Policies that have kept the American economy open to international competition and have fostered the removal or reform of outdated government regulations have given American firms a new competitive vitality and have once again placed the United States at the top in many competitiveness rankings. The flexibility and innovative capacity of American firms and workers gives the U.S. economy the capacity to respond to new competitive challenges in the global marketplace and to reduce the risks to them posed by greater exposure to global competition.

The fact that the United States is in a relatively strong competitive position overall in terms of its productivity, its capacity to apply new technologies, and its ability to respond to market shifts does not mean that the nation is equally competitive in all industrial, service, and commodity sectors. Increasingly, the United States has a strong comparative advantage in subsectors or niches that are technology- and skill-intensive. Interestingly, this is the case even in sectors such as textiles, footwear, and glassware, industries in which the United States had experienced a strong erosion of comparative advantage in previous decades. At the same time, the United States retains a strong comparative advantage across a wide range of agricultural products and other natural resources, although even in this area there appears to be a trend toward high-value specialty products.

A regional analysis of data on comparative advantage indicates a significant regional variation in the comparative advantage of U.S. exports, but it is not clear whether that is due to geographic considerations or to differences in the ability of exporters from different countries that are U.S. competitors to deal with local regulatory and business practices. In a number of cases, a weak U.S. export performance in particular regions can be correlated with known difficulties concerning the regulatory regime in the countries involved. This weak performance might be explained by a greater reluctance of American firms, or legal inhibitions imposed on U.S. firms by U.S. law, to circumvent restrictive regulations or business practices. This fact raises the possibility that negotiated reforms in such regimes could enable the United States to capture a larger share of such markets.

The benefits of trade do not come without costs. One of those costs is that firms producing goods or services competing with imports, and their typically less-skilled employees, have been losing income. This, in turn, has had a negative impact on communities that host such firms. Trade, together with technology, has contributed to a growing income inequality between educated and skilled workers and the entrepreneurially minded on one hand and less educated workers on the other. In turn, this has fostered public uncertainty about the advantages of expanded trade. The challenge for trade policy in the new economic environment is to spread the gains from expanded trade and investment more widely in the population. The first task is to deliver the large gains to be achieved from further global integration. Then, these gains must be distributed fairly within and across countries to achieve both internal political support and external consensus on a package of new and continuing liberalizations. Neither of these challenges can be met without overcoming the overwhelming misunderstanding of the issues involved.[1]

THE U.S. STAKE IN TRADE

Over the last two decades, the importance of trade relative to the U.S. economy as a whole has grown significantly. American trade, as measured by imports and exports combined, grew by a whopping 1,261 percent in nominal terms between 1970 and 1994, far exceeding the 566 percent increase in nominal national output. In 1970, export and import transactions constituted about 11 percent of gross domestic product. By 1994, this amount had increased to 24 percent, an increase of 118 percent. And even though most countries significantly increased their openness, the U.S. increase is unmatched by that of any of its major trading partners. International trade has indeed become an ever more important influence on the U.S. domestic economy.

The same increased openness is also seen at the finest level of disaggregation. In the United States, for example, both the number of firms with export sales and the intensity of those sales has surged in the past 10 years. Small-firm export participation has grown strikingly, and small-firm exports have grown just as fast as exports of the top 50 U.S. exporters. Table 3.1 illustrates this point.

SECTORAL PRODUCTIVITY, COMPETITIVENESS, AND COMPARATIVE ADVANTAGE

Over the past 25 years, sectoral productivity shifts have radically altered U.S. competitiveness, giving the nation strong performance in high-technology, skill-intensive niches in the industrial structure. These productivity-based trends are far more important than more traditional indicators of sectoral competitiveness such as unit labor costs and industry investment would suggest. Productivity-based niche competition is the source of the strong U.S. position in the coming global economy.[2]

The movement in the rankings of industries with respect to their labor productivity level also has been significant. This can be observed in Table 3.2, which ranks various industry sectors according to their productivity (measured by value added per employee) in two periods, 1972 and 1993.

The large productivity growth figures in a number of industries, combined with the ranking shifts shown in Table 3.2, suggests that the United States is beginning to specialize in high-productivity growth sub-industries while simultaneously abandoning many low-productivity growth sub-industries. Roughly speaking, low-value-added production is being replaced with high-value-added production and low-productivity jobs are being replaced with high-productivity ones. Workers as well as employ-

TABLE 3.1. EXPORT PARTICIPATION AND INTENSITY
        BY SMALL AND LARGE U.S. FIRMS

	1987	1992
Small Plants[a] (less than 250 employees)		
Participation (% of all plants)	12	19
Intensity (% of sales)	10	12
Large Plants[a] (more than 250 employees)		
Participation (% of all plants)	49	59
Intensity (% of sales)	10	14
Very Largest Exporters (top 50 firms)		
Intensity (% of sales)	14	16

[a] Manufacturers only.
Source: J. David Richardson and Karin Rindal, *Why Exports Matter: More!* (Washington, DC: Institute for International Economics and the Manufacturing Institute, 1996), pp. 15, 17, based on U.S. Census of Manufacturers and *Fortune* magazine.

ers and shareholders reap these gains. And to the extent that global integration is the agent force in this niche specialization, the gains displayed should be credited to it.

EXPORTS AND PRODUCTIVITY AT THE PLANT LEVEL

The lesson that global engagement creates significant opportunity for gains applies not just "in the large," but on the plant floor too. One of the most surprising empirical regularities to be discovered in the past 20 years is the strong correlation between export engagement and a myriad of corporate and workforce performance indicators.[3]

Among other things, export engagement is strongly correlated with labor productivity. This finding, in turn, helps to explain why the gains from global integration today seem to involve productivity gains as well as the more conventional efficiency gains.[4]

The productivity gap between export-engaged workers and others in the United States is striking.[5]

TABLE 3.2. PRODUCTIVITY RANKINGS OF MANUFACTURING SECTORS

Industry	1993 Rank	1972 Rank
Telephone communications	1	20
Steel	2	16
Commercial banks	3	9
Cotton & synthetic broadwoven fabrics	4	15
Petroleum refining	5	8
Hydraulic cement	6	12
Farm & garden machinery	7	3
Agricultural chemicals	8	17
Household furniture	9	6
Dairy products	10	18
Paints and allied products	11	11
Grain mill products	12	19
Men's & boy's suits and coats	13	5
Industrial inorganic chemicals	14	10
Hotels and motels	15	2
Crude petroleum & natural gas production	16	1
Motor vehicles and equipment	17	14
Structural clay products	18	7
Tobacco products	19	13
Bakery products	20	4

- Exporting plants had higher average labor productivity in 1992 than nonexporting plants, as was also true in 1987. Exporters thus enjoyed a productivity "premium."

- The crude average productivity premium is quite large. The productivity premium for exporting (relative to nonexporting) plants is almost 40 percent on average for plants of all sizes, locations, and industries. Of course, some of that raw premium is due to the fact that exporting plants typically are larger and located in high-productivity industries and states. But the productivity premium turns out to be still quite large for exporting plants that are comparable to nonexporters in size, industry, and location, as follows.

- Value-added per employee in 1992, one measure of productivity, was almost one-sixth higher in exporting plants than in comparable nonexporting plants.

- Small exporters enjoyed a 1992 productivity premium of the same magnitude relative to comparable small nonexporters. This figure is up from a premium of one-seventh in 1987 between comparable small plants. (This is, of course, not as impressive as the raw average differences, which are due largely to exporters on average being in high-productivity industries.)

- Large exporters were even more productive in 1992. Their productivity premium relative to comparable nonexporters was almost one-fifth in 1992, up from less than one-sixth in 1987. (The raw average differences are, of course, again even larger.)

Trade provides an interpretation of these trends along somewhat unfamiliar lines. Openness to trade implies not just ordinary price competition but quality or "attribute" or productivity competition as well. Global competition between the cream of the quality and productivity competitors, both firms and workforces (and regional polities), inevitably involves their separation from the milk.

This fact has both bad- and good-news aspects. The bad-news aspect is that the low-performing marginal firms will decline and possibly die. The good news is that there is room for the displaced workers in the expanding high-performing marginal firms, although moving may require costly acquisition of new skills and work habits.

The productivity advantage for export-engaged firms, in turn, helps explain why employment growth and employment stability are so much more favorable for exporters than for nonexporters.[6]

• Employment growth between 1987 and 1992 at plants that started or continued exporting during that time was up to 18.5 percent greater than at comparable plants that did not export.

• Large plants that started exporting between 1987 and 1992 "grew jobs" 13 percent faster than comparable large plants that did not export at all. Large plants that exported continuously through this period "grew jobs" almost 16 percent faster.

• By implication, exporting plants are better able to cope with unwelcome business slumps through attrition or through slowing the normal hiring process, instead of having to release workers outright.

• By implication, communities with large numbers of export-reliant plants are more likely to enjoy growing tax bases and are less likely to face falling real-estate prices.

• Exporting plants were less likely to close their doors between 1987 and 1992 than comparable nonexporting plants.

REVEALED COMPARATIVE ADVANTAGE INDICATORS

It is apparent that the United States has experienced noticeable structural change over the last two decades. Industries have risen and industries have fallen. To keep jobs and a good standard of living, countries must shift factors of production from the declining industries into the ascendant ones. Labor, capital, and other resources need to move to uses that produce the greatest return, even if that means shrinking some important sectors of the economy.

The reallocation of resources will almost surely reflect America's comparative advantage. The commodity pattern of trade will reflect relative productivity and costs as well as the influence of nonprice factors, such as goodwill, quality, and the availability of servicing and repair facilities.

How does the United States compare to its trading partners in comparative advantage? What do productivity trends contribute to the answers?

TABLE 3.3. U.S. REVEALED COMPARATIVE ADVANTAGE, 1980 AND 1994
(ONE-DIGIT SITC PRODUCT GROUPS)[a]

SITC		1980	1994
0	Food and live animals chiefly for food	128.4	137.2
1	Beverages and tobacco	94.8	137.0
2	Crude materials, inedible, except fuels	137.9	141.2
3	Mineral fuels, lubricants and related materials	40.2	41.8
4	Animal and vegetable oils, fats and waxes	135.6	106.3
5	Chemicals and related products, N.E.S.	141.9	140.5
6	Manufactured goods classified chiefly by material	77.1	82.7
7	Machinery and transport equipment	103.1	99.4
8	Miscellaneous manufactured articles	82.2	78.4
9	Commodities & trans. not classified elsewhere	122.9	129.6

[a] RCA indicators for 1980 and 1994 vis-à-vis all regions for all one-digit SITC product groups.

A good indicator of trade specialization is an index developed by the late economist Bela Balassa to measure revealed comparative advantage (RCA).[7] The "revealed" comparative advantage of any country can be indicated by its trade performance with respect to other countries.

RCA measures a country's relative share in the exports of a particular product to a particular region or country. To place small and large countries on the same footing, the number is adjusted to take into account the exporting country's share in the exports of all manufactured goods to the importing country or region involved. Values greater than 100 indicate that a country's exports are relatively specialized in that industry.

The indicator of export specialization helps to identify areas of strength and of weakness, as these are revealed by past export performance. Table 3.3 shows the RCA as reflected in trade between the United States and all regions of the world in 1980 and 1994. The calculation in this table is based on the broadest category of industry groupings, the one-digit Standard Industrial Tariff Classification (SITC) used by the U.S. government. Looking across the sectors at the numbers for 1994, the United States shows a strong comparative advantage in sectors 0 to 3, covering food products and natural resources, basically reflecting traditional trade theory and the relative richness of the nation's natural resources. The United States also clearly shows a comparative advantage in chemicals and related products. In contrast, it shows a comparative disadvantage in manufactures at this most aggregate level, especially for the miscellaneous manufacturing category. U.S. strengths in manufacturing show up at a more disaggregated level of measurement, where the numbers capture U.S. strengths in technology.

Table 3.4 shows more detailed data for SITC product groups 6 to 9, in which the United States does not show a strong overall comparative advantage at the one-digit level. The rank-ordered numbers indicate that at this more detailed level, the United States shows a considerable comparative advantage in many manufacturing products, including products such as glassware, textile fabrics, floor coverings, and specialty fabrics in which the United States might be thought to have lost global competitiveness. Generally, the product categories in which the United States is competitive are products containing high-value content such as advanced technology or up-to-date designs. What would become even more apparent with an analysis of even more disaggregated data is that U.S. competitive strength is increasingly focused on particular product niches containing technology- or skill-intensive inputs.

GEOGRAPHIC COMPETITIVENESS AND COMPARATIVE ADVANTAGE BY REGION

Regional-oriented U.S. trade negotiations involve not just knowing which sectors and types of workers are globally competitive or uncompetitive, they require knowledge of which countries and which sectors therein show the greatest opportunities for U.S. export growth. The most promising negotiating partners today may be very different from the principal trading partners in the past.

A comparison of U.S. trade patterns in the early 1980s and the early 1990s shows a change in the regional revealed comparative advantage of U.S. exports.

- In the early 1980s, three major trading areas accounted for roughly equal "quarters" of U.S. trade: the European Union (EU), Asia, and the border countries of Canada and Mexico. The rest of the world composed the remaining quarter.

- U.S. trade with Asia and the border countries has increased tremendously over the last decade, by roughly 7 percentage points each. Tables 3.5 and 3.6 show that the share of U.S. exports to these groups increased from 21 to 28 and from 23 to

TABLE 3.4. U.S. REVEALED COMPARATIVE ADVANTAGE, 1994
(THREE-DIGIT SITC CATEGORIES)[a]

SITC		RCA Value
899	Other miscellaneous manufactured articles	171.6
712	Steam & other vapour power units, steam engines	159.6
896	Works of art, collectors pieces & antiques	146.7
792	Aircraft & associated equipment and parts	144.9
872	Medical instruments and appliances	141.3
721	Agricultural machinery and parts	140.7
711	Steam & other vapour generating boilers & parts	138.0
874	Measuring, checking, analyzing instruments	133.9
892	Printed matter	133.7
741	Heating & cooling equipment and parts	129.6
723	Civil engineering & contractors plant and parts	127.3
659	Floor coverings, etc.	126.7
692	Metal containers for storage and transport	123.5
898	Musical instruments, parts, and accessories	123.2
691	Structures & parts of structures; iron, steel, aluminum	121.6
679	Iron & steel castings, forgings & stampings; rough	119.9
621	Materials of rubber (e.g., pastes, plates, sheets, etc.)	119.9
657	Special textile fabrics and related products	118.3
742	Pumps for liquids, liquid elevators and parts	114.1
728	Machine & equipment specialized for particular industry	114.1
714	Engines & motors, nonelectric	112.6
745	Other nonelectrical machine tools, apparatus & parts	112.5
727	Food processing machines and parts	112.2
744	Mechanical handling equipment and parts	109.3
776	Thermionic, cold & photo-cathode valves, tubes, parts	105.9
882	Photographic & cinematographic supplies	104.6
665	Glassware	103.4
743	Pumps & compressors, fans & blowers, centrifuges	102.9
656	Tulle, lace, embroidery, ribbons, & other small wares	101.4
893	Articles of materials described in division 58	100.8
695	Tools for use in hand or in machines	98.5
651	Textile yarn	98.1
736	Machine tools for working metal or metal carbon parts	96.3

[a] RCA indicators for 1994 vis-à-vis all regions for selected three-digit SITC categories within one-digit product categories 6 to 9. Arranged in descending RCA values.

30 percent respectively, while U.S. imports from them increased from 29 to 40 percent and 23 to 27 percent respectively. As a result, in the early 1990s the Asian countries, as a group, became the Unit-

TABLE 3.5. U.S. EXPORT GEOGRAPHIC STRUCTURAL CHANGE

	1980–82 Average	1992–94 Average
Total Market[a]	100.0	100.0
Border Countries	23.0	30.0
Canada	17.2	19.6
Mexico	5.9	10.4
Asia[b]	21.2	27.7
Japan	9.7	10.5
Korea	2.3	3.5
Taiwan	1.8	3.4
China	1.5	2.0
Hong Kong	1.1	2.1
European Union[c]	26.7	22.6
United Kingdom	5.8	5.4
Germany	4.9	4.7
France	3.7	3.4
Latin America[d]	6.8	5.1

[a] Includes 48 countries: all countries included in the table's regional groupings as well as six East European countries, Australia and New Zealand, Norway and Switzerland, and India, South Africa, Egypt, Israel, and Saudi Arabia.

[b] Includes China, Hong Kong, Indonesia, Japan, Korea, Malaysia, Philippines, Singapore, Taiwan, and Thailand.

[c] Includes 15 countries: Austria, Belgium, Denmark, Finland, France, Germany, Greece, Ireland, Italy, Luxembourg, Netherlands, Portugal, Spain, Sweden, and the United Kingdom.

[d] Includes Argentina, Brazil, Chile, Colombia, Peru, and Venezuela.

Source: Stats Canada, World Trade Data Base (1995).

ed States' largest trading partner, accounting for more than one-third of U.S. trade; the border countries and the EU account for the second and third largest shares.

Analysis of revealed comparative advantage at a regional level reveals a surprising diversity of sectoral U.S. comparative advantage across trading partners. "Niche" comparative advantage in a particular sub-industry in Europe may be counterposed to U.S. disadvantage in exactly the same niche in North American markets. Strong U.S. growth in European export penetration may be counterposed against weak U.S. export growth in Canadian and Mexican markets in exactly the same niche.

In some cases these regional differences are the result of differences in the inclination or ability of exporters from a particular country to break through restrictive local regulations or

TABLE 3.6. U.S. IMPORT GEOGRAPHIC STRUCTURAL CHANGE

	1980–82 Average	1992–94 Average
Total Market[a]	100.0	100.0
Border Countries	23.2	27.3
Canada	18.8	19.9
Mexico	4.3	7.3
Asia[b]	29.0	40.3
Japan	14.9	17.4
Taiwan	3.4	4.3
Hong Kong	2.4	5.0
Korea	2.3	3.1
China	0.7	2.7
European Union[c]	17.8	18.6
United Kingdom	5.0	4.0
Germany	4.6	5.0
France	2.2	2.7
Latin America[d]	5.3	3.6

[a] Includes 48 countries, all countries included in the table's regional groupings as well as six East European countries, Australia and New Zealand, Norway and Switzerland, and India, South Africa, Egypt, Israel, and Saudi Arabia.
[b] Includes China, Hong Kong, Indonesia, Japan, Korea, Malaysia, Philippines, Singapore, Taiwan, and Thailand.
[c] Includes 15 countries: Austria, Belgium, Denmark, Finland, France, Germany, Greece, Ireland, Italy, Luxembourg, Netherlands, Portugal, Spain, Sweden, and the United Kingdom.
[d] Includes Argentina, Brazil, Chile, Colombia, Peru, and Venezuela.
Source: Stats Canada, World Trade Data Base (1995).

business practices or to accommodate to a different cultural, social, or legal environment. In other cases these differences are due to geographic factors, differences in natural endowments, or simply the result of geographically concentrated corporate strategies. Long-standing investment and trading relationships also may help explain why a country's exporters are relatively more successful in penetrating some markets as compared to other markets.

To illustrate these points, we have calculated the RCA indicators for U.S. trade with the major regions.[8] Table 3.7 provides a regional analysis of revealed comparative advantage at the three-digit level for industry sectors in which the United States has an overall comparative advantage. The table shows substantial regional variation in U.S. trade performance in these sectors. In a number of these sectors there is a strong possibility that American exporters are less inclined or prevented by U.S. laws from overcoming restrictive government regulations or business practices, or that other countries' exporters have developed long-term investment or trading relationships that enhance their ability to overcome local conditions. At a minimum, sectors showing a large regional variation deserve a closer look.

Table 3.8 shows a somewhat longer list of products at the three-digit level in which the United States does not show a relative comparative advantage vis-à-vis the world as a whole but nevertheless shows considerable competitive strength in some regions. This table illustrates that comparative advantage is less immutably fixed by a specific set of natural endowments and is much more open-ended in today's world, where competitive advantage often depends on technology, design, and managerial skill at the firm level. As noted earlier, a more disaggregated set of data would show that specialization takes place in specific niche products and that trading relationships between mature economies are characterized by extensive two-way trade.

Table 3.9 presents the list of 25 products at the three-digit SITC level for which the United States shows the least revealed comparative advantage in trade with all regions. What is interesting about this list is that in virtually all of these products, the United States shows competitive strength in at least one region of the world.

LIVING-STANDARD DISPERSION INDICATORS AND IMPLICATIONS

The gains from trade seem unequally distributed, no matter how large their overall size. This is a major problem. Increasingly, the gains from global engagement seem concentrated in only some groups within a country and in only some countries.[9] Others in society gain less, and still others seem to lose.

Economists are confident that the gains to the gainers generally exceed the losses to the losers.[10] But that only guarantees that an economy's mean standard of living rises. The problem is that the economy's median standard of living—the living standard of the most typical income earner in the very middle of the income distribution—may not rise. Defined this way, global integration may not benefit the typical citizen. And the broader economic problem

TABLE 3.7. U.S. REVEALED COMPARATIVE ADVANTAGE WITH KEY REGIONS, 1994
(PRODUCT CATEGORIES WITH STRONG OVERALL ADVANTAGE)[a]

SITC		All Regions[b]	EU15[c]	Border Countries[d]	Japan	Asian Tiger[e]	ASEAN[f]	Latin[g]
723	Civil engineering & contractors plant and parts	127.3	74.3	148.7	21.6	178.7	204.3	134.2
659	Floor coverings, etc.	126.7	65.9	124.0	316.5	196.7	100.7	137.3
692	Metal containers for storage and transport	123.5	80.6	99.4	313.6	101.6	179.5	132.0
898	Musical instruments, parts and accessories	123.2	133.3	115.7	117.5	119.7	169.4	137.8
691	Structures & parts of structures; iron, steel, aluminum	121.6	86.1	92.6	264.2	170.1	200.8	128.6
679	Iron & steel castings, forgings & stampings; rough	119.9	84.8	132.4	144.2	95.6	144.3	82.9
621	Materials of rubber (e.g., pastes, plates, sheets, etc.)	119.9	137.3	115.9	42.1	173.5	42.8	131.9
657	Special textile fabrics and related products	118.3	89.8	124.8	156.3	123.3	84.8	64.3
742	Pumps for liquids, liquid elevators and parts	114.1	88.2	136.0	48.1	173.8	201.4	93.9
728	Machines & equipment specialized for particular industry	114.1	83.6	118.1	99.3	182.2	195.0	140.0
714	Engines & motors, nonelectric	112.6	106.0	83.1	280.0	158.8	195.1	93.5
745	Other nonelectrical machine tools, apparatus & parts	112.5	90.8	132.6	70.1	104.8	197.7	141.1
727	Food processing machines and parts	112.2	70.6	131.3	127.3	167.6	199.8	140.2
744	Mechanical handling equipment and parts	109.3	91.9	104.8	28.0	139.4	198.8	136.6
776	Thermionic, cold & photo-cathode valves, tubes, parts	105.9	132.8	124.3	101.9	107.6	198.7	140.4
882	Photographic & cinematographic supplies	104.6	79.1	112.8	125.3	197.7	125.9	125.0
665	Glassware	103.4	51.5	101.3	343.1	94.2	109.9	122.3
743	Pumps & compressors, fans & blowers, centrifuges	102.9	63.1	132.6	21.4	148.5	145.4	75.6

[a] RCA indicators for three-digit SITC product categories selected for their overall comparative advantage.
[b] Includes 38 countries: all countries included in the table's regional groupings as well as Australia, New Zealand, China, South Africa, Egypt, and Israel.
[c] Only includes Austria, Belgium, Denmark, Finland, France, Germany, Greece, Ireland, Italy, Luxembourg, Netherlands, Portugal, Spain, Sweden, and the United Kingdom.
[d] Canada and Mexico.
[e] Includes Hong Kong, Korea, Singapore, and Taiwan.
[f] Only includes Indonesia, Malaysia, Philippines, and Thailand.
[g] Only includes Argentina, Brazil, Chile, Colombia, Peru, and Venezuela.
Source: Computed based on Stats Canada, World Trade Data Base (1995).

TABLE 3.8. U.S. REVEALED COMPARATIVE ADVANTAGE WITH KEY REGIONS, 1994

(PRODUCT CATEGORIES WITH WEAK OVERALL ADVANTAGE) [a]

SITC		All Regions[b]	EU15[c]	Border Countries[d]	Japan	Asian Tiger[e]	ASEAN[f]	Latin[g]
695	Tools for use in hand or in machines	98.5	90.4	133.4	63.0	52.7	156.4	110.3
651	Textile yarn	98.1	82.2	96.0	91.0	136.3	47.0	79.0
736	Machine tools for working metal or metal carbon, parts	96.3	77.4	137.2	42.7	135.9	181.1	114.1
871	Optical instruments and apparatus	95.9	126.1	118.3	90.2	76.3	47.5	141.2
716	Rotating electric plant and parts	95.0	91.0	81.1	31.4	114.3	170.0	118.6
663	Mineral manufactures, N.E.S.	95.0	92.5	82.2	69.3	162.1	158.0	97.7
725	Paper & pulp mill machines, machines for manufacture of paper	92.4	52.2	114.7	101.1	196.6	203.9	112.6
718	Other power generating machinery and parts	92.1	52.8	121.1	17.8	194.5	133.0	123.3
713	Internal combustion piston engines & parts	89.7	73.5	106.4	15.8	190.2	202.9	80.9
774	Electric apparatus for medical purposes (radiolog)	89.6	57.4	140.4	148.0	217.3	201.9	146.6
793	Ships, boats and floating structures	88.9	51.9	67.1	91.8	57.5	187.2	136.5
773	Equipment for distributing electricity	88.5	139.2	76.9	88.0	65.8	44.9	121.4
778	Electrical machinery and apparatus, N.E.S.	86.3	97.2	96.5	50.7	67.5	95.7	127.3
655	Knitted or crocheted fabrics	86.1	104.0	122.9	180.9	13.9	170.7	126.8
684	Aluminum	85.0	75.5	62.5	261.6	220.3	196.9	35.4
689	Miscellaneous nonferrous base metals employed in metallurgy	83.7	93.9	78.7	227.2	55.5	55.4	24.6
737	Metal working machinery and parts	83.3	41.2	82.8	18.7	107.7	204.8	122.4
764	Telecommunications equipment and parts	80.6	153.8	85.7	54.8	65.4	40.0	144.6
722	Tractors fitted or not with power takeoffs, etc.	80.4	58.8	100.9	15.0	190.1	202.4	131.0
791	Railway vehicles & associated equipment	80.1	85.1	57.4	56.7	220.6	195.8	105.3
761	Television receivers	62.2	142.8	23.7	17.2	77.1	1.2	147.7
662	Clay construction materials & refractory construction materials	60.7	15.1	91.3	89.4	191.9	108.8	45.2
884	Optical goods, N.E.S.	60.5	75.5	133.4	37.6	22.3	58.6	141.3
881	Photographic apparatus and equipment, N.E.S.	59.8	100.0	121.9	22.8	46.3	24.3	143.2
724	Textile & leather machinery and parts	58.8	26.7	155.0	21.3	74.0	194.9	113.6
894	Baby carriages, toys, games and sporting goods	56.7	109.5	100.7	166.7	18.6	12.8	104.4

[a] RCA indicators for three-digit SITC product categories selected for their overall weak comparative advantage.
[b] Includes 38 countries: all countries included in the table's regional groupings as well as Australia, New Zealand, China, South Africa, Egypt, and Israel.
[c] Only includes Austria, Belgium, Denmark, Finland, France, Germany, Greece, Ireland, Italy, Luxembourg, Netherlands, Portugal, Spain, Sweden, and the United Kingdom.
[d] Canada and Mexico.
[e] Includes Hong Kong, Korea, Singapore, and Taiwan.
[f] Only includes Indonesia, Malaysia, Philippines, and Thailand.
[g] Only includes Argentina, Brazil, Chile, Colombia, Peru, and Venezuela.
Source: Computed based on Stats Canada, World Trade Data Base (1995).

TABLE 3.9. U.S. REVEALED COMPARATIVE ADVANTAGE WITH KEY REGIONS, 1994 (PRODUCT CATEGORIES WITH STRONG OVERALL DISADVANTAGE)[a]

SITC		All Regions[b]	EU15[c]	Border Countries[d]	Japan	Asian Tiger[e]	ASEAN[f]	Latin[g]
666	Pottery	11.7	10.3	93.0	2.5	6.2	1.0	45.5
672	Ingots and other primary forms, of iron or steel	15.4	7.4	53.8	1.5	218.2	203.0	2.1
762	Radio-broadcast receivers	20.2	58.4	57.7	15.1	2.4	0.4	27.3
661	Lime, cement, and fabricated construction materials	29.8	4.6	43.2	149.2	101.8	68.4	7.3
885	Watches and clocks	31.4	61.3	119.3	28.0	9.5	40.6	99.4
897	Jewelry, goldsmiths and other articles of precious metals	36.3	18.9	88.2	241.7	39.1	24.8	6.8
671	Pig iron, spiegeleisen, sponge iron, iron or steel	36.6	29.4	76.2	169.9	227.8	191.4	3.0
674	Universals, plates and sheets, of iron or steel	44.7	5.6	80.4	6.3	22.7	31.7	18.5
677	Iron/steel wire/wheth/not coated, but not insulated	49.5	12.6	67.6	8.4	24.9	85.3	33.2
654	Textile fabrics, woven, other than cotton/man-made fiber	49.7	32.5	93.1	62.2	50.3	71.6	54.3
697	Household equipment of base metal, N.E.S.	50.7	33.6	60.5	178.8	14.5	11.7	61.2
685	Lead	50.8	25.4	13.4	238.0	217.2	199.1	24.2
673	Iron and steel bars, rods, angles, shapes & sections	53.7	10.1	70.5	7.7	72.4	178.4	27.5
676	Rails and railway track construction material	55.4	13.5	81.5	1.6	127.9	186.6	138.4
667	Pearls, precious & semi-precious stones, unworked/worked	56.7	54.5	116.8	274.7	140.9	52.7	2.3
894	Baby carriages, toys, games and sporting goods	58.8	109.5	100.7	166.7	18.6	12.8	104.4
724	Textile & leather machinery and parts	58.9	26.7	155.0	21.3	74.0	194.9	113.6
681	Silver, platinum & other metals of the platinum group	59.8	94.9	49.7	283.9	218.2	61.9	5.0
881	Photographic apparatus and equipment, N.E.S.	60.5	100.0	121.9	22.8	46.3	24.3	143.2
884	Optical goods, N.E.S.	60.7	75.5	133.4	37.6	22.3	58.6	141.3
662	Clay construction materials & refractory construction materials	60.7	15.1	91.3	89.4	191.9	108.8	45.2
761	Television receivers	62.2	142.8	23.7	17.2	77.1	1.2	147.7

[a] RCA indicators for three-digit SITC product categories selected for their overall weak comparative advantage.
[b] Includes 38 countries: all countries included in the table's regional groupings as well as Australia, New Zealand, China, South Africa, Egypt, and Israel.
[c] Only includes Austria, Belgium, Denmark, Finland, France, Germany, Greece, Ireland, Italy, Luxembourg, Netherlands, Portugal, Spain, Sweden, and the United Kingdom.
[d] Canada and Mexico.
[e] Includes Hong Kong, Korea, Singapore, and Taiwan.
[f] Only includes Indonesia, Malaysia, Philippines, and Thailand.
[g] Only includes Argentina, Brazil, Chile, Colombia, Peru, and Venezuela.
Source: Computed based on Stats Canada, World Trade Data Base (1995).

is that global integration may not benefit middle-class citizens as a group.

The corresponding political problem is that further global integration, by itself, may not be democratically supportable: Globalization could be something shunned by a democracy, not embraced. One solution, of course, is global integration and . . . where the blank describes any companion policies that could compensate groups that otherwise would vote no on global integration. As in AIDS therapy, often "cocktails" of policies taken together have the most impact, more than the sum of their isolated benefits: global integration and, say, middle-class education benefits, enhanced tax relief for the working poor, effective retraining inducements for those with skills of shrinking value, and so on. The challenge is to discover the politically supportable recipes of ingredients.

The same problem also can be described as overly narrow diffusion of the gains from global integration. Both economically and politically, policies that cause large and diffuse increases in living standards are best.[11] Diffusion of the gains from trade is as important as realizing them. Gains that are too concentrated are not necessarily good, no matter how large they are on average.

The same problem, and the same potential solutions, exist across countries. The gains from global integration seem especially large for some countries, smaller for others, and possibly negative for a few.[12] Almost all estimates show that gainers gain more than losers lose. But that only guarantees that the average (mean) global standard of living rises. The standard of living of the median country—the one in the middle of World Bank and other income rankings—might not rise much, if at all. So global integration might not benefit the typical country much, nor the vast group of middle- and lower-income countries.

The economic and diplomatic problems are similar. Further global integration may be politically insupportable among, say, all the members of the World Trade Organization. The gains are not diffuse enough. But possible solutions are similar too. Cocktails of policies can, in principle, draw in the countries least benefited. The challenge is to find the winning therapeutic policy mix, which might be different for each country. Global integration and greater technical assistance? . . . environmental grants and technology? . . . tighter security arrangements? . . . educational and cultural exchanges? . . . debt relief?

But what is the evidence that the recent gains from global integration are unequally distributed within and between countries? Are these problems really significant or merely hypothetical?

Diffusion Within Countries

Within countries, income inequality has been rising for the industrial market economies and falling among most others. Global integration's contributing influence is controversial.

A more precise summary is that patterns are diverse but follow clear central trends. For industrial market economies, conventional measures show little trend in the early 1980s and growing inequality in the late 1980s and early 1990s, especially outside of continental Europe.[13] For nonindustrial countries at all levels, the central trend over the 1980s and 1990s has been declining inequality.[14]

With these trends as context, growing dispersion of the within-country gains from global integration would seem to be primarily a problem for Europe and the United States. Since these areas have initiated the most important regional and global market integration over the past half century, this fact poses a particularly serious challenge to the momentum of world trade negotiations.

Within the United States, the role of global integration in these trends is well researched. Both "trade" and technology contribute to wage shifts between skill groups that create these trends. The influence of both is illustrated in Figure 3.1.

The message from the figure is clear. Time is a greater enemy of lower-skilled workers than trade is. First, note that U.S. export industries long have required a larger number of educated workers relative to the number required by import industries. Second, note that export and import industries both have shifted steadily toward requiring a relatively smaller number of less-educated workers. Finally, note that the time effect is much greater than the gap effect. While the relative size of the gap between the two lines grew slightly, both sets of lines shrank by more than half during the 20-year period shown. Both export and import industries reduced by more than half the number of less-educated workers needed for each more-educated worker.

It is remarkable that very similar shifts over time have been observed even in developing countries. There is growing consensus that these shifts reflect skill-biased technological change going on in parallel in a number of countries.[15] Skill-biased technolog-

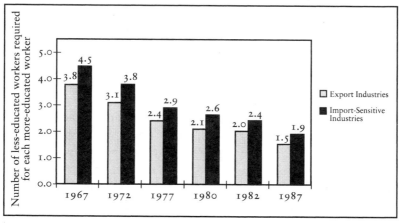

FIGURE 3.1 NUMBER OF LESS-EDUCATED WORKERS REQUIRED FOR EACH
MORE-EDUCATED WORKER IN EXPORT AND IMPORT-SENSITIVE INDUSTRIES
IN THE UNITED STATES

Source: J. David Richardson and Karin Rinal, *Why Exports Matter: More!* (Washington, D.C.: Institute for International Economics and the Manufacturing Institute, 1996), p. 30, based on table 1 of Robert E. Baldwin and Glen G.Cain, "Shifts in U.S. Relative Wages: The Role of Trade, Technology, and Factor Endowments," National Bureau of Economic Research Working Paper No. 5934, February 1997.

ical change is a shift in production methods toward more-skilled labor services and away from those that are less skilled. There may be only small impacts on measures of overall labor productivity, because these cases represent replacement of one worker with another (albeit one who is more skilled). But there will be large impacts on the relative rewards of the skilled successor and the less-skilled displaced worker.

Skill-biased technological change has several possible sources: One is worldwide computerization, another is worldwide outsourcing of intermediate components and business services. Trade, investment, and technology transfer can be vehicles for these technological trends. Computer trade has grown stunningly, and the recent Information Technology Agreement will only make it grow faster. International trade in components and business services continues to grow strikingly. Communications innovation and the declining cost of information make certain forms of skill-biased technological change global instead of local and therefore a source of growing worldwide wage dispersion rather than merely a localized phenomenon.

The compensation gap between export-engaged workers and others in the United States also should be mentioned. In fact, 50 percent of the widening gap in payroll shares between more- and less-skilled workers in U.S. manufacturing between 1973 and 1987 (and virtually all of the widening wage gap) can be explained by the growth of exporting plants and the shrinkage of plants that do not export.

Diffusion Across Countries

Across countries, income distribution has been characterized by hollowing out, describing two contrasting trends. Upper-middle-income countries are converging on high-income industrial countries in their average (mean) standard of living. But lower-middle-income countries have been slipping behind the higher groups, and some have been falling back toward low-income groups.[16]

The degree to which global integration has been responsible for these trends is, of course, controversial.[17] The World Bank's 1996 *Global Economic Prospects*, however, finds a strong correlation between growth in average living standards and integration with the global economy.[18] Indeed the patterns are striking. Whether global integration is measured as an attribute (level of integration) or as a momentum (speed of integration), globally integrated and globally integrating countries enjoy faster growth and more above-average standards of living than do others. The more integration impetus, the better, with the strongest and fastest integrators closing the standard-of-living gap rapidly on the high-income industrial countries. Countries that are moderate, weak, and slow/low integrators into the global economy are not only growing more slowly in living standards, they also are falling farther and farther behind the high-income industrial and industrializing countries, and most are suffering stable or declining living standards. The projection of these trends to 2005 in Figure 3.2 shows no relief except from the absolute decline in the standards of living in those countries that are least globally engaged.

Of course, one response to these trends is that these countries should get on board the globalization train. That was in fact the strong plea used during the Uruguay Round and may contribute to the more optimistic outlook for standard-of-living growth running up toward 2005 (Figure 3.2). But if the gap in gains continues to widen, or, worse, if high-income countries renege on their back-loaded textile/apparel and other Uruguay Round trade opening concessions, how can new global integration possibly be sustained? It could be diplomatically insupportable. Without

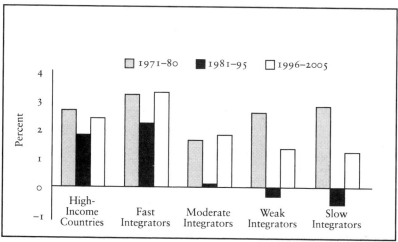

FIGURE 3.2 MEDIAN REAL PER CAPITA GDP GROWTH
BY INTEGRATION CATEGORY, 1971–2005

Source: World Bank, *Global Economic Prospects and the Developing Countries* (Washington, D.C.: World Bank, 1996), p. 31.

compensatory agreements on other matters, the gains to the small number of big gainers would in some sense be too big, and the gains to the big number of small gainers would be too small. And what would be the substance of such compensatory agreements? That is the global political challenge.

WHAT IT ALL MEANS

The global economy in the new century offers a different set of opportunities from in the old, and a different set of risks. The new opportunities involve growth-enhancing gains from trade—cheaper, higher-quality components, capital goods, education, and technologies rather than merely cheaper consumer goods. The new risks involve political fallout from misunderstanding and from narrow diffusion of these dynamic gains.

The new gains from global integration reward those who are savvy, agile, and skilled at identifying specialized business niches. Those are workers, firms, and countries. What they identify increasingly in the global economy are those niches in which to specialize their efforts and those in which to depend on the savvy, agility, and skills of others. The former become exported activities and those that promote investment (and even professional migration) abroad; the latter become sources of imports and inward investment.

The new risks from global integration are the opposite face of the new rewards. Workers, firms, and even countries that reflexively try to preserve traditional competence and protect those who refuse to adapt will face increasingly high costs—of forgone momentum. Forgone momentum will entail sluggish growth, ensuing social instability, unattractive investment opportunities, and reduced rewards to education, experience, and research and development.

But the market does not guarantee wide dispersion of the gains from trade. If they are narrowly distributed, or if enough workers, firms, and countries merely perceive (however mistakenly) that they are, there will be no political support for policies that engage global integration further and no international consensus for new global trade-liberalizing negotiations.

The United States and its trading partners today, therefore, face one large political problem and several related trade-offs. Solving the political problem according to selections made within the trade-offs will necessarily involve creativity, judiciousness, persuasion, and strong leadership.

The Majoritarian Problem

Further steps toward global integration are inevitably political. Not just border policy, but internal policies with cross-border effects will face pressures for rationalization. Yet if the median voter or the middle-income countries are not made better off by further global integration, how feasible is further integration in systems of democracy and consensus (as opposed to systems of meritocracy and coercion)? Deeper still in the same spirit, how then could further global integration be defended as desirable? Arguments that rising tides lift all the boats are inherently suspect anyway, but all the more so when the majority of boats seem anchored so far up river, out of range of the benefits of global integration, that the tide never reaches them. The problem is to make a majority of the boats ocean-going.

The Big Emerging Trade-Offs

Without solutions to this problem, unsavory trade-offs emerge. One trades off the dynamic gains from trade and their distribution, forcing countries to choose between productivity and growth impetus and avoiding marginalization or hollowing out of the middle class. This trade-off confronts industrial countries especially, since in others, global integration seems to have equalizing internal distributional effects.

There is a closely related trade-off between current generations and future generations. Failure to engage in further global integration may make economic prospects slightly more promising and secure for today's middle-age, middle-class households in industrial countries and for the poor among them. But as a result, the next generation may pay a high price 20 years from now.

More constructively, the most promising bequests that current generations can leave to their offspring are the skills, savvy, corporate culture, and social infrastructure necessary to engage the global marketplaces of the new millennium: cultural and language skills; technological, geographical, and scientific competence; workplace adaptability, mobility, and flexibility; and so on. Like all bequests, this one also costs current generations. But if this account of global integration is accurate, it can be persuasively defended in terms of intergenerational equity.[19]

Possible Policy Approaches

From this assessment of the economic context of U.S. trade policy, three promising directions for trade strategy emerge.

- *Therapeutic cohabitation.* Global integration is most likely to succeed when trade policy is paired with other issues that allow for exchanges of concessions that pull peripheries in. Political reciprocity is naturally built into such negotiating cocktails. Between countries, companion issues might include debt relief or environmental technology grants. Within countries, companion issues almost surely should include adjustment policies such as corporate rationalization (and privatization), worker mobility and retraining, and regional-national revenue sharing.[20]

- *Innovative Adjustment.* The adjustment agenda has been seriously neglected. Sectoral safeguards need reviving and rationalization, including credible means to lift safeguards over time. More thought needs to be put into voluntary buyouts of those adversely affected by trade, financed perhaps by special but temporary taxes on international transactions. Some of these buyouts might be arranged even on a cross-country basis.

• *Constructive Regionalism.* Regional trade liberalization initiatives should result in gains that diffuse widely within and between the participating countries.[21] That can best be accomplished through geographically contiguous groupings that facilitate the mobility and adaptability of the resources needed for adjustment. These regional trade groupings also should focus on economic sectors that will generate widely shared benefits.

NOTES

1. Economic misunderstanding among the populist public is one obvious side of this. But economists are guilty of misunderstanding too. They often have misunderstood their populist opposition. Economists have demonized protectionism so successfully that they now religiously refuse to have any serious exchange with devils who worry about the effect of globalization on community, rights, fairness, or the environment. "Those things are important," they say, "but border barriers to markets are neither their cause nor wise instruments to encourage them." As often is the case, demonization is the enemy of understanding. For a careful account of these themes, see Chapters 4 and 14 and Dani Rodrik, *Has Globalization Gone Too Far?* (Washington, DC: Institute for International Economics, 1996).

2. Although the focus here is on industrial sectors because the data are richer, the same opportunities for niche-based gains exist for trade in services, trade in corporate control (foreign direct investment), and trade in technology, whether protected by intellectual property protection or not. Opportunities for niche-based gains are not merely due to export potential. The gains from niche-determined imports of outsourced and other components are just as large as export gains and show up as productivity gains (again) for the firms that purchase them from abroad—imported components, business services, management prowess, and technology.

3. For a detailed summary of this evidence for the United States and cites for the corresponding research for Israel, Bulgaria, and Australia, see J. David Richardson and Karin Rindal, *Why Exports Really Matter!* (Washington, DC: Institute for International Economics and the Manufacturing Institute, 1995) and their *Why Exports Matter: More!* (Washington, DC: Institute for International Economics and the Manufacturing Institute, 1996). The evidence for the United States comes from a number of sources: researchers such as Bernard and Jensen at the Census Bureau's Center for Economic Studies, using the U.S. manufacturing censuses and annual surveys; the exhaustive U.S. exporter data base compiled at the U.S. Commerce Department by William Kolarik and summarized in William F. Kolarik and Scott G. Ellsworth, *A Profile of United States Exporters: Initial Findings from the Exporter Data Base* (Washington, DC: U.S. Department of Commerce, ITA, Office of Trade and Economic Analysis,

September 1993); surveys such as Paul Swamidass, "Export Induced Manufacturing Plant Characteristics" (unpublished ms., 1995, compiled by the Manufacturing Institute of the National Association of Manufacturers and others). The evidence for other countries can be found in Arye Bregman, Melvyn Fuss, and Haim Regev, "High Tech and Productivity: Evidence from Israeli Industrial Firms," *European Economic Review* 35 (1991), pp. 1199–1221; Simeon Djankov and Bernard Hoekman, "Trade Re-Orientation and Post-Reform Productivity Growth in Bulgarian Enterprises" (unpublished ms., August 28, 1996); and Henry Ergas and Mark Wright, "Internationalization, Firm Conduct and Productivity," paper presented at a conference on the international integration of the Australian economy, Loombs Centre, Kirribili, July 11–12, 1994.

4. For an argument that there is causal connection, see Richardson and Rindal, *Why Exports Matter: More!*, pp. 21–23. For a cautious inability to find a causal connection of exporting on productivity in Colombia, Mexico, or Morocco, see Sofronis Clerides, Saul Lach, and James Tybout, "Is 'Learning by Exporting' Important? Micro-Dynamic Evidence from Columbia, Mexico, and Morocco" (National Bureau of Economic Research Working Paper no. 5615, August 1996).

5. The following is from Richardson and Rindal, *Why Exports Matter: More!*, pp. 10-12.

6. Ibid., p. 13.

7. Bela Balassa, *Studies in Trade Liberalization* (Baltimore, MD: Johns Hopkins Press, 1967). The RCA index for a particular industry is defined as the share of the country's exports of the industry in total manufacturing exports of the country divided by the share of global exports of such product in total global manufacturing exports.

8. Six Eastern European countries, Norway, Switzerland, India, and Saudi Arabia (included in previous tables) are not included here.

9. For example, "eight developing countries accounted for two-thirds of foreign direct [investment] inflows in 1990–93, while half of all developing countries received little or none." World Bank, *Global Economic Prospects and the Developing Countries* (Washington, DC: World Bank, 1996), p. 1.

10. Indeed, economists estimate that the gains are quantitatively bigger than ever because of the way global integration enhances productivity and growth and disciplines distortions of market power.

11. The economics of this argument spring from the pathbreaking work of John Rawls's *Theory of Justice* (1971) and those who have continued in a similar tradition. But they do not require Rawls's extreme simplification or abstraction. They require only assent to the principle that of two policies with the same effect on mean standards of living, the one that raises the median most is generally to be preferred.

12. Even in traditional thinking, adverse movements in a country's terms of trade could impose losses. Alongside new gains from trade via productivity, growth, variety, and monopolistic undermining are a few new reasons why, in exceptional cases, a country actually might lose from global liberalization.

13. See OECD, *Employment Outlook* (1996), table 3.1, pp. 61–62, and World Bank, *World Development Report* (Washington, DC: World Bank, 1986–1997). The former uses ratios of earnings of the marginal worker in the top decile of wage earners to the median and the median to the marginal worker in the bottom decile. The latter uses income or consumption shares of the top decile or quintile to the bottom quintile.

14. Based on World Bank, *World Development Report*, 1986–1997. Exceptions with more varied patterns include Brazil and Thailand.

15. Eli Berman, John Bound, and Stephen Machin, "Implications of Skill-Biased Technological Change: International Evidence" (National Bureau of Economic Research Working Paper No. 6166, September 1997).

16. For detail, see Ishac Diwan and Ana Revenga, "Wages, Inequality, and International Integration," *Finance and Development*, September 1995, pp. 7–9; Lant Prichett, "Divergence, Big Time" (World Bank Policy Research Working Paper no. 1522, 1995); and Danny T. Quah, "Convergence Empirics Across Economies with (Some) Capital Mobility," *Journal of Economic Growth*, 1 (March 1996), pp. 95–124.

17. Ramon Moreno, "Are World Incomes Converging," Federal Reserve Bank of San Francisco Weekly Letter No. 93–41, November 26, 1993, for example, observes that the clustering at the bottom could be explained by measured declines in investment and productivity growth in low- and middle-income countries from 1982 to 1992. The controversial 1993 World Bank study of the East Asian miracle attributed much of the clustering at the top to global integration by outward-oriented converging countries.

18. The measure of integration is either (a) the level of or (b) the time change (early 1990s over early 1980s) in a simple average of four integration indicators, all standardized to be comparably measured: the ratios of trade and foreign direct investment to gross domestic product; the country's sovereign credit ratings as determined by the publication *Institutional Investor*; and the share of manufactures in exports.

19. In these matters, the trade-offs and opportunities confronting today's societies have somewhat the same character as those confronting insular, agrarian, traditional societies of a century ago. Current generations in those times may not have gained from the forces pressing them toward education, urban relocation, industrialization, specialization, and interdependence (instead of self-sufficiency), but it would be ludicrous to argue that their children and grandchildren did not gain.

20. Perhaps core standards for labor relations and industrial relations, in relative preference to further intellectual-property rationalization.

21. And that, of course, keep the gains positive by circumscribing their preferential and diversionary effects.

Chapter 4

Gaining Support for Trade from the American Public

Ellen L. Frost

To be credible and effective, a national trade strategy needs broad public support. Within the next few years, a number of key developments will highlight the presence—or absence—of such support. The effort to renew authority to implement trade agreements (so-called fast-track authority), the possible expansion of the North American Free Trade Agreement (NAFTA), the need to address China's entry into the world economy, the planned elimination of the global system of quotas on textiles and apparel, and many other controversial issues will keep trade on or near the front burner of American political life.[1]

These initiatives are almost certain to trigger some form of public debate. Gone are the days when trade policy could be formulated and negotiated behind closed doors. Too many Americans are caught up in it, and too many interests are at stake. Whole new sets of actors have emerged, and congressional interest has intensified. Trade has been both oversold and demonized. The media have fastened onto trade-related controversies and are unlikely to let them lapse back into relative obscurity.

In economic terms too, trade is here to stay. The United States ceased to be even relatively self-sufficient decades ago.

The sum total of exports, imports, and returns on investment is now equivalent to over 30 percent of U.S. gross domestic product (GDP), up from 13 percent in 1970. Given the higher-than-average wages and productivity levels prevailing in export-competitive industries, no U.S. president will pass up the chance to expand exports. But that means reducing import barriers as well, which is politically less popular.

The question is, can this debate proceed in such a way as to deepen Americans' understanding of trade policy and to build public support for trade in the process? How should the protrade side of the debate be framed, and who should make the case?

U.S. ATTITUDES TOWARD TRADE

As of the mid-1990s, trade is nowhere near the top of the list of American concerns. Crime, drugs, and immigration greatly overshadow it. Nevertheless, anxiety about trade can burst into flame rather suddenly, only to die down again a short time later. At such times trade becomes a scapegoat for the nation's economic and social ills. The 1996 presidential campaign of Pat Buchanan was by no means the first example.

Such explosions could happen again because there is no clear foundation of support for trade. Americans have a sense of inevitability about trade, but they do not necessarily like it or understand it. Accordingly, attitudes toward trade often are inconsistent. When asked about goals, for example, many times individual respondents are simultaneously willing to restrict trade (to preserve jobs and punish "unfair" traders) and *un*willing to restrict trade (to preserve consumer choice and stimulate competition).

Without a doubt, the collapse of the Mexican economy—sparked by the collapse of the peso in December 1994—dealt a serious setback to supporters of free trade, at least in the short term. Before the Mexican economic crisis, the public felt that NAFTA was "mostly good" for the U.S. economy by a margin of 50 percent to 31 percent.[2] Scarcely had the wounds of the NAFTA fight healed, however, when Mexico was once more in the public eye. The combination of the perceived U.S. "bailout" of the Mexican economy and the temporary collapse of U.S. export prospects imprinted the following equation in the public mind: "Trade" = NAFTA = Mexico = disaster. This image persists despite the fact that U.S. exports to Mexico have more than fully recovered.[3]

On the other hand, the public also is registering more long-term confidence about America's future as a trading nation. Only

21 percent of the American public believes that Japan is a "critical" threat to American competitiveness, down from 63 percent in 1990. According to one poll, fully 57 percent of Americans rate the country's ability to deal with foreign economic competition to be either "excellent" or "good," up 15 points from 1991. Compared with the late 1970s, there has been a steady decrease in the percentage of Americans who believe that retaining tariffs is necessary, from 57 percent in 1978 to 48 percent in 1994.[4]

American attitudes toward trade tend to divide on the basis of age, class, and education. Those most likely to perceive the benefits of trade include the young (under 30), those with higher incomes, and those with higher levels of education. Least supportive are women over 40, the elderly, those with lower incomes, members of labor unions, and those with a high school education or less.

Job Creation and Job Security

In the United States, as in most countries, jobs are the number-one trade issue. Whatever else Americans may feel about trade, majorities believe that trade reduces the overall number of jobs and that job losses from foreign competition are an "extremely" or "very" serious problem.[5]

At first sight, the persistence of this fear is a paradox. Some 11 to 12 million new jobs have been created in the United States since 1993, as compared with a million or less in Europe and Japan. The unemployment rate is currently quite low (around 5 percent). Moreover, job turnover is a normal feature of the American labor market: On average, 400,000 Americans change jobs every *week*; about 15 percent of the workforce each year. So why are Americans feeling that their jobs are threatened by trade?

A general answer is that Americans have enormous misconceptions about the economy. According to poll data published in the *Washington Post*, the average American thinks the number of jobless people is four times higher than it actually is. Seven in ten Americans believe that there are fewer jobs than there were five years ago. They are similarly misinformed about inflation, the budget deficit, and foreign aid.[6]

The specific link between anxiety and trade appears to spring from the general restructuring of the American job market that occurred in the late 1980s and early 1990s. Prodded by the Japanese challenge and galvanized by the information revolution, many companies began to consolidate and/or disperse their operations, shedding large numbers of workers in the process. Large corporations that had always seemed like secure sources of employment underwent drastic streamlining. Whole communities have been decimated by the closure of a plant that had always been part of the landscape.

The number of people (mostly Americans) employed by *Fortune* 500 companies shrank from 16.5 million in 1979 to 11.5 million in 1995.[7] The number of permanent dismissals, as opposed to temporary layoffs, has grown by at least a third since 1980, reaching 40 to 45 percent by 1993.[8] These displaced workers are more likely to be older, white collar, and relatively well educated.[9]

The sudden collapse of the Mexican economy in 1994–95 crystallized American anxiety about trade. In 1993 then U.S. Trade Representative Mickey Kantor had predicted that NAFTA would result in 200,000 new export jobs related to Mexico. But instead of hiring additional workers to service the growing Mexican market, companies were forced to retrench. In 1995 Public Citizen turned Kantor's arithmetic around and calculated that 600,000 jobs had been lost.[10] A month before the 1996 presidential election, Pat Choate, Ross Perot's vice presidential candidate, claimed that 500,000 U.S. jobs had been "lost to Mexico because of NAFTA alone."[11] Although the Mexican economy is recovering, Mexico remains a lightning rod for the whole debate over trade and jobs and serves as a vivid reminder that the job creation argument should not be oversold.

It is a political fact of life that job losses associated with imports are more visible than job gains associated with exports. The same is true when a company shuts down a domestic operation and invests overseas. In a poll published in 1996, the percentage of respondents who said that corporate downsizing is bad for the economy was virtually the same as those who said that trade agreements have cost U.S. jobs (59 percent and 54 percent, respectively).[12] Feeling injured and helpless, many Americans turn their anger against trade. As they see it, trade agreements result in less control of their lives.

This sense of grievance is exacerbated by the lack of effective support programs designed to help displaced workers. Adjustment and training opportunities have not kept pace with the expansion of trade. The planned strengthening of adjustment assistance and "lifetime learning" programs, which Secretary of Labor Robert Reich advocated with conviction in 1993, has not taken place.

Not only has the federal budget been scaled back across the board; there is considerable doubt as to whether past efforts have been effective, and if not, whether the federal government should play a role in the adjustment process at all.

In the past, argues Harvard economist Dani Rodrik, societies accepted the social and economic disruptions that accompany the liberalization of the market in return for some degree of "cushioning" by governments as well as growth. This welfare function still receives public support in the United States and elsewhere, but governments are increasingly unwilling and/or unable to sustain their end of the bargain. Rodrik believes that this situation creates a tension between the consequences of globalization and the social legitimacy of free trade.[13]

Wages

When asked if trade pulls wages down, two-thirds of American respondents say yes.[14] This fear is an offshoot of two more general concerns about wages.

The first is wage stagnation. From 1973 to 1995, wages grew by only about 1 percent per year, compared with 3 percent from 1960 to 1973. To be sure, overall compensation has risen, but what people feel is what goes home in their pockets, not what goes for health insurance and other benefits.

The second is a growing wage gap. The "skill premium"— that is, the gap between the first-time wages of high school and college graduates—has risen by 18 percent.[15] The income disparity between the richest and poorest end of the population spectrum has widened as well. Economists are divided as to what exact role, if any, trade plays in this trend. What is clear is that participation in the high-stakes global economy offers both greater rewards and higher risks.

These concerns are exacerbated by the job fluctuations described earlier. It is widely believed that a majority of displaced workers end up accepting jobs that pay significantly lower wages. Two recent studies suggest that this wage loss is on the order of 10 percent, and one indicates that the gap persists even after six or more years have passed.[16]

Fear of competing with low-wage countries takes root in this soil. During the 1996 presidential campaign, candidates Bob Dole, Pat Buchanan, and Ross Perot sought to turn this fear to their advantage. At the Republican Convention in August 1996, for example, Senator Dole stated, "We must commit ourselves to a trade policy that does not suppress pay and threaten American jobs."

The exact link between imports and wages is a matter of debate among economists. What seems clear is that imports are a catalyst accelerating the transition to a more efficient allocation of resources. Those left behind are the workers in America's least competitive industries, who suffer from low productivity and receive lower-than-average wages. These are often the industries facing competition from imports.

By contrast, jobs in export-oriented sectors pay 5 to 15 percent more than the average wage. These jobs appear to be expanding. According to the Council of Economic Advisors, two-thirds of the net growth in full-time employment between February 1994 and February 1996—8.5 million jobs—occurred in industries or occupation groups paying above-median wages.[17] Many if not most of these are in globally competitive sectors.

Fairness

Many Americans have a general impression that foreigners do not "play fair."[18] This suspicion may date from the earliest days of the republic, when George Washington urged his compatriots to avoid "entangling alliances." According to at least one seasoned observer, former U.S. Trade Representative Mickey Kantor reinforced "latent public suspicion of trade" by repeatedly suggesting that other countries' trade promises cannot be trusted.[19] That is why he placed so much emphasis on the need for enforcement.

Perceptions of unfairness tend to center on Japan. According to a respected poll, 71 percent of the American public and 80 percent of U.S. leaders think Japan practices "unfair" trade. By contrast, the perceptions that the European Union is unfair are 35 percent and 27 percent, respectively.[20] A significant majority, however, thinks that President Clinton is making progress in opening markets in Japan.[21] From now on, the focus of concern about unfairness is likely to be on China, whose growing trade surplus with the United States is second only to Japan's.

A new variation on the theme of unfairness is the American version of what Europeans call "social dumping." This ugly term refers to countries that are perceived to be capturing markets and/or luring investment by taking advantage of low labor standards and inadequate environmental protection. Unlike Europeans, Americans have no interest in a "social charter" or in anything else that smacks of excessive government intervention in the economy. But they share with Europeans a fear that they will be unable to compete against low-wage workers and environmentally unregulated industries. Thus labor standards and environmental protection are not marginal concerns. Rightly or wrongly, they influence the definition of fair competition.

Corporate Responsibility

At first sight, it is hard to understand why a number of environmental groups have joined forces with supporters of organized labor and worker rights advocates to oppose the expansion of trade. The two make an odd couple. Some environmentalists advocate a "zero-growth" world economy and an austere lifestyle that seem alien to labor's traditional goals.

What brings environmentalists and labor activists together is concern about the behavior of multinational corporations. As they see it, these corporations are abandoning workers and communities to pursue profits around the world. In so doing they are destroying U.S. jobs, undermining health and safety standards, exploiting foreign workers, and polluting the global environment. Their chief executive officers receive exorbitant salaries, but they are subject to no oversight and no governance. No one elects them, but their decisions affect millions of people. By paying foreign workers inadequate wages and forcing them to work in substandard conditions, they are simultaneously exploiting poor people overseas and depriving Americans of jobs. Where economists see an efficient allocation of resources based on a global division of labor, the new anti-NAFTA, anti–World Trade Organization (WTO) coalition sees corporate greed and a blow to democracy.

There is an interesting parallel between these concerns and the broader movement known as communitarianism, which stresses the needs of the community as well as the individual. According to communitarians, the exclusive pursuit of private interests erodes both the social environment and the institutions of civil society.[22] Some Americans see trade and investment in these terms.

Sovereignty

Americans broke away from foreign rule in the 18th century and have remained wary of conniving foreign princes ever since. Proud of their independence, and occasionally paranoid about foreign influence, most of them recoil from any suggestion of "world government."

A new coalition, uniting elements from both the right and left wings of the political spectrum, invoked this fear in their fight against both NAFTA and the Uruguay Round.

Specifically, these groups claimed—erroneously—that NAFTA would force Americans to lower their health, safety, and environmental standards. The WTO was described as a "world court" with power to change U.S. laws. They compared the WTO to the U.N. General Assembly, with its one-nation, one-vote system; the United States, they said, always would be outvoted.

But members of the antitrade coalition make at least one valid point. Just as then British Prime Minister Margaret Thatcher accused the European Commission of a "democratic deficit," so these groups point out that trade decisions affecting ordinary people are made in Geneva behind closed doors, by unelected officials who are not accountable to the public. Americans recognize that rules-based international trade necessarily implies that each country accepts limits on its sovereignty, but they have a right to insist that the WTO is at least reasonably accessible and accountable to ordinary citizens.[23]

Moral Purpose

Many observers have noted that Americans feel more comfortable supporting foreign policy when it is presented in a moral framework. By the same token, Americans need to feel that if they are bearing some of the costs of free trade, they are doing so in a good cause. Those who advocate a more open trade and investment climate will have to invoke more than the pocketbook. Thus far the only major link between trade and moral concerns is a negative one, namely trade sanctions against governments that support terrorism, suppress human rights, invade another country, or otherwise violate international norms. In recent U.S. legislation directed at Cuba, Iran, and Libya, the extension of extraterritorial claims and restrictions against foreign nationals has enraged America's trading partners. This is not a new phenomenon; witness the fight over the Soviet gas pipeline in the early 1980s. Supporters of these measures believe that normal trade and investment are favors or privileges that should be withdrawn in response to bad behavior. These measures, however, rarely achieve their stated goals.[24]

In the long run, the growth of market-oriented economic policies is linked not only to a higher standard of living but also to a more tolerant, inclusive, and democratic political system. Trade and investment introduce modern and open ways of thinking and acting that encourage the expression of human rights and peaceful behavior and thus ultimately threaten dictatorial, aggressive regimes. They also create communities of mutual well-being whose citizens are less likely to wage war against one another than they would in the absence of economic links.

ELEMENTS OF A NONPARTISAN TRADE STRATEGY

Stakeholders

A major challenge is to expand the trade coalition beyond traditional protrade groups in order to reach new "stakeholders" in the international trading system. These stakeholders might be categorized as follows: business, labor, consumer groups, academics, members of Congress, nongovernmental organizations (NGOS), and local leaders.

Business. Efforts to mobilize support for trade from new elements of the business community should pay special attention to small and medium-sized companies. Not only do they help to counter the image of "fat-cat" corporations profiting from trade while laying off American workers; they are also the most dynamic sources of new jobs and new exports. Other good candidates are service industries such as insurance and accounting; agribusiness; tourism; high-technology industries such as telecommunications, aerospace, and medical equipment; and state and local chambers of commerce.

Labor. Working people everywhere have a vital interest in trade. Thus far the major unions remain hostile to further trade liberalization, but both the quantity and quality of U.S. jobs will be a central theme of any trade debate. In that context it is important not to "oversell" trade, as may have been done in the case of NAFTA. Open trade does not create jobs per se; it facilitates a more efficient allocation of resources. Those resources then can be redeployed to create and serve new markets, thus creating new job opportunities. Stating the advantages of trade this way will help to avoid the charge of "broken promises," such as those cited by opponents of NAFTA, when immediate gains were not achieved.

Consumer Groups. In the United States, consumers are natural allies of free trade and have been for some time. The role of trade in dampening inflation and keeping down the cost of living are natural themes. New target audiences for these groups could be young people and older Americans.

Academics. Intellectuals in the United States lack the prestige that they enjoy in other societies, but they have a place in the debate. A study conducted at the Institute for International Economics, for example, calculated that trade protection costs the United States roughly $70 billion per year, or more than 1 percent of GDP. The average consumer loss per job "saved" is a breathtaking $170,000.[25] Studies of this kind, if conducted rigorously, lend credibility to protrade arguments.

Members of Congress. Article I of the Constitution vests the power to regulate commerce with foreign nations in Congress. As the scope of trade policy expands, it is worth thinking about how Congress receives, organizes, channels, and applies information about trade. Many members of Congress would like to support trade more actively, but they lack credible arguments and relevant local data.

Elected representatives witness the effects of trade firsthand, in their states or districts. According to political consultants, trade offers a platform from which candidates for Congress can display personal attitudes and leadership qualities (positive or negative).

Nongovernmental Organizations. In December 1996, on the eve of the WTO's first ministerial meeting, WTO Director General Renato Ruggiero addressed more than 150 NGOs, calling them "a bridge, an essential link" between the WTO and the public.[26] Most NGOs are relative newcomers to trade and bring little intellectual capital to trade dicussions, but they already have had a policy impact and will be key players in any future debate. Labor and environmental groups are already mobilized, and other NGOs (e.g., church groups) have begun to speak up on trade as well. Addressing their suspicions, and giving them a seat at the trade policy table, will be crucial to the legitimacy of any trade strategy.

Local Leaders. Local leaders are also relative newcomers to the trade debate, but their links with "real people" and "real business" in their communities make them invaluable participants. Such leaders include governors, mayors, members of state legislatures and city councils, educators, journalists, businesspeople, selected union leaders, and representatives of port authorities or other transportation systems. Local leaders are all too aware of the negative affects of trade when, for example, a local plant closes. They can be made more aware of the potential to increase exports of locally provided goods and services.

The Message

Any national trade strategy must be devised with the interests of these stakeholders in mind. The message conveying such a strategy must not only address these interests but also take account of the general public's concerns identified above, namely jobs, wages, fairness, corporate responsibility, sovereignty, and moral purpose.

A well thought out trade policy is likely to contain at least three major thrusts: open and contestable markets, expansion of the rule of law, and transparent institutions. A strategy based on these components addresses several of the concerns identified earlier: job creation, wages, fairness, and (arguably) sovereignty. It addresses only indirectly, if at all, job security, corporate responsibility, and moral purpose.

The message conveying a national trade strategy must both reflect and transcend this distinction. It is important for Americans to understand what trade can and cannot do. Just as trade cannot be blamed for all social ills, it cannot solve them all either. Ultimately, there is no substitute for sound domestic economic and social policy. To be effective, the trade message needs to be expressed in a context that is broader than the scope of the trade strategy.

With respect to concerns most directly related to trade policy, an appropriate theme of the message would be fair competition. Since American prospects in the world export market are currently extremely good, competitive themes might play well. It is important, however, to cast this aspect of the message in "win-win" language rather than in "win-lose" or "trade war" terms. Doing so is both right on the merits and reassuring to our trading partners, who scrutinize U.S. trade policy messages with great care.

With respect to concerns beyond the scope of trade policy, the message must be that trade is not an appropriate tool. Instead, debate should center on domestic policies to strengthen competitiveness and promote adjustment to corporate relocations, such as education, worker retraining, and community development.

That leaves the issue of moral purpose. The indirect linkage between trade and moral purpose could and should be strengthened. At the very least, one can cite a definite link between trade and human well-being. When the world trading system was established in the wake of World War II, it was seen as a key component of a comprehensive institutional order. The architects of the General Agreement on Tariffs and Trade correctly believed that their work was bound up in the overall quest for recovery, peace, prosperity, and democracy. During the Cold War, U.S. foreign policy also had a strong moral purpose.

Now that the threat of communism has disappeared, it is possible to move the debate to a higher level. Themes might include the contribution that trade can make to sustainable development, rising labor standards, and human rights. A broader set of themes might pick up on the notion of trade as a catalyst not only for economic growth but for healthy social and political development. In such circumstances peace, freedom, and democracy are more likely to flourish. This train of reasoning may require inventing both a new vocabulary and a new set of conceptual linkages.

CONVEYING THE MESSAGE

Conveying the message about trade should proceed in a top-down, bottom-up fashion. Primary responsibility rests with both government officials and leaders from the private sector. In addition, individual citizens bear some responsibility for acquiring knowledge about trade, just as they do about other important national issues.

The Role of Education

Trade is beginning to be taught in schools, especially at the high school level. It enters the curriculum in two main ways. First, some 30 states now require the teaching of economics at the high school level. An international unit usually is included in the curriculum. A typical case study is the U.S.-Japan trade relationship.

Second, many states require a high school social studies course that covers contemporary history, geography, and world affairs. In New York State, for example, the course extends for two years and is aimed at ninth and tenth graders. Such courses typically include units on China and Japan, where trade is a natural topic.[27]

Certain states have launched programs of their own. The State of Washington, for instance, brings together representatives from the port authority, the business community, and the schools for summer seminars on trade. Students discuss trade in the classroom in the morning and visit a factory or port facility in the afternoon. Such initiatives, however, appear to be few and far between.

In response to this new interest in trade, a few new teaching tools have appeared. Organizations such as the Asia Society and the Japan Society have launched educational programs aimed especially at high school teachers. These programs include daylong seminars, newsletters, and videos. Members of the Business Roundtable have developed discussion materials to use with their employees. The President's Export Council has initiated a "Virtual Trade Mission" for high school and junior college students, complete with multimedia presentations, workbooks, and opportunities for discussion with public and private sector representatives engaged in trade. One enterprising company even has invented a board game, unfortunately named "Trade Wars," in which each player represents a group of countries.

The Role of the U.S. Government

With the partial exception of the Commerce Department and the Agriculture Department, U.S. government officials have not engaged in systematic "outreach" to the public to explain trade policy. Commerce and Agriculture officials have largely concentrated on export promotion. Sometimes a major congressional vote will produce a flurry of speeches (notably NAFTA and the Uruguay Round votes), but trade policy as a whole—including the vital contribution of imports and investment to jobs, growth, and productivity—is rarely discussed outside the Washington Beltway.

Limited budget resources and the press of daily business help to explain this gap. But the pattern must change. Opponents of trade already have taken advantage of call-in radio shows to lambast NAFTA and the WTO and to stir up fear and resentment. They are also active on the Internet. Op-ed pieces attacking free trade appear regularly—far more regularly, in fact, than regular editorials defending international commerce.[28] Supporters of more open trade and investment should learn a lesson from their antagonists and become much more active in the media.

Needless to say, personal commitment and interest from the president are essential. Any U.S. president has the advantage of the "bully pulpit." President Clinton made several important speeches about trade at the beginning of his first term, but apparently he was counseled to drop the subject. He should consider not only speeches and radio broadcasts but also events that could be highly publicized. One could be a "National Trade Summit" similar to the 1993 "Economic Summit" held at Little Rock, Arkansas. Another could be a "World Trade Summit," as suggested by economist C. Fred Bergsten.[29] A third could be a bipartisan trade policy commission charged with identifying the major "stakeholders" and connecting them with U.S. government officials through a series of local and regional meetings.

Regional and Multilateral Institutions

Regional and multilateral trade institutions, particularly the WTO, should do their part to overcome public fears about trade. Their tasks now include creating user-friendly educational materials for the public and expanding access to meetings and information for designated nongovernmental organizations and individuals. The WTO recently has taken a step in the right direction by producing two simple brochures and a video, and more documents are being "derestricted" and circulated. Access for nongovernmental groups, however, remains minimal. The United States is pressing actively for greater access and a more "transparent" modus operandi, but diplomatic traditions die hard.

The Role of Stakeholders

There is strong evidence that people change their views on trade if they are given correct information. Obviously, such information must be credible. Along these lines, a successful trade strategy will require mobilizing all of the stakeholders and suggesting assignments corresponding to what they do best. For example, the Business Roundtable has produced a clear, factual booklet and a video about trade. Thanks to electronic mail, the various groups engaged in trade education can communicate easily and share lessons learned.

Each state, city, and locality will need to tailor the trade message to its own circumstances. In many places there is a World Trade Center or other trade-oriented association. These private sector groups can play an important role in reaching and educating new stakeholders. In San Francisco, for example, the Bay Area World Trade Center has launched a weekly "Open Forum" where questions can be addressed to trade experts from a number of companies and banks without charge.

The Media

The partners in a new trade coalition should think more boldly and creatively about the media. For example, *Parade* magazine runs a weekly column on what teenagers think. Why not an annual essay contest on "Why Trade Is Important to the U.S." with a $5,000 prize? *TV Guide* would be another good target. There could be a national prize for local reporting on the links between a local community and the international economy—showing, for instance, that losses from imports were offset by exports or that the local community college depended in part on foreign students.

Opinion leaders from different walks of life could be asked to write Op-ed pieces about what trade means to them or to mention trade in television spots. Such leaders could include celebrities and sports stars. A model of sorts is talk show host Oprah Winfrey's exhortation to Americans to read more. The trade equivalent of a "national spokesman" or "goodwill ambassador" also could be considered.

Television offers numerous opportunities. Perhaps a public service announcement could be devised with a snappy message about trade. If trade is a key ingredient of economic health, then analogies with the antismoking campaign are not totally farfetched. The Advertising Council of America might become a player in a trade campaign, especially since the advertising industry is now exporting its services. For similar reasons, the Motion Picture Association might become involved in an effort to reach film viewers.

Above all, a trade strategy should make increased use of *local* TV and radio. Community programming, talk shows, and local newscasts are logical targets.

The popularity of the Internet argues strongly for a web page for trade. Users could have access to up-to-date information from both government agencies and educational institutions. Such a forum could provide a rapid response to pseudofactual allegations of the sort issued by the Perot campaign.

CONCLUSION

A successful public diplomacy campaign in support of a trade strategy will require time, planning, and money. But there is arguably little choice. Opponents of trade expansion are waiting for the right moment to launch another attack. They have shown how far a simple message can carry (e.g., the infamous "giant sucking sound") and how much can be achieved by unpaid volunteers.

Happily, the outlook is promising. Global circumstances are favorable; trade opportunities are expanding all around the globe. Trade is not painless, nor is it a cure-all. It should not be oversold. But given adequate information and a message that is attuned to American concerns, the public will readily recognize that the very nature of trade—with its vital mixture of choice, competition, opportunity, and freedom—reinforces all that is best about the United States.

NOTES

The author gratefully acknowledges the assistance of Frederick L. Montgomery, who provided valuable analytical insights and extensive editorial suggestions.

1. Throughout this chapter, the word "trade" is used in its broadest sense, to include goods, services, investment, government procurement, intellectual property protection, and other economic activities encompassed by existing or proposed global trade rules.

2. John E. Rielly, *American Public Opinion and U.S. Foreign Policy, 1995* (Chicago: The Chicago Council on Foreign Relations, 1996).

3. U.S. exports to Mexico in the first half of 1996 were up 27 percent over the corresponding period in 1993. Office of the United State Trade Representative, "North American Free Trade Agreement: Information Package," August 13, 1996.

4. Ibid., p. 29.

5. Committee for Free Trade and Economic Growth, "Contrary to Conventional Wisdom, Americans Support Free Trade, National Survey Finds," press release, July 17, 1996.

6. Richard Morin and John M. Berry, "A Nation That Poor-Mouths Its Times," *Washington Post*, October 15, 1996, sec. A, p. 1.

7. David Hale, "Is the U.S. Yield Curve Discounting Increased Political Risk?" *The Weekly Money Report* 29 (1996): 2.

8. Ibid., p. 2.

9. Council of Economic Advisers, "Job Creation and Employment Opportunities: The United States Labor Market, 1993–1996" (photocopy), p. 9.

10. "NAFTA's Broken Promises," in Public Citizen, "The Economic, Environmental, and Social Costs of and Response to Economic Globalization," information packet for the International Forum on Globalization Congressional Briefing, Washington, DC, May 10, 1996. For more detail, see Public Cit-

izen, "NAFTA's Broken Promises: Job Creation under NAFTA," September 1995, and the Commerce Department's rebuttal, released on September 4, 1995.

11. Pat Choate, "We're Trading Away Our Jobs," *Washington Post*, October 6, 1996, sec. C, pp. 1–2.

12. "Policymakers vs. the Public," *Washington Post*, October 15, 1996, sec. A, p. 6.

13. Dani Rodrik, *Has Globalization Gone Too Far?* (Washington, DC: Institute for International Economics, 1997), pp. 90–92.

14. Ibid.

15. Susan M. Collins, "Adjusting to Labor Market Disruptions from Trade and Other Economic Changes" (in conference report "International Trade and the U.S. Economy, Second Conference," Washington, DC, May 1996), p. 36.

16. Council of Economic Advisers, "Job Creation and Employment Opportunities," p. 11.

17. Ibid., p. 4.

18. See the discussion in Clyde Prestowitz, *Trading Places: How We Allowed Japan to Take the Lead* (New York: Basic Books, 1988), pp. 75–81.

19. Marc Levinson, "Kantor's Cant," *Foreign Affairs* 75, no. 2 (1996): 2, 7.

20. Rielly, *American Public Opinion and U.S. Foreign Policy*.

21. John Maggs, "Majority Back Clinton on Japan, JofC [*sic*] Poll Says," *Journal of Commerce*, September 8, 1995, sec. A, p. 1.

22. See, for example The Communication Network, "The Responsive Communitarian Platform: Rights and Responsibilities" (undated photocopy); and "Promoting a Return to 'Civil Society,'" *Washington Post*, December 15, 1996, sec. A, p. 1. The link between trade and communitarianism is discussed in Susan Aaronson, *Trade Is Everybody's Business* (Alexandria, VA: Close Up Publishing, 1996), pp. 139–140.

23. Susan A. Aaronson, *Trade and the American Dream* (Lexington: University Press of Kentucky, 1996), pp. 172–76.

24. Gary Hufbauer, Jeffrey J. Schott, and Kimberly Ann Elliott, "Economic Sanctions Reconsidered," Working Paper (Washington, DC: Institute for International Economics, 1990).

25. Gary Hufbauer and Kimberly Ann Elliott, *Measuring the Costs of Protection in the United States* (Washington, DC: Institute of International Economics, 1994), p. 11.

26. *Reuter European Business Report*, December 8, 1996, http://www.wto96.org/news/intl/o8ina107%2D25.html.

27. Instructional materials for teaching trade in high schools include: Susan A. Aaronson, *Trade Is Everybody's Business*; Susan A. Aaronson, *Are There Trade-Offs When Americans Trade?* (Alexandria, VA: Close Up Publishing, 1996); Agency for Instructional Technology, *Economics at Work: Teacher's Guide*, Module 3, Lesson E: "All Over the World," 1996; Lucien Ellington, et al., *The Japanese Economy: Teaching Strategies* (New York: Joint Council on Economic Education, 1990); Randy Charles Epping, *A Beginner's Guide to the World Economy* (New York: Vintage Books, 1992); Michael Hart, *Trade: Why Bother?* (Ottawa: Centre for Trade

Policy and Law, 1992); Gary Mukai and Truc Truong, *U.S.-Japan Relations: The View from Both Sides of the Pacific, Part III: Introduction to International Trade* (Stanford, CA: Stanford Program on International and Cross-Cultural Education, 1994); Russell D. Roberts, *The Choice: A Fable of Free Trade and Protectionism* (Englewood Cliffs, NJ: Prentice Hall, 1994); *Social Studies School Service Catalog* (Culver City, CA: Social Studies School Service, 1996); Trade Wars (a board game) (Naiad Corporation, 1991); and World Trade Organization, *WTO: Trading into the Future* (Handbook and video) (Geneva: World Trade Organization, 1996).

28. A 1995 survey of media coverage about Mexico and related trade issues found that editorials supported more open trade with Mexico by a margin of 2 to 1, while opinion pieces and letters reflected opposition in the order of 4 to 1. "Study Shows Mexico Is a Mixed Bag in American Media," press release from Carma International.

29. C. Fred Bergsten, "Globalizing Free Trade," *Foreign Affairs* 75 (1996): 114–115.

Chapter 5

Workforce Training: Investing in Human Capital or Antidote To International Trade?

Howard Rosen

Proponents of liberal trade cite two main reasons for more worker training. First, and most important, they argue that training offers a means to help workers who lose their jobs due to increased import competition. They argue that, through training, displaced workers can acquire skills that will help them regain employment, perhaps in positions that pay higher wages and offer greater job security. Second, since export-related jobs tend to be skill-intensive, they argue that a better-trained workforce could improve supply conditions for increased U.S. exports.

Beyond the trade policymaking community, however, Americans have more of a love-hate relationship with the issue of workforce training.

On the one hand, developing an educated workforce—"investing in human capital"—is considered by some to be as important, if not more important, than traditional investment in plant and equipment. In a competitive environment, firms must invest continuously to maintain the most up-to-date capital stock, but this capital stock can only be as productive as the skills of the people who use it. In order to realize fully capital-stock investments, employers also need to invest continuously in workforce skills, especially as goods and services become more and more "knowledge-intensive."

On the other hand, government-supported training programs consistently come under attack—along with virtually all other programs that create public jobs or pay unemployment benefits—as being costly, ineffective, and wasteful. Critics argue that if training yields positive returns, the market will provide it: Firms will find it in their interest to train their workers, thus precluding the need for government intervention. Another criticism is that the government does not have the expertise to train, let alone the foresight to know what skills people will need.

Thus, while there is general agreement that worker training is beneficial, there is no consensus in the United States on who should supply it or how it should be supplied. Without this consensus, it becomes increasingly hard to "buy" support for further trade liberalization by promising training and other worker adjustment programs. Indeed, as noted by Ellen Frost and others in this volume, if proponents of trade liberalization hope to gain broad-based public support for future trade negotiations, workers will have to feel that they share in the benefits of these negotiations. Simply extolling the virtues of workforce training will not be enough. Training will have to be an offer to enable workers at least to maintain their living standards in light of technological change, defense conversion, and trade liberalization.

As part of a new, comprehensive trade policy, the United States needs to develop and implement both a lifetime learning system to ensure that workers' skills are continually updated and enhanced, and benefit packages for dislocated workers that encompass job search assistance, skills assessment, counseling, referral services, access to retraining programs, and adequate income support.

THE ECONOMIC RATIONALE FOR WORKFORCE TRAINING

It is generally agreed that improved workforce skills raise economic efficiency and contribute to wealth creation. Greater productivity growth benefits the economy as a whole and enables wages for individuals to rise. By boosting worker productivity, training can decrease costs and increase profits for firms.

However, very little empirical evidence measures the contribution of training to productivity. This paucity is due primarily to the difficulty in measuring the effectiveness of training programs and their short- and long-term effects on workers and the economy. Methodologies to measure the impact of training on productivity are inadequate and almost nonexistent; accurate evaluations entail labor-intensive, costly studies that must be conducted over lengthy periods of time and should incorporate variables beyond the actual training program.[1] Since only a minority of firms make a serious investment in training, credible data are scarce.

This lack of concrete empirical evidence serves as a convenient tool for both proponents and critics of public support for training. Proponents point to empirical studies that have shown repeatedly that workers with more skills have higher incomes than those workers with less skills.[2] They also point to anecdotal evidence that suggests that those firms that invest in their workers tend to outlast and outperform firms that do not. By contrast, critics of public-sponsored training view training as something that the market will supply if it is left to function freely. They argue that since individuals and firms reap the direct benefits of training, they should bear its costs directly. In so doing, individuals and firms create a demand both for skills and for training programs, and the market can respond to those demands. Government intervention in this process will simply result in a misallocation of training resources.

While proponents of government-sponsored training programs might not have solid data for their claims, what does seem clear, despite the dearth of empirical data, is that critics' market-based arguments are flawed. The market for worker training is imperfect and will not necessarily best serve the needs of individuals, firms, or the economy as a whole. Indeed, there are several drawbacks to leaving training purely to the private market.

First, consider a firm's demand for training. Because a firm cannot "own" an employee, it is unlikely to reap the full returns of an investment in training—there is no way of preventing a trained employee from taking a job with another firm. This "free-rider" problem can be alleviated only if all firms train their workers. Since this is not the case, employers will underinvest in training.

Second, privately funded training, both within and between firms, tends to be focused on those who need it least. Firms may provide more training to white-collar workers, who already have more education. Moreover, those firms that are fairing well are most likely to spend on worker training. At an individual level, the people who need training the most tend to be the same ones who have the fewest financial resources. They cannot enslave themselves or promise not to file for bankruptcy, and these limitations make it difficult to "borrow against" their future skills.

Various schemes have been put forward to correct for these market failures. In general, however, the schemes that place the onus solely on private individuals and firms solve only part of the problem. For example, proposals are made that a firm that lays off workers should provide training benefits as part of its separation package. This might work in some instances, but not all firms could pay for "exit training." Indeed, many firms find it difficult to fully fund their workers' pensions. Requiring these same firms to provide training might force a hard choice between training today and a pension tomorrow.

Another suggestion is that the hiring firm should be responsible for providing training to prospective employees. This way firms would ensure that their workers have the skills they want and need. Under "entrance training" schemes, firms might pay the cost of training in order to lure workers away from other firms. In this way, firms might be enticed to contribute somewhat more toward training. However, such schemes might encourage firms to hire those workers who already have some or all of the necessary skills. An individual firm might get better-trained workers, but there would be little incentive to hire unemployed people and pay the expense of training them.

Thus, although the private sector can and should play a role in workforce training, it is not enough to leave training to the private sector alone. Government has a legitimate role to play in filling the gaps in these private schemes.

In fact, government-sponsored training makes sense in economic terms. The government can use tax revenues to finance training with the expectation that the trained worker will become reemployed and begin paying taxes again. The present value of the future stream of tax revenues (plus unemployment benefits not paid) could be much larger than the current cost of training.

Moreover, the government has a strong interest in realizing the positive externalities associated with training. By encouraging productivity enhancements and labor market flexibility, training helps keep an economy close to full employment and, more generally, helps in achieving sustainable improvements in living standards.

Turning to international trade liberalization efforts, effective training programs can help ensure that the gains of these liberal-izations are shared broadly within the population, which in turn might foster continued public support for more liberalization. Re-ciprocal market-opening agreements can place pressures on domes-tic import-competing industries, resulting in possible downsizing and layoffs. The government may choose to compensate those work-ers adversely affected by the liberalization via more training, in order to capture the gains of freer trade to the overall economy—greater consumer choice, lower prices, and expanded exports.[3]

TRAINING IN THE UNITED STATES

Training can be viewed as a two-by-two matrix: training for active and for dislocated workers, provided and financed by the private sector or the government. In the United States, active worker training has been primarily the responsibility of the pri-vate sector, and dislocated worker training has become the respon-sibility of the government. According to the American Society for Training and Development, U.S. companies currently devote approximately $55 billion annually to formal training.[4] Aver-aged across the nation, U.S. firms spend slightly more than 1 per-cent of payroll on training. Most of this investment is concentrated among a handful of firms—just 0.5 percent of all employers spend 90 percent of the formal training dollars. Compared to Japanese companies, U.S. companies train a relatively small number of employees. (See Figure 5.1.)

Based on the 1991 Current Population Survey, the Bureau of Labor Statistics reports that only 16 percent of the workforce par-ticipated in some kind of employer-provided formal training. This includes on-the-job training (15 percent of workers), school-ing (13 percent of workers), and other kinds of training (7 percent of workers). By industry, 21 percent of all training was performed in professional and related services; 20 percent in manufacturing industries; 12 percent in finance, insurance, and real estate; and 11 percent in transportation, communications, and utilities.

Training also tends to be focused on younger, educated work-ers. Almost two-thirds of those workers who received some kind of employer-based formal training had at least some college edu-cation. Thirty-eight percent of workers receiving training were col-lege graduates, and an equal percent of workers receiving training had a high school degree or less. Thirty-one percent of those workers receiving training were between 35 and 44 years old, and 29 percent were between 25 and 34 years old.

Another study by the U.S. Small Business Administration found that firms with more than 500 employees are more than twice as likely to provide formal training to new hires as firms with fewer than 25 employees.

One proposal aimed at fostering more private sector–financed training would have required all firms with more than 50 employees to invest at least 1.5 percent of payroll for training for all employees, not just for top managers, as in many current cases. Such a requirement would have represented a training guarantee under which firms could either conduct their own training or contribute the equivalent amount to a national fund that would be used to finance training. This idea, commonly known as "play or pay," was popularized by candidate Bill Clinton in 1992. Unfortunately, the idea did not find its way into President Clinton's legislative

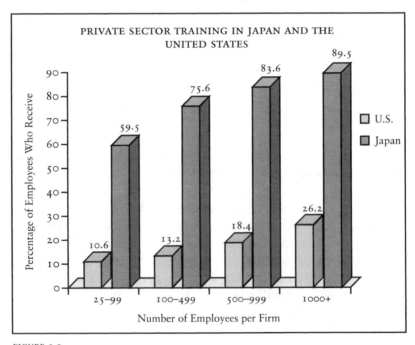

FIGURE 5.1

Source: Organization for Economic Cooperation and Development.

program once he was in office, and it has since fallen from public debate.

Only very weak incentives are in place to encourage individuals to undertake continuous retraining on their own. Under existing tax law, individuals can deduct from their taxable income expenses only for training for their *current* job, not for future jobs. The Clinton administration has suggested expanding this tax deduction to include training expenses for a current or future job, but no action was taken in the 1997 tax bill. In addition, the United States is the only industrial nation without a formal system for establishing national standards in particular skills. There have been recent efforts to develop such standards, but budget cutbacks and political conflict over the content of standards could significantly curtail this exercise.

U.S. GOVERNMENT–FINANCED
TRAINING PROGRAMS

In the United States, government-sponsored labor market adjustment programs are based on two overlapping approaches. The first offers assistance to dislocated workers generally, whereas the second offers assistance to targeted populations—workers who have been adversely affected by specific government actions, such as defense conversion, stepped-up pollution controls, or trade agreements. Table 5.1 briefly describes both kinds of assistance programs.

The largest program under the more general approach was the Jobs Training Partnership Act (JTPA), as later revised by the Economic Dislocation and Worker Adjustment Assistance (EDWAA) program. These programs are decentralized programs through which federal benefits are distributed locally. Specifically, JTPA offers job search assistance, classroom training, on-the-job training, relocation assistance, and prelayoff assistance to dislocated workers, defined as those people who have been laid off and are unlikely to return to their previous industry or occupation. The EDWAA changes, passed as part of the 1988 Omnibus Trade and Competitiveness Act, call for: (1) the creation and use of state rapid-response units; (2) states to pass on at least 60 percent of JTPA/EDWAA funds to sub-state areas; and (3) half of those sub-state funds to be spent on training rather than job search assistance and related activities.

An early review of JTPA by the U.S. General Accounting Office suggested that less than 10 percent of eligible displaced workers received benefits in the first three years of the program.[5] Another early evaluation of the program suggested that older workers and those with less education were less likely to be served by JTPA than their representation in the population of displaced workers might indicate. These findings suggest that those individuals who are most in need of assistance are the ones least likely to receive it under JTPA programs for displaced workers.[6] The number of people who participated in JTPA between 1985 and 1989 totaled only 18 percent of dislocated workers during that period.[7] Although this program may assist those workers who participate, it appears much too small to alleviate overall adjustment pressures in the economy at large.

The Trade Adjustment Assistance (TAA) program is the largest targeted government-sponsored labor adjustment program. Under TAA, workers who lose their jobs due to import competition are eligible for generous income support (cash benefits), limited training benefits, and other employment services, such as job search and relocation assistance. Similar programs offer assistance to workers adversely affected by the Clean Air Act, by defense conversion, and by the North American Free Trade Agreement (NAFTA).

There is some evidence that workers covered under these special programs face a more difficult adjustment process and thus deserve additional public assistance. For example, workers adversely affected by trade liberalization tend to be older and less skilled than other dislocated workers. In the case of defense conversion, workers may be geographically concentrated, thus subjecting them to higher adjustment burdens.

At the same time, the proliferation of smaller programs has resulted in a maze of discretionary paths for workers to navigate. This maze has proven particularly confusing during periods of higher general unemployment, when workers from the same firm or even the same plant may be eligible for different benefits, but each on an exclusive (not cumulative) basis. Indeed, a recent report by the General Accounting Office found that the U.S. government currently supports 163 separate labor adjustment programs, across 15 federal agencies, costing more than $20 billion a year.[8] Unfortunately, so far efforts toward harmonization have been unsuccessful. To date, the United States does not provide a comprehensive,

TABLE 5.1. U.S. LABOR MARKET ADJUSTMENT PROGRAMS

Program	Eligibility	Benefits	Financing
Job Training Partnership Act/ Economic Dislocation and Worker Adjustment Assistance	Dislocated workers defined as those who have little possibility of returning to their previous jobs. All benefits are determined and distributed at the state and local level.	Job search assistance, training, and relocation benefits. Possibility of needs payments if enrolled in training. All benefits are determined and distributed at the state and local level.	Federal share is budgetary outlay by congressional appropriation. Three-quarters of funds are allocated to states based on matching formula, of which 60 percent must be further distributed to sub-state level. Half of all JTPA/EDWAA funds must be allocated for training, $1 billion in FY 1994 and $1.3 billion in FY 1995.
Trade Adjustment Assistance	Workers previously employed by firms that have been certified by U.S. Department of Labor as being hurt by imports.	Income maintenance payments set at unemployment insurance (UI) level for up to 52 weeks (inclusive of regular UI benefits) and may be extended for an additional 26 weeks. Payments conditioned on enrollment in training. Job search assistance, training, and relocation benefits available.	Financed entirely through budgetary outlay by congressional appropriation. $128 million for benefits and $99 million for training in FY 1994, $179 million for benefits and $98 million in training in FY 1995.
Clean Air Act	Workers adversely affected by implementation of acid rain regulations.	Same as JTPA. Needs-related payments are conditioned on training.	$50 million additional congressional appropriation to JTPA for FY 1990.
Defense Conversion Act	Workers displaced by cutbacks in defense programs.	Same as JTPA.	$150 million additional congressional appropriation to JTPA for FY 1991.
NAFTA Transition Adjustment Assistance	Workers adversely affected by NAFTA.	Expanded Trade Adjustment Assistance benefits.	$2 million for benefits and $8 million for training in FY 1994; $33 million for benefits and $32 million for training in FY 1995.

unified system that ensures access to training for all those who need it. Moreover, as seen in Tables 5.2 and 5.3, the United States spends significantly less than other developed countries on labor market assistance and training programs.

THE POLITICS OF WORKER TRAINING AND TRADE

Plenty of historical evidence indicates that politicians find it easier to vote for measures that may cost jobs if the legislation includes a provision to help adversely affected workers. Accordingly, worker assistance programs often have been used to "buy" congressional support for particular legislation. Generous training and income maintenance programs were considered a small cost for securing congressional passage of international trade agreements. For example, TAA was created in 1962 as part of an attempt to garner labor support for the Trade Expansion Act of 1962—the legislation that authorized U.S. participation in the Kennedy Round GATT negotiations. In order to gain support for the Tokyo Round of GATT negotiations, Congress liberalized TAA eligibility requirements and enriched the TAA benefit package as part of the Trade Act of 1974. As part of the Omnibus Trade and Competitiveness Act of 1988, which granted negotiating authority for the Uruguay Round, Congress enacted EDWAA.

Ironically, current concern over the impact of trade on employment and wages has come at the same time that congres-

TABLE 5.2. GOVERNMENT EXPENDITURES ON LABOR MARKET PROGRAMS, 1980 TO 1990 (PERCENT OF GDP)

Country	Training	Unemployment Compensation	All Labor Market Programs
Canada	0.22	1.58	2.09
France	0.28	1.34	2.87
Germany	0.23	1.30	2.32
Japan	NA	0.36	0.52
United Kingdom	0.22	0.94	1.62
United States	0.10	0.38	0.62

Source: Organization for Economic Cooperation and Development, *Labor Market Policies for the 1990s* (Paris: OECD, 1990), Table 14.
Note: U.S. data include Perkins Act vocational training.

sional support for trade-related labor market adjustment programs has eroded. Legislation implementing NAFTA included only a small, highly targeted program for workers adversely affected by changes in trade with Mexico and Canada. In fiscal year (FY) 1996, while a great many workers were eligible, only about 2,000 workers actually received benefits under this program. Tens of thousands of others either chose to take benefits under some other federal program or got lost in the shuffle. As for the Uruguay Round implementing legislation, no provision for worker adjustment was included.

These recent cases suggest that the old model of "buying" support for trade agreements with the promise of worker training programs is no longer viable. By contrast, a comprehensive lifetime learning system would help ensure opportunities for workers to gain new skills continuously and also might go a long way toward ensuring broad-based support for trade liberalizing agreements.

PRINCIPLES FOR BUILDING A COMPREHENSIVE LIFETIME LEARNING SYSTEM

Structural changes in the U.S. economy require new thinking about how to encourage labor market flexibility. These changes are significant enough to require new thinking about adjustment policy, not just tinkering with existing programs. Technological change, defense conversion, and trade liberalization: Each results in long-

TABLE 5.3. TRAINING PROGRAMS IN SELECTED INDUSTRIALIZED COUNTRIES

Country	Participation (% of Labor Force)	Average Duration (in Months)	Total Spending (% of GDP)	Expenditures per Participant (in U.S. $)	Expenditures per Participant (% of Average Income)
Canada	1.1	6	0.22	$7,000	37
France	2.3	2.5	0.28	$4,600	27
Germany	1.5	8	0.25	$7,200	37
United Kingdom	1.4	NA	0.22	$5,000	31
United States	1.0	3.5	0.05	$1,800	9

Source: Organization for Economic Cooperation and Development, *Labor Market Policies for the 1990s* (Paris: OECD, 1990), Table 5.

run benefits for the economy as a whole, yet each also brings concentrated costs in the short run. These costs can threaten society's
willingness to accommodate change. The challenge to public policy is to minimize the short-run costs in order to preserve the long-
run benefits.

Unfortunately, the current discussion of labor adjustment
programs is far too often motivated by a desire to reduce budgetary
expenditures rather than by a desire to establish programs that succeed. It is ironic that, at a time when American workers are facing more pressure than ever due to changes in technology,
globalization, and corporate downsizing, the current buzzword in
Washington about training and labor market programs is "consolidation." If enacted, "consolidation" could lead to *less* government
resources for training and possibly less effective programs.

What is needed is not consolidation but rather harmonization and enhancement. The United States needs a comprehensive
adjustment program that assists dislocated workers, encourages
labor market flexibility, and improves national competitiveness.
The challenge is to provide a program that is expansive enough
to provide assistance to all workers, regardless of cause of dislocation, yet flexible enough to enable tailoring benefits to best suit
an individual worker's needs. The following principles can provide guidance in meeting this challenge:

- *Training should be seen as a means toward an end, not an end
  in and of itself.* The primary objective should be to assist workers to meet the challenges of productive work. To do so, there
  must be jobs available and workers must have access to good and
  timely information concerning these employment opportunities, skill requirements, and available training programs.

- *Training should not be solely for the purpose of getting a job.* Recent
  evidence suggests that those firms willing to make serious investments in their workers are more likely to succeed in the globally competitive world market. Although there are still many
  questions concerning what constitutes a "high-performance"
  workplace, firms that spend more than the national average on
  worker training do seem to reap a high return.[9]

- *Training should be part of a system of "lifetime learning."* The
  lifetime learning model includes basic education, the transition
  from school to work, active worker training to improve skills,

and training to assist dislocated workers move from job to job. Lifetime learning is an ongoing process for which everyone is eligible and in which everyone continuously participates in order to expand his or her skills and knowledge.

• *Existing education resources and training programs should be molded into a unified system coordinated at the local, state, and national levels.* This system should conform to the "lifetime learning" model. Public schools, junior colleges, and adult education systems are all valuable resources. They need to be integrated into a cohesive system that serves to update our workforce constantly.

• *Where appropriate, the government should finance labor market programs delivered to workers by the private sector.* Government sponsorship helps ensure that the costs and burdens associated with labor market adjustments are spread relatively evenly throughout the economy, rather than concentrated in the declining segments and sectors that are least equipped to confront the challenges of adjustment.

• *Dislocated worker benefits should be determined by a person's prospects for reemployment, not cause of unemployment.* The benefit package should encompass job search assistance, skills assessment, counseling, referral services, adequate income support (covering at least 50 percent of lost wages), payments or vouchers for retraining programs, and extended income and benefit payments, including health care payments, through the training period.

• *The government should introduce tax incentives for both individual and company-sponsored training.* Incentives will both help support training efforts financially and help establish lifetime learning as a national priority.

• *In assessing worker training programs, returns to individuals and the economy should be considered over the long term.* Evaluations that compare a worker's salary immediately before and after training are misleading.

POLICY RECOMMENDATIONS

First, the U.S. government should implement a harmonized, econ-omy-wide program to assist dislocated workers, regardless of the cause of dislocation. Economic change is pervasive enough to warrant this program, and the increased complexity of the econ-omy makes it almost impossible to determine the cause of an indi-vidual worker's dislocation. Efforts to identify regional or sector-specific expressions of these causes, such as the impact of increased trade due to NAFTA, have resulted only in a prolifera-tion of targeted programs, each inadequately funded, and there-fore ineffectual.

Second, any future program should aim at combining the pos-itive attributes of both TAA and EDWAA. TAA, as an entitlement, makes income maintenance and training available to all eligible workers. Although income maintenance is necessary for workers to undertake serious retraining, some programs offer income maintenance payments only if sufficient residual funds remain after providing other benefits. EDWAA, for example, does not guarantee benefits. On the other hand, it tries to provide a rapid response to dislocated workers, using states and localities to identify work-ers in need.

Third, future programs aimed at assisting dislocated work-ers should have sufficient funds both to encourage training and to provide income maintenance during the period of training. Under TAA, dislocated workers must be enrolled in training to qualify for income maintenance payments. It may not be necessary to go as far as the TAA requirements, but training should be central to any new program. Indeed, the continued enhancement of skills is vital to successful employment in today's knowledge-based econ-omy. Over the last 20 years, skilled workers have fared much bet-ter that unskilled ones. Less skilled workers are much more likely to lose their jobs due to economic downturns, technological advances, and increased globalization.

Finally, training should reflect the demands of the labor mar-ket. Experience suggests that among all the various formats, on-the-job training tends to have the highest success rate in getting workers employed and lowering earnings losses. Although this for-mat may not fit all workers, evidence indicates that the effective-ness of training increases the closer it is linked to actual employment. One option would be to provide training vouchers to dislocated workers. These workers then could take the vouchers to potential employers who might be willing to hire them and provide training necessary to perform well in the new job. Another option is to provide tax credits to firms in order to encourage more worker training, particularly for dislocated workers.

It is far too easy for proponents of liberal trade policies to call for more training as an antidote to increased import competition yet do nothing about building political support for that training. Similarly, it has been easy for the Clinton administration and Congress to speak about the virtues of training without actually establishing or funding adequate programs. There needs to be a better balance between rhetoric and action. A closer link between changes in trade policy and government labor market adjustment programs should be considered. For example, the provision of trade relief might be conditioned on allocating public and private resources to worker training and adjustment benefits. "Labor-impact" accounting, similar to environmental impact statements, might encourage Congress to address the adjustment burden associated with trade liberalizing legislation.

A more flexible labor market is crucial to meeting the challenges of the international economy. This flexibility is an important reason why the U.S. economy has performed so much better in the 1990s than Europe or Japan. However, the U.S. government should encourage flexibility at the least cost to American workers. Existing U.S. adjustment programs are too small and short-sighted to support a flexible labor force. Serious adjustment programs must provide for better training opportunities coupled with adequate income maintenance so that workers can undertake the kind of retraining they need.

NOTES

1. Examples of these other variables include location of the worker, before-and-after training, age, sex, and prior work history.

2. See, for example, Frank Levy, "Is Anxiety About Living Standards Justified?" and Larry Mishel and Jared Bernstein, "Trouble in Paradise: Eroding Wages and Growing Income Inequality." Both papers are included in *Running in Place*, papers commissioned by the Competitiveness Policy Council (Washington, DC, September 1996). On the other hand, there is no evidence that the "skill premium" would remain if more workers were skilled.

3. For a more detailed discussion, see C. Michael Aho and Thomas O. Bayard, "American Trade Adjustment Assistance After Five Years," *The*

World Economy 3, no. 4 (December 1980); and Gary Clyde Hufbauer and Howard F. Rosen, "Trade Policy for Troubled Industries," *Policy Analyses in International Economics* 15 (March 1986).

4. Laurie Bassi, "Expenditures on Employer-Provided Training" (American Society for Training and Development July 1996, Washington, DC, photocopy).

5. U.S. General Accounting Office, *Dislocated Workers: Local Programs and Outcomes Under the Job Training Partnership Act*, GAO/HRD 87-41 (Washington, DC: U.S. General Accounting Office, March 1987).

6. Margaret C. Simms, "The Effectiveness of Government Training Programs" (paper prepared for the U.S. Department of Labor, Commission on Workforce Quality and Labor Market Efficiency).

7. See U.S. Department of Labor, "Summary of Title III Program Performance for Program Year 1989" (photocopy); and Diane Herz, "Worker Displacement Still Common in the Late 1980's," *Monthly Labor Review* 114, no. 5 (May 1991).

8. U.S. General Accounting Office, *Dislocated Workers*.

9. For example, some departments within Motorola spend approximately 6 percent of payroll on training as compared to 1 percent of payroll for the majority of U.S. companies. Motorola is certainly not sorry about its investment. On the contrary, other companies are trying to learn how to emulate Motorola's success.

Chapter 6

Domestic Policy Requirements for a Liberal Trade Regime

Marina v. N. Whitman

These are perilous times for extending the liberalization of international trade and investment. The trade-bashing views of Republican presidential contender Pat Buchanan and Reform Party presidential candidate Ross Perot may be extreme, but talking tough on trade is popular with Americans across the political spectrum. The bipartisan vision of Presidents George Bush and Bill Clinton of expanding the North American Free Trade Agreement (NAFTA) into a hemispheric trade alliance has been put on indefinite hold. And having pressed hard to bring the fledgling World Trade Organization (WTO) into being, the United States periodically threatens to undermine its authority by acts of "aggressive unilateralism" in trade disputes. Nor is such behavior confined to the United States. U.S. Treasury Secretary Robert Rubin commented after a recent meeting of the Group of Seven (G-7) finance ministers that every one of his counterparts had noted an increase in economic nationalism in his own country.

In the words of Peter Kenen and Barry Eichengreen, two leading analysts of the international economy, ". . . the ability of governments to manage change internationally has depended importantly on their ability to manage it domestically."[1] But what are the domestic policy requirements for an open international trade regime? In order to shed some light on this question, we need to look back at the domestic policy context in which trade liberalization flourished in the quarter century or so following World War

II. We need to look also at the factors that stimulated the emergence of a "new protectionism" in the industrial nations since 1973–protection that relies on nontariff barriers and administrative measures. Armed with whatever insights can be gleaned from these relationships, guidelines can be developed for both macroeconomic and microeconomic policies that can offer the greatest likelihood of minimizing protectionist pressures in American politics and policymaking.

Perhaps the most critical factor underpinning the postwar momentum of trade liberalization was the unique role and position of the United States. As the world's economic and technological hegemon, the United States could sustain a leadership role in the global liberalization of trade and payments even when other countries did not make reciprocal commitments to open their markets to U.S. goods.

A second reason for the greater acceptability of trade-liberalizing moves was the fact that national economies in general, and the U.S. economy in particular, were far less open and thus less vulnerable to external disturbances than they are today. The share of exports and imports in the American gross domestic product (GDP) has roughly doubled over the last several decades, in part as a result of successive rounds of multilateral tariff reductions. Even more important is the fact that, unlike today, balance-of-payments positions and exchange-rate pressures were not dominated by huge and often virtually instantaneous movements of capital across international boundaries. Capital was relatively immobile between countries, and capital controls were regarded as an acceptable trade-off for the ability to sustain both a system of pegged exchange rates and independence of domestic monetary policies.

Finally, and most relevant from the point of view of the present trade discussion, was the existence of an implicit *domestic* compact regarding economic stability and income distribution. This took the form of a commitment both to ensure growth rapid enough to maintain full employment and to maintain a variety of "welfare state" measures through which the losers in an increasingly open market economy were at least partially compensated by the winners (via unemployment insurance and other income-maintenance schemes).

While the period between the end of World War II and 1973 was marked by sustained, if somewhat discontinuous, progress toward a more open and rule-based global economy, the 25 years since the watershed year of 1973 stand in sharp contrast. Since then, average tariff levels have continued to fall through successive rounds of multilateral trade negotiations. But increased resort to a wide variety of nontariff barriers, both formal and informal, has both slowed the momentum toward trade liberalization and led to an increase in trade distortions. The reasons for these developments are not hard to find: a sharp slowdown in economic growth in the industrial nations accompanied either by high and persistent unemployment in most continental European nations or by wage stagnation and increased earnings inequality in the United States. These developments have heightened economic insecurity and, with it, economic nationalism and protectionist pressures.

There is clearly an urgent need to renew the Bretton Woods bargain that underpinned the quarter-century thrust toward liberalization of economic transactions across international boundaries. But the old conditions that made that bargain possible no longer prevail. The economic dominance of the United States has eroded, as other nations have converged toward American levels of income and industrialization and their industries have encroached on America's global market share. Although the United States today once again leads the rankings in multidimensional measures of "global competitiveness," it can no longer take that position for granted. And the resulting sense of economic insecurity, together with the end of the Cold War and its alliance burdens, have led the United States to pursue a tenor of reciprocity in trade-liberalizing agreements that it frequently was willing to forgo in the earlier postwar years.

The end of American global economic dominance was accompanied by the end of American insulation from transnational economic disturbances. The United States can no longer conduct domestic macroeconomic policies without regard to their cross-border consequences and the resulting attenuation of their effectiveness in achieving economic goals at home. This is partly a result of the increased share of exports and imports in the U.S. economy. But the greatest impact has come from developments in financial markets. Advances in information technology and financial innovations have made capital controls obsolete and have vastly enhanced the magnitude, speed, and sensitivity of capital flows across national boundaries.

The result has been a significant limitation on the conduct of monetary policy, even in the world's largest and least interdependent economy. Furthermore, capital movements are now more important than trade flows in determining a nation's international payments position and movements in its exchange rate. Today no government, not even that of the United States, can count on its own intervention to neutralize the impact of market forces on its currency's value and thus on its domestic economy.

Finally, two goals of government policy that seemed relatively feasible and noncontroversial in the 1950s and 1960s have become more problematic today: the maintenance of full employment and the alleviation of difficulties for those who lose out because of free trade and the free movement of capital. The implied promise of the Phillips curve, that government could trade off a lower unemployment rate for a higher steady-state rate of inflation, was devastated by the stagflation of the late 1970s and early 1980s.

More recently, faith in and political support for income-maintenance and income-redistribution measures have fallen victim to concerns about both their budgetary costs and their tendency to create rigidities that render an economy less able to respond promptly and flexibly to economic change. For all these reasons, designing domestic economic policies that will minimize pressures to restrict or distort market access across international boundaries is far more challenging today than it was a quarter century ago.

MACROECONOMIC POLICIES AND EXCHANGE RATES

Twenty-five years ago, one of the strongest arguments offered in favor of a flexible exchange rate system was that, in the words of economist Milton Friedman, it makes the case for free trade clear and simple. In the 1970s many economists argued that the automatic adjustment mechanism of flexible exchange rates would make it unnecessary to resort to trade restrictions or capital controls to shore up a deteriorating balance-of-payments and reserve position. Furthermore, such flexibility would free up macroeconomic policy to focus on the needs of the domestic economy.

The experience of the past quarter century has taught that life is not so simple. The 1996 *Economic Report of the President* takes pains to remind us that, in a world of high capital mobility, the exchange-rate changes induced by domestic macroeconomic policies may widen as well as narrow imbalances on the current account.[2] And exchange rate changes may be far from neutral in their impact on the domestic economy.

The volatility of exchange rates has increased enormously since the end of the Bretton Woods system in 1971. But, contrary to widespread belief, it is not short-term rate volatility—as measured by increases in the standard deviations of daily, weekly, or even monthly rates—that significantly affects domestic economic activity. Such risks can be hedged at relatively low cost by a wide variety of financial derivatives or minimized through the matching of assets and liabilities in particular currencies. It is not surprising, therefore, according to economists Reuven Glick and Clas Wilborg, that a substantial body of empirical work "lends no support to the conventional presumption that firms face more risk under floating exchange rates, and that exchange rate flexibility reduces international trade."[3]

Much more significant and troublesome in their impact on domestic economic activity are persistent misalignments, lasting several years, of real exchange rates defined in terms of purchasing power parity or underlying economic fundamentals.[4] Such misalignments alter the global competitive positions of domestic firms and industries in ways that cannot be offset easily by financial instruments or strategies. Furthermore, the costs of the labor market reallocations and other adjustments associated with a loss of competitiveness are likely to be long-term rather than merely transitional. "When domestic firms in a given industry contract and their foreign competitors expand, effects may persist even beyond the subsequent reversal in the exchange rate," conclude economists Kathryn M. Dominguez and Jeffrey A. Frankel. "Once American firms lose market share, they may have trouble winning it back."[5]

It is no wonder, then, that such exchange-rate misalignments create pressures for trade measures to ease the impact on affected industries. A study covering the United States and the nations of the European Community over the period from 1969 to 1986 indeed found that the demand for nontariff protection, as measured by the frequency with which petitions for antidumping, subsidy-countervailing and safeguard actions were filed, is strongly associated with the appreciation of the real exchange rate.[6]

The overvaluation of the dollar in the late 1960s and early 1970s, just prior to the U.S. unilateral abrogation of the Bretton Woods system of pegged exchange rates, gave rise to the highly protectionist Burke-Hartke bill (although it never became law). And the dollar overvaluation in the first half of the 1980s not only produced several protectionist legislative proposals but also forced President Ronald Reagan, in the words of his own secretary of the treasury, to "grant more import relief to U.S industry than any of his predecessors in more than half a century."[7]

Persistent misalignments of real exchange rates can occur for a variety of reasons. However, in a flexible-rate regime, one of the primary reasons is domestic macroeconomic policy or, more precisely, the monetary-fiscal mix employed to stimulate or restrain the domestic economy. An excessively expansionary stance in fiscal policy, such as characterized the Reagan administration during much of the 1980s, exerts upward pressure on the real interest rate and thus on the exchange rate for two reasons. The first is that the government borrowing requirements created by the fiscal deficit push up the cost of debt. The second is that when the Federal Reserve is concerned about what it regards as excessive fiscal stimulus, it responds by tightening up on the monetary side in order to combat inflation.

Benign neglect was the initial response of the Reagan administration to the substantial appreciation of the dollar in both nominal and real terms in the early 1980s. The appreciation was regarded as a reflection of foreigners' confidence in the American economy and economic policy. Only as the U.S. current account deficit widened to unprecedented levels and American firms increasingly complained about their loss of competitiveness and market shares did the administration become concerned about the crowding out of domestic production in export and import-competing industries. This concern was reflected in the 1985 joint "Plaza Communiqué" by the Group of Five (G-5) countries stating that "some further orderly appreciation of the non-dollar currencies is desirable."

Despite the commitment to cooperation, the tendency of the U.S. government over the next few years was to pressure Germany and Japan to adjust their macroeconomic policies in order to reduce current-account imbalances rather than to modify its own. Only toward the end of the decade, after the 1987 Louvre agreement, which stated that exchange rates were "now consistent with economic fundamentals," did a more orderly pattern of cooperation emerge, however briefly. And, even then, the emphasis was primarily on coordinated intervention in exchange markets, the effect of which was almost certain to be short-lived in the absence of supporting changes in domestic monetary policy.[8]

According to C. Randall Henning, an associate fellow at the Washington-based Institute for International Economics, the episode just described is merely one example of the repeated cycles of neglect and activism that have characterized U.S. policy toward exchange rates since the 1960s. "The exchange rate was treated as the residual of domestic macroeconomic policies until it created a severe problem for the balance of payments and trade policy," he has written. He contrasts this inconsistency with the behavior of Germany and Japan, which, he argues, have employed such tools as foreign exchange intervention, capital controls, the extent to which they permit an international role for their currencies, and domestic monetary policy with a much more sustained and explicit focus on the exchange rate. This is true, he asserts, even though their balancing of the tension between the procompetitive view of the exchange rate (favoring undervaluation) and the anti-inflation view (biased toward overvaluation) has been different and, within each country, has varied over time.[9]

TRADE DEFICITS, DOMESTIC POLICIES, AND POLICY COORDINATION

The major guideline for domestic macroeconomic policy that emerges from these lessons of history is to avoid combinations of monetary and fiscal policy that lead to sustained currency misalignments, which have in the past exacerbated pressures for trade protection. The next question is: What institutional changes are likely to be helpful in implementing this general guideline?

The first requirement is to free up fiscal policy so that it can once again be utilized as a tool for macroeconomic stabilization. Doing so means achieving reductions in future increases in government spending including both so-called discretionary programs and the currently "untouchable" entitlement programs, Social Security and Medicare. It also means eschewing promises of aggregate tax cuts. Only by such a combination of spending and tax policies can we hope to achieve a federal budget that is in balance or even in slight surplus at full employment. Until that occurs, fiscal policy will continue to be, in effect, paralyzed as a tool for achieving domestic economic goals.

This paralysis is a problem for two reasons. First, if monetary policy is the only macroeconomic policy measure available to stimulate or restrain the domestic economy, the likelihood of arriving at a monetary-fiscal mix that has undesirable effects on the exchange rate is substantially increased.[10] More fundamentally, however, the American combination of extremely low private savings and government dissaving, in the form of a budget deficit, makes inevitable a deficit in our trade balance with the rest of the world (generally called the current account deficit), assuming we are to maintain a reasonable level of domestic investment. This is because any gap between aggregate domestic saving, both public and private, and domestic investment must be filled by an inflow of capital from abroad. And the mirror image of this capital inflow is, as a matter of accounting identity, our deficit on the current account.

Seen from this perspective, exchange-rate changes and the shifts in trade flows that they produce are an inevitable by-product of the capital flows required to fill the gap between domestic savings and investment. An appropriate monetary-fiscal mix is indeed desirable to avoid medium-run swings in exchange rates that create disruptive shifts in trade flows and in the mix of economic activity between sectors, such as manufacturing, that are engaged in international trade and those, such as retail trade, that are not. But monetary policy alone cannot do the job.[11] In the words of the 1996 *Economic Report of the President,* "To shrink or eliminate the current account deficit, either the government budget deficit must be narrowed, or private saving must rise relative to investment, or both."[12] And because no one has yet figured out how to boost the savings patterns of America's citizens, fiscal policy is key to shrinking our trade deficit.

Once fiscal policy is again available as a discretionary tool, a further step would be to institute processes that could help to coordinate and reconcile the three major goals of macroeconomic policy: fighting inflation, avoiding recession, and ensuring appropriate exchange rates. One suggestion is to use the National Economic Council within the executive branch as the focal point for action.[13] In addition, it has been suggested that the input of private sector views regarding the exchange rate be institutionalized somewhere in the policy formulation process. Doing so may require including on the agenda of the President's Advisory Committee on Trade Policy and Negotiations (ACTPN) periodic discussion of the current exchange-rate situation and its competitive impact.[14]

Such an inclusion would be appropriate, given that the impact of hard-won moves toward trade liberalization, particularly in the form of tariff reductions, can be more than offset by a misalignment of the exchange rate. A dramatic recent example of such a situation is the early experience of NAFTA, where the anticipated gains from liberalized trade with Mexico were overwhelmed by the effects of that nation's financial crisis and the severe domestic recession and steep devaluation of the peso that ensued. The impact of these developments on the U.S.-Mexican trade balance sharply eroded political support for NAFTA in the United States and doubtless has made more difficult the promised extension of the agreement to other Latin American countries.

Finally, such moves toward a more coherent domestic approach to the exchange-rate impact of macroeconomic policy could be complemented and reinforced by a revival and reform of the G-7 coordination process, which has fallen into disuse in recent years.[15] The G-7 should be the forum for regular discussion of exchange-rate relationships and of how macroeconomic policies might be modified, when there is general agreement that a substantial misalignment exists.

A previous effort along similar lines, the so-called objective indicators exercise adopted at U.S. urging by the G-7 heads of state at their Tokyo summit meeting in 1986, failed largely because the United States' G-7 partners were suspicious of U.S. motives. Nevertheless, this might be an opportune time to revive the G-7 coordination process, as the U.S. current account deficit appears to be heading toward a record $180 billion level for 1997. This process could provide a useful framework within which to encourage Japan to pursue macroeconomic policies consistent with a continuing movement away from reliance on export-led growth. We could enlist the support of our G-7 partners in questioning the appropriateness of China and Taiwan accumulating dollar reserves in order to hold down appreciation of their currencies and thus stimulate their exports, despite the fact that both countries have large and growing trade surpluses. And we could discuss with our European partners the fact that several of them appear to be encouraging depreciation of their currencies relative to the dollar in an effort to stimulate their economies and put a dent in their persistently high unemployment rates.

The very salience of these issues makes them particularly sensitive, however, and increases the amount of diplomatic skill that will be required to revive the coordination process. At the very least, if there is to be any hope of using such a process to avoid both competitive undervaluations and enforced overvaluations, the lessons of earlier failures must be taken to heart. One lesson is to avoid making any process overly ambitious or overly mechanical. Even more important, the burden-sharing in the form of course corrections in domestic policies must be perceived as reciprocal and fair. Finally, and most fundamentally, both the United States and other leading industrial nations must recognize that trade balances are primarily home-grown, the result of domestic macroeconomic policies, and should not become a source of trade friction or an excuse for restrictive trade measures.[16]

TRADE, JOBS, AND LABOR MARKETS

Even when the exchange rate is in accord with economic fundamentals, the intertwined processes of trade and foreign investment are bound to create winners and losers by affecting the distribution of income in the domestic economy.[17] And because the overall benefits of a more open trading system tend to be both small, relative to the total size of the domestic economy, and widely diffused, trade liberalization is always vulnerable to becoming hostage to its much larger distributional effects.

By far the most prominent of these distributional effects is the impact of trade flows on wages and/or employment in particular industries, communities, regions, and occupational or income groups. Patterns of trade protection reflect this fact. A survey of empirical studies of trade protection in advanced industrial countries, primarily focused on the United States, concludes that industries with high levels of protection are likely to be labor-intensive, low skill, and low wage. They also are likely to be beset by high or increasing import penetration or to be in decline. Finally, such industries are likely to be regionally concentrated and to be little involved in intraindustry trade.[18]

This pattern of protection suggests strongly that a major function of trade barriers is to ameliorate, or perhaps delay, the costs of trade-related adjustments in labor markets. That is, protection appears to be focused on situations where labor shifts are likely to be large. This is the case where interindustry rather than intraindustry trade is involved or where industries are regionally concentrated. Protection also appears to be biased in the direction of those seen as most vulnerable and least able to bear the costs of adjustment, that is, low-skill, low-wage workers in threatened or declining industries. However, some protection favors low-skilled relatively high-wage workers, who have a great deal to lose.

The fact that the politics of trade and trade policy tend almost everywhere to focus heavily on the labor market or "jobs" aspects is nothing new. Two developments have intensified this focus in recent years, however. One is the increasing "footlooseness" of the other major factors of production: capital and technology, along with the steady increase in the importance of trade in the economies of the United States and Western Europe. The other is deteriorating performance of labor markets in virtually all industrial nations in recent years, including a near-universal slowdown in the growth of real earnings. Along with it have come either a significant increase in unemployment or underemployment, in Europe and Japan, respectively, or a substantial increase in income inequality, in the United States and other English-speaking countries.

The simultaneous emergence of these developments has pushed to the forefront concerns about the impact of trade on labor markets, concerns variously subsumed under the rubrics of "deindustrialization" in the United States, "delocalization" in Western Europe, and "hollowing out" in Japan. Although the views of Ross Perot and Pat Buchanan are extreme, they do resonate with widely held concerns about the impact of trade on employment, wages, and the distribution of income.

In fact, the preponderance of economic analysis suggests a verdict of "not guilty" as regards the impact of trade on aggregate employment and wage levels and a hung jury, so far, as regards its relationship to increasing inequality in earnings. On the first point, several studies by the Organization for Economic Cooperation and Development (OECD) have found a positive (although small) relationship between exogenous increases in trade and employment in tradable-goods sectors, except for those countries—the United States and the United Kingdom—that experienced substantial deterioration in their current accounts over the period.[19] But the negative impact of the trade deficit is somewhat beside the point, because the employment effects of domestic demand dominate the effects of changes in the trade balance in all the countries studied.

And, even given the factors that currently constrain fiscal policy, all industrial nations have access to those macroeconomic tools with which they can impact the level of domestic demand.

In regard to the relationship between trade and job quality, the increased role of trade and foreign direct investment often is blamed for the stagnation of real earnings in the United States since 1973 and for the elimination of "good" jobs, by which generally is meant well-paid production worker jobs in manufacturing. In fact, however, the slowdown in real compensation is attributable largely to the slowdown in the growth of labor productivity over the same period.[20]

There is also evidence that expanded trade creates good jobs rather than destroying them. A 1995 study found that, holding other characteristics constant, U.S. exporting plants paid better, particularly to production workers, and experienced faster growth of both wages and employment than nonexporters over the period from 1976 to 1987. An earlier study found, furthermore, that exporting industries tend to be associated with high wage premiums and import-competing industries with low ones (the two major exceptions are autos and steel), thus reinforcing the positive relationship between trade and the creation of well-paid jobs.[21]

The issue that has generated the most controversy within the economics profession is whether globalization is making the rich richer and the poor poorer—that is, whether trade has been a major factor in the growth of earnings inequality. The jury is still out on this question, which has spawned an enormous theoretical and empirical literature. But the general consensus appears to be that trade accounts for a relatively small proportion of the increase in earnings inequality that has characterized the United States in recent years, while skill-biased technical change appears to be a much more important—indeed, the dominant—factor.[22]

Whatever the results of economic analysis, public concern about the impact of trade on labor markets is not likely to disappear. While trade does not reduce either employment or wages in the aggregate, increases in trade, even if balanced, or changes in trade patterns are unquestionably associated with job displacement. The net job impact on particular industries, communities, and even regions of the country can be substantial. Some studies have found, furthermore, that workers displaced by trade tend to bear a heavier burden of adjustment, in the form of longer periods of unemployment and larger permanent earnings losses, than the average for workers displaced by other shifts in the pattern of economic activity.[23]

A development that may in fact be intensifying the relationship between labor reallocation processes and attitudes toward trade and trade policies is the increasing reliance, in the United States as well as in other leading industrial countries, on *external* (i.e., between firm) rather than *internal* (i.e., within firm) mechanisms to reallocate labor in response to market signals.

A number of cross-country studies have noted convergence among Western industrial nations toward a weakening of employment stability.[24] For the United States, the evidence regarding an overall decline in job tenure is somewhat mixed for the post-1973 period as a whole, although job tenure has clearly declined for less-educated workers. But a comparison of the job-loss rate during the modest recovery of 1991 to 1993 with that during the severe recession of 1981 to 1983 provides preliminary evidence of a secular decline in job security,[25] particularly for more educated workers and for reasons linked to corporate restructuring and downsizing.

Another manifestation of the internal-to-external shift in the United States was the tendency for U.S. manufacturing firms to become smaller and more specialized over the 1980s.[26] This suggests a reduced enthusiasm for internal diversification as well as organizational changes associated with advances in information technology that encourage outsourcing and reductions in vertical integration. But probably the most striking manifestation of a heavier reliance on market-mediated reallocation mechanisms is the increased use of a "peripheral" or "contingent" workforce consisting of temporary or part-time workers or contract services. In the United States, while the proportion of the workforce accounted for by part-time or self-employed workers has remained relatively stable, the share accounted for by temporary employees and business services has tripled between 1982 and 1992, albeit from a very small base.

This shift toward a greater reliance on external as opposed to internal processes of labor market adjustment appears to be a rational response to changes in the economic environment confronting the major industrial nations since 1973. One is the slowdown in aggregate growth rates, which demands greater flexibility for downward adjustments, thus increasing the need to exercise the "hard" disciplines of the marketplace. Another is the increased incidence of large and unanticipated economic shocks. Even the most enthusiastic supporters of internal labor markets recognize that, because custom exerts a strong inertial pull in these markets, their efficiencies are greater when change is gradual and predictable, less so when it is radical and unanticipated. The reinforcing effect of rapid advances in information technology has been described already.

Finally, an increase in the intensity of global competition has heightened pressures to increase competitiveness by reducing labor costs. It is always easier to reduce such costs when workers move from one firm to another than to cut the wages of a person who remains with the same company, even if his or her job function or responsibilities change. Therefore, such pressures tend, once again, to stimulate the substitution of hard external disciplines for softer internal ones.

COMBINING ECONOMIC FLEXIBILITY
WITH ECONOMIC SECURITY

While these changes may be a rational response to developments in the external economic environment, they shift some of the costs of adjustment away from firms and toward workers. Together with the labor market difficulties experienced in the United States and other countries since 1973, worker displacement increases the pressure for protectionist measures. Many trade restrictions apparently are intended to cushion or postpone the transitional costs of labor market adjustment. This fact suggests, in turn, the importance of instituting policies that reduce friction and enhance "employability security" in labor markets as well as policies that reduce the growing inequality in earnings between skilled and unskilled workers. ("Employability security" means the individual's ability to find a new job, at roughly the same or better pay, with minimum search time, when his or her old job disappears.)

Two broad categories of measures aim at improving the functioning of American labor markets by combining economy-wide flexibility with an acceptable level of individual economic security. One is education and training to enhance the work-related skills. Periodic training opportunities are needed to ensure employability in a world where several changes of jobs and even occupations over a working lifetime are rapidly becoming the norm. The second is workers' ability to carry pension rights and health insurance with them when changing employers or moving in and out of the workforce.

On the education front, no one has the answer as to why the United States—with the best system of higher education in the world—does such a relatively poor job of preparing students who are not college-bound for the workforce. The public debate over education vouchers and charter schools suggests an interest in experimentation and innovation that should yield valuable insights.

As for lifelong training, both on and off the job, the private sector has been forging ahead on its own. The number of people over 35 attending college has increased significantly in recent years, and more and more firms are providing or subsidizing ongoing training for their employees, either voluntarily or as the result of collective bargaining.[27] Government could support such developments by encouraging innovative cooperation among employers, high schools, and community colleges. But the most obvious innovation would be to remove the current bias in the tax system against training that would broaden an individual's work-related skills and thus enhance employability security even when a person's current job disappears. Current tax law makes educational expenses tax-deductible only if they are relevant to an individual's present job, but not if they would enhance the likelihood of qualifying for a new employer or a different occupation.

Recent legislation has increased the portability of health insurance for working Americans, but further improvements are still needed. Legislative and regulatory changes also have reduced the period of time required before an individual's contingent pension rights become permanent (known as vesting) and have increased the reliability of such vesting, but the ongoing shift among companies from defined-benefit to defined-contribution pension arrangements has done the most to enhance portability. Finally, the increasing number of workers engaged in various nontraditional employment relationships, including temporary, part time, and self-employment, contributes to the flexibility of the American economy. But, as a recent report by the Committee for Economic Development (CED) entitled *American Workers and Economic Change* argues, if such workers are not to be second-class citizens in the workplace, it is important that pensions, health care, and unemployment insurance be extended to them on a proportionate basis.[28]

In addition to extending eligibility, the contribution of the unemployment insurance (UI) system to improved labor market adjustment would be enhanced by a number of reforms to align it more closely with the realities of the modern workplace. These realities include not only the substantial increase in nontraditional employment arrangements but also the heightened importance of structural unemployment relative to cyclical layoffs (where the expectation is a recall to the same job). The CED report also makes a number of useful suggestions along these lines, in particular ". . . that the UI system be better integrated with effective reemployment services, and that states be given broad discretion to use reemployment incentives . . . in their UI systems."[29]

In addition to increasing the portability and coverage of the traditional forms of work-related benefits, resistance to labor-market adjustments might be decreased if firms were to give workers a "piece of the action" that they can take with them when they leave. In particular, there has been a great deal of negative publicity and some political fallout when corporate downsizing has resulted in both job losses and a rise in the company's stock price. Although this association has been somewhat exaggerated in the press,[30] its adversarial impact could be alleviated if an element of stock-based compensation were extended to nonmanagement employees. Such stock ownership would tend not only to enhance an employee's commitment to the firm but would enable the individual to share in the firm's success even if the employer-employee relationship is terminated.

While the emphasis here is naturally on the role of public policy in improving adjustment processes in labor markets, many of the relevant innovations fall within the purview of the private sector. Some relate to the policies of individual firms—above and beyond what is required by law—on such matters as advance notice, severance pay, outplacement services, job retraining, extended health benefits, and assistance to communities. Of particular interest are initiatives undertaken collectively by groups of firms, such as a recent proposal to the Business Roundtable (BRT) to establish a BRT-sponsored National Jobs Bank program to match needs for new employees with available people on a membership-wide basis and to establish a clearinghouse to enable member companies to share best practices in creating portable health care and pension benefits.

An alternative mechanism is provided by temporary-help firms that place employees with operating companies with whom they have contracts. The category of "business services and temporary employees" represents the fastest-growing segment of the American economy, more than tripling in size over the decade from 1982 to 1992. Furthermore, such arrangements are no longer confined to low-skill casual labor; they now include doctors, lawyers, accountants, engineers, executives, and many other skilled occupations. Such firms could provide, on a proportional basis, many of the noncash benefits available to companies' permanent employees. Some temporary-help companies are already beginning to offer benefits such as guaranteed levels of employment days per year, paid vacations, and/or access to retirement plans to "core" contract employees who meet certain longevity and availability criteria.

Finally, labor unions have the potential to play a constructive role in facilitating the reallocation of labor in response to structural change. So far the shift toward a heavier reliance on external as opposed to internal adjustment mechanisms and the associated changes in the implicit social contract between firms and their employees have been accompanied by a steady decline in the proportion of workers who belong to unions, particularly in the private sector, and a concomitant decline in union power.

If this decline is to be reversed and unions are once again to play a meaningful role in the design and operation of the American workplace, a change in the nature of unions will have to accompany the changing nature of firms. One of the more radical and difficult aspects of such a shift would be union acceptance of a growing substitution of employability security for the traditional concept of job security. This might involve, for example, focusing the "security" aspects of collective bargaining on such issues as the provision of educational subsidies or generalized training to enhance an individual's capacity to compete in the job market rather than on guarantees of a certain level of employment or on restrictions on downsizing or outsourcing. Because a successful outcome might well result in workers moving out of the jurisdiction of the union doing the bargaining, this shift in institutional emphasis would be a bitter pill to swallow. Some of the more farsighted companies and unions have recognized the need and begun to wrestle creatively with these issues, but the evolution of American labor unions into organizations that protect workers' rights without rigidifying labor markets remains a major challenge.[31]

Along with measures to reduce friction in labor markets, policies aimed at reversing or at least halting the increase in income inequality among Americans with different skill levels are likely to play a role in reducing pressures for protection. High on the list, once again, are policies to increase the effectiveness of basic education, improve the efficiency of the school-to-work transition, and provide for lifelong skill enhancement through training both on and off the job. Education and training are at best long-range propositions, however, and their effectiveness will vary widely. Some form of wage subsidy would have a more immediate impact on the earnings and employability of low-skill and therefore low-wage workers. This in turn suggests that it would be better to deal with the acknowledged problems of the existing earned income tax credit (EITC) by reforming it than by scrapping it.[32] In addition to measures to assist the working poor, many of the proposals already discussed to update and better integrate the social safety net of unemployment and welfare benefits would be particularly important to those who, because of low skills and poverty need such services most frequently and acutely.

Probably no aspect of American trade has given rise to so much public concern as the rapid increase of manufactured imports from developing countries and the associated increase in foreign direct investment (FDI) in these countries by U.S.-based firms. The importance of such investment is greatly exaggerated in the public mind. In recent years only about 3 to 5 percent of the total production of goods by foreign affiliates of American firms was exported from developing nations to the U.S. market. Nevertheless, the belief that such trade and investment are eroding the economic position of low-skill workers in this country is a significant source of pressure for protection.

Several prominent observers have suggested that WTO involvement in the promotion of international labor standards could be useful in maintaining political support for trade liberalization. (See Chapter 14 in this volume.) The issue of labor standards and the accompanying one of environmental standards are high on the list of issues that need to be confronted by both multilateral and regional trade organizations. But they need to do so in ways that minimize the use of threatened trade sanctions as the major instrument of pressure on nonconforming countries. Proposals for sanctions only increase suspicions in the developing world that the United States is engaging in disguised protectionism. If implemented, sanctions could stand in the way of the economic growth and increasing affluence which historically have been associated with improvement of labor standards and working conditions.

In addition, voluntary measures, whether undertaken within the United States or in conjunction with producers in other nations, could play a useful role in reducing what Geza Feketekuty, one of the editors of this volume, has called the "moral outrage and reduced legitimacy of international competition" produced by egregious exploitation of workers in other countries. Product labels that assure the consumer that exploitative practices have not been used in the item's production are one such voluntary measure. Carpet manufacturers in a number of industrial nations recently have initiated such a process to certify that their products did not involve the use of child labor in other countries. Similarly, several major U.S. clothing manufacturers have introduced codes of conduct for subsidiaries and suppliers in developing nations, although effective enforcement continues to be an issue for both these initiatives. The International Standards Organization (ISO) is exploring broader development of such voluntary standards. The ISO has gained widespread recognition for its worldwide standards for ensuring quality production processes (the ISO 9000 standards) and is now extending its reach to environmental standards as well (ISO 14000 standards).

THE ROLE OF ECONOMIC GROWTH

Whatever measures are introduced specifically to assist workers in making job transitions, economic growth is the most effective way to ease adjustment to structural change. It is not surprising, therefore, that empirical studies have found that, along with exchange-rate misalignment, high unemployment or a low overall growth rate is a major factor in trade protection.[33] Thus policies directed toward accelerating an economy's aggregate growth rate can play an important role in reducing pressures for protection.[34]

Because the overall rates of growth and inflation in the United States have both been at low levels for several years, the question of whether the Federal Reserve might be retarding the growth rate by an overcautious monetary policy has been an on-and-off debate over the past few years.[35] By all the standard measures, however, the U.S. economy contains little or no slack that could be eliminated by a more stimulative monetary policy. For the time being, additional stimulus would be more likely to produce an increase rather than a decrease in long-term interest rates, which are critical to the level of economic activity.

Once again, however, it is important to pay close attention to the monetary-fiscal mix. In the words of the recent CED report entitled *American Workers and Economic Change,* "As we restore a growth-oriented fiscal policy, monetary policy should be responsive to the short-term restrictive impact of the new fiscal policy."[36] The same report goes on to urge ". . . that monetary policy should cautiously explore the possibility that structural changes have raised the level of economic activity that is compatible with low inflation." As suggested in the preceding paragraph, the reactions in the long-term bond markets are likely to provide the best guide available as the Fed treads this uncharted path. So far the long-term bond market has been comfortable with a combination of 2.5 to 3 percent growth and 5 percent unemployment.

A sustained increase in the real growth rate of the American economy and in the compensation rate of American workers will require a reversal of the still-unexplained slowdown in the growth of aggregate productivity that has occurred since 1973. Because no one knows just why the slowdown occurred, there are no clear-cut prescriptions for how to reverse it. Virtually all observers agree, however, that policies to encourage an increase in the low rates of savings and net investment in the United States would be a good place to start.

A lower federal budget deficit would stimulate growth by reducing interest rates. Added fiscal stimulus could come from structural changes on both the taxing and the spending side of the government budget. On the taxation side, this would require a shift from the current emphasis on tax cuts per se (the U.S. aggregate rate of taxation is already the lowest among the major industrial countries) to a focus on changes in the tax structure that would encourage savings and productivity-increasing investment more than the present system does. One move in this direction would be to exempt a greater proportion of savings from taxation while reducing or eliminating the deduction for interest on home mortgages.[37] On the government spending side, the need is, according to the CED report, to ". . . redirect public expenditures toward productive investment by reforming and restraining entitlement transfers (which enlarge private consumption) and redesigning or curtailing activities that are 'investments' in name only."[38]

A healthy aggregate growth rate is conducive to the preservation of economic openness, which in turn stimulates the growth of productivity and aggregate economic activity. The role of trade in enhancing the quality of jobs, in terms of the level and growth of wages and the growth of employment, has been noted already. A recent study by the McKinsey Global Institute reinforces this observation. It cites a series of case studies showing that global competition is necessary for an industry to be on the leading edge of technology. Purely domestic competition, however intense, is not sufficient.[39]

Regulatory reform also could play a useful role in stimulating growth. Reforms could include a shift to regulatory measures that make use of market-based incentives, employ risk-based and cost-benefit standards in establishing priorities, and focus on outcomes while giving regulators and firms broad latitude in determining how to achieve those outcomes. Such reforms could alleviate the higher costs imposed by many current regulatory approaches while preserving the underlying social goals.

Finally, government should take every opportunity to encourage a shift in the private sector away from downsizing as the major route to increasing profitability and toward a greater emphasis on innovation and growth—a shift that may in fact already be under way. Aside from exploiting its possession of a bully pulpit, the U.S. government should maintain its support for basic research and development that traditionally has stimulated private-sector growth but that is currently on the endangered species list. While resisting any temptation to try to "pick winners and losers" via industrial policies, taxpayers should support the initiatives of the Commerce Department's National Institute of Standards and Technology (NIST) to encourage the diffusion of new technologies, particularly to small and medium-size firms that might otherwise not have access to them.

CONCLUSION: DOMESTIC STABILITY
AND ECONOMIC OPENNESS

Economists tend to regard the benefits of a liberal trade regime as self-evident and its opponents as self-serving, but political scientists and historians remind us forcefully that support for such a regime depends importantly on the citizenry's degree of satisfaction with the functioning of the domestic economy. In *The Great Transformation,* published in 1944, the philosopher-political scientist Karl Polanyi argued that the major disruptions in labor markets, associated with the pre-1913 increase in global economic integration, led directly to the collapse of the world economy after the first World War. In more measured tones, but still disquieting to supporters of economic openness, economic historian Jeffrey Williamson has argued that ". . . the inequality trends [within rich countries] which globalization produced prior to World War I were at least partly responsible for the interwar retreat from globalization." Williamson asks whether ". . . the world economy of the next century [will] also retreat from globalization because of its inequality side effects?"[40]

Postwar policymakers in the major industrial countries responded to these lessons of history with what political scientist John Ruggie has termed "the compromise of embedded liberalism."[41] This "compromise" took different forms in different countries, but the aim was to combine international economic liberalization with domestic stability through government commitment to stabilizing domestic employment and output and to compensating, at least partially, those who lose from increased economic integration.

Today the challenge is to update the "Bretton Woods bargain," but to do it with policies that take full account of the lessons painfully learned during the half century since the end of World War II. There is no stable trade-off between unemployment and inflation. The extensive social safety nets developed by many European countries have surprisingly high costs, not only in budgetary terms but in the loss of economic flexibility and ability to respond to structural change. Finally, efforts to reduce income inequality, through such redistributive measures as highly progressive marginal rates of income tax, are likely to retard rather than encourage economic growth.

We need to minimize the costs of adjustment to structural change and to halt or reverse the increase in earnings inequality in order to preserve political support for economic openness. But this must be accomplished in ways that enhance rather than reduce the economy's flexibility to respond to change. On the macroeconomic side, it is critical to ensure that the nation's monetary-fiscal mix does not produce a sustained misalignment of exchange rates, which is virtually certain to produce pressures for trade protection. Even more fundamentally, public policies must be grounded in an understanding that trade deficits cannot be reined in by trade liberalization abroad or trade restriction at home, since they are largely the home-grown result of domestic saving, investment, and budget policies.

Microeconomic measures are also important. In particular, there is a need for policies to facilitate job-to-job transitions, to enhance the earning power of low-skilled workers by upgrading their skills, and to increase the real growth rate of the overall economy on a sustainable basis. Such initiatives could play a significant role in reconciling the political and social demand for personal economic security with the demands for economic flexibility engendered by a commitment to the global marketplace.

NOTES

1. Peter B. Kenen and Barry Eichengreen, "Managing the World Economy Under the Bretton Woods System," in Peter B. Kenen, ed., *Managing the World Economy: Fifty Years After Bretton Woods* (Washington, DC: Institute for International Economics, 1994), p. 53.

2. *Economic Report of the President, 1996* (Washington, DC: Government Printing Office, 1997).

3. Reuven Glick and Clas Wilborg, "Exchange Rate Regimes and International Trade," in Benjamin J. Cohen, ed., *International Trade and Finance: New Frontiers for Research* (New York: Cambridge University Press, 1997), and studies cited there.

4. Morris Goldstein, *The Exchange Rate System and the IMF: A Modest Agenda* (Washington, DC: Institute for International Economics, 1995), p. 73, concludes: "All of this [evidence] supports the argument that the main shortcoming of the existing exchange-rate system falls in the area of misalignments of real exchange rates, not with the short-run variability of those rates." In principle, such prolonged misalignments can occur under either a fixed or a flexible exchange-rate regime. Two leading experts observe that the earlier view, which regarded misalignments as more likely to occur under fixed rates, seemed relevant to the dollar in 1970 and before, while the opposite view, which is much more prevalent today, seems relevant to the dollar in the 1980s and 1990s. Rudiger Dornbusch and Jef-

frey A. Frankel, "Macroeconomics and Protection," in Robert M. Stern, ed., *U.S. Trade Policies in a Changing World Economy* (Cambridge, MA: MIT Press, 1987), p. 103.

5. Kathryn M. Dominguez and Jeffrey A. Frankel, *Does Foreign Exchange Intervention Work?* (Washington, DC: Institute for International Economics, 1993), p. 35.

6. Enzo Grilli, "Macro-economic Determinants of Trade Protectionism," *The World Economy* 11, no. 3 (1988): 313–326.

7. I. M. Destler and C. Randall Henning, *Dollar Politics: Exchange Rate Policymaking in the United States* (Washington, DC: Institute for International Economics, 1989), p. 146.

8. For an exhaustive discussion of the conditions under which exchange-rate intervention can be effective, see Dominguez and Frankel, *Does Foreign Exchange Intervention Work?*

9. C. Randall Henning, *Currencies and Politics in the United States, Germany, and Japan* (Washington, DC: Institute for International Economics, 1994), pp. 310–327.

10. For a contrary view, see C. Fred Bergsten and C. Randall Henning, *Global Economic Leadership and the Group of Seven* (Washington, DC: Institute for International Economics, 1996), pp. 100–109.

11. Because of the strong exposure of manufacturing to international trade, swings in exchange rates and trade flows tend to fall particularly heavily on blue-collar workers.

12. *Economic Report of the President, 1996,* 259.

13. Destler and Henning, *Dollar Politics,* pp. 161–164; Henning, *Currencies and Politics,* pp. 356–357.

14. Such an arrangement would provide better overall policy integration, in my view, than Henning's suggestion (p. 353) for a separate, parallel "private sector advisory group" on exchange rates.

15. For a discussion of the reasons for this decline, see Bergsten and Henning, *Global Economic Leadership,* chap. 5.

16. In particular, the United States would have to achieve a domestic saving-investment balance that would make it less reliant on capital inflows from such surplus countries as Japan to hold down its own interest rates. This dependence has made the U.S. government somewhat schizophrenic about the yen-dollar and mark-dollar exchange rates.

17. The following section draws heavily on Marina v. N. Whitman, "Labor Market Adjustment and Trade: Their Interaction in the Triad," in Benjamin J. Cohen, ed., *International Trade and Finance: New Frontiers for Research* (New York: Cambridge University Press, 1997).

18. Dani Rodrick, "What Does the Political Economy Literature on Trade Policy (Not) Tell Us That We Ought to Know?" Working Paper 1039, National Bureau of Economic Research, 1996.

19. Organization for Economic Cooperation and Development, *The OECD Jobs Study: Evidence and Explanations,* Parts I and II (Paris: OECD, 1994). The word *exogenous* is crucial here. Because of the endogeneity of the trade balance over the business cycle—imports are more sensitive to changes in income than are exports—observed patterns are counterintuitive:

Increases in trade deficits tend to be associated with a fall rather than a rise in the unemployment rate.

20. *Economic Report of the President, 1996*, p. 61.

21. A. B. Bernard and J. B. Jensen, "Exports, Jobs, and Wages in U.S. Manufacturing 1976–87," *Brookings Papers on Economic Activity: Microeconomics* (1995), pp. 67–112; Lawrence Katz and Lawrence Summers, "Industry Rents: Evidence and Implications," *Brookings Papers on Economic Activity: Microeconomics* (1989), pp. 209-290.

22. Robert Z. Lawrence, *Single World, Divided Nations? International Trade and OECD Labor Markets* (Washington, DC: Brookings Institution, 1996), and references cited there.

23. J. David Richardson, "Income Inequality and Trade: How to Think, What to Conclude," *Journal of Economic Perspectives* 9, no. 3 (1995): 33–57, and references cited there.

24. See references in Whitman, "Labor Market Adjustment and Trade," 1997

25. Henry S. Farber, "The Changing Face of Job Loss in the United States, 1981–1993," Working Paper 360, Princeton University Industrial Relations Section, 1996.

26. Michael Useem, *Investor Capitalism* (New York: Basic Books, 1996), p. 2, and *Fortune* (December 1993): 76.

27. German and Japanese employers provide substantially more on-the-job training than do their American counterparts. In both countries, however, traditional pay structures have the effect of making workers themselves bear a larger share of the training costs than in the United States.

28. Committee for Economic Development, *American Workers and Economic Change* (New York: Committee for Economic Development, 1996).

29. Ibid., p. 13–14.

30. Useem points out, *Investor Capitalism* (p.146), that analysis of share-price reactions to a number of company layoff announcements between 1979 and 1987 found that "[i]n the days immediately following layoffs announced as part of general restructurings, stock prices rose an average 4 percent. Downsizing announced simply as a cost-cutting measure, however, depressed stock prices an average 6 percent."

31. See "Why America Needs Unions but Not the Kind It Has Now," *Business Week*, May 23, 1994, and U.S. Department of Labor and U.S. Department of Commerce, Commission on the Future of Worker-Management Relations, *Report and Recommendations*, (Washington, DC: Government Printing Office, 1994).

32. In *Single World, Divided Nations* (p. 172), Lawrence argues that "[t]he ideal system would combine American efficiency with European compassion. A deregulated labor market and a generous earned income tax credit would do exactly that." Exempting the wages of low-wage workers from part or all of payroll taxes is another possibility. Both would avoid the negative impact of increases in the minimum wage on the demand for low-skill workers.

33. Grilli, "Macro-economic Determinants"; Dornbusch and Frankel, "Macroeconomics and Protection," p. 96, and references cited there.

34. Rodrik argues provocatively that "big government" is also positively associated with economic openness. A larger share of government expenditure in gross domestic product, he asserts, mitigates the risk associated with economic openness by reducing the variability of real income. Dani Rodrick, "International Trade and Big Government," in Benjamin J. Cohen, ed., *International Trade and Finance: New Frontiers for Research* (New York: Cambridge University Press, 1997).

35. Taking an even more controversial position in a recent issue of *Foreign Affairs*, Ethan Kapstein argues strongly that restrictive *fiscal* policies are retarding growth throughout the industrialized world. The equally strong assertions to the contrary by two of the most highly regarded international economists, Paul Krugman and Robert Lawrence, in the subsequent issue of *Foreign Affairs,* make for a lively debate. Ethan B. Kapstein, "Workers and the World Economy," *Foreign Affairs* 75, no. 3 (1996): 16-37; Paul Krugman, "Workers and Economists: First, Do No Harm," *Foreign Affairs* 75, no. 4 (1996): 164-170; and Robert Z. Lawrence, "Workers and Economists: Resist the Binge," *Foreign Affairs* 75, no. 4 (1996): 170–173.

36. The CED report defines such a growth-oriented fiscal policy as "a modest structural (or "high employment") federal budget *surplus*" (p. 10).

37. Substituting a tax on consumption, such as a sales or value-added tax, for some part of the payroll tax also could increase growth by making added employment more attractive to either workers or employers or both.

38. Committee for Economic Development, *American Workers*, p. 39.

39. Martin L. Bailey and H. Gersbach, "Efficiency in Manufacturing and the Need for Global Competition," *Brookings Papers on Economic Activity: Microeconomics* (1995), pp. 307–358.

40. Jeffrey G. Williamson, "Globalization and Inequality Then and Now: The Late 19th and Late 20th Centuries Compared," Working Paper 5491,"National Bureau of Economic Research, 1996.

41. John G. Ruggie, "International Regimes, Transactions, and Change: Embedded Liberalism in the Postwar Economic Order," *International Organization* (Spring 1982): 195–231.

Chapter 7

Strategies for Multilateral Trade Liberalization

Gary C. Hufbauer and Jeffrey J. Schott

Throughout the postwar period, multilateral trade negotiations have been the centerpiece of U.S. trade policy. The United States has been the demandeur of all eight rounds of trade talks under the General Agreement on Tariffs and Trade (GATT). U.S. participation in GATT and its successor, the World Trade Organization (WTO), serves a straightforward and important objective: to promote U.S. trading interests.

Multilateral trade negotiations give the biggest bang for the buck. U.S. negotiators parlay their commitments to trade reform into reciprocal liberalization by dozens of important trading partners. Regional pacts may produce deeper liberalization in specific areas, but none matches the comprehensive coverage of national trade practices contained in multilateral accords that have been negotiated in GATT.

Liberalization of foreign trade barriers has been a cornerstone of the U.S. export-oriented strategy of the 1990s. This strategy has successfully tempered political demands for new protection that heated up in response to record U.S. trade deficits. U.S. export growth (up about 50 percent since 1990) has created a political counterforce to the protectionist lobbies of import-competing industries and, at the same time, has contributed to higher U.S. wages. Exporting firms pay wages about 15 percent better than comparable nonexporting firms, and their workforce numbers grow more steadily over time.[1]

Moreover, unlike early postwar trade pacts, recent trade negotiations both regionally and in GATT have yielded asymmetric commitments to trade liberalization in which developing countries outdo their industrial country counterparts. For example, in the Uruguay Round, the United States agreed to a package of agreements that basically required it to cut industrial tariffs on average by 2 percentage points and to eliminate textile quotas over ten years (but leaving half of them intact until the end of the transition period). In return, WTO members agreed to accept new multilateral obligations on intellectual property and services and to cap agricultural subsidies (matching U.S. cuts previously enacted in domestic legislation). In addition, developing countries agreed to bind most of their tariffs and cut them on average by one-fifth of base levels that often ranged between 15 and 40 percent.[2]

In mercantilistic arithmetic, vis-á-vis developing countries, the United States "gave" tariff concessions averaging 2 percentage points in the Uruguay Round bargain and "got" tariff concessions ranging between 3 and 8 percentage points, plus a bountiful harvest of nontariff reforms. Were he alive today, the noted mercantilist Thomas Mun, author of *England's Treasure by Foreign Trade* (ca. 1628),[3] would applaud the procession of U.S. trade representatives who achieved this coup: William Brock, Clayton Yeutter, Carla Hills, and Mickey Kantor.

Future talks are likely to follow the same pattern and produce substantial new market access opportunities abroad in return for limited changes in existing U.S. practices and policies. After all, most developing countries—the big growth markets of the 21st century—still have tariff barriers of 10 to 30 percent, plus quotas and other restrictions on agriculture with tariff equivalent rates often exceeding 100 percent. Moreover, they maintain nontariff barriers on most service activities that translate into tariff-equivalent barriers of 50 percent and higher, plus assorted restrictions on investment that serve to constrain U.S. exports.[4] These barriers form the major targets of the next multilateral trade negotiation (MTN). Thus U.S. politicians should be champing for a new MTN: Where else can the United States get something for virtually nothing!

If MTNs are such a good deal for the United States, why is U.S. enthusiasm for multilateral trade liberalization seemingly so frayed? Although memories of Pat Buchanan's 1996 primary campaign are fading, and while few people may have noticed the Republican platform warning about the insidious World Trade Organization, the underlying protectionist sentiments remain strong. They add up to underwhelming support for the WTO and new multilateral initiatives. According to one poll, 51 percent of Americans believe that trade agreements cost jobs.[5]

A common but not comforting explanation for the current mood is trade fatigue. The years 1993 and 1994 were landmarks in the postwar trade agenda: The North American Free Trade Agreement (NAFTA) and the Uruguay Round were ratified; Asia Pacific Economic Cooperation forum (APEC) members pledged to achieve free trade and investment by 2010 (for developed members) and 2020 (for developing members); and the Western Hemisphere countries promised to complete their own free trade negotiations by 2005.

U.S. negotiators are justifiably proud of these accomplishments but fear overloading the political circuits by adding to the ongoing adjustment burden of U.S. industries and workers generated by recently concluded trade reforms. Instead, they argue that WTO members should digest the latest pacts before feasting again at the negotiating table.

To be sure, prior multilateral agreements were followed by lengthy pauses. After the conclusion of the Kennedy Round in 1967, it was six years before the Tokyo Round was launched in 1973. After the conclusion of the Tokyo Round in 1979, it was seven years before the Uruguay Round was launched in 1986. The arithmetic of simple progressions suggests that eight years would be required to recuperate from the double whammy of NAFTA and the Uruguay Round—and that could take us to the year 2002!

Politicians are an impatient lot. Waiting six, seven, or eight years before talks even start, much less bear fruit, is long past their electoral horizon. So, based on the old math, new approaches must be used to fill the negotiating calendar while multilateral liberalization gets under way. New approaches are necessary both to deliver political fruit during the careers of leading members of Congresspeople and cabinet secretaries and to keep trade liberalization moving forward.

Trade fatigue does not tell the whole story behind American doubts. Two new impediments—obstacles that were barely evident in the run-up to the Tokyo Round or the Uruguay Round—now confront U.S. policymakers.

First, the persistence of earnings stagnation for the U.S. workforce could not be anticipated in 1973 and was barely noticed in 1986. While few economists blame international trade and investment for the slow measured growth of U.S. productivity (and only modest growth even with an intellectually defensible revamping of the consumer price index), many economists think that globalization explains part of the growing earnings differential between skilled and unskilled workers. More to the political point, the majority of Americans hold globalization responsible for a less secure environment in the workplace and for lower pay than they deserve.

Second, remaining U.S. trade barriers are concentrated in textiles and apparel, agriculture, and a handful of services. The profile of U.S. protection thus has come to resemble the view around Jackson Hole, Wyoming: a relatively flat valley surrounded by sharp pinnacles. If another multilateral round means business for the United States, it means flattening the Grand Tetons—a fate postponed in eight prior rounds of multilateral negotiations. Threatened U.S. firms are sure to fight like General Custer at the Little Big Horn, because they are surrounded and have nowhere else to go.

Of course, with the passage of time, it is easy to forget the obstacles and alternatives that confronted Presidents Lyndon Johnson, Richard Nixon, and Ronald Reagan when they launched trade rounds. The Kennedy Round and the contemporaneous U.S.-Canada Auto Pact both represented dramatic free trade ripostes to protectionist threats: in the first case, the challenge of the European Common Market with its common external tariff that portended severe discrimination against U.S. exports; in the second case, a looming trade war over Canadian auto subsidies. Nixon's endorsement of the Tokyo Round was bedeviled by the politics of Vietnam and the Cold War. Reagan's push for the Uruguay Round was obstructed by the inflated value of the U.S. dollar, European intransigence over agriculture, and developing country resistance to GATT rules on services, investment, and intellectual property.

In other words, obstacles to multilateral talks are a familiar sight in postwar trade history. The obstacles change shape from decade to decade, and as they evolve new launch strategies are required.

FOUR LAUNCH STRATEGIES FOR LIBERALIZATION

Four main strategies can be used, in combination, to pursue negotiated trade liberalization over the next few years. They are:

- Multilateral trade negotiations, similar to the Kennedy Round (1963–67), the Tokyo Round (1973–79), and the Uruguay Round (1986–94) conducted under the auspices of GATT but modified to take advantage of the new institutional structure of the WTO that accommodates continuing negotiations.

- Regional trading arrangements, exemplified by the European Union, the Australia-New Zealand Closer Economic Relations Agreement, the North American Free Trade Area, the Association of Southeast Asian Nations (ASEAN) Free Trade Area, and South America's customs union, MERCOSUR, but now broadened to encompass continent-bridging initiatives such as APEC and the Free Trade Area of the Americas (FTAA).

- Sectoral negotiations designed to widen market access. A very early example is the regime for civil aviation—bilateral Air Service Agreements negotiated within a multilateral framework. In the Tokyo Round era, plurilateral accords covered sectors such as dairy and beef. More recently, WTO negotiations have focused on a troika of service sectors (financial services, basic telecommunications, and maritime) as well as the information technology agreement.

- Bilateral negotiations focused on specific sectors and issues. This style is well known from U.S. bouts with Japan over goods and services ranging from citrus, to semiconductors, to insurance.

In addition to liberalization achieved by trade negotiations of one sort or another, several countries have liberalized on their own intiative. Two outstanding examples in the past 15 years are New Zealand and Chile; but, in fact, a great many countries have relaxed their trade and investment barriers in the context of overall economic reform.[6]

Unilateral liberalization must be applauded when it occurs. But the political arithmetic of mercantilism ("exports are good, imports are bad") is too deeply ingrained in the public's mind for unilateral liberalization to substitute for negotiated liberalization. Indeed, mercantilistic doctrines are deeply entrenched when it comes to liberalizing highly protected sectors, such as agriculture, textiles and apparel, telecommunications, and financial services—all targets of opportunity for the 21st century.

Multilateral Rounds

Early GATT rounds typically were held among a small group of elite officials at European resorts such as Torquay, Annecy, and Geneva. Starting with the Dillon Round (1961–62), these became much bigger affairs, and by the time of the Uruguay Round (1986–94), the GATT show had become a 15-ring circus, involving hundreds of public officials, private business advocates, and nongovernmental watchers.

There are three strong arguments for multilateral rounds of trade negotiations. First, with broad subject matter coverage, this approach plays to every country's mercantilistic sentiments. It can harness broad coalitions in favor of the final package. To cite but one example, in the Uruguay Round package, the United States "won" on intellectual property and "lost" on textiles and apparel. By the same mercantile arithmetic, India's score was just the reverse. Broad coverage ensures that nearly every country has sectors where the ensuing liberalization works to the benefit of its exporting industries.

Second, ongoing multilateral negotiations act as a break against the introduction of new barriers while the talks are in progress. Sometimes this is achieved by formal standstill arrangements (although, on close inspection, such provisions always have loopholes); but to a greater extent, the seawall against new protection is constructed from the mood of continuing negotiations. This is what C. Fred Bergsten, director of the Institute for International Economics, calls the "bicycle theory" of trade negotiations; only by maintaining forward progress can the global trading system avoid tipping over into protectionism.

Third, multilateral rounds are so central to the international economy that they engage the attention of presidents and prime ministers. In fact, just launching past rounds required a concerted push from top leadership in the United States, the European Union, Japan, and Canada. Top leaders from these same countries and others have had to instruct their ministers, at crucial junctions, to reach a deal.

Juxtaposed against the advantages of multilateral rounds are some obvious disadvantages. In the first place, the very size of multilateral talks—the number of countries and the number of topics—makes them daunting, multiyear exercises. At the conclusion of each of the last three multilateral rounds, many negotiators, weary from the international battles and domestic debates, muttered "Never again."

The time scale of multilateral rounds has attracted a second set of objections. Business firms with an immediate agenda to pursue—for example, opening the telecom market in India, or closing counterfeit factories in China—are wary that their issues will become part of a larger drama with many acts and that satisfaction on their issues will be delayed until the last scene. This fear has prompted U.S. trade officials to concentrate on "deliverables": negotiations that produce results in a year or two.

Equally serious is the fact that the "launch price"—the political energy that top leaders must invest to get talks under way—is far higher today than in the past. In the United States, Europe, and Japan, a new round of talks means that leaders must confront a series of antiglobalization themes—stagnant wages, high unemployment, wider differentials between skilled and unskilled workers, and corporate downsizing. While Patrick Buchanan and Ross Perot in the United States and the late Sir James Goldsmith and Philippe de Villiers in Europe all scored poorly in the polls, their ideas carry more resonance than their candidacies.

Beyond the broad ideological debate, a new multilateral round would carry the premise of free trade to sectors that, so far, have retained most of the vestiges of protection dating back to the 1950s: dairy and speciality crops (such as peanuts, tobacco, and fresh vegetables) in the United States and Canada; most of agriculture in Europe and Japan; high tariffs and nontariff barriers against textile and apparel imports in nearly all industrial countries; contingent protection (notably antidumping legislation) in both the United States and Europe; and a surprising range of sectors insulated by opaque barriers in Japan.

Finally, a new WTO round inevitably will prompt a major debate on the social agenda—the extent to which labor, environmental, and corruption questions should be tied to trade talks. Many Europeans and North Americans believe that free trade and investment with Asia and Latin America must be accompanied by upward harmonization of social standards. If that cannot be achieved, they want to have the power to ban or label imported goods that embody "deficient" production processes. Asian and Latin American nations reject the social agenda themes, both as an intrusion on their sovereign rights and as a disguised attempt to create new protective barriers, akin to the antidumping laws.

To meet these challenges, the WTO agenda must be comprehensive, encompassing initiatives both to unravel residual protection and to extend multilateral disciplines into new areas not adequately covered by WTO rights and obligations. The negotiating package needs to be large enough to afford the opportunity for trade-offs between sectors and issues—otherwise WTO members will not be able to sell the reform of long-entrenched trade barriers to their domestic constituencies.

Fortunately, the new institutional structure of the WTO accommodates continuing negotiations on a rolling agenda of issues, much as we proposed in our blueprint for the Uruguay Round more than a decade ago.[7] Not all the issues on the WTO agenda need to be started, or completed, at the same time. Indeed, a new WTO "round" could well take the form of a series of "roundups," in which trade ministers use their biennial meetings to: foster decisions on interissue trade-offs needed to close some negotiations; extend talks on other issues; and add new topics to the negotiating agenda.

Roundups essentially would be consecutive rounds rolled together; they would avoid the problems of past GATT rounds by producing minipackages on a regular basis and adding new items to the negotiating agenda.[8] WTO negotiations likely will still need to package agreements together, as in past GATT rounds, but the packaging can now be more flexible because of the institutional structure of the new trade organization.

Regional Trade and Investment Arrangements

In the last 15 years, most innovations in trade and investment issues were pioneered in regional arrangements. The European Union invented the concept of mutual recognition for product standards and is implementing Europe-wide rules for ensuring competitive markets. The United States and Canada devised the first comprehensive rules for liberalizing services within a free trade area. The United States and Mexico, in the context of NAFTA, ultimately will achieve free trade in agricultural products. Australia and New Zealand have rid themselves of antidumping legislation, opened their air services markets, and applied the concept of mutual recognition to professional qualifications. APEC declared a vision of free trade and investment for its members; together its members add up to half the world's economy.

What's wrong with regional innovation? Not much, but a cadre of professional economists worry that regional groups will deflect trade into inefficient patterns; create a spaghetti of conflicting rules, each backed by entrenched interests; and generally undermine the process of multilateral liberalization.[9] Eventually, according to the critics, a "battle of blocs" will erupt as regional groups confront one another.

These worries are too apocalyptic. In theory, regional trade arrangements could spoil five decades of success with a multilateral system. In practice, they have been far more constructive than destructive, notwithstanding severe shortcomings, such as the European Common Agricultural Policy, the NAFTA rules of origin, and the MERCOSUR's sky-high protection of automobiles.

Appropriate concerns with regional arrangements lie elsewhere. In the first place, the political energies required to construct and defend a regional zone of free trade and investment may detract from the energies available for the multilateral system. This clearly happened in Europe in the 1980s: While the Uruguay Round negotiations were under way, the European Union was simultaneously and distractingly engaged with the difficult task of building Europe 1992. The same regional preoccupation is again taking place, with Europe's expansion to the east, its run-up to monetary union, and the adoption of the euro as currency of the realm.

By contrast, for the United States, negotiation of NAFTA enabled its trade officials to establish high benchmarks on services, intellectual property, investment, and agricultural rules for subsequent display in GATT talks. Following the Mexican peso crisis of December 1994, however, and the ensuing rescue plan organized by the U.S. Treasury, defense of NAFTA has put very substantial demands on its champions in the executive branch and Congress. Moreover, the Mexican crisis curbed Clinton's enthusiasm for talking about trade in the 1996 presidential campaign. Turning to South America, it is conceivable that Brazilian preoccupation with expanding the reach of the MERCOSUR and with protecting key sectors such as automobiles and information technology, could attenuate that nation's interest in the multilateral system.

The second concern with regional arrangments is that they may find it increasingly difficult to accept less affluent countries as members. Europe is going through agonies as it tries to draw the line at the Visegrad and Baltic countries, not wanting to admit

Ukraine, Bulgaria, and Romania, much less Turkey, Tunisia, Algeria, and Morocco. The United States is wary about expanding NAFTA to include Chile and the Caribbean and Central American nations, much less Colombia or Venezuela. Aussies and Kiwis are going through a national debate on their ties to Asia; and a formal arrangement between the Australia–New Zealand Closer Economic Relations group and the ASEAN countries now seems remote. Almost by definition, developing countries have social problems—exploited workers, environmental degradation, drug trafficking, the abuse of human rights. These problems offer powerful arguments against membership in regional groups dominated by advanced industrial countries.

Bilateral (or Small Plurilateral) Negotiations

Bilateral negotiations are an essential feature of a multilateral trading system. Much of the hard negotiating work within big rounds is done bilaterally (or in small groups) between the parties with the strongest commercial interests—on tariffs, quotas, standards, services, and so forth. After the multilateral agreement is signed and ratified, and members disagree on their rights and obligations, the ensuing disputes usually occur in a bilateral context. The current U.S.-EU dispute over cattle raised with hormone additives, played out within the WTO framework, provides one illustration. The Kodak-Fuji case provides another.

But an additional other category of bilateral negotiations exists outside the framework of the multilateral (or regional) system; and this is what observers usually have in mind when using the term (not counting bilateral deals that serve to close markets). An old example is the U.S.-Canada auto dispute in 1963 and 1964, which led to the Auto Pact, signed in 1965. More recent examples are the U.S.-China negotiations, in 1996, on the enforcement of copyright protection in China; and the ongoing U.S.-EU talks, supported by the Transatlantic Business Dialogue, on mutual recognition of standards, testing, and manufacturing practice norms within the pharmaceutical and other industries.

At times, such bilateral talks have threatened the commercial interests of outside parties. Back in the 1970s, this was true of U.S.-Japan beef negotiations: In response to U.S. demands, Japan opened its protected market to a very limited extent, but it also shifted some of its purchases from Australian to U.S. beef. More recently, in the U.S.-Japan semiconductor agreement of the 1980s,

European producers were rightly concerned that price floors would be determined at the expense of their commercial interests.

These are exceptions. More often bilateral negotiations, if they succeed, result in agreements that respect multilateral norms. For example, when Japan relaxes its laws limiting large retail stores, Taiwan toy exporters should benefit just as much as U.S. film exporters.

Bilateral market access talks frequently go nowhere. Neither side has adequate legal rights or commercial clout to persuade the other. The case may not be resolved, even after years of talk. Nevertheless, in many instances, the issue rolls over as an agenda item for the next multilateral round of trade negotiations. In fact, an accumulation of bilateral issues can help set the stage for a multilateral round.

Market Access by Sector Agreements

From time to time, the leading commercial powers have agreed to liberalize trade and investment on a sectoral basis. Usually these agreements do not encompass all countries, and frequently they lead to partial rather than complete relaxation of trade barriers. Old examples are the networks of bilateral treaties and agreements that establish a common framework for ship and air traffic between countries. A recent example is the Agreement on Government Procurement, signed by 22 WTO members, that is not part of the Single Undertaking of the WTO. The two latest examples are the Information Technology Agreement (ITA), endorsed by the APEC leaders at their 1996 meeting in Subic, the Philippines, and initialed at the Singapore WTO Ministerial in December 1996, which covers $500 billion of world trade in computers, semiconductors, and software; and the WTO Basic Telecommunications Agreement, signed in April 1997, which will dramatically liberalize protective regulatory regimes that cover some $600 billion of telecommunications services.

In fact, the WTO's "built-in agenda"—negotiations mandated by the agreements concluded in the Uruguay Round—amounts to a series of sectoral talks. The first three subjects were financial services, maritime transportation services, and basic telecommunications. None of these talks produced an agreement by its initial deadline, and all three were given new calendars; since the initial deadline, however, the highly successful Basic Telecom Agreement was hammered out. Future talks are scheduled on government procurement, agriculture, and services (as well as financial services and maritime services), together with lesser topics. Meanwhile, the Organization for Economic Cooperation and Development (OECD) is working on its Multilateral Agreement on Investment (MAI), which the industrial countries hope to sell in concept (if not in language) to the WTO. Many observers are skeptical, both of the built-in agenda and the MAI, so long as they remain independent sectoral talks. The ITA and Basic Telecom deals have converted some skeptics. Moreover, just as frustrated bilateral negotiations in an earlier era helped launch the Kennedy, Tokyo, and Uruguay Rounds, so frustrated plurilateral talks can provide the makings of a "roundup" that leads to a full-blown multilateral round in the future.

Complementarity Between Negotiating Modes

It is easy to play armchair general and conjure up conflicts between negotiating modes. But that is a game we leave for academic economists.[10] There are some potential conflicts. However, with a little imagination, trade officials can use the different approaches to complement one another rather than conflict. The most important complementarities deserve mention.

All the negotiating styles, short of a multilateral round, can be used to keep the bicycle moving while the political forces in Washington, Brussels, Tokyo, and elsewhere gather strength to launch a new round. By drawing on the strengths of each trade negotiating approach, some problems can be addressed over the next two or three years, and many more problems can be framed for a multilateral round.

In other words, business leaders should not worry that their grievances will be forgotten for years while negotiators wine and dine in Singapore, Geneva, and other culinary centers. Quite the contrary. As in the Kodak-Fuji dispute, the U.S. trade representative will go forward with WTO cases, even when victory is not a sure bet. The same aggressive approach will be taken in NAFTA. Even when disputes are lost, something is gained: a better understanding, especially by trade experts, of where the international rules need to be extended or fixed.

Meanwhile bilateral and sectoral initiatives will be pursued to widen market access. In a few instances, such as the celebrated Information Technology Agreement reached at Singapore, they will succeed. In far more cases, market access initiatives will stall, but they will help create an agenda for the forthcoming multilateral negotiations.

Whatever the success of bilateral and sectoral initiatives, it is not obvious that the European Union, China, and India—to name three big players—will engage quickly in new multilateral talks. Indeed, the European Union (at French behest) already has demanded that farm trade talks not restart until 2000, the date previously agreed in the Uruguay Round accord. The best way for the United States to keep pressure on recalcitrants is to launch negotiations for a Free Trade Area of the Americas, and to keep the APEC process moving smartly forward. With these devices, the United States buys insurance against intransigience by big players in the world economy.

To recapitulate, U.S. trade negotiators must practice a three-step dance: bilateral and sectoral access talks on any issue, just as soon as it becomes "ripe"; FTAA and APEC negotiations to push regional free trade initiatives and induce other major trading countries to reciprocate; and multilateral roundups in the WTO by the year 2000 to link these initiatives together.

CONVINCING THE PUBLIC

In selling free trade and investment to the American public, the simple point needs to be made again and again: Foreign barriers restrict U.S. exports far more severely than American barriers limit U.S. imports. The United States has some protective pinnacles and a handful of investment restrictions. But where the United States has isolated barriers, Asia and Latin America have massive walls. Tariff averages of 10 to 20 percent are common even in countries dedicated to open markets, such as Chile, Argentina, and Malaysia. Other countries, not so dedicated, such as Brazil and Korea, complement their tariff barriers with opaque nontariff measures. Important East Asian countries such as China, Indonesia, and Thailand publish tariffs in the 20 to 40 percent range, buttressed by assorted nontariff barriers. In South Asia, protection in Pakistan and India gets started at tariff equivalent levels of 40 percent. All these countries wall off large segments of their economies—mining, transport, power, telecommunications, finance—from foreign investment. Even Europe and Canada severely restrict U.S. exports of agricultural products and television shows.

The essence of the next multilateral round is to ensure that U.S. firms can, in the future, sell their goods and services abroad just as easily as foreign firms already can sell their products in the United States. To achieve this objective, not only must tariffs and quotas be abolished, but investment restrictions also must be lifted. Without additional U.S. investment abroad, the growth of U.S. exports will be severely constrained.

Government speeches alone cannot sell the American public on the merits of open markets. The voice of business also must be heard. In the years since ratification of the Uruguay Round accords in 1994, corporate America has been missing in action as a force for liberalization. To be sure, the computer and semiconductor industry did a first-rate job at designing and selling the Information Technology Agreement; and U.S. telecom carriers (AT&T, MCI, Sprint) worked with their industry colleagues abroad to push the Basic Telecom Agreement. But year in and year out, most firms routinely take for granted the benefits of an international system that delivers open markets.

Specifics tell the story. Retailers such as Sears and Neiman Marcus are shy to advertise the fact that bargain merchandise from China, Indonesia, and Mexico fills their shelves. Each retailer fears that if it advertises its great foreign merchandise, other retailers will answer with patriotic "We stock America" slogans (as Wal-Mart already does). The result: collective silence. Instead, the big retailers could use their trade associations to put together advertising campaigns that engagingly tell the story of global purchasing—what it means in quality and price for the American public.

Firms that produce for export markets are just as bad. How many GE, Boeing, or Caterpillar workers know that their jobs are supported by export sales? A few, but not that many. Among employees of firms that supply these industrial giants, ignorance of export markets is almost universal. Exporting firms and their suppliers ought to put in each worker's pay slip, every month, a simple factual statement describing the percentage of earnings attributable to export sales and naming the main export products and markets.

HEAVY LIFTING ELSEWHERE

Environmental standards, labor rights, and corrupt practices are important issues. But a multilateral round of trade negotiations is not necessarily the place to answer all questions. There are two reasons why advocates consign environment, labor, and corruption to the WTO: First, they want trade sticks to prompt action in laggard countries; second, they want flexible trade rules that permit discrimination against foreign goods manufactured in a context that abuses social norms. Two examples will illustrate these propositions. If Indian officials corruptly sell telecom rights to a European consortium, some U.S. firms might want to bedevil consortium members, and their Indian associates, when those firms try to sell goods or services in the U.S. market. If Canadian trade unions can persuade Ottawa to enact a labeling requirement for athletic shoes made with child labor, the unions do not want the label questioned by a WTO dispute panel.

Advocacy arguments for trade linkage are understandable. But the WTO round already will be a big show, just dealing with existing trade and investment barriers. It should not be the only show in town. Talks should be launched on other issues, but headed by different institutions and drawing in other ministries from national bureaucracies.

For example, an invigorated International Labor Organization (ILO) could devise norms on the use of child labor. And these norms could be built into the International Standards Organization's (ISO's) proposed standards series for labor (the ISO 25000 series). The WTO Singapore Ministerial Declaration opens the door for an approach along these lines, with its call for cooperation between the WTO and the ILO.

To take another example, a new Global Environmental Organization might develop common rules for global and transborder environmental issues. And the World Bank and its sister institutions could create affirmative standards to be followed in public procurement to guard against corruption.

In each subject area, linkages could be forged—at the end of the day, not at the beginning of negotiations—with the trading system. Rules could be devised for individual WTO members to exclude products manufactured with tainted processes. In exceptional cases, the WTO might authorize all its members to retaliate against specified countries or companies for their breach of international norms. But the trade linkages should be forged only after international agreement has been reached, in competent bodies, on the applicable substantive standards.

THE NEXT STEPS

By the year 2000, world trade in goods and services will top $8 trillion. If the U.S. share of world exports remains constant, U.S. sales abroad will increase by $260 billion over 1995 levels. Such a windfall has great political appeal, especially if it is achieved by relaxing the market access barriers of other countries.

The key to reaping these rewards lies in convincing Americans that global trade pays off in a better standard of living.

The challenge for President Clinton is to persuade the American public that trade agreements open far more doors to U.S. goods and services than they close doors to U.S. factories. With that all-important shift in public opinion, Clinton should be able to convince Congress to restore fast-track trade negotiating authority. Serious regional or multilateral talks require fast-track legislation that gives the president comprehensive authority to abolish U.S. trade barriers and thus substantially expands the executive branch's existing power to pursue talks on a short list of zero-for-zero sectors left over from the Uruguay Round. Without fast track, anything negotiated internationally stands an excellent chance of being renegotiated in Congress. Recognizing this situation, trading partners will hold back their offers and thus make it harder for U.S. negotiators to bring home the best deal possible.

President Clinton's window of opportunity to obtain fast track is brief. Second-term presidents rarely enact major legislation during their last two years in the White House, especially when the opposition controls Congress. These considerations should prompt the Clinton administration to make a big push for fast track in 1997.

Fast-track authority might last to the year 2002, with interim deadlines and with the possibility of extension. This timetable would ensure that the next president will bring back some of the important results for congressional approval. In other words, President Clinton may not be present at every finish line (a plus for some congressional Republicans). But, with interim deadlines, President Clinton will wrap up some of the negotiations, and he can fire the starting gun for all of them, a plus for Democrats.

By taking these initiatives, President Clinton could build a bridge to carry the traffic of global commerce in the 21st century.

NOTES

1. J. David Richardson and Karin Rindal, *Why Exports Matter: More!* (Washington, DC: Institute for International Economics and the Manufacturing Institute, 1996).

2. Jeffrey J. Schott assisted by Johanna W. Buurman, *The Uruguay Round: An Assessment* (Washington, DC: Institute for International Economics, 1994).

3. Thomas Mun, *England's Treasure by Forraign Trade, or the Ballance of Forraign Trade is the Rule of our Treasury* (London, 1664).

4. See Bernard Hoekman, "Tentative First Steps: An Assessment of the Uruguay Round Agreement on Services," Centre for Economic Policy Research Discussion Paper No. 1150 (London: CEPR, 1995); Gary Clyde Hufbauer, "Surveying the Costs of Protection: A Partial Equilibrium Approach," in Jeffrey J. Schott, ed. *The World Trading System: Challenges Ahead* (Washington, DC: Institute for International Economics, 1996); and Edward M. Graham, "Direct Investment and the Future Agenda of the World Trade Organization," in Jeffrey J. Schott, ed. *The World Trading System* (1996).

5. United States Information Agency (USIA), Judy Aita, Staff Correspondent, "Poll Shows Americans Remain Skeptical of Trade Pacts," New York, November 8, 1996.

6. A number of cases are analyzed in Demetrius Papageorgiou, Michael Michaely, and Armeane M. Choksi, eds., *Liberalizing Foreign Trade* (Cambridge: Basil Blackwell, 1991).

7. Gary Clyde Hufbauer and Jeffrey J. Schott, *Trading for Growth: The Next Round of Trade Negotiations,* Policy Analyses in International Economics 11 (Washington, DC: Institute for International Economics, 1985).

8. Jeffrey J. Schott, ed., *The World Trading System: Challenges Ahead* (Washington, DC: Institute for International Economics, 1996).

9. Jagdish Bhagwati and Arvind Paragariya, eds., *The Economics of Preferential Trade Agreements* (Washington, DC: The AEI Press, 1996.)

10. See, for example, Paul Wonnacott and Ronald J. Wonnacott, "Liberalization in the Western Hemisphere: New Challenges in the Design of a Free-Trade Agreement," *North American Journal of Economics and Finance* (1995).

Chapter 8

From Here to Free Trade:
The Quest for a Multilateral/Regional
Synthesis

Ernest H. Preeg

The 50 years of the multilateral trading system have been an extraordinary success story marked by the reduction of barriers to trade and the stimulation of economic growth throughout the world. During the 1980s, however, a fundamental restructuring of trade—and the trading system—began. It continues to gather momentum in the 1990s and requires, in turn, fundamental rethinking of U.S. trade strategy.

Many aspects of this changing structure of trade relationships have received wide-ranging attention. Economic globalization is a central phenomenon, drawing national economies more closely together in terms of trade, international investment, and cross-border technology transfer. National companies are becoming more and more oriented to international markets. Governments are caught between political pressures to resist import competition and the imperative to craft more open trade policies in order to maintain a competitive position in world markets. On balance, governments have pursued the trade liberalizing route, thus reinforcing the globalization process. Moreover, trade liberalization has been proceeding at three levels—multilaterally through the Uruguay Round, regionally through various free trade initiatives, and unilaterally as a matter of national self-interest by many developing and former and remaining communist countries.

This greatly changed, multifaceted context of trade relationships, compared with only a decade ago, presents complex challenges for U.S. trade strategy formulation in the period ahead. Two critical developments in policy orientation, however, constitute the point of departure for developing a strategy and will be decisive for the outcome.

The first critical development is that free trade, as distinct from progressive trade liberalization, now has become an explicit policy objective. This situation is most obvious in the proliferation of regional free trade initiatives under way in Europe, the Americas, and across the Pacific. But it also emerged in the latter phase of the Uruguay Round through "zero-for-zero" tariff elimination by sector by the industrial countries, which resulted in a more than doubling—from 20 percent to 44 percent—of the share of nonagricultural imports by these countries that will be free of duties on a most-favored-nation (MFN) basis. Since the Uruguay Round, industrial and some newly industrial countries continued this sectoral free trade approach through the Information Technology Agreement (ITA), which phases out remaining tariffs on information technology and telecommunications goods. This achievement brought the duty-free share of industrial country nonagricultural imports to about half. Initiative for such sectoral—as well as regional—free trade objectives comes largely from multinational corporations, which seek to rid themselves of border payments and achieve a more predictable market for their internationally oriented investment and distribution strategies. Governments also find the free trade outcome easier to explain to voters because it delivers "reciprocity" in market access.

The second critical policy development is that regional free trade agreements have political momentum and are rapidly approaching parity with MFN commitments as the organizing principle for trade relationships. The European Union is negotiating agreements in Eastern Europe and the Mediterranean basin that will lead to a free trade grouping of over 40 countries. The intended Free Trade Area of the Americas (FTAA) will include another 34 countries, and the free trade objective of the Asia Pacific Economic Cooperation forum (APEC) would add 14 more (some of them, like China and Japan, very large). Thus three-quarters of the members of the World Trade Organization (WTO) are committed to regional free trade between now and 2020. In trade terms, the share of global exports within free trade agreements will increase from about 45 percent today to 70 percent, if these objectives are achieved. In addition, a Transatlantic Free Trade Agreement (TAFTA), encompassing another 7 percent of world exports, is under preliminary review. In view of these two developments— free trade as an explicit policy objective and near parity between the multilateral MFN and regional free trade components of the overall trading system—the central question of trade strategy ahead is how to manage the interaction of these developments and to what end. Should multilateral and regional objectives continue to be pursued on largely separate "tracks" or integrated toward some common goal? If the latter, what role should free trade play, including the possible objective of multilateral free trade? And how should free trade be defined as an operational objective? In sum, the trade strategy challenge facing the United States and the world is how to develop a multilateral/regional synthesis with particular attention to the uneven process now under way.

These strategic questions can best be answered in terms of three basic scenarios for trade negotiations over the coming five to ten years. The first scenario is to pursue the current two-separate-tracks course. This basically amounts to an extrapolation of official trade policy objectives at the multilateral and regional levels. The second scenario is for a WTO free trade "Grand Bargain," adopting the label of C. Fred Bergsten, director of the Institute for International Economics in Washington, who has put forward the most detailed proposal along these lines. The third scenario is for a multilateral/regional synthesis based on an extension and integration of regional free trade groupings, featuring a TAFTA initiative as the key catalytic step. In my view, this third scenario is the preferable approach for building a strengthened and truly multilateral trading system over the coming ten years, although it is also at some cost to the concept of universality. But it is clearly a more complex strategy to evaluate as well as to implement.

The Current Two-Separate-Track Approach

This scenario reflects the WTO action program at the multilateral level, with existing free trade agreements in Europe, the Americas, and the Asia-Pacific region moving forward at the regional level on differing time schedules. Under this approach, the multilateral and regional trade liberalization tracks are, in effect, pursued independently of one another, linked only by the vague concept of "gradual convergence" toward free trade at some undefined future point. The multilateral WTO track receives rhetorical priority, as expressed by the WTO director-general, Renato Ruggiero: "Maintaining the primacy of the WTO rules and dispute settlement system is vital, not as an end in itself, but in order to avoid a bedlam of competing and contradictory jurisdictions."[1] But the supposed primacy of multilateralism is belied by actions at the regional level. Europeans, in particular, appear disingenuous in pledging allegiance to the multilateral trading system while at the same time moving forcefully to create a preferential regional trading bloc among one-third of the WTO membership. Surely the intent of the 40-plus members of the anticipated European grouping is not to create a bedlam of competing and contradictory jurisdictions but rather to assert the primacy of European rules over WTO rules and dispute settlement procedures.

Within this two-separate-track scenario, the WTO action program is important to consolidate and extend market-access commitments within the multilateral trading system. First the Uruguay Round agreement must be effectively implemented. The greatly strengthened dispute settlement mechanism will be critically tested. Implementation of the complex and politically charged Uruguay Round commitments in the agriculture and textile sectors will require political courage, particularly by governments of industrial countries. The post–Uruguay Round WTO action program, perhaps leading to a new round of multilateral negotiations, is based on the "built-in agenda" of commitments for further negotiations contained in the Uruguay Round agreement, in particular for the financial and basic telecommunications sectors in 1997 (achieved with great success in basic telecom), public procurement by 1999, and agriculture and services more generally by 2000. Possible new areas for negotiation, based on the Singapore ministerial declaration issued in December 1996, include investment and competition policies, transparency in government procurement,and the trade-environment linkage. Overall, it is a very ambitious agenda.

One area of further trade liberalization within the WTO that remains vague is reduction or elimination of tariffs and related border restrictions such as quotas, import licenses, and currency restrictions. These are the traditional centerpieces of multilateral negotiations under the General Agreement of Tariffs and Trade (GATT) and, of course, the core of regional free trade agreements. The conundrum facing the WTO is the great asymmetry between the industrial countries and the emerging market countries in Asia, Latin

America, and Central/East Europe. Industrial countries have eliminated or are in the process of eliminating tariffs, on an MFN basis, on half of their nonagricultural imports. Most of their remaining tariffs are either very low or in the textile sector subject to a rigidly negotiated ten-year Uruguay Round arrangement. The emerging market countries, in contrast, bound most of their tariffs in the Uruguay Round against future increase, but generally at very high levels of 20 to 40 percent or more, often well above actual rates. Moreover, quotas, import licensing requirements, and currency restrictions abound. This asymmetry in market access presents a major problem for any further "zero-for-zero" tariff elimination by industrial countries. It was, in fact, a contentious issue for the pharmaceutical industry and other sectors in the final phase of the Uruguay Round because it created "free rider" benefits for advanced developing countries. The ITA includes limited participation by some, not all, developing countries. In any event, it is difficult to envisage how comprehensive tariff reduction or elimination, and removal of other border restrictions to trade, can be negotiated within a WTO context of "reciprocity." In order to reach a target of free trade, developing countries, contrary to all tradition and practice, would have to slash barriers far more than the industrial countries.

A final issue of concern for the projected WTO action program is its leisurely pace. Negotiations in most cases would not begin for another two to three years, and a new round would begin no sooner than the year 2000, with concrete results not anticipated before 2005 at the earliest.

The regional free trade track under this first scenario, in contrast, likely will proceed more rapidly and concretely, certainly in Europe and probably in the Americas. In the process, it will shift the balance between the two tracks further toward comprehensive regional free trade relationships. Three aspects of this regional course stand out.

The first important aspect of the regional track is the enormous significance of the broadening process of free trade within Europe. For four decades, regional free trade between European Community countries and countries of the European Free Trade Association was a contained relationship, viewed as the exception to the MFN rule of the GATT multilateral system, and an essential element of Western cohesion against the hostile Soviet bloc. Now this contained group is expanding to the east and south with no clear limits. Ten countries in Central and Eastern Europe have in place or are negotiating free trade association agreements with the European Union, as a stepping-stone to full membership. Turkey is engaged in negotiation of a customs union with the European Union. And free trade agreements exist or are being negotiated with more than ten other Mediterranean Basin countries. This whole integration process portends wide-ranging political as well as economic benefits, for the region and the global order. But it also fundamentally alters member-state relationships, inside and outside of Europe, and within multilateral institutions. Within the WTO, for example, all 40-plus members of the European grouping will be obliged or tend to follow the unified position of the European Union representative, and to cast 40-plus votes in decision-making, compared with one vote each for the United States and Japan.

The most far-reaching implication of the momentum for EU expansion to the east, however, is the evolving economic relationship with Russia and Ukraine. If political and economic reforms in these two countries muddle forward over the next several years, the compelling next step would be for them to apply for associate, free trade arrangements with the European Union similar to those of the Baltic and Central European nations. The European Union then would be in a position of not being able to say no to regional free trade even if it wanted to. Western Europe is the natural market for Ukraine and European Russia, and the greater the economic success of Poland and other Central European economies, based heavily on free access to the EU market, the stronger will be the Western European magnet. The European Union and Russia, in fact, already have agreed in principle to discuss a possible free trade agreement as early as 1998 if reforms go forward in Russia. Ukraine has even more incentive for an early free trade agreement with the European Union, as a counterbalance to excessive economic dependence on Russia, and already is pursuing free trade with Central European countries. These European developments, again, could have broad positive consequences, but at a cost to transatlantic solidarity with the United States. Even preliminary discussion of an EU-Russian free trade arrangement, whereby Russian exports to the European Union would have preferential access compared with U.S. exports, raises difficult questions in Washington, including the rationale for maintaining a troop presence in Western Europe. At the same time, EU-Russian economic integration appeals to European nationalists, especially in Russia and France, as a means to consolidate a Europe from the Atlantic to the Urals and thus to regain status as a global power independent of the United States.

The second important aspect of the regional track is what can be called bridging the north/south divide. In contrast with the asymmetry of reciprocity that is a conundrum within the WTO, regional free trade initiatives have moved forward with little regard to the "special and differential treatment" for developing countries that is fundamental to multilateral tradition and practice. Mexico, for example, agreed within the North American Free Trade Agreement (NAFTA) to eliminate its much higher levels of import restrictions on a more-than-reciprocal basis with the United States and Canada. At the same time, in the Uruguay Round Mexico offered only modest tariff reductions and agreed only to bind many sensitive tariffs at 40 percent, or double the actual level. Similar reciprocal free trade agreements have been negotiated between the European Union and the emerging market economies in Central Europe and are the basis for preliminary free trade discussions in the Americas and APEC, although in the latter case, at least, with a longer phase-in period for developing countries. It is difficult to overemphasize this distinction in institutional negotiating context between the GATT/WTO and what has been happening at the regional free trade level.

The third important aspect of the regional track is the evolving definition of what is meant by a free trade agreement. At a minimum, such an accord should lead to the elimination of tariffs on nonagricultural imports as well as closely related border restrictions such as quotas, import licensing requirements, and currency restrictions. Agriculture should be included to a large extent, if not completely. Trade in services, protection of intellectual property, subsidies, government procurement, and investment policies should be included in forthcoming free trade agreements. Most of these trade-related policies are only partially included, if at all, in the multilateral WTO. A "comprehensive" approach to free trade is vital to ensure that the elimination of border restrictions is not nullified by other government policies and to reflect the broadening interrelationships between trade in goods and services, investment, and technology transfers.

In sum, this first scenario of two separate tracks has many positive elements for continuing the trade liberalizing process of past decades, mostly in the direction of "gradual convergence." It could set the stage for a reappraisal five or ten years hence as to how to achieve a more definitive convergence between the multilateral and regional free trade dimensions of the overall trading system. There is a strong likelihood, however, that under this scenario, regional groupings will strengthen and deepen their relationships at a faster pace than will the WTO multilateral structure. This situation could cause a disturbing drifting apart of Europe and North America, in particular, as well as growing concerns in Asia if the APEC free trade course does not produce early concrete results. Therefore, it is useful to consider alternative trade strategies to achieve a more definitive multilateral/regional synthesis during the coming five to ten years.

A WTO GRAND BARGAIN

The simplest way to achieve convergence between the multilateral trading system and the various regional free trade agreements in place or in process would be to negotiate the elimination of remaining tariffs and other restrictions to trade on an MFN basis within the WTO. Such a multilateral free trade approach has been proposed from time to time over the years, most recently by Fred Bergsten.[2]

Bergsten terms his proposal a "grand bargain" between the industrial and developing countries. The former provide "insurance" that their markets will remain open, "including procedural safeguards against subtle methods of undoing prior market opening." The latter offer free and full access to their more highly protected markets. In Bergsten's vision, agreement would be reached at a WTO trade summit meeting to achieve global free trade by 2010, "with a possible extension to 2015 or 2020 for the poorest nations."

The central question about the grand bargain proposal is whether it is politically feasible over this short- to medium-term time frame, whereby the negotiation of global free trade would be inserted at an early date into the WTO action program, and indeed, become its centerpiece. In terms of U.S. interests, almost all of the bargain would appear feasible, given strong presidential leadership. U.S. tariffs are already generally very low, and much would be gained for U.S. exports through free access to highly protected developing country markets. Global free trade in agriculture was the explicit and staunchly pursued U.S. objective in the Uruguay Round. In any event, since the United States is already committed to free trade in the Americas and with East Asia, political support for a global deal—essentially adding transatlantic free trade to the pot—should be relatively easy to obtain. The difficult issues for the United States would be an early phase-out of textile and apparel tariffs and "more stringent multilateral disciplines" on antidumping duties, which Bergsten explicitly cites as one of the not-so-subtle methods of undoing prior market opening. But some arrangement for these issues probably could be negotiated if America's trading partners did their part of the bargain.

It is precisely the willingness of others to respond to the grand bargain proposal, however, that raises serious questions about its political feasibility. It requires greater specificity as to what an acceptable free trade agreement would encompass. Certainly all border restrictions on nonagricultural trade would have to be phased out. Agriculture would have to be included in a major way, although perhaps not completely in the initial phase. Investment policy is now clearly linked to trade in a growing number of bilateral and regional agreements and would have to be part of the grand bargain. Intellectual property rights, trade in services, and government procurement, while all included in the Uruguay Round agreement, would require further commitments by developing countries. Competition policy, broadly defined, also is making its way into trade deliberations as an important dimension of overall market access relationships. It certainly would have to be part of an agreement that placed more stringent multilateral disciplines on antidumping duties. All of these trade and trade-related policies, in sum, presumably would have to be part of a WTO grand bargain, as they are, for example, in the NAFTA/FTAA regional free trade context.

Whether the more advanced developing countries, in particular, would be prepared to negotiate such a comprehensive free trade agreement, for implementation by 2010 is surely doubtful. Four examples of critical participants indicate that such a grand bargain is, at a minimum, premature:

- India has undertaken market-oriented reforms over the past several years but is far from freeing its imports of all tariffs and non-tariff border restrictions. It objected to discussion of investment policy within the WTO until the eve of the Singapore meeting and almost certainly would resist the grand bargain in which it would have to take more far-reaching liberalization measures than any other major WTO member.

- The Association of Southeast Asian Nations (ASEAN) could be receptive in principle to a WTO free trade initiative, as they were to the APEC regional free trade objective. But their performance to date in implementing APEC is not encouraging. Some ASEAN members decry the U.S. trade policy approach that entails binding market-access commitments and highly legalistic rules and procedures. They favor a more informal, flexible Asian approach. But the U.S. approach is what the GATT/WTO multilateral trading system is all about. It is therefore highly doubtful that ASEAN countries would be any more forthcoming in the WTO than they have been in signing up to a specific plan and schedule for APEC free trade.

- China is likely to become a WTO member within the time frame of the grand bargain proposal. But China poses a mind-boggling challenge for quick integration into a comprehensive free trade relationship. The Chinese trading system is far from market-oriented. And Chinese insistence on membership in the WTO as a developing country does not bode well for early acceptance of free trade parity with the industrial countries by 2010, as required by the grand bargain.

- Russia, too, can be expected to join the WTO over the next few years. But with a trading system still in a state of semidevelopment and uncertain decentralized control, a more modest association arrangement with the European Union is a more practical next step for Russian convergence toward a longer-term free trade objective.

There are also, of course, major questions as to whether Europe and Latin America would be prepared to negotiate a free trade arrangement with East Asia. Long-standing concerns about unbridled import competition from Asia constitute one motive for these countries to maintain their free trade horizons at the regional level. Only the North American countries are committed to free trade with Japan, China, and other East Asians. And even in the United States, to some extent at least, the quiescence of the U.S. Congress and public about this FTAA commitment is due to its still unspecified content.

There is finally the question of WTO's institutional capability to handle such a wide-ranging initiative. It took five years, beginning in 1981, to launch the GATT Uruguay Round, another eight years to negotiate an agreement, and a further ten years to implement it. WTO procedural complexities, based on the one-nation-one-vote principle, grow along with its burgeoning membership. The establishment of WTO credibility as the multilateral foundation for the global trading system should not be threatened by overly ambitious objectives during its initial years of operation.

In conclusion, a WTO grand bargain does not appear politically feasible at this time. With the current strategy of separate regional and multilateral tracks also inadequate, the best trade strategy for both the United States and the world in the near future could be an extension and integration of regional free trade.

AN EXTENSION AND INTEGRATION OF REGIONAL FREE TRADE

Regional free trade is already the objective for nations accounting for 75 percent of the WTO membership and 70 percent of world trade. Thus an alternative to a WTO-based grand bargain would be a direct linkage between the principal regional trade groupings to form a dominant free trade core within the multilateral trading system. This core could then be expanded as circumstances permit. Currently the European, Western Hemisphere, and Asia-Pacific groupings are the principal candidates for this amalgamation, but an early move faces problems similar to those of a WTO grand bargain. Among the major obstacles are the slower pace of the APEC free trade process and the unwillingness of Europe and Latin America to offer free access to their markets for Asian exporters. One additional regional initiative, however, could play an immediate catalytic role in integrating all of the major groupings on an accelerated step-by-step basis, thereby greatly diminishing the threat of a drift into rival regional blocs. The initiative would be a Transatlantic Free Trade Agreement.

A TAFTA has received belated attention since 1994, but discussion thus far has been incomplete and disjointed, in part because North Atlantic governments have essentially backed into the subject. At the time, both the European Union and the United States were negotiating free trade agreements with much of the rest of the world, and it was becoming a more and more glaring anomaly for the North Atlantic Treaty Organization (NATO) allies, who had formed the central axis of the GATT trading system for almost 50 years, not to be considering free trade across the Atlantic. But the United States and the European Union, while establishing a New Transatlantic Agenda at a summit meeting in Madrid in December 1995, went no further than indirect reference to a TAFTA by calling for a study of a possible future reduction or elimination of trade barriers.

Thus, at the official level, currently there is no serious consideration of a possible TAFTA. This failure is especially unfortunate because the implications of an agreement are momentous, consisting of three interacting dimensions. The first and least important dimension involves the trade and income effects of a TAFTA, both for members of the agreement and for nonmember trading partners. The second dimension is the impact on the trading system—in particular, the dynamic of such an initiative on the evolving relationship between the multilateral and regional tracks. The third dimension concerns broader foreign policy considerations in connection with U.S. leadership in a greatly changed post–Cold War world order.

The economic benefits of a TAFTA between the European Union and the NAFTA countries are difficult to assess, especially with respect to the more dynamic effects of structural changes induced in the member economies. For the nonagricultural sector, there are first the direct effects of tariff elimination: Relative prices change, stimulating more trade, existing plants benefit from larger-scale production, and a slightly higher aggregate level of savings and investment is realized. Additional "dynamic" gains from trade are obtained to the extent companies restructure their production and marketing patterns and make new investment decisions in response to the more predictable—and competitive—transatlantic market permanently free of border restrictions. Still further gains would accrue from other elements of a TAFTA, such as inclusion of investment and competition policies, public procurement, telecommunications regulation, and industrial standards.

The trade and income effects for the direct impact of tariff elimination are estimated to be quite small—a 2 percent increase in exports at most. The additional dynamic effects, while almost certainly much larger, do not lend themselves to reliable quantification and can best be judged in more qualitative terms by surveys of corporate intent, which have not yet been done.[3]

In any event, the trade and investment effects of a TAFTA would be relatively small, on balance positive for all members, and should not provoke the kind of protectionist public reaction that attended the NAFTA ratification in the United States, when voters feared job losses to cheap Mexican labor. Likewise, any adverse trade impact on nonmembers should be small. Half or more of nonagricultural imports already would be duty-free on an MFN basis, thanks to the Uruguay Round. No tariffs would be increased through formation of a free trade agreement. And some tariffs might be harmonized downward during the course of negotiations.

Agriculture often is cited as a stumbling block for a TAFTA, but it need not be so, as it accounts for only about 5 percent of transatlantic trade. The European Union is not prepared to make specific commitments for free farm trade at this time. But a general statement of ultimate intent, together with substantial liberalization, based on the Uruguay Round "built-in agenda," should produce an acceptable result. The Uruguay Round agreement stipulates new negotiations for liberalizing the agricultural sector by 2000. A U.S.-EU agreement on another five-year phased reduction of MFN tariffs and export subsidies, patterned on the Uruguay Round commitments, would constitute a substantial benefit to all agricultural exporting nations. In addition, those agricultural products largely traded across the Atlantic could be subject to a phase-out of tariffs within TAFTA, as occurred in EU free trade agreements with Central European nations. In any event, the European Union needs to reform its agricultural policy further to accommodate full membership for Central Europeans. To this end, greater use could be made of income support payments to small farmers, as permitted by the WTO.

The second dimension of a TAFTA initiative—its impact on the trading system—could be far-reaching and would depend in large part on how the initiative is managed. There are four largely distinct relationships to consider: (1) Europe and the Western Hemisphere; (2) the advanced 2010 East Asian countries in APEC; (3) other major trading nations; and (4) the WTO.

Europe and the Western Hemisphere

The relationship between Europe and the Western Hemisphere is the only one that can be projected with reasonable confidence. A TAFTA almost certainly would have to be open-ended through an accession clause, as is NAFTA. European countries linked by free trade with the European Union and participants in the Western Hemisphere free trade area would all be offered associate or full membership to form an extended TAFTA. In fact, all of these relationships should be moving forward in parallel and should reach a decisive stage as early as the late 1990s. There also should be a positive attitude on all sides to attain an extended TAFTA. Central European and South American countries should be comfortable politically and would benefit economically from free access to both the EU and NAFTA markets, while EU and NAFTA members would no longer face high tariff walls in South America and Central Europe. In other words, the regional free trade objectives in Europe, the Western Hemisphere, and across the Atlantic should be mutually reinforcing toward accelerated implementation.

The Asia-Pacific 2010 APEC Countries

Countries of the Asia-Pacific region are committed to achieving free trade by 2010 within the APEC context. The nations likely to reach that goal are Japan, Australia, New Zealand, and perhaps South Korea, Singapore, and Taiwan. Japan would be key, but Tokyo currently is unable to decide what specific 2010 course to take. Japan is unwilling to support a preferential arrangement in the Asia-Pacific region, but Tokyo understands that MFN free trade by all APEC members is unrealistic. An extended TAFTA, however, even at an early stage of active consideration, would create a strong incentive for Japan to decide on its free trade course and would permit a new and more appealing option through association with the extended TAFTA. The anticipated investment agreement by the Organization for Economic Cooperation and Development (OECD) could provide a bridge to a free trade agreement, because it would involve European nations, Canada, the United States, and Japan. Japan would have to be more forthcoming in opening its rice market if it were to affiliate with TAFTA. But that will become easier over time as Japanese rice farmers age and dwindle in number. As for its relationship with East Asia, Japan could act with uncharacteristic boldness by following the long-standing example of Singapore and Hong Kong and eliminate its remaining low nonagricultural tariffs on an MFN basis within the extended TAFTA (suitably renamed), on the assumption that other APEC members would reach free trade by 2020 in their own Asian manner.

Other Major Trading Nations

An extended TAFTA would include half of world trade. Linkage with the 2010 Asia-Pacific countries would raise this share considerably higher, leaving relatively few major trading nations outside the core free trade relationship. Numerous least-developed countries account for a very small share of world trade and would continue to receive preferential trade treatment. The remaining major countries would be ASEAN members, China, India/Pakistan, and Russia/Ukraine, and their relationships with the core free trade grouping would vary considerably. ASEAN countries and China are committed to free trade within the Asia-Pacific region by 2020. India and Pakistan, in contrast, remain exclusively engaged within the WTO multilateral trading system. Russia and Ukraine likely would find an early TAFTA free trade association attractive. Initial reactions from these trading partners probably would be critical. An early objective of the leaders of the TAFTA-extended grouping vis-à-vis these other countries would be to demonstrate that the free trade relationship is not exclusionary and is based on reducing rather than raising trade barriers.[4] The longer-term objective would be to integrate the remaining countries within the core grouping while recognizing that they need more time and should proceed at their own pace.

The WTO

The final step for a multilateral/regional synthesis would involve integrating the core free trade agreement with the WTO. A TAFTA extended to European and Western Hemisphere countries already would include most WTO members and global trade, and further extension to the APEC 2010 countries would add much of the remainder. Integrating this arrangement within the WTO thus would require more than simply depositing documents in Geneva. Some significant changes in the current WTO structure would be required. A name change to the World Trade and Investment Organization (WTIO) is likely in the next few years. Conditional MFN status between members of the free trade grouping and others, at least for some parts of the core agreement, presumably would be necessary. Voting procedures also would have to be amended as they apply to implementation of parts of the core free trade agreement. The net result, however, should be a greatly enhanced multilateral trading system. Within this system, the multilateral/regional synthesis would be definitively realized, with procedures established to broaden the inner free trade grouping as other nations become willing and able to participate. Moreover, the whole process of assimilation could be assisted by multilateral actions mandated by the WTO work program, perhaps in the context of a new round of multilateral negotiations.

This scenario of a TAFTA initiative for the overall trading system demonstrates the powerful dynamic that would be unleashed. The critical role of political leadership and management in reaching this goal cannot be overemphasized. Relationships between TAFTA leaders and those of other major trading nations—Japan, China, ASEAN, India, Russia, and Brazil—will be critical to the outcome. These relationships, moreover, go beyond trade or even a broadened trade/investment/technology relationship. A wide range of foreign policy interests will be influenced by trade strategies pursued in the period ahead, particularly with respect to a TAFTA decision. For many observers, indeed, the foreign policy dimensions of a TAFTA initiative are paramount.

THE FOREIGN POLICY AND LEADERSHIP DIMENSION

Economic globalization, including the deepening integration of national economic policies, has far-reaching foreign policy consequences, especially in the post–Cold War circumstances in which long-standing East-West security alliances have lost most of their raison d'être. Foreign policy interests need to be reordered with greater emphasis on economic relationships, but not to the exclusion of reformulated national security interests and broader geopolitical considerations. The difficulties in such a reordering are evident in the evolving multilateral/regional structure of the world trading system.

A major foreign policy question facing the United States is whether the Atlantic Alliance, post–Cold War, is drifting apart in politico-economic terms into what could become rival regional blocs, and, if so, how the choice of trade strategy over the next several years could affect the outcome. European nations are focused on historic opportunities to the East and on troubled neighbors in the Mediterranean Basin. The declining U.S. troop presence in Europe makes the United States an increasingly distant ally. The United States, in parallel, is shifting its geographic priorities to the Western Hemisphere and across the Pacific, largely in pursuit of commercial interests. In each case, a central policy objective is a regional free trade arrangement with inevitable exclusionary consequences across the Atlantic. Trade and investment continue to flourish between Europe and North America, but multinational companies tend to adjust to whatever policy frameworks are encountered, and the current course may not maintain the long-standing transatlantic political/security/economic cohesion. As one European leader concluded: "The glue, which kept us together for so long, has lost its strength."[5]

There is no question that a TAFTA would produce a new cohesive construct for the industrial democracies of Europe and North America, enabling them jointly to confront post–Cold War challenges to global stability and security. TAFTA would greatly reduce, if not eliminate, the threat of drift into rival geopolitical groupings. As noted earlier, future extension of the European free trade grouping to Russia and other former Soviet republics would not create the same foreign policy difficulties for the United States and the European Union with a TAFTA in place. Within Europe, the objective of political integration and economic union would not be threatened by a phasing-out, across the Atlantic, of the remaining common external tariff, which is already quite low and no longer the major cohesive element it once was for the European Community.

The most complex foreign policy implications for a TAFTA would arise with respect to Asia. A careful assessment of how this relationship would be managed should be an important part of an overall TAFTA evaluation. A tentative judgment is that it could be managed to positive effect. Japan and South Korea, as industrial democracies, should continue to be drawn more closely together with Europe and North America through various political and economic forums, including the WTO and the OECD. A TAFTA could work to accelerate this process. ASEAN members, India, and other Asian nations all have to be given assurances that a faster track to free trade elsewhere is not pursued at their expense. The Chinese relationship would require the most careful attention. But a trade strategy, with the United States at the center of a more cohesive grouping of industrial democracies in Europe and the Western Hemisphere, could provide a stronger basis, compared with the current course, for the difficult and long-term objective of positive Chinese participation in the global political and economic systems.

Any successful trade strategy—especially a TAFTA initiative—will require strong and sustained political leadership. Forward-looking U.S. leadership, moreover, will remain essential for at least the five to ten years addressed here. In the 1990s the European Union has displayed more pronounced leadership on trade issues than it once did. But its decision-making procedures are cumbersomely slow, and its preoccupation with regional objectives continues. Japan is reluctant to take on a global leadership role commensurate with its economic power. Newly industrial nations are more actively engaged than a decade ago, but they still tend to react to initiatives taken by the OECD countries.

Traditional U.S. leadership, however, has been conspicuously lacking in recent years, especially since 1995. The earlier Uruguay Round and NAFTA initiatives were concluded and regional free trade objectives in the Western Hemisphere and the Asia-Pacific region were agreed to in principle by 1994. Little follow-up has taken place since then. The U.S. response to interest by others in a TAFTA since 1994 is especially revealing. Canadian Prime Minister Jean Chrétien and various European leaders called for a serious look at a TAFTA in view of the proliferation of regional free trade initiatives elsewhere. The U.S. response initially was one of disinterest, then grudging agreement to an EU proposal in May 1995 to give TAFTA "the serious study it deserves," and then dilution of the study proposal by the time of the December U.S.-EU summit in Madrid, whereby indirect reference to examine ways of "further reducing or eliminating tariff and non-tariff barriers" limited examination of a possible TAFTA to its narrow technical aspects.

This hiatus in U.S. trade policy leadership is due, in part, to domestic politics and the decision of leaders in both major parties to downplay support for a liberal trade policy in the run-up to the 1996 elections. It also reflects a post–Cold War tendency to view U.S. global interests in more narrowly defined commercial terms and thus to avoid global strategizing where trade policy plays a major role but not the only role. And finally, the hiatus reflects an intellectual vacuum within the U.S. government, a simple lack of interest or capacity to give serious consideration to the broader questions of trade strategy. The "vision thing" remains in bipartisan disrepute.

It was not always this way, of course. The leaders in the United States and Europe who created the Bretton Woods system, including GATT, in the wake of the Great Depression and the devastation of World War II combined vision with forceful action. So too did the postwar leaders who launched the Marshall Plan, NATO, and the Common Market to achieve both a democratic reconciliation between France and Germany after three wars in three successive generations, and a political-security bulwark against the external Soviet threat. By comparison, the circumstances of the post–Cold War world, while far from trouble-free, present extraordinarily positive opportunities. The industrial democracies are broadening in geographic scope and influence. The rapid growth of international trade and investment constitutes a massive positive sum game from which all nations should benefit. The leadership challenge today is to build on dynamic growth rather than to reconstruct crippled nations.

The leadership focus for trade strategy, beginning in 1997, is not clear. For governments, the biannual WTO ministerial meetings are large and unwieldy gatherings. The annual Group of Seven (G-7) economic summit meetings of the major industrial nations are dominated by finance ministers whose principal interest lies in macroeconomic policy and international financial markets rather than trade strategy. The informal "Quad" relationship of trade ministers from the United States, the European Union, Japan, and Canada comes closest to a high-level trade strategy grouping, at least among the industrial countries, but trade ministers tend to be hard bargainers over immediate interests rather than longer-term strategizers.

In any event, discussion of trade strategy at this important juncture should be more broadly based than intergovernmental deliberations. Legislators, private sector leaders, and others outside of government need to become engaged. An assessment of the full consequences of a TAFTA, for example, would benefit from a U.S.-European parliamentary dialogue and consideration by private sector leaders within the recently established Transatlantic Business Dialogue. An Eminent Persons Group, which played a catalytic role in formulating the Asia-Pacific free trade objective, also should be formed to evaluate a TAFTA initiative. But this group should consist principally of former statesmen and other distinguished public and private sector leaders, rather than of economists/technocrats, as was the case with APEC, since the questions to be addressed in a TAFTA initiative are of broader political and institutional scope.

The challenge of getting from here to free trade is more than a phrase. It is an operational objective going forward at both the multilateral and regional levels. How the objective is pursued, including the quest for a synthesis between the multilateral and regional tracks, requires urgent consideration and probably bold action. It is also too important a task to be left to governments alone.

NOTES

1. From a speech given in Ottawa on May 28, 1996.
2. C. Fred Bergsten, "Globalizing Free Trade," *Foreign Affairs*, May 1996, pp. 105-120.
3. The up to 2 percent estimate is taken from Richard Baldwin and Joseph Francois, "Transatlantic Free Trade: A Quantitative Assessment," unpublished ms., May 1996. The survey of corporate intent could be undertaken by the private-sector Transatlantic Business Dialogue established in 1995.
4. An anticipated negative reaction from Asians is the most frequent argument made against a TAFTA, argued most strenuously by proponents of APEC, and a full consideration of their concern is in order. A starting point for explaining a TAFTA in positive terms to Asian trading partners would be: A TAFTA would do nothing more than achieve the free trade objective already engaged across the Pacific between North America and East Asia as well as in other regions. Indeed, in the process under way toward global free trade, the North Atlantic nations should be among the first rather than the last to eliminate border restrictions to trade on a regional basis since they are the most mature and open industrial economies, with import barriers already much lower than in other regions, including zero tariff on an MFN basis for half of nonagricultural imports. Moreover, no trade barriers would be raised to Asian exporters in the formation of a TAFTA.
5. The quote is attributed to the Belgian prime minister, Jean-Luc Dehaene, in Bruce Stokes, ed., *Open for Business: Creating a Transatlantic Marketplace* (New York: Council on Foreign Relations, 1996), p. 2.

Chapter 9

A Geoeconomic Strategy for the 21st Century

Bruce Stokes

Geopolitics—the art and practice of traditional foreign and security policy as defined during the Cold War—is a paradigm that no longer provides adequate policy solutions to the problems facing the United States as it enters the 21st century. A geoeconomic paradigm—a discreet foreign economic policy designed to open markets for U.S. exports and investment—is now needed to deal with the challenges created by the growing dependence of the U.S. domestic economy on the global marketplace.

In the last few years, the United States has crossed an economic threshold of historic significance. Once primarily a continental economy, America is rapidly becoming a truly international economy. Exports have become an animating force behind much of domestic economic growth and job creation. This profound change in the nature of the U.S. marketplace is rapidly blurring the distinction between foreign policy and economic policy.

In the future, the impact on the domestic economy of problems facing U.S. exporters and investors abroad will become almost indistinguishable from traditional domestic economic concerns. As exports become a concern on Main Street as well as on Wall Street, and the economic fortunes of congressional districts are increasingly tied to the global economy, foreign economic policy will become an ever greater domestic political issue. As a result, U.S. trade policy will become much more aggressive and results-oriented as U.S. economic self-interest in business conditions abroad grows.

In the past, the pursuit of traditional foreign and security policy concerns was viewed as separate from and, at times, contradictory to the goals of foreign economic policy. But with the growing integration of the U.S. economy into the world economy, such distinctions are increasingly irrelevant. In this new economic and political environment, Washington can ill afford to compartmentalize foreign policy and international economic policy. The ability of the United States to provide diplomatic leadership and a security umbrella around the world will increasingly depend on the health of the U.S. economy and the growth it derives from its engagement with the world. Continued voter support for traditional foreign policy activities will be contingent upon public perception of tangible benefits from the global marketplace. And these benefits will best be realized through the achievement of traditional diplomatic and security goals—security, stability, democratization, and a balance of power.

In the future, geopolitical interests and emerging geoeconomic concerns will increasingly converge.

A GLOBAL ECONOMY

The U.S. economy that for decades permitted a neat division between foreign policy concerns and international economic interests no longer exists. A new U.S. economy is emerging—one dependent on access to foreign markets and imports from abroad—that will inevitably shape a new U.S. foreign policy deeply rooted in economic affairs.

Two generations ago the United States had a continental economy. What really mattered for the economic well-being of average citizens was the commerce and job creation that took place in the vast expanse between the shores of the Atlantic and the Pacific. There was a yawning divide between economic policy, which by definition was domestic economic policy, and foreign policy.

Today the United States is in transition from an inward-looking to an outward-looking marketplace. In 1970 trade—both imports and exports—was equivalent to 13 percent of the gross domestic product (GDP). By 1996 trade was nearly 30 percent of GDP.[1]

Rising imports have stretched the buying power of American consumers and widened their choices, bringing them fuel-efficient cars, cutting-edge consumer electronics, and affordable shoes and apparel. Moreover, competition from abroad has stimulated a dramatic improvement in the productivity and quality of U.S. manufacturing.

Even more dramatic has been the transformation of the United States from a bystander in the export game to an export superpower. Since 1994 the United States has exported more than any other nation. A third of U.S. economic growth in recent years can be attributed to sales overseas.[2] And export-related jobs accounted for 23 percent of private industry new-employment growth between 1990 and 1994.[3]

Economic developments abroad, once peripheral to the core issues driving the domestic U.S. economy, will increasingly be a central determinant of the nation's economic well-being. For example, world demand for imports is expected to more than double by the year 2007. For the United States simply to maintain its current share of world import consumption, it will have to double exports—no mean feat. This challenge is particularly difficult in Asia, where the U.S. share of imports into the region, excluding Japan, declined to 14.2 percent in 1995 from 17.5 percent in 1980.[4]

If the United States fails to maintain its current share of the world's consumption of imports and, more important, if it continues to lose share in the world's fastest-growing markets, then domestic economic consequences could be severe. The relative contribution of exports to the U.S. economy will suffer. Proportionally fewer well-paying jobs will be created. Economic growth could slow.

SIMILAR OBJECTIVES

To avoid that fate requires a geoeconomic policy that does not supplant traditional geopolitical policy but embraces its goals and pursues them for economic purposes.

In the past, U.S. foreign policy has pursued a range of mutually consistent and self-reinforcing objectives: security for the United States, global and regional stability, a balance of power, and democratization.

In the future, U.S. foreign economic policy will increasingly be guided by these same aims, because the achievement of U.S. economic self-interest in the global marketplace necessitates many of the same political and social preconditions as required to achieve U.S. foreign policy goals during the Cold War.

Security

For the past two generations, the preservation of America's security has been synonymous with the avoidance of nuclear conflagration. As long as atomic arsenals remain, strategic deterrence, arms control, and nonproliferation will continue to be critically important objectives for U.S. foreign and security policy. But other threats to national security have now arisen. Primary among these is any erosion in the vitality and strength of the U.S. economy.

In the immediate post–World War II period, the relative size and strength of the U.S. economy permitted the nation the luxury of maintaining an army in Europe, of building up a global network of military alliances, of providing the economic assistance that rebuilt the war-torn nations of Europe and Asia, and of opening its markets to foreign goods to restart the engines of growth around the world.

In the 1990s, the economic foundation for that robust foreign and security policy has eroded. The United States is no longer the preponderant world economic power. Moreover, despite its recent success, the U.S. economy is still growing on average about a third slower than it did in the 1950s and 1960s.

At the same time, the cost of an active foreign and security policy remains. Expansion of the North Atlantic Treaty Organization (NATO) is expected to add billions of dollars to defense spending. The commitment of U.S. forces in Bosnia and the Persian Gulf only underscores the continued need for a costly U.S. military presence in disparate parts of the globe.

With other claims on the federal budget—Social Security, Medicare, and Medicaid—all growing faster than government revenues, prospects for spending on defense and diplomacy depend as never before on the performance of the economy. As recent experience has demonstrated, that performance is increasingly dependent on exports and earnings from investments abroad. If the Pentagon, the State Department, the White House, and Congress want to continue to afford the pursuit of traditional foreign policy, they must first realize that foreign economic policy—opening markets for U.S. exports and investment in order to sustain domestic economic growth—is a tool to achieve their ends.

Stability

Stability has long been a U.S. foreign policy goal in a dangerous world where instability could sow the seeds for military conflict. But now stability is also a business-driven need, because peaceful, functioning societies make good markets and stable suppliers.

Social, political, and economic uncertainties make consumers and investors cautious, slowing growth and the resultant demand for U.S. goods and services. Before the Third World debt crisis in the early 1980s, Latin America was one of the largest markets for U.S. exports. When financial instability arose, that market almost disappeared overnight.

During the Cold War, the United States supported expansionary economic growth in Southeast Asia and elsewhere because strong economies were less likely to fall prey to communism. For the future, U.S. ambitions remain the same, but the rationale is different.

The United States needs vibrant Southeast Asian economies to fuel consumption of American products. Recent growth in the region, in the range of 6 to 9 percent per year, drove demand for an annual increase in imports of about $16 billion. With recent levels of U.S. market penetration, this translated into an additional $2 billion a year in U.S. sales to the region. Any slowing of growth in these nations, as is now likely, will also slow the expansion of U.S. exports, which will reverberate back through the domestic U.S. economy, translating into fewer good-paying jobs and slower economic growth.

This new stake in the stability of overseas markets was dramatically demonstrated by the U.S. response to the Mexican peso crisis of 1994. In the early part of the century, the United States invaded Mexico to defend its economic interests. This time arms were twisted among the Group of Seven (G-7) nations, and unprecedented sums were mobilized internationally to minimize disruption in the economy of America's second-largest trading partner. Subsequent U.S.-inspired reforms at the International Monetary Fund (IMF), including the creation of a special account to call on in similar crises, were an attempt to institutionalize the response to a threat to geoeconomic stability.

In the past strategic planners put a premium on political stability because any disturbance of the status quo could provide a
dangerous opening to communism. Clearly, the dangers of political instability remain. And there always will be economic fallout
from political turmoil. But the equation now clearly runs in both
directions, and economic instability will increasingly be seen as a
threat to the political status quo. In the future, geoeconomic policymakers are likely to spend more and more of their time wor-
rying about how to build institutions, how to create financial reserve
armies, and how to exercise diplomatic leverage in the pursuit of
stability.

Balance of Power

During the Cold War, it was Washington's goal to avoid the rise
of a hegemonic strategic power that could threaten the security of
the United States. Today the nation has a similar interest in blunt-
ing the emergence of economic powers that can challenge its
commercial interests.

For example, in Asia, Japan exercises rising influence through
the widespread investments of its corporations, through the pre-
dominance of its foreign aid, and through the compelling attraction of its model of economic development. If this influence is allowed
to continue unchecked, Asia-wide business networks, organized
on the *keiretsu* model dominant in Japan, may emerge to the
detriment of the United States. These networks would bring exclusionary ties between suppliers and producers and would effectively
lock out many U.S. companies from the rapidly growing auto and
electronics sectors of East Asia. Japanese-funded infrastructure projects would go primarily to Japanese firms. And government rules
and regulations would be drafted based on the Japanese legal model
that effectively excludes open participation by U.S. and most
other foreign firms.

Chinese influence is currently less pervasive but potentially more
significant. The size of the potential Chinese market, the region-
wide uncertainty about China's strategic intentions, and the close
ties between the overseas Chinese and the mainland ensure a
growing Chinese imprint on economic developments in Asia.

The United States faces a similar balance-of-power challenge
in Latin America, where Brazil—with the region's largest economy and a government that is less committed to open markets than

the United States—has emerged as a self-styled alternative pole for economic influence south of Mexico. Brasilia has already cobbled together MERCOSUR, a customs union with Argentina, Paraguay, and Uruguay, which has displayed sufficient staying power to attract Chile into an association agreement. The Brazilians tout MERCOSUR as a Latin alternative to the North American Free Trade Agreement (NAFTA). By raising some external tariffs while lowering internal ones, MERCOSUR already is distorting trade and investment patterns in ways that adversely affect U.S. interests, forcing U.S. automakers to build plants in MERCOSUR countries rather than export to the region from the United States.

In the face of these challenges, Washington again finds itself needing to play balance-of-power politics around the world. But the goal this time is to maximize U.S. influence over policies and practices that affect the ability of U.S. enterprises to compete in global markets, whether through trade or investment. And the tools are foreign economic policy, not carrier fleets.

Japan's influence in Asia needs to be countered with increased foreign aid to the region (mostly channeled through the World Bank), new help for U.S. companies attempting to do business there (notably through the Export-Import Bank and the Overseas Private Investment Corporation), and pressure on regional governments to adopt meaningful antitrust policies. China is best handled in a multilateral context, by admitting it to the World Trade Organization (WTO) only under terms that ensure Chinese commitment to core trade disciplines. And Brazil's influence in Latin America can best be offset by a reinvigoration of U.S. efforts to create a Western Hemisphere free trade area.

Democratization

The creation and sustenance of democracy has long been a goal of U.S. foreign policy. In the immediate postwar period, democracies were cast as bulwarks against communism in the global struggle with the Soviet Union. But democratization often was a principle ignored in practice. Many times Washington propped up friendly governments—in Iran, Indonesia, Guatemala—even if they were authoritarian, just to keep them from going communist.

In the future, the pursuit of U.S. economic self-interest necessitates a reaffirmation of American commitment to true democratization. This course is required, not out of any philosophical commitment to one particular form of governance or as part of some new global ideological conflict, but because American business functions best in a democratic environment characterized by due process, the rule of law, and transparency in decision-making.

Free market advocates often argue that capitalism breeds democracy. But democracy—in effect a consumer-driven polity—is also fertile ground from which a consumer-driven economy can grow. Citizens freely able to make decisions about their own governance are less likely to accept passively bureaucratic or corporate decisions about what they can buy and at what price. Moreover, voters in a democracy have the opportunity to change governments and thus change the direction of economic policy in their own interests.

A consumer-oriented market will be an open one, because only when consumers can freely pick between imports and domestically made products can they exercise their democratic prerogative. Experience suggests that American firms fare quite well in such an environment because of their competitive advantage in the production of a range of goods and services.

Of course, a democratic form of government does not necessarily ordain an open, fully democratic marketplace, as bitter experience in dealing with Japan testifies. For this reason, it is incumbent on U.S. economic foreign policy—unlike traditional foreign policy—to support deeper democratization abroad.

Access to a foreign market for U.S. exporters or investors is useless without the rule of law to defend that access and make it meaningful. If U.S. assets can be seized with no recourse in the courts, U.S. corporations may refuse to do business in a country or pursue only the most lucrative investment opportunities to compensate for the high risk. In fact, the absence of a functioning legal system has been one of the primary obstacles to U.S. investment in the former Soviet Union. The cost to the Russian economy of limited foreign investment is obvious.

The absence of due process and a lack of transparency in decision-making also can negate U.S. access to foreign markets. Government regulatory decisions can level a playing field for domestic and foreign producers or tilt it in favor of indigenous firms. In Japan, for example, U.S. firms have found that bureaucratic actions have been used to close ostensibly open markets for products such as photographic film. If U.S. firms do not have the opportunity to exercise basic democratic oversight—to see proposed regulations before they go into effect, to comment on them, to appeal if they object to them—then the benefits of competing in a foreign market can be severely limited.

GEOECONOMIC TOOLS AND THEIR CONSEQUENCES

To achieve these geoeconomic goals, U.S. policymakers will need both a strategic vision and the tools to realize it.

The foundation of that vision is the recognition that the nature of the U.S. economy has changed in fundamental ways and that a radically new approach to international affairs is needed in the new economic environment. This approach must operate simultaneously on three levels: global, regional, and bilateral. And it must be supple enough to accommodate a blurring of traditional distinctions between orthodox foreign policy and international economic policy.

Postwar geopolitics was a strategy devised to deal with the global confrontation of two nuclear superpowers. But in a world where the United States is merely one of several major economic powers, albeit the strongest, and where power will be measured by the vitality of one's economy, not the size of one's nuclear arsenal, U.S. interests will best be served by a system of global economic rules. Thus a new geoeconomic vision requires a renewed American commitment to multilateralism. The United States was the driving force in the creation of the modern international trading system. Now, more than ever before, the United States has an economic stake in the success of that regime. Washington should take the lead in pushing for the elimination of all remaining tariffs, for multilateral disciplines for competition and investment policy, and for labor and environmental standards. Whether this effort is under the auspices of the WTO or of some other international forum will depend on the particular issue.

In addition, Washington has a vested interest in seeing that the WTO works. In principle, most future trade disputes should be taken to the WTO. But increasing the volume of the WTO caseload is not sufficient. Such cases need to produce results that directly benefit U.S. economic interests. The United States must insist that for the WTO to enjoy American support, it must produce real market openings and a tangible balance of benefits from trade and investment liberalization.

U.S. multilateral efforts should not be limited to the WTO. In approving loans, the World Bank and the IMF have long used the relative openness of borrowers' markets as a loan criteria, but often a minor one. U.S. representatives to these lending institutions need to demand that a commitment to market access become a major determinant for future lending.

The regional aspect of a new strategic vision is already largely in place. It began to take shape during the Bush administration, with the launching of negotiations for NAFTA. The Clinton administration extended that vision with the annual summits of the Asia Pacific Economic Cooperation forum and its Free Trade of the Americas initiative. The goal of these efforts was to build a network of regional free trade areas that will compete against each other in their market-opening efforts and push other nations to move more rapidly toward lowering trade barriers. Such regional undertakings permit experimentation, allowing for differences based on culture and level of development, before innovations are multilateralized.

The United States is the only major economy at the center of all three of these initiatives, not unlike the American role in the regional security systems built up during the Cold War. In such a pivotal position, Washington can help drive the regional economic integration process to ensure that it maximizes American economic self-interest. This position also permits the United States to play one region off against the other, to offer up the huge U.S. market as an incentive to those regions willing to lower their own trade and investment barriers.

The only piece missing from this geoeconomic puzzle is a transatlantic free trade initiative (TAFTA). TAFTA is a good example of the new interrelationship between economic and strategic goals. Europeans, worried about waning U.S. commitment to their security and concerned about American ambivalence over NATO expansion, were the first to suggest deepening the transatlantic economic relationship to help offset any tension in the relationship over security matters. But a more economically oriented United States has been skeptical, pushing the Europeans to place meaningful market opening initiatives on the negotiating table. A TAFTA will come into being only if Europe realizes that the game has changed and that, for Americans, economic concerns are no longer the handmaiden of security interests.

Finally, the United States must continue its efforts to open markets one by one, when that tactic is likely to achieve the best economic results for the country. This will require new bilateral trade tools and a willingness to use them. In addition, as the substance of bilateral trade negotiations increasingly shifts toward traditionally domestic forms of regulation, the United States itself must be willing to consider changes in standards and testing procedures, antitrust policy, and similar regulatory practices.

While aggressive unilateralism will remain an important arrow in any American president's quiver of policies, such a trade tool does pose grave new risks in the new era of growing U.S. dependence on exports. U.S. trade policy has always been subject to abuse by powerful special interests. This temptation will only grow as the economic rationale for trade assertiveness becomes more convincing. In the future, the number of proverbial squeaky wheels seeking to shape U.S. actions to fit individual corporate agendas or to bend them to the will of powerful members of Congress will only multiply. Without a strategic vision of multilateral, regional, and bilateral action to solve a prioritized list of U.S. market-opening problems around the world, geoeconomics could rapidly devolve into a series of increasingly acrimonious and ultimately self-destructive one-on-one trade confrontations.

Washington's forays into the exercise of geoeconomic policy are likely to be fraught with such turmoil. Much of what will be done will be new, both for the practitioners and for their foreign counterparts. Mistakes will be made. Feathers will be ruffled. Most important, actions will be taken that are without precedent because the United States is embarked on a new direction in foreign affairs growing out of new domestic economic conditions.

On the trade front, Washington can be expected to pursue market opening aggressively. At best, such assertiveness will be an irritant to Japan, Korea, China, and other governments. At worst, it will engender new diplomatic tensions and, for foreigners, call into question the reliability of the United States as an ally.

Japan obviously will be the target of much of this market-opening pressure. American assertiveness may stir nationalistic sentiments in Japan. If, as in the past, Japan drags its feet in opening its market, new calls will be heard in Congress for a reassessment of the U.S.-Japan security relationship.

Even more important in the long run is the likelihood of greater U.S. trade tensions with China. As China's trade surplus with the

United States surpasses that of Japan, U.S. attentions will focus on opening the vast Chinese market to more U.S. exports. Such initiatives inevitably will fan the flames of Chinese nationalism and provide the military in Beijing with new rationales for resisting Bully Boy America.

Trade concerns also will engender newfound American interest in foreign governance, a concern that many nations will find intrusive.

America's growing need for open markets abroad makes it the natural ally of many foreign nongovernmental organizations and consumers who have a stake in an open society. For example, Japanese consumers who would benefit from the lower prices of imported rice have a common cause with American rice producers hoping to sell more in the Japanese market. But U.S. efforts to reach out to those groups, to help them in their efforts to change policies in their own countries, will lead to charges of meddling in domestic affairs. The fact that the distinction between domestic and foreign affairs has been hopelessly muddled by the globalization of economies will not ease the tensions that are inevitable.

At the same time, the U.S. economic stake in stability will raise potential policy contradictions between long-run U.S. interests in democratic systems and short-run U.S. concerns about predictable, disturbance-free business environments. For example, a fully democratic Indonesia would afford U.S. business greater access to that burgeoning market by reducing the nepotism and cronyism that determines the outcome of so many commercial deals in Jakarta. But preservation of the status quo may be best for existing U.S. interests there, who have found ways to make money despite the corruption. Moreover, a messy transition from authoritarian rule to a more open system would be costly for all parties involved.

Finally, the growing U.S. stake in the global economy will provide a new rationale for continued U.S. military engagement in the world. For example, despite the debate in the United States about the continued stationing of U.S. troops in Japan, America's interest in Asian stability will only grow. Open markets in Asia are worthless to U.S. exporters if the region is beset with civil strife and military tensions. Any security problems that slow growth will adversely affect demand for U.S. products.

But the mode of providing that security may change over time as the rationale becomes more explicitly economic. The United States is likely to have a prolonged economic stake in maintaining some military presence in Japan and Korea, given the huge American trading relationship with those two countries. But America's growing trade and investment relationship with China and Southeast Asia lacks a parallel forward military presence to secure it. The loss of the Subic Bay base in the Philippines has never been replaced. Some day a basing arrangement with Singapore or Vietnam may be needed.

In the end, the transition from a foreign policy shaped by geopolitics to one driven by geoeconomics will be a tortuous experience of fits and starts. It will take time for the U.S. policy process to internalize the profound implications of this transformation. The start-stop nature of U.S. trade policy toward Japan, alternately aggressive and accommodationist, reflects the complexity of this evolution. For some time to come, our perceptions of the future are likely to be colored by perceptions formulated in the past that no longer reflect current economic conditions. But the implications for the domestic U.S. economy of trade and foreign investment conditions around the world are now so formidable, it is only a matter of time before geoeconomic policy is the new operating principle for America's relations with the rest of the world.

NOTES

1. Bureau of Economic Analysis, U.S. Department of Commerce, homepage.
2. *Economic Report of the President, 1995* (Washington, DC: Government Printing Office, 1996), p. 225.
3. *Trade and Investment Reference Manual* (The Business Roundtable, 1996).
4. International Monetary Fund, *Direction of Trade Statistics,* various years.

Chapter 10

U.S. Trade Policy Toward Japan and China: Integrating Bilateral, Multilateral, and Regional Approaches

Merit E. Janow

The last several U.S. administrations, both Republican and Democratic, have stressed the importance of pursuing a multilevel international trade strategy toward the nation's trading partners. This notion that policymakers can and should make simultaneous use of multilateral, bilateral, and regional approaches is therefore not novel. The challenge of the coming years has less to do with the availability of these different dimensions than it does with the issue of how they can best advance the goals of U.S. trade policy. Nowhere is this more evident than in U.S. relations with Japan and China, where new trade policy initiatives are needed, especially greater use of multilateral and regional approaches.

U.S.-JAPAN TRADE AND ECONOMIC RELATIONS

Few, if any, bilateral economic relations have been more contentious than those between the United States and Japan, even though Japan is the United States' second largest trading partner, after Canada. Large bilateral trade deficits, coupled with continuing concern about the closed nature of Japanese markets, have produced a steady stream of trade disputes between the United States and Japan over the past 20 years.

A central goal of U.S. trade policy in the postwar period has been the development of a multilateral, rule-based trading system, embodied in the principles and commitments of the General Agreement on Tariffs and Trade (GATT). Japan's participation in each of the eight multilateral trade negotiating rounds over the last half century has been a high priority for U.S. administrations and for Japan's government.

Most recently in the Uruguay Round, Japan's eventual willingness to make concessions in the agricultural sector and its cooperation in a variety of other areas were essential in bringing the negotiations to a successful close. As a result of past multilateral negotiations, Japan has reduced or eliminated most of its formal quantitative restrictions on imports at the border, and its formal tariff rates on goods (apart from agriculture) are among the lowest in the industrial world.

Yet historically, GATT dispute settlement procedures have been used only infrequently to resolve trade disputes between the United States and Japan. Since Japan joined GATT in 1955, the United States has invoked GATT procedures to challenge the Japanese government for violating GATT agreements on only nine occasions.

Thus, although Japan's participation in GATT has been essential, the ironic fact is that U.S.-Japan trade tensions have been addressed in GATT only rarely. At least two reasons for this state of affairs suggest themselves. First, in some past instances, Japan itself requested that a matter be handled quietly between the two countries rather than under the glare of multilateral processes. Second, in other instances, it appears that a combination of the weaknesses of GATT dispute settlement procedures, the absence of multilateral disciplines with regard to the matters under dispute between the United States and Japan, and the perceived effectiveness of bilateral negotiations all have combined to cause U.S. policymakers to question whether GATT would prove an effective forum for resolving the dispute in question.

As a result, most disputes have been addressed bilaterally. Over the course of the postwar period, the United States and Japan have entered into over 100 bilateral understandings on trade and economic matters.[1] The vast majority of these have been negotiated so as to be consistent with multilateral principles.

During the period from 1988 to 1992 alone, the United States and Japan negotiated some 13 bilateral trade agreements.

The range of matters covered by these agreements included government procurement practices, regulatory practices, and some combination of government and private restraints that have limited access to Japan's market.[2] In addition to those areas covered by formal agreements, the United States and Japan reached bilateral understandings on a number of other sectoral and structural issues.[3]

There is no established way to evaluate the results of these negotiations. One study conducted during the Bush administration estimated that the 13 sectors covered by new bilateral agreements negotiated during that administration produced an increase in U.S. exports of some 57 percent, which meant that exports to Japan in those sectors were growing at a rate of roughly twice as fast as exports to Japan overall.[4] Of course, these numbers do not indicate how much of this growth can reasonably be attributed to the bilateral agreements as opposed to some combination of market trends and changes in government policies.

These gains notwithstanding, by the end of the Bush administration concerns began to surface regarding the Japanese government's implementation of several of the agreements as well as the effectiveness of some of the less formal bilateral understandings involving glass, automotive, and insurance markets. More generally, Japan's current account surplus (with all countries taken together), which stood at $117 billion in 1992, remained a lightning rod for criticism due to the relatively limited role imports played in the Japanese market.

Indeed, many of these very same sectoral, structural, and macroeconomic concerns proved to be the focus of trade attention during the period from 1993 to 1995. During this time, the Japan problem came to be viewed as one having at least two distinct dimensions: the problem of Japan's continuing macroeconomic current account surpluses accompanied by the need for assurances from the Japanese government that it would address those surpluses over the medium term; and the need for the Japanese government to make additional commitments to correct long-standing sectoral problems.

This twin emphasis on macroeconomic and sectoral measures was reflected in the Framework Agreement with Japan negotiated in July 1993. While this agreement did produce an agenda and certain timetables, it did not reflect agreement about which substantive measures would be taken to remedy the perceived problems.

Not long after the Framework Agreement was concluded, it became apparent that all of the major sticking points in its negotiation remained serious problems in the negotiations that followed. There were at least five general sources of tension, reflecting disagreement as to: the nature of the market access problem in Japan; the nature of Japanese government control over the economy; the degree of specificity appropriate for bilateral agreements, as reflected in the U.S. use of terms, such as "quantitative indicators," "numerical targets," and "objective criteria"; the so-called "two-way-street issue," which reflected the Japanese government's desire to be able to raise its own issues regarding the U.S. market; and the enforceability of commitments.

None of these sticking points represented an entirely "new" problem in U.S.-Japan trade negotiations. Negotiators on both sides of the Pacific have found these same issues to be difficult for some years, and frustrations have grown over time. What was new, however, was the relatively greater emphasis the Unitied States placed on numerical indicators or objective criteria in measuring results as well as the public expectations Washington created for these numerical indicators.

For at least a year, the two sides engaged in largely philosophical and acrimonious debates. Eventually, over the course of the ensuing two and a half years, the two governments entered into more than 22 new agreements. Once again, there is no established way to evaluate the results of these agreements. However, evidence suggests that trade in areas subject to agreements has grown at a faster rate than overall trade. For example, an April 1996 report by the Council of Economic Advisers (CEA) argued that in goods sectors where the United States reached trade agreements with Japan under the World Trade Organization (WTO), the Framework Agreement, and other bilateral initiatives, U.S. exports had grown by 85 percent—or roughly three times faster than the overall growth of exports to Japan.[5]

Importantly, the CEA report also notes that a substantial reduction in Japan's current account surplus occurred over this period, but this reduction was driven largely by macroeconomic factors and structural shifts occurring within the Japanese economy.

Despite this record of achievement, an examination of the years under discussion reveals heightened Japanese bureaucratic resistance to the pattern of bilateral trade negotiations with the United States and more dissatisfaction on both sides of the Pacific as to both the effects of agreements reached and the process involved in reaching them. Japanese government officials are more willing than they once were to rebut U.S. allegations as to the closed nature of the Japanese market and less willing than in the past to resolve issues through bilateral consultations.[6]

Such resistance seems to stem from a number of factors that have continuing relevance for future negotiations. First, although many Americans have overemphasized the ability of the Japanese government to remedy trade problems, for its part that government consistently has underemphasized the role it can and does play in managing or influencing competition within its borders. Second, there is increased resistance in Japan to government bureaucrats using informal and nontransparent administrative guidance. Where the rubber meets the road on this issue is with U.S. government pressure on the Japanese government to remedy allegedly discriminatory or anticompetitive business practices. U.S. demands for greater Japanese imports in the glass, paper, semiconductor, and other sectors have been unpopular because the Japanese government characterized such pressure as serving to strengthen the hand of the Japanese bureaucracy.

Third, in the absence of internationally agreed upon rules regarding these structural and business issues, Japanese government circles are more unwilling to take up such concerns bilaterally. This resistance has been heightened by the passage of the Uruguay Round agreement, which now strengthens WTO dispute settlement and covers a broader range of matters than had been the case historically. The lead case here is the unwillingness of the Japanese government to hold bilateral consultations with the U.S. government on the complaint lodged by Eastman Kodak Company alleging barriers to the sale and distribution of consumer photographic film despite a finding by the U.S. Trade Representative that Japanese government practices were "unreasonable" under Section 301 of the 1974 Trade Act. Instead, the Japanese government said that the proper forum in which to air the governmental aspects of the complaint was the WTO and that the allegedly anticompetitive business features fell solely within the jurisdiction of Japan's Fair Trade Commission.

Fourth, a bilateral negotiating dynamic has developed in recent years between the United States and Japan that has failed to generate domestic support in the latter country. Although numerous bilateral accords have been struck, in Japan these agreements have been widely characterized as representing victories for free-market–oriented Japanese officials, who had successfully repelled proto–managed trade by U.S. officials. Whatever the merits of this claim, a general perception developed in Japan that the United States was seeking managed outcomes. This perception, adroitly cultivated by the Japanese government during a period of domestic recession, had a profoundly negative effect on the negotiations. It also had the unfortunate consequence of making allies of Japanese and European officials on the issue of the U.S. approach; and the Europeans seemed to hesitate not for a moment in their criticism of it—with little public discourse on the substantive concerns driving U.S. policy. This dynamic successfully united Japanese bureaucrats and politicians, thereby providing cover for those interests in Japan that have been reluctant to address trade problems identified by U.S. negotiators.

For the moment, the reduction in Japan's current account surplus, and the resolution of many of the specific bilateral disputes have combined to quiet U.S.-Japan trade relations. Nevertheless, U.S. policymakers and business leaders continue to express concern about sectoral issues and the slow pace of regulatory reform. This is likely to heighten with increased exports to the United States in the months ahead.

IMPLICATIONS FOR U.S.-JAPAN ECONOMIC RELATIONS

Although the speed of economic change in Japan may be a source of disappointment for many Americans *and* Japanese, the direction of change is promising. Market-based and other pressures are chipping away at barriers and resulting in a relatively more open Japanese economy. A consensus seems to be emerging in Japan supporting further economic deregulation and regulatory reform. The current reform agenda, if implemented, suggests much more than a modest tinkering with the system—especially in the area of financial sector deregulation and regulatory oversight procedures. Moreover, Japanese politicians and executives regularly state that failure to implement economic deregulation will imperil Japan's future growth prospects.

Importantly, Prime Minister Ryutaro Hashimoto has actively pushed forward an administrative reform agenda that could prove quite important for Japan's economic future. He has urged the American public to recognize that he has become "Hashimoto the Reformer." And various steps already have been introduced that will, by their very nature, result in still further changes—for example, the lifting of the restrictions on holding companies will likely bring consolidated tax returns; the removal of the remaining restrictions under the foreign exchange law should facilitate cross-border investment and capital raising; the introduction of some price discounting and new entry into the tightly controlled airline industry may prompt further deregulation; and so on.

While it is more difficult to restructure in a slow-growth economy than in one that is booming, the domestic economic logic for economic deregulation becomes more compelling when one considers Japan's constrained fiscal environment. Economic deregulation would enable firms to move into more promising lines of business and would benefit consumers. The results could be larger private spending, both for investment and consumption. Deregulation also would reduce government intervention in the economy. It offers the possibility of an improved business climate for potential new market entrants, both foreign and domestic.

Moreover, as many Japanese and foreign economists have argued, the prolonged recession and appreciation of the yen against the dollar in the years from 1993 to mid-1995 highlighted distortions within the Japanese economy. Export-oriented firms faced the strongest pressures to adjust in order to remain competitive in world markets and therefore adjusted the most. As Japan's Finance Vice Minister, Eisuke Sakakibara, has noted, the automotive, semiconductor, and machine tool sectors remain world-class competitors.[7] Yet firms in protected markets, heavily regulated sectors, or sectors that produce nontradable goods and services did not face these same pressures and adjusted less. Productivity gaps among different industries in Japan have increased.

Will these powerful economic arguments in favor of deregulation prevail in Japan's policy environment? Many small steps are being taken and some significant initiatives are on the table, but I can be only cautiously optimism about broad-based changes. One source of concern has to do with public attitudes.

A sentiment often heard in Japan is that economic deregulation is a necessity but must be accomplished with limited disruptions. In other words, all must gain, there can be no significant losers. A "convoy" approach to deregulation whereby the process is "managed" to limit deregulation's negative effects suggests a highly constrained process. If this approach prevails, it could put the brakes on the various gains from deregulation, including job creation. As many Japanese observers have noted, risk-taking remains underrewarded in Japan, and there has been insufficient effort to either manage or measure risk.[8]

Other obstacles are structural and institutional. From a distance, government deliberations on deregulation often appear to be aimless. Excessive attention seems to be paid to preparing lists of existing laws and regulations, which are then linked to efforts to reduce the aggregate number of such laws and regulations. Bureaucrats in Japan always have exerted a high degree of control over policy, and expertise on economic issues resides primarily in the bureaucracy. This pattern appears fairly stable. [9]

What does this recent record of trade disputes as well as the changes under way in Japan suggest for bilateral trade policy?

A Greater Need for U.S. Multilateral Initiatives and Demonstrated Commitment to WTO Mechanisms

Dispute settlement procedures in GATT (now the WTO) have been significantly improved as a result of the commitments made during the Uruguay Round.[10] The new WTO dispute settlement rules address many of the flaws of the earlier system.

The procedural improvements in dispute settlement will permit both Japan and the United States to assess more accurately the costs and benefits of alternative approaches to remedying a dispute. A country can, of course, still chose to ignore a WTO panel ruling, but by doing so it will face more identifiable consequences: It will be obliged to pay compensation if it loses a WTO case, or, if it chooses not to pay such compensation, it is likely to be subject to WTO-authorized counterretaliation from the winning party. Thus, while compliance with panel rulings cannot be forced, noncompliance will be recognized and retaliatory measures legitimated.

If fairly administered, these improvements should contribute to the effectiveness of the WTO as a vehicle for resolving disputes related to matters that it covers.

Vigorous U.S. use of multilateral dispute settlement procedures on WTO covered matters will be essential to the future of U.S.-Japan trade relations for several reasons. First, use of the WTO will ensure that the organization operates up to its full potential.

Second, active use of WTO dispute settlement is not only consistent with U.S. policy and history but will serve to demonstrate that the United States remains committed to the development of a multilateral rule-based system. Despite the fact that the United States remains the most active plaintiff in the WTO, one often hears it said in Asia that the United States is less committed to seeking multilateral remedies and more inclined to pursue regional or bilateral approaches at the expense of the multilateral system. U.S. policymakers need to step up their public diplomacy in order to address negative public perceptions abroad. Third, the fact that multilateral disciplines now cover a broader range of matters provides the opportunity to address a wider range of trade disputes that could arise between the United States and Japan.

Nevertheless, disputes between the United States and Japan on matters not covered by the WTO are certain to arise, and there is substantial room for improvement in a number of the new areas, such as services, investment, and competition policy.

Improving Bilateral Dispute Resolution

The improvements in the WTO dispute settlement process do not as matter of law restrict the ability of the U.S. government to take unilateral trade action under Section 301 or related self-help remedies. There is no ambiguity in the U.S. legislation implementing the Uruguay Round on this point.

The more complex question for the future relates to how bilateral negotiations can be used effectively to induce foreign governments to ameliorate practices that are deemed unreasonable by the U.S. government and are not covered by multilateral disciplines.

The effective exercise of Section 301 will become more constrained by virtue of those improvements to GATT that are now embodied in the WTO. Additionally, the range of WTO-consistent retaliation has been reduced by virtue of the expanded matters covered by international rules. Finally, Japan is more resistant to bilateral dispute resolution and more inclined to take the position that the existing WTO rules are the only standards to which it must conform.

Moving Forward: Where U.S.-Japan Trade Discussions Can Usefully Go from Here

In the past, the sectoral trade negotiations that have been the most successful have tended to combine: a globally competitive U.S. industry committed to penetrating the Japanese market; a willingness on the part of the U.S. government to apply bilateral and multi-lateral economic and political pressure on the Japanese government for corrective measures; the ability of the Japanese government to deliver on those requests; constituencies in Japan that support U.S. demands; negotiated measures that provide an effective context for follow-up; and the identification of market access priorities that reinforce market trends.[11]

Although it is not possible to anticipate every sectoral issue that is likely to surface, one can be confident that old issues will resurface and new issues will arise. At least three broad policy areas need attention by U.S. policymakers. These include: sustained focus on economic deregulation; increased efforts to address anti-competitive business practices; and continued efforts to encour-age even more transparency and due process in government actions through active engagement with proreform constituencies in Japan.

Addressing Private Business Practices

Increasingly, private business practices have surfaced as a source of bilateral trade tension between the United States and Japan. Numer-ous bilateral agreements have contained a competition policy feature, usually taking the form of affirmative statements by the government of Japan that it will vigorously enforce the Antimo-nopoly Act, and occasionally resulting in commitments to encour-age proactively greater import penetration of competitive foreign goods and services in particular sectors. The second approach has been particularly controversial, with little agreement between the United States and Japan as to the market effects of the practices identified and considerable divergence of opinion as to the appro-priate role of governments in punishing, deterring, or influencing the private conduct identified as problematic by the United States.

Although many policymakers in both Japan and the United States acknowledge that business practices can impede access to international markets, no comprehensive international frame-work of rules or principles cover business practices under either trade or competition disciplines. While this issue is surfacing prominently in disputes involving the United States and Japan, it is a much broader international problem, requiring U.S. and other trade and antitrust officials to consider more fully effective respons-es at the international level.

Pursuing Economic Deregulation in Japan

The costs to the Japanese economy of failing to continue the process of further economic deregulation, and the domestic pressures in favor of deregulation, are sufficiently great that in the years ahead Japanese government and private sector leaders are likely to push for some version of reform. This does not mean that the paths chosen will be those most desired by Japan's major trading partners.

Many cross-pressures also exist within Japan. It is entirely possible that if a perceived trade-off exists among increased efficiency, higher imports, and increased unemployment on the one hand, and inefficiency, lower imports, and fuller employment on the other, there will be overwhelming pressure to choose the latter approach. This fact alone suggests that international attention to economic deregulation in Japan is important.

While such international attention will not eliminate sectoral disputes between Japan and its trading partners, nor substitute for needed Japanese attention to competition policy and its enforcement, foreign attention to deregulation and competition policy is both necessary and desirable. It could contribute to debates already under way in Japan and could help ensure that whatever deregulation occurs does so in a manner that fully recognizes the international consequences of the paths chosen.

Indeed, the challenge for U.S. policymakers is to ally themselves with those groups in Japan supportive of changes that happen to coincide with the interests of the United States, Japan, and the global economy.

Over the long term, progress in achieving expanded market access can be assured only if measures undertaken to open markets have some domestic support in Japan. In fact, such support has existed for a number of U.S. trade initiatives with Japan in the past. For example, such support was especially evident at certain points during the Structural Impediments Initiative (SII) as well as in the course of the beef and citrus negotiations, among others.[12]

In one sense this was not surprising, because U.S. negotiators took great pains to identify those issues that would benefit U.S. firms and yet were already contentious domestic issues within Japan. For example, when the United States identified the large scale retail store law as an impediment to new market entrants seeking to establish larger retail chains, Japanese retail chains were already pressing for reform.[13]

Moreover, in a number of other sectoral negotiations, it was not U.S. pressure as such but rather public support in Japan for U.S. negotiating objectives that obliged Japanese government officials and politicians to go farther than they might otherwise have chosen. This dynamic is hard to achieve but increasingly important, especially with respect to matters that are not fully covered by international rules.

U.S. ECONOMIC AND TRADE RELATIONS WITH CHINA

In contrast to U.S. relations with Japan, which, despite bilateral trade frictions, are firmly grounded and multifaceted, most dimensions of U.S. policy relations with China remain volatile and fragile. In recent years U.S. economic and trade relations with China have been clouded by a number of contentious sectoral issues that have been made all the more difficult to resolve because of the serious nontrade issues between both countries, including nuclear proliferation, security, and human rights.

On the economic front, a central challenge facing U.S. policymakers in dealing with China is to pursue an overall approach that is effective in promoting Chinese adherence to global international economic norms.

Economy and Recent Reforms

The magnitude and speed with which China has reformed and opened its economy to foreign trade and investment is a development of historic significance that is changing the global economic landscape. By some estimates, China may become the world's largest economy by early in the next century.[14]

From 1949 to 1979 China was essentially hostile to foreign capital, lacked exposure to international finance and technology flows, and was bent on achieving near total self-reliance. Starting in 1978, Chinese leaders began to introduce a number of important economic reforms.

Since then China has gone through several stages of reform that have decentralized economic policymaking to local governments; permitted the expansion of private businesses and the introduction of various market-based reforms; eliminated price controls on a broad range of products; and opened up wider areas to foreign investment. The result of these and other measures has contributed to very dramatic improvements in economic growth. Between 1979 and 1995 China's real gross domestic product (GDP) more than quadrupled; over the past 10 years its real GDP has grown by an on average of 9.6 percent annually.

In the 17 years since China embarked on its open-door policies, it has become a major world trading country and a major recipient of foreign investment.

A few statistics are illuminating. Since 1985 foreign direct investment (FDI) on a realized basis has expanded by nearly a factor of 20. According to the United Nations, in 1995 China was second only to the United States as a recipient of world FDI and accounted for over a third of all direct investment in developing countries.

On the trade front, as recently as 1979, China's total trade was $20.7 billion; in 1995 its total trade was a staggering $280 billion. U.S.-China trade patterns have played an important role in this upward trend. The countries established diplomatic relations in January 1979 and signed a bilateral trade agreement in July of that year. In 1989 China was the tenth largest trading partner of the United States in terms of total trade. By 1996 China had become its fourth largest trading partner—after Canada, Japan, and Mexico. In 1996 the United States exported nearly $12 billion in goods to China and imported more than $51 billion of goods and services. As a result, the United States is experiencing its second largest bilateral trade deficit with China, over $39 billion. For a number of months in 1996 and 1997, the U.S. trade deficit with China exceeded its trade deficit with Japan.[15]

Indeed, while Chinese statistics indicate that on a global basis China is experiencing a small trade surplus, the United States records a large trade deficit with China, and this deficit has grown at a faster rate than the United States' deficit with any other major trading partner.[16]

Trade flows aside, official U.S. trade policy engagement with the Chinese government really began in earnest only in the 1990s. Since China was not a member of GATT, that engagement occurred largely in the context of bilateral negotiations, although these talks occurred against the backdrop of GATT working party discussions.

Trade Disputes Between the United States and China

U.S. trade policy engagement with China has centered on three separate but related issues: concerns about intellectual property theft; concerns about China's overall trade regime, which came to be reflected in a bilateral negotiation on market access; and negotiations with China regarding the terms and conditions of its entry into the WTO.

Intellectual Property Issues

With the growing importance to the U.S. economy of industries dependent on intellectual property, protection of American intellectual property rights abroad has, over the last decade, become a top priority of U.S. trade policy. Hence Washington pressed for the issue's inclusion in the Uruguay Round and also modified its domestic laws, adding a so-called special 301 provision into the 1988 Trade Act.[17] In the late 1980s and early 1990s, as a result of that statute and the information compiled by trade associations, U.S. policymakers came to see intellectual property theft in China as a major trade issue.

In spring 1991 China, India, and Thailand were designated as countries of priority concern under the intellectual property provisions of U.S. trade laws.[18] The ensuing negotiations were contentious and involved a high degree of brinkmanship on both the U.S. and Chinese sides—a pattern that has continued in all subsequent bilateral trade negotiations between the two countries.

In these negotiations, the United States argued that:

- Reforms that it was seeking would increase *investor confidence* in the Chinese economic system, which was consistent with China's interest in expanding foreign direct investment, especially high-technology investment;

- Reforms would foster *inventor confidence,* which was important for China's future, given its tremendous reservoir of talented people who were increasingly likely to produce new intellectual property;

- Reforms were in any event *necessary to bring China's intellectual property regime up to world standards,* including those of other developing economies, as well as to the standards that were being negotiated in the Uruguay Round;

• Reforms were necessary to *restore equality and fairness* to U.S.-China trade and to restore a healthy and fair bilateral trade relationship.

Chinese government officials tended to argue that China was in the process of fundamentally reforming its economy, evidencing its commitment to an increasingly open market; however, China remained a developing country that needed more time to introduce the reforms sought by the United States. Further, the U.S. government failed to appreciate the substantial steps that China had taken and intended to undertake to further reform its economy. Finally, the U.S. government was expecting more from China than was reasonable or than it expected from other trading partners at comparable stages of development.

On November 26, 1991, the U.S. Trade Representative determined that insufficient progress had been made in resolving U.S. intellectual property concerns. The USTR decided to extend investigations until January 16, 1992, but threatened to impose retaliatory sanctions on some $1.5 billion of Chinese goods if an agreement was not reached by that date. The Chinese government indicated that any retaliation would be met with counterretaliation. A settlement eventually was reached on January 16, 1992, and took the form of a Memorandum of Understanding (MOU).

In that MOU, China agreed to a number of steps in each of the core problem areas identified by the U.S. government and agreed to bring its intellectual property regime (IPR) up to world standards.[19]

Over the next two years, even as China began to implement the 1992 agreement, U.S. executives and trade officials grew increasingly concerned about the Chinese government's apparent inability or unwillingness to end rampant piracy. As a result, on June 30, 1994, the USTR again initiated another special 301 investigation designed specifically to focus on the problems of enforcement.[20] On February 4, 1995, the USTR determined that the talks had failed to achieve sufficient progress; it threatened to retaliate against some $1.08 billion of Chinese goods, effective February 26, 1995. China threatened counterretaliation.[21] An agreement to resolve the dispute was signed on March 11, 1995.

This IPR deal was the most detailed enforcement agreement of its kind ever entered into between the United States and a foreign country. The steps agreed to were consistent with the provisions on enforcement contained in the WTO's agreement on trade-related intellectual property rights (TRIPS) but far more detailed. The 1995 deal contained not only a broad range of undertakings that will be implemented by the Chinese government to address systemic barriers to inadequate enforcement but also pledged the United States to certain collaborative efforts. In addition, the Chinese government took visible symbolic steps to demonstrate that it was doing all it could to protect intellectual property. For example, the government invited U.S. intellectual property groups to accompany Chinese officials on raids.[22]

Intellectual property enforcement problems in China did not end with the negotiated agreement of 1995. Indeed, the International Intellectual Property Alliance (IIPA) estimated China was still the single largest foreign pirate of U.S. intellectual property.

On April 30, 1996, the USTR once again designated China under its special 301 laws, saying that it had yet to comply with the 1995 IPR agreement. Although USTR officials noted a number of steps that had been taken, they drew particular attention to China's failure to take action against the thirty or more factories that were mass-producing and exporting pirated works. On May 15, 1996, once again the USTR published a list of products under consideration for retaliatory sanctions that amounted to some $2 billion. And yet again China threatened to impose countersanctions.

On June 17, 1996, the USTR announced that China was taking steps to fulfill the 1995 agreement. In particular, the USTR cited as evidence the fact that China had closed a total of 15 compact disc (CD) factories; begun a new initiative to identify underground CD plants; stepped up the activities of the Ministry of Public Security; placed a moratorium on the establishment of any new CD factories; issued regulations that "virtually ban the importation of CD presses and other manufacturing equipment"; and strengthened border enforcement, among other measures.[23]

As a result of these bilateral negotiations, China has joined a number of international intellectual property conventions, prepared numerous domestic laws and regulations on intellectual property, and developed domestic institutions that are responsible for administration in these areas.

The Market Access Negotiations

While the first special 301 proceedings were under way in 1991, the U.S. government also was engaged in broad-based consultations with the Chinese government on a variety of practices seen as inhibiting access to China's market. In the fall of 1991 the Bush administration initiated a Section 301 investigation directed at four general areas and requested the Chinese government to undertake various short-, medium-, and longer-term remedial measures.[24]

This 301 investigation was the broadest and most comprehensive Section 301 investigation ever undertaken by the U.S. government.[25] It was aimed at addressing immediate problems and promoting long-term economic reform in China.

In the ensuing negotiations, the U.S. government stressed that its willingness to support China's entry into the WTO was linked to the successful resolution of the market access dispute. Indeed, a central argument advanced by the U.S. government was that the commitments being sought were reforms that China would be obliged to undertake if it were to join the WTO. The hope was that this would stimulate China's interest in making the desired adjustments in its trade regime.

Yet on August 21, 1992, the USTR once again determined that the negotiations had failed to address the outstanding issues and threatened to impose $3.9 billion in trade sanctions unless an agreement was reached by October 10, 1992. Again China threatened counterretaliation. On October 10, after nine rounds of negotiations, the two governments finally reached an agreement and entered into an MOU.

In that MOU, China pledged to reduce or eliminate a wide variety of nontariff barriers such as quotas, licensing requirements, controls, and other restrictions on imports of industrial and agricultural products; and to eliminate some import substitution policies. China also committed to undertake a number of measures to make its trade regime more transparent.

The U.S. government, for its part, committed to "staunchly support" China's entry into the GATT/WTO and to reduce export controls on computer and telecommunications equipment exports.

Although the U.S. government continues to raise concerns about Chinese trade practices in a number of sectors, it also has credited China with doing much to implement the 1992 agreement.

This recent history of U.S. disputes with China over intellectual property and market access suggests that despite accusations, defiant gestures, and mutual finger-pointing, bilateral accords can be reached that both the United States and China accept and welcome. What accounts for this success? At least seven factors appear to have been important.

First, there has been relatively little discernible disagreement within the U.S. administration as to the importance of the trade issues raised with China and therefore relatively little evidence that the United States was prepared to abandon its core requirements.

Second, the importance of the U.S. market for Chinese goods presumably provided the United States with some leverage and served to induce Chinese officials to make adjustments in their trade regime.

Third, imposition of sanctions obviously would deny China most-favored-nation (MFN) treatment for some portion of U.S.-China trade, yet as large as those threatened retaliations were, they were but a fraction of Chinese exports to the United States. Spillover effects on the annual MFN review could have proven much more problematic to Chinese exporters and the Chinese economy.

Fourth, although this is not certain, probably some within China believed the changes sought by the United States on balance would benefit the Chinese economy or would otherwise be necessary for China to join the WTO.

Fifth, despite the strong rhetoric described earlier, the linkage of trade threats with failure to provide adequate trade and economic rights has not generated the vitriol that trade threats for noneconomic objectives have engendered.

Sixth, although there have been instances when a number of China's other trading partners have expressed concern about U.S. "unilateral" tactics, overall the international trading community has either remained on the sidelines or quietly supported the substance of U.S. trade policy requests.

Seventh, bilateral trade tension has occurred against the backdrop of China's strong interest in joining the WTO.

In sum, this process of bilateral negotiations can be credited with contributing to the development of a law-based and more transparent trade and intellectual property system. It is not yet clear, however, whether the revised legal framework can be equated meaningfully with enduring change within China and greater domestic respect for rights and legal processes.

China and the WTO

China has had observer status at GATT since 1983 and formally applied for GATT membership in 1986. At least part of its motivation for joining GATT appears to have been political, reflecting an interest in gaining admission before Taiwan. China also may have seen GATT admission as a way of eliminating the annual U.S. review of MFN. Additionally, some U.S. analysts of China argue that reformers in China view the GATT/WTO accession process as a useful one for adjusting domestic institutions that stand in the way of broader-based economic reform.

Whatever the motivation, China's interest in joining GATT and now the WTO has been a major priority, and China has taken a number of steps to bring its trading regime into greater conformity with WTO standards. A draft accession protocol was developed in Geneva in 1994, and consultations bilaterally and in the WTO working party continue actively.

However, many steps remain to be taken. At various points, U.S. officials have cited the following areas as major sticking points: insufficient offers on market access for goods, services, and agriculture; unresolved issues related to trade rules; and insufficient disciplines on agricultural supports, subsidies, and China's industrial policies.

A major point of ideological contention in the negotiations for WTO accession has centered around the question of whether China should be considered a "developing country" for WTO purposes. This designation would permit China a much longer time frame to comply with WTO rules. Chinese negotiators often have publicly stated that, given the changes that the country has already undertaken, withholding membership until China's economy has made a full market transition would be unreasonable. The United States and other WTO members have argued that, for many purposes, China is already a developed country, thus its admission to the WTO must be granted only on "commercially sound" terms.

WTO membership would provide China with several advantages:

- *Status and prestige.* In recent years, China has joined many international organizations as part of its opening to the outside world. GATT (now the WTO) is the only major international organization in which China does not have membership.

- *Ability to shape future international trade rules.* Once it joins the WTO, China will participate actively in WTO deliberations and will therefore help shape future rules that will govern the international trading system.

- *Access to Information.* Joining the WTO will provide China with access to information about the policies and practices of other countries that affect its export opportunities.

- *Depoliticization of trade relations.* As a member of the WTO, many of China's trade disputes may be taken out of a bilateral context; and China will have full recourse to dispute settlement procedures in the WTO.

- *Improved investor confidence.* By joining the WTO and, more important, through the commitments it makes by virtue of joining, Beijing will demonstrate China's long-term commitment to a market-based system. This will underscore the seriousness and stability of the domestic reforms that China is putting into place and help ease the fears of foreign investors.

- *Institutionalizing and binding MFN treatment of Chinese exports.* Unless a country opts out of applying WTO benefits to China, China will be able to receive MFN treatment.

While these advantages of WTO membership are important, in the last several years the Chinese government's official position on joining the WTO has fluctuated between hot and cold. A number of possible explanations can be invoked for these shifts in China's official posture. Perhaps the long process has taken its toll; after ten years of effort, Chinese negotiators may believe that their very expression of interest gives negotiating partners excessive leverage. Thus it is now common to hear Chinese negotiators assert that, given China's size, by excluding China the WTO would limit its own importance. China's perception of U.S. public opinion also may have tempered its expectations of U.S. support for China's WTO accession.

A more troubling interpretation is this: China no longer sees the economic benefits of joining the WTO to be as compelling as it once did, after appraising the economic and social pain that could accompany some of the changes sought by the United States and the WTO working party. China's protection of state-owned enterprises may prove to be an area of particular difficulty for Chinese officials. [26] Furthermore, the promise of MFN treatment may no longer be seen as the powerful inducement it once was. All countries but the United States already provide durable MFN treatment for Chinese exports. Even the United States, which goes through an annual review process, has extended MFN for more than 15 years.[27]

Thus, while China's accession to the WTO would reduce the ability of countries to withdrawal MFN treatment unilaterally and would thereby introduce a greater degree of predictability into China's trade relations, the concrete economic gains could, in part, be offset by the social and economic adjustment costs that could accompany the necessary reforms. Some U.S. scholars have argued that Chinese negotiators who are committed to joining the WTO are finding it increasingly difficult to obtain the consent of key domestic interests.˙

OVERALL IMPLICATIONS

The political challenge associated with economic reform has been formidable, but Chinese-style economic reform, however gradual and piecemeal, has succeeded in creating a dynamic nonstate sector that has so far kept reform alive.[28] Growing numbers of Chinese have come to recognize that the inherent risks of market-based competition are preferable to the security suggested by state plans.[29] And, despite very slow improvement in state-owned industrial firms, the economy as a whole has grown rapidly and living standards have risen considerably.

Nevertheless, China still has a long way to go before it has a well-functioning market economy. And it is apparent that China's internal politics will remain unsettled for many years.

What Does This Suggest for U.S. Policy?

It is almost certain that the continuing transformation of the Chinese economy and the still-unsettled state of China's internal political economy will generate points of economic friction between the United States and China. U.S. trade policy toward China therefore will need to be framed with full recognition that it could take years before China's trade and economic system becomes predictable and stable. This fact makes it all the more necessary to put U.S.-China trade and economic relations on firmer and more normal footing.

U.S. policymakers have long argued that their central goal is to further integrate China in the international community by pursuing a policy of "comprehensive engagement."[30] Expanding high-level political contacts between Washington and Beijing, including reciprocal state visits between President Bill Clinton and President Jiang Zemin, is an important step to address the political dimensions of this problem. Indeed, exchanges between senior officials from various agencies should be regularized. But additional actions also are needed.

Within the United States, the most important step for U.S. policymakers is to rebuild a bipartisan policy toward China. Doing so will require leadership from the White House and close cooperation with Congress.

In the economic sphere, China's admission to the WTO appears to be—and rightly should be—a top trade priority for the U.S. government. Every effort should be undertaken to drive this process forward. It is not only in China's interest to join the WTO, but it is very much in the U.S. national interest. China's entry into the WTO could (and indeed should) result in substantial improvements in access to its market. Entry would commit China to further systemic economic reforms and perhaps strengthen the hand of modernizers within the country.

China's admission to the WTO also would permit many U.S.-China trade frictions to be addressed in a multilateral framework rather than through bilateral means. Chinese officials often state that the United States is erecting the major obstacles to China's admission. The willingness of some important trading nations to assert their support for China's prompt admission to the WTO has only exacerbated China's perception that the process is a political one, not driven by the economic commitments that the country is prepared to undertake as part of its WTO entry process. It will not be easy to correct this perception, but greater efforts are necessary. In this sense, improved cooperation between the United States, the European Union, Japan, and other Asian countries is both necessary and desirable.[31]

China's accession to the WTO also is important because, once this step has been taken, the United States and the WTO working party can move ahead with Taiwan's admission. Taiwan is now the seventh largest overseas market for U.S. goods. China's accession to the WTO also could have potentially important implications for Hong Kong. It is unclear how China would react to a long-term situation where Hong Kong was itself a member of the

WTO (albeit as a customs territory) while China remained outside of the WTO.

Of course, the United States should not support China's entry into the WTO on any terms that China proposes. It is essential that the WTO working party obtain specific commitments from China regarding the measures that it will undertake in the short term, as well as the phase-in of reform measures over the longer term. The key issue is not whether to admit China to the WTO—there is international consensus on the importance of China's accession—but on what terms. Looking ahead, U.S. policymakers should further consider multilateralizing the review mechanisms that are built into the protocol and multilateralize the various forms of international assistance to China as it builds more modern economic systems. The latest IPR agreement may provide a useful model.

It is difficult to predict how China will utilize the WTO once admitted. It might, for example, try to use the WTO to slow the pace of global trade liberalization. It may refuse to bring its regime into compliance with agreed-upon timetables. Indeed, Western countries may find that the rules of the game, including the rules of international trade, will be challenged by conflicting Chinese social and political values. These are risks that the United States should undertake. The potential gains from China's entry will be significant, both in terms of improved market access and, more important, in terms of an improved framework in which to engage China on problems that will arise. Moreover, once China is admitted, the United States then will have multilateral as well as bilateral tools available to encourage China's compliance with WTO principles and, if necessary, to challenge China's practices under established international disciplines.

CONCLUSIONS

U.S. foreign economic and trade policy rests on the assumption that the continued vitality of both the Japanese and the Chinese economies is important not only for each of these countries but also for U.S. global foreign and economic policy objectives.

At this time, the economies of both Japan and China are undergoing substantial changes that bespeak greater openness to imports and, in China's case, enormous potential for inward investment.

U.S. trade policies, therefore, need to build on the market-driven processes under way in both economies.

In terms of trade policy, these factors suggest that multilateral, bilateral, and regional instruments should be applied in complementary and consistent ways. Especially important will be more active use of multilateral instruments where the subject matter of a trade dispute is covered by WTO rules.

This is also an important time to consider, especially in the context of U.S.-Japan trade disputes, expanded international engagement on practices that remain largely outside of multilateral disciplines, in areas such as investment, services, and competition policy. The Singapore WTO meetings established that new initiatives need to be undertaken in the WTO on these important new frontiers of international trade. Doing so, in turn, will require leadership from U.S. trade and competition authorities.

The inclusion of these new areas into the international trade agenda bespeaks a new economic reality: Few areas of economic policymaking are purely domestic in nature. This fact necessarily requires not only more international attention to domestic economic policies but increased coordination within governments.

Over the long term, the importance of Japan, China, and indeed Asia to the United States also points to the need for more expertise on Asia at all, but especially senior, levels of government.

In the future, there is likely to be some diminution in the effectiveness of bilateral trade negotiations both as a matter of practical application and principle. The ambit of matters that are likely to be resolved successfully through bilateral consultations is likely to become more circumscribed, and bilateral leverage will require greater sophistication in its application. Especially important in this regard is the structural agenda with Japan, which remains underdeveloped. The United States can more vigorously engage Japan in a plurilateral as well as a bilateral context on the twin problems of competition policy enforcement and economic deregulation.

Whether on specific sectoral issues or structural matters, U.S. policymakers also need to seek more effectively constituencies within both Japan and China that support U.S. trade policy objectives. Doing so will be a lengthy and taxing process but will prove critical over time if further nondiscriminatory market-oriented trade policy reforms are to prove sustainable.

With respect to China, the United States needs to put its commercial relations on a more stable footing. China is a difficult country to deal with, and trade relations are, of course, only one dimension of broader U.S. political, security, and economic relations. But steps could be undertaken to put U.S.-China economic relations on a firmer footing by expanding senior policy-level exchanges between U.S. and Chinese officials; by removing China from the annual review of MFN; by more vigorous work to conclude a WTO protocol; and by more effective coordination with other U.S. trading partners that share analogous concerns about the Chinese market. Active and ongoing efforts to develop a bipartisan China policy within the United States are inescapable.

And finally, in today's world of more assertive, affluent, and more economically and politically complex Asian countries, the United States is challenged to modify its exercise of leadership. There is no single or easy answer. Bilateral, plurilateral, and multilateral dimensions of U.S. trade policy all need to be adjusted to contemporary economic and political realities.

NOTES

1. Not all of these are "agreements" for U.S. trade law purposes. This aggregate number is based on a compilation of U.S.-Japan agreements prepared by William Piez and includes the basic Treaty of Friendship, Commerce, and Navigation; bilateral sectoral agreements; voluntary restraint agreements (VRAs); science and technology agreements; financial services agreements; the Market Oriented Sector Specific (MOSS) talks; the Structural Impediments Initiative (SII) undertakings; and the agreements covering civil aeronautics; among others.

2. During the Bush administration, the United States and Japan concluded four agreements covering Japanese government procurement practices (in computers, satellites, supercomputers, and construction services); five agreements covering Japanese government telecommunications standards, regulations, and licensing procedures (in third-party radio and cellular telephone, telecommunications equipment, and three agreements on international value-added telecommunication services); one agreement covering technical standards (in wood products); and three broad market-access agreements involving some combination of government and private conduct (in semiconductors, paper products, and amorphous metals).

3. These included, for example, expanded access to Japan's market for automotive parts and vehicles, its glass sector, enhanced intellectual property protection for foreign sound recordings, nondiscriminatory access to Japanese private standard-setting bodies, reduction of import restraints for certain agricultural products, and many other areas. Discussions on structural issues started in the Reagan administration under the MOSS talks, continued in an expanded fashion during the Bush

administration in the context of the SII, and have continued in select areas during the Clinton administration.

4. Carla A. Hills, "Targets Won't Open Japanese Markets," *Wall Street Journal*, June 11, 1993, p. 10.

5. Council of Economic Advisers, "U.S. Trade Policy With Japan: Assessing the Record," April 12, 1996.

6. This point was brought home vividly in a 1996 speech by then-Ministry of International Trade and Industry Vice Minister Yoshihiro Sakamoto, who suggested that the era of bilateral negotiations was over.

7. See Dr. Eisuke Sakakibara, "Reforming Japan," *The Economist*, March 22, 1997, p. 89.

8. See Arthur M. Mitchell, "Can the Big Bang Change Japan?" photocopy, on file with M. E. Janow.

9. As I have argued elsewhere, while expertise on economic matters resides in the bureaucracy, this fact should not be interpreted to mean that politicians are mere window dressing. Bureaucrats in Japan often appear to have difficulty reaching agreement on issues when domestic private interests or other bureaucrats oppose the proposed policy matter. Resolving problems appears especially difficult when issues cut across the jurisdiction of several ministries. In such circumstances, Japanese politicians (including those who are affiliated with such interests) often have played an important role in brokering compromises. Merit E. Janow, "Japan's Uncertain Politics," testimony before the House Foreign Relations Committee, October 1995.

10. As many analysts have noted, the basic improvements include: stricter time frames; automatic establishment of a panel upon request; automatic adoption of panel reports unless the Dispute Settlement Body (DSB) decides the contrary by consensus; the opportunity for appellate review of a panel report; surveillance of implementation; and in the absence of conformity, automatic approval by the DSB of a request for authorization to suspend concessions unless the DSB decides by consensus to reject such a request.

11. Merit E. Janow, "Trading with an Ally: Progress and Discontent in U.S.-Japan Trade Relations" in G. Curtis, ed., *The United States, Japan and Asia* (New York: W. W. Norton, 1994), pp. 53–95.

12. Not all issues in the SII generated support in Japan, but the initiative was on the right track insofar as it augmented a process of affording heightened attention to structural barriers in Japan that continues to this day—with regard to the need for deregulation, the existence of price gaps, cartels, excessive bureaucratic discretion, more public accountability, and so on.

13. A poll by *Asahi Shimbun* in May 1990 showed some 58 percent of the respondents in favor of reducing regulations over large stores.

14. "The Titan Stirs," *Economist*, November 28, 1992, p. S3. (Calculations based on figures from the World Bank.)

15. Various statistical tables, ITA/Department of Commerce, http://www.ita.doc.gov.

16. The size of China's trade surplus with the United States is itself a subject of some controversy. Nicholas Lardy of the Brookings Institute has argued that Department of Commerce figures overstate the Chinese surplus by as much as $11 billion for 1995 because they include gross margins that Hong Kong entrepreneurs earn on Chinese goods that they reexport from Hong Kong to the United States and fail to include U.S. goods sold to Hong Kong and then reexported to China. See prepared statement of Nicholas R. Lardy, U.S.-China Intellectual Property Rights Agreement and Related Trade Issues, Joint Subcommittee Meeting, House Committee on International Relations and Senate Committee on Foreign Relations, March 7, 1996.

17. Specifically, Section 182 of the Trade Act of 1974 was amended by Section 1303 of the Omnibus Trade and Competitiveness Act of 1988 to require the U.S. Trade Representative to identify "priority foreign countries" that violate U.S. intellectual property rights. Under this "Special 301" provision, the USTR is required to initiate a 301 investigation of priority foreign countries that fail to provide "adequate and effective protection of U.S. intellectual property rights" or that "deny fair and equitable market access to U.S. firms" that rely on intellectual property protection. The statute requires the USTR to seek negotiations with such nations to end such violations and to recommend to the president retaliatory measures to halt such violations if they have not ceased within six to nine months of the investigation.

18. The investigation covered four areas: (1) lack of copyright protection for works not first published in China; (2) deficient levels of protection under China's copyright law and regulations; (3) inadequate protection of trade secrets; and (4) deficient patent laws and regulations, particularly the failure to provide product patent protection for chemicals, including pharmaceutical and agrochemical. USTR press release, January 16, 1992.

19. China committed to revise its patent law to extend the term of protection to 20 years, to ease compulsory licensing requirements, and to provide administrative protection for pharmaceuticals and agrochemicals. In the copyright area, China committed to join the Berne Convention; agreed to provide protection for sound recordings; agreed to treat computer software as literary works; issued new copyright regulations and amended its copyright law; and committed to set up new intellectual property rights tribunals. China also agreed to promulgate new trade secrets legislation, among other measures.

20. The USTR cited in particular the establishment of some 26 compact disc factories in China producing pirated CDs, along with continuing trade barriers restricting access to China's market for movies, videos, and sound recordings. It called on China to take immediate measures to curb piracy by closing down and conducting raids on CD producers, instituting structural changes to improve IPR protection over time (including the creation of an effective border enforcement regime, the introduction of a copyright verification system, and improved access to intellectual property tribunals), and providing greater access for U.S. intellectual property–based products.

21. China indicated that it would retaliate against the big three United States car makers and suspend new ventures with U.S. companies in the automotive, chemical, and audiovisual sectors if the United States implemented the threatened sanctions. For example, the Shanghai Automotive Industry Corp. warned that "bids by both Ford and General Motors (GM) to take part in a planned one billion dollar auto assembly joint venture could be derailed by a trade war." Tiffany Bown, "U.S. Businessmen in China Welcome Copyrights Agreement," *Agence France Presse*, February 27, 1995, available in WESTLAW, ALLNEWS Database.

22. Press reports indicate various other steps. For example, Ren Jianxin, president of the Supreme People's Court of China, told Parliament that Chinese courts "jailed 341 people for trademark infringement in 1994 and will intensify their battle against piracy this year." "China Vows to Enhance Copyright Protection," Reuters News Service, Far East, March 13, 1995, available in LEXIS, News Library, TXTLNE File. He also announced the establishment of special tribunals in several cities to handle intellectual property disputes. The Administration for Industry and Commerce (AIC), a branch of the state authorized to enforce copyright, "raided seven manufacturers, wholesalers or retailers in Beijing of pirated Sega game machines and software on March 9" at the request of Sega Enterprises Ltd. "China Raids Video Game Machine Pirates, Sega Says," Reuters World Service, March 15, 1995, available in LEXIS, World Library, TXTLNE File.

23. Testimony of Ambassador Charlene Barshefsky before the House Ways and Means Committee, September 12, 1996.

24. These included: selected product specific and sector-specific import prohibitions and quantitative restrictions; selective restrictions on imports made effective through restrictive import license requirements; selected technical barriers to trade, including standards, testing and certification requirements, and policy toward phytosanitary and veterinary standards that create unnecessary obstacles to trade; and the failure to publish laws, regulations, judicial decisions, and administrative rulings of general application and pertaining to customs requirements, restrictions, or prohibitions on imports or affecting their sale or distribution in China.

25. This market-access 301 probably came closest to what Congress thought the administration should undertake under the so-called Super 301 provisions introduced in the 1988 Trade Act.

26. For example, in June 1994, China announced its intention to design national industrial policies for its "pillar industries." Pillar industries were seen as those with large output, use of advanced technology, and large and potentially significant foreign markets. Sectors such as machinery and electronics, construction materials, petrochemicals, aircraft, telecommunications, automobiles and auto parts are examples. Although the WTO does not prohibit countries from pursuing industrial policies, some national industrial policies could violate international trade rules. The WTO has prepared a paper describing these features for the explicit purpose of alerting the Chinese government to such a possibility. *Inside U.S. Trade*, April 5, 1996.

27. Testimony by Nicholas Lardy, Senior Fellow, Brookings Institution, before the House Ways and Means Trade Subcommittee, September 19, 1996.

28. Susan Shirk, *The Political Logic of Economic Reform in China* (Berkeley: University of California Press, 1993).

29. Ibid.

30. This was outlined by Winston Lord, testifying before the Senate Foreign Relations Committee on United States policy on China, who defined this strategy as the pursuit of U.S. interests "at the levels and intensity required to achieve results" and "to continue pushing [those] interests forward on as many fronts as possible." Prepared testimony of Winston Lord, assistant secretary East Asian and Pacific Affairs, Department of State, Before Subcommittee on East Asian and Pacific Affairs of the Committee on Foreign Relations, Federal News Service, Congressional Hearing Testimonies, 1995 WL 10384528, March 8, 1995.

31. This was stated well by former Under Secretary of State Robert Zoellick in testimony before the Committee on Banking and Financial Service of the U.S. House of Representatives on July 29, 1996: "We want China to accept the rules. We want China to perceive that adherence to norms of behavior will benefit it as well as others. And we want China to recognize that these requirements are not a form of American political Diktat, but rather the principles of a system designed for mutual advantage."

Chapter 11

Contestability, Competition, and Investment in the New World Trade Order

Edward M. Graham

The 1996 ministerial meeting of the World Trade Organization (WTO), held in December in Singapore, authorized the formation of working parties to examine whether issues pertaining to trade and investment and trade and competition policy should result in new or changed rules in the body of multilateral trade law. These decisions reflect a growing recognition that, even though successive rounds of multilateral trade negotiations have resulted in significant reduction or elimination of tariffs and other "traditional" nontariff barriers, substantial impediments to market access still exist that do not fall into the category of traditional barriers to trade.

Such barriers are found mostly beyond the national frontier. They are not the result of measures imposed at the border, designed to impede imports. Rather they are a result of both public and private sector policies and practices that are internal to the domestic economy of a trading nation. Such measures often take the form of domestic regulatory policies that favor incumbent firms, retarding or preventing market entry by foreign firms either via imports or direct investment. Market access also can be impeded by industrial policies that grant subsidy and subsidy-like advantages to favored domestic firms. In addition to government policies, private business practices also can create market-entry barriers. These can take many forms, such as exclusive distribution networks, cross-share-holding arrangements that restrict or prevent foreign direct investment (FDI) via takeover of existing firms, and supplier cartels.

Taken together, private practices and public policies can have a combined effect that creates very substantial barriers to market entry. Although such barriers are not specifically border measures, in some cases they arguably have been created with the intent to favor domestically owned firms over foreign-owned or controlled ones. For example, the recent WTO dispute case lodged against Japan by the United States was based on allegations that certain laws and policies in Japan pertaining to the market for photographic film, although in the form of domestic regulation, have discriminated against sales by foreign firms. The European Union asked to be included as a third-party participant in this case. Kodak, whose complaint initiated this case, maintains that private practices in Japan restricted its ability to increase its share of this market. Fuji, the dominant seller of film in Japan, in turn argued that certain practices of Kodak in the United States foreclosed Fuji's ability to expand sales of its product in the U.S. market.[1]

Such barriers hinder the international contestability of markets. A contestable market is one in which barriers to new entrants are sufficiently low that incumbent firms must behave competitively in order to foreclose new entry by rival firms. This implies competitive pricing—prices that are maintained at levels that would prevail if a large number of firms competed in the market. If prices are at competitive levels, consumers will capture the benefits of competition even if there are few sellers in the relevant markets. Firms in contestable markets for technologically advanced products and services also must constantly strive to improve the products or services they offer and to introduce new products at a satisfactory rate. Otherwise, new rivals will overtake them in the marketplace.

As a consequence, contestable markets are ones in which allocative efficiency is high because prices are competitive and quantities sold are commensurate with demand at low prices. Under these circumstances, resources allocated to production of the relevant products and services ensure that there is neither undercapacity nor overcapacity. Because rates of innovation tend to be high in contestable markets, these markets tend to be dynamically efficient as well.

No market can be fully contestable. Some production process-es are characterized by very high fixed costs, so that only one sup-plier of the good or service associated with this process can operate efficiently in a market. For example, historically, the fixed cost of creating a network of cables and switching devices need-ed to provide basic telecommunications services was very high, and, in most regions, only one such network could be economical. In such cases of "natural monopoly," new entry is effectively blocked by high fixed costs; a second supplier would not be able to gar-ner enough revenue in competition with the incumbent supplier to cover these costs. Nonetheless, even for natural monopolies, the goal of public policy can be to maintain as much contestability as is possible. For example, whereas the provision of basic telecom-munications services might function in a noncontestable market, the market for value-added services sold over the network could be contestable. To maintain contestability in the market for such services, public policy might require that the basic service provider allow all sellers of such services access to the network, providing of course that such sellers pay fees to the basic provider to cover the provider's costs.[2]

It is thus argued that increased international market contestability should be the main goal of trade policy.[3] However, this goal sure-ly should extend well beyond trade policy *per se*. In nations hav-ing domestic competition policy,[4] maintaining contestability in domestic markets also can be a major goal.[5] This suggests a natural com-plementarity between trade policy and competition policy. If a mar-ket is internationally contestable, it likely is domestically contestable as well.[6]

There also can be a natural complementarity between the goals of competition policy and those of international investment pol-icy, especially that policy affecting FDI. FDI entails the extension of business operations of firms based in one nation into the mar-kets of other nations. In such situations, the "parent" firm is the investor and the overseas operation under its control is the invest-ment. An internationally contestable market is one that is, almost by definition, open to entry by foreign firms. If foreign firms choose to enter such a market, it is because they believe that they can offer better products or lower prices than can domestically owned rival firms. Open entry benefits consumers and, in addition, may induce domestic firms to improve their products or increase their efficiency. Thus open policies toward FDI are consistent with increased international market contestability. A question that naturally presents itself is whether WTO rules should include obligations of nations to maintain open policies toward direct investors. These, then, are the issues that the new WTO working parties will explore in depth.

BARRIERS TO MARKET CONTESTABILITY

If contestability is such a desirable end, one that embraces the goals of liberal trade policy, investment policy, and competition policy, why do governments pursue policies that are inconsistent with increased contestability? One reason is that in some cases, increased efficiency can be at variance with increased contestability. While such cases do exist, it is important not to overstate their frequency.

It is especially important to beware of false claims of efficiencies that do not exist. Such claims often are advanced by incumbent sellers wishing to defend policies or practices that shelter them from competition. Worldwide, for example, the leaders of telecommunications monopolies claim that increased competition would lead to decreased efficiency in the provision of telecommunications services and hence reduce consumer welfare. Serious analysis reveals that the opposite is true: Increased competition in the provision of telecommunications services results almost invariably in consumer welfare gains, not losses.[7] The challenge for public officials thus is not to limit competition in this sector but rather to find ways to increase contestability in the face of a high degree of natural monopoly that characterizes the provision of basic telecommunications service.

Indeed, most of the resistance to increased contestability is based on the concern that contestability tends to reduce rents garnered by incumbent firms and/or to reduce the ability of regulatory officials and other government agents to exercise powers over the relevant economic activities. Perhaps the strongest resistance to increased contestability comes from industries characterized by regulatory capture, ones where government regulators view their job precisely as defending incumbent sellers rather than maximizing the public interest.

The wisdom of such regulatory capture is being examined and questioned worldwide. In the United States and the United Kingdom, for example, deregulation began in earnest during the late 1970s, under the administrations of Jimmy Carter and Margaret Thatcher. In other nations, for example Japan and Taiwan, deregulation with the intent of reducing or eliminating regulatory capture has only begun much more recently. Nonetheless, in these two nations, the trend is clear. Of course, appropriate regulation is necessary in industries characterized by market failure. In fact, most government regulation in most countries began with a recognition of some sort of market failure. Such situations persist. Also, in some sectors, regulation is warranted to enforce standards of sanitation, safety, or health. The challenge for regulators is not to overregulate and, in particular, to guard against necessary regulations turning into measures guarding the interests of incumbent firms over potential new entrants. In other words, it is important to guard against regulation that suppresses the contestability of markets.

Changing circumstances can alter the need or desirability of regulation. The trend toward increased globalization of many industries leads to greater contestability. A danger is that a vicious circle might persist in cases where regulation originally designed to correct market failure will reduce international contestability of the relevant sector and hence, on the surface, provide a rationale for continued regulation.

CONTESTABILITY AND THE ARGUMENT FOR INVESTMENT POLICY IN THE WTO

The argument in favor of new rules on FDI in the WTO is as follows: (1) Increased globalization of markets for many goods and services is a trend that makes these markets increasingly contestable,[8] and (2) new investment rules in the WTO will impede governments from implementing measures or continuing existing measures that can offset the trend toward increased contestability of markets. Also, investment rules can serve to offset, or force governments to take steps to offset, private practices that can reduce contestability. Some examples are illustrative.

During the four decades spanning from roughly the Great Depression to the first oil crisis, the number of firms supplying the U.S. auto market declined precipitously, largely because of rising fixed costs of creating and upgrading dealer networks and rising fixed costs of developing and introducing new automobile models. Rising fixed costs led to the auto market becoming less and less contestable.

One consequence was that the surviving firms were increasingly able to appropriate rents in terms of higher prices from buyers of automobiles. Much of this rent in turn was captured by unionized workers. By the time of the first oil crisis, hourly compensation in the auto industry far exceeded the national average for workers in manufacturing, and the premium paid to auto workers could not be explained by their higher marginal productivity. Also, the design of U.S.-produced automobiles began to ossify. Chassis-on-frame body design prevailed, even though this design was obsolete by the early 1960s, and overly heavy autos were powered by fuel-guzzling, environmentally unfriendly V-8 engines. Thus the consequences of the lack of contestability were manifest: The market became dominated by an oligopoly of three firms that kept prices above those that could prevail in a competitive market. Product improvement was sluggish, and, by 1974, most U.S. autos were inappropriate for the changing market that, even before the onset of the energy crisis of 1974, already had begun to demand smaller, more fuel-efficient cars.

This shifting demand was met to a large extent by imports, especially from Japan. To enter the U.S. market, Japanese firms did face significant barriers. They had to invest in distribution facilities and after-market service networks.[9] Japanese autos not only embodied characteristics that the U.S. market had begun to demand, but also the quality of the product seemed to be higher, in terms of reliability and such characteristics as finish and precision. The benefits to U.S. consumers were manifest.

And yet, pressures mounted throughout the 1970s and into the early 1980s to limit imports of Japanese autos. The U.S. auto producers and the United Auto Workers were both adversely affected by the increased contestability of the market, and they worked tirelessly to persuade the U.S. government to implement measures to reduce imports. Voluntary export restraints were introduced early during the Reagan administration, in spite of its outstanding rhetorical commitment to the principles of free markets and free trade.[10] The quotas were set, however, at high enough levels so that the share of the total market held by Japanese firms was not reduced.

In response, Japanese firms upgraded the quality of products that came into the United States under quotas—in a sense, the Lexus replaced the Corolla—and established U.S. production facilities via foreign direct investment. U.S. policy welcomed Japanese plants located in states such as Tennessee and California. These facilities began to come on line during the middle to late 1980s. Local production by Japanese auto firms was not something that the U.S. automakers found that they could thwart as easily as imports. One consequence was that their U.S. rivals—the Detroit "Big Three"—were forced to upgrade their own products and find ways to cut their own costs. These firms, in a word, had to adjust their strategies to ones appropriate to a contestable market.

The big winner became the U.S. public. Compared to 15 or even 10 years ago, U.S. consumers have a choice of many more automobile models, and the average price of autos has fallen as a percentage of disposable personal income. Automobiles produced by domestic firms are no longer technically obsolete or, in terms of product characteristics, out of touch with market demand.

This example of the U.S. auto market illustrates that globalization of an industry fosters contestability; indeed, in this instance, globalization reversed what had been a trend toward less contestability.

Of equal importance, the United States avoided imposing restrictions on foreign investment as a response to the Japanese auto challenge. Legislation was introduced into the U.S. Congress during the middle 1980s that would have put domestic content requirements on cars manufactured domestically, a law that clearly was intended to discriminate against Japanese auto manufacturers. Other even more discriminatory measures were called for by a number of prominent parties. The domestic content bill would have been in violation of new world trade rules proposed by the United States, which were at the time under negotiation in the Uruguay Round but not yet in effect. These rules were implemented with the completion of the round under the aegis of the Agreement on Trade Related Investment Measures (TRIMs). The TRIMs agreement forbids domestic content requirements being placed on foreign investors as a condition of entry by national or subnational governments. The legal foundation is that these requirements are inconsistent with Article III of the General Agreement on Tariffs and Trade (GATT), national treatment for imports. In the end, Congress did not pass the domestic content bill.

Indeed, in the United States and some other advanced countries, treatment of FDI is already largely consistent with market contestability. In such nations, the main purpose of an international agreement on FDI would be to ensure that future governmental measures remain consistent and, in particular, to impede new legislation that hindered contestability. In many developing nations current policy regimes are anything but consistent. Many of these regimes were put into place during the 1960s and 1970s, a period of backlash against the colonial legacy by much of the developing world and fears of "neocolonialism" in much of the rest of the world. By and large, policies in the developing nations are moving away from the regimes put in place during this period, regimes that in retrospect have retarded economic development. Indeed, during the early 1990s the trend toward liberalization of policies toward FDI began more and more to resemble a stampede.[11] An international agreement on investment would, for these nations, serve as something of a beacon. It would establish universal norms against which national policies could be calibrated, and it would help to guide policymakers as they further liberalized these policies. Alas, certain developing nations, including ones that might benefit greatly from such a beacon, are opposed to an international agreement.

The member nations of the WTO were able to reach a consensus during the Uruguay Round on a limited WTO agreement on FDI, the TRIMs agreement. This agreement does in fact prohibit certain government measures that might reduce market contestability. In addition to domestic content requirements, they include export performance requirements and trade balancing requirements as conditions for entry. But these prohibited measures far from exhaust the arsenal that governments can deploy to discriminate against foreign direct investors. Thus there is widespread feeling among both policymakers and analysts that a much more comprehensive agreement on investment should be concluded.

The main provisions of such an agreement would include all of the following key items:

1. An obligation of governments at both national and subnational levels to extend national treatment to foreign investors on both a pre- and postestablishment basis.[12] Preestablishment national treatment is sometimes termed "right of establish-

ment." Under this provision, governments would be obligated to grant to foreign-controlled affiliates treatment under law and policy that was no less favorable than that granted to similar business entities under domestic control. This obligation would be a natural extension of GATT Article III, which requires that imported goods, once they clear the frontier, receive under law and policy a treatment no less favorable than that accorded to similar products produced domestically.

Governments could register exceptions and "derogations" (temporary exceptions) to national treatment, but these would have to be listed to make them "transparent." One objective of negotiations would be for governments to pressure each other to minimize such exceptions.

2. An obligation of governments to grant investors and their investments from every nation party to the agreement most-favored-nation treatment. All investors and their investments would be granted a treatment no less favorable than that granted to those investors from the most-favored nation.

Again, certain exceptions might be allowed to this obligation on a transparent basis.

3. Nations would be obligated to provide foreign investors with certain protection: No investment of a foreign investor could be expropriated except for a purpose consistent with the due process of law, on a nondiscriminatory basis, and with prompt and just compensation. And foreign investors would be allowed normal business transactions, such as transfer of funds, free movement of personnel who are not nationals of the country in which the investment is located, and so forth.

4. Governments would be obligated to curtail or refrain altogether from applying certain measures to foreign investors or their investments that have the effect of reducing market contestability. These would include additional trade-related measures not now covered by the existing TRIMs agreement. Also, many of the existing subsidies and subsidy-like measures ("investment incentives") used by governments in efforts to attract foreign direct investment might be curtailed or abolished.[13]

5. Importantly, the agreement would establish procedures for resolving disputes arising out of interpretation of the obligations, including alleged violations by governments. Parties with "standing" under this agreement would include foreign investors

as well as governments. (Under the WTO's current dispute settlement procedures, only member governments have "standing" to bring disputes to the WTO.) Care would have to be taken, however, to ensure that these procedures did not enable private parties to pursue "frivolous" cases, for the purpose of harassing competitors. Such an outcome could discourage market contestability rather than enforce it.

A number of agreements already exist that establish limited obligations on some governments along these lines. The extant agreements include over 900 bilateral investment treaties (BITs) and certain regional agreements, such as chapter 11 of the North American Free Trade Agreement (NAFTA). This chapter in fact contains almost all of the provisions just outlined. It applies, of course, only to Canada, Mexico, and the United States. The Asia Pacific Economic Cooperation forum (APEC) has endorsed a set of "Nonbinding Investment Principles" (NBIP) that embody, often in rather ambiguous language, most of these provisions, but, as the name implies, these are not binding upon nations. Rather they are seen as "principles to which the member nations [of APEC] might aspire." The member nations of the Organization for Economic Cooperation and Development (OECD) are, at this writing, negotiating a "multilateral agreement on investment" (MAI) that probably would embody most if not all of the provisions outlined. However, this agreement would attract few signatories outside the OECD countries, even though in principle non-OECD member nations are free to join the MAI. At a number of meetings held in international organizations during the past year, government representatives of numerous non-OECD nations have expressed reluctance to join an agreement when their governments did not take part in the negotiations.

The result of the various initiatives is something of a crazy quilt of international rules. They are often inconsistent with one another and with certain provisions of existing WTO agreements.[14] It would make sense that a single agreement be struck within the WTO, one consistent with other WTO obligations.

Whether the WTO actually will implement rules along these lines remains to be seen. The ministerial decision at Singapore to create a working party to investigate trade and investment was in fact a compromise between one group of nations that wanted some sort of work in this area to proceed (this bloc was led by Canada and Japan, with support from the European Union and a number of developing nations) and another group, led by India and Malaysia, that sought to block such work. The United States did not in fact oppose formation of the working party but rather opposed any effort to begin negotiations until after the OECD MAI exercise has been concluded. The United States contended that, given the position of many WTO member nations, any agreement that might emerge from WTO negotiations at this time would embody low standards, and that higher standards could be achieved within the OECD. "Higher standards" presumably means an unqualified statement of the principle of national treatment and relatively short lists of exceptions and derogations.[15]

The group of developing nations most actively opposed to trade and investment in the WTO argued that such an agreement would impede them from pursuing policies necessary for economic development without foreign domination. Many of the policies that those nations seem eager to preserve—such as the right to screen proposed investments by foreign interests—are contrary to the spirit of contestability. The record of such screening is, at best, dubious. Nonetheless, certain developing countries continue to impose arbitrary and discriminatory policies on the local activities of foreign firms.

This group of developing countries was led by India, which has one of the lowest rates of foreign direct investment in proportion to its size of any nation,[16] and Malaysia, which has one of the highest rates. This is an odd couple. The growth record of India has been dismal, whereas the growth rate of Malaysia has been remarkable. In fact, in many ways Malaysia serves almost as a laboratory of how a developing nation might use FDI to its benefit. Malaysia has in fact already pursued very open policies toward foreign investment, ones that are de facto rather far removed from the rhetoric of Prime Minister Mahatir Mohammed. Indeed, it is not clear how acceptance of the international obligations just listed would serve to reduce the benefits of FDI to the Malaysian economy (or, as some Malaysians have claimed, impose risks to national autonomy and sovereignty).

India, on the other hand, almost surely could benefit from a heavy dose of policy reform in order to make its markets function better. India is a nation rich in human capital. It has, for example, produced more scientists and engineers holding advanced university degrees than all but a handful of nations. It has the potential to enter an era of rapid growth, following neighboring countries in East Asia. Greater contestability of markets would be one important goal of a reform program. And a more open policy toward FDI would be one important means of implementing this goal.

Thus Malaysia's opposition to an agreement on FDI at the level of the WTO seems quite contrary to the policies the nation actually is pursuing. And India seems determined to defend policies that have failed to deliver anything but frustration to its own aspirations to become a major economic entity.

In the end, trade and investment survived as one of the WTO "new issues," but the ultimate outcome remains to be seen.

THE ROLE OF COMPETITION POLICY IN FOSTERING INTERNATIONAL CONTESTABILITY OF MARKETS

The role of competition policy at the multilateral level is even more controversial than the role of investment policy. This controversy extends even to strong advocates of market contestability. While there is agreement among such advocates that competition policy has a role to play in maintaining market contestability at some level, there is sharp disagreement whether competition policy should be implemented at the international level or only at the national level.[17]

Also, even if there were a consensus that multilateral competition policy would be a good thing, it faces a number of potent obstacles. Foremost is that, among nations that have competition policies and enforcement mechanisms in place, standards vary significantly from jurisdiction to jurisdiction. This variance occurs at the level both of substantive rules and enforcement vigilance. For example, with respect to enforcement, in the United States certain violations of antitrust law are criminal offenses, whereas in Europe all violations are treated as noncriminal civil offenses.[18] At the level of substance, certain practices in the United States that would be subject to the "rule of reason," (their legality would depend on specific circumstances) are per se illegal in Europe. In particular, certain vertical arrangements and practices that are illegal in Europe are subject to "efficiency defenses" in the United States.

However, European law often grants sectoral exemptions to illegal practices, whereas U.S. law does not.

The roles of competition enforcement agencies is also quite different. Directorate General IV of the European Commission acts as both an investigatory/prosecutorial agency and, to some extent, a judiciary agency. The United States has two such agencies, the Federal Trade Commission and the Antitrust Division of the Department of Justice, whose roles are limited to investigation and prosecution.[19] The judicial role in the United States is played by the U.S. court system. Private parties whose interests are aggrieved by alleged violations of antitrust law can sue in U.S. courts without going through the enforcement agencies; indeed, private antitrust cases are an important aspect of U.S. competition policy. In Europe, there are no such "private rights of action." In Japan, private cases are possible but not common. Parties in Japan who believe that their interests are adversely affected by alleged violations of antimonopolies law more commonly notify the Japanese Fair Trade Commission (JFTC).

These differences preclude one possibility for internationalization of competition law, notably that there be global "harmonization." The differences in substantive and enforcement standards are simply too great to allow harmonization.

However, nations seem to agree that a subset of restrictive business practices that most impedes international contestability of markets is particularly undesirable.[20] In other words, nations might agree to international standards for selected practices, even if these same nations cannot reach a consensus on competition standards writ large.

New York University law professor Eleanor Fox suggests that certain identified practices could be incorporated in a new agreement within the WTO that might be labeled trade-related antitrust measures or TRAMs, in the spirit of the existing agreements on trade-related investment measures and on trade-related aspects of intellectual property rights (TRIPs). These practices would include, in Fox's judgment: cartels with boycotts; vertical arrangements that tend to foreclose "outside" vendors or block established channels of distribution to new entrants; and monopolistic discriminations and exclusions.

Fox herself acknowledges that, while agreement on the first of these could be relatively straightforward, the second and third are problematic. It already has been noted that vertical arrangements that create elements of exclusivity also can enhance efficiency. And differences between U.S. and European doctrine exist with respect to substantive policy toward vertical arrangements, with the United States generally allowing efficiency defenses for arrangements that might be prohibited outright in Europe. Similar differences exist between U.S. and European doctrine with respect to the rights of firms to refuse to deal. The United States allows such refusal by monopolistic firms except under specific circumstances, whereas European policy holds that "dominant" firms have a duty not to discriminate among customers or refuse to deal.

How might such an agreement fit into the existing WTO rules pertaining to trade? One possibility would be to create the code as an extension of the existing Article XXIII of GATT, paragraph 1 of which deals with "nullification or impairment":

> If any [member nation] should consider that any benefit accruing to it directly or indirectly under this Agreement is being nullified or impaired or that the attainment of any objective of the Agreement is being impeded as the result of
>
> (a) the failure of another [member nation] to carry out its obligations under this Agreement, or
>
> (b) the application by another [member nation] of any measure, whether or not it conflicts with the provisions of this Agreement, or
>
> (c) the existence of any other situation the [aggrieved member nation] may, with a view to the satisfactory adjustment of the matter, make written representations or proposals to the other [member nation or nations] which it considers to be concerned. Any [member nation] thus approached shall give sympathetic consideration to the representations or proposals made to it.

Paragraph 2 of Article XXIII indicates that if no satisfactory adjustment is effected between the disputing nations, the issue can be brought before the WTO dispute settlement panel. Indeed, from the language of this article, it would seem logical that impairment of market access by a private business action that might itself be remedied by competition policy is tantamount to nullification or impairment of a benefit (in this case, increased exports enabled by the reduced border measures brought about by GATT) as a consequence of (c), "the existence of any other situation." Thus, under the article, it would seem legitimate that "written representations or proposals" be made by the aggrieved nation (the country that suffers reduced exports) to the offending nation (where the market access barrier exists).

However, there are two flaws in this logic. The first is that in 1960, a GATT Working Party recommended against the application of Article XXIIIc as a means to address restrictive private business practices, arguing that the application of GATT was limited to governmental actions. This recommendation was adopted by the GATT "contracting parties" (in today's language, the WTO member nations) and hence is now considered part of WTO law. The second flaw is that WTO Dispute Settlement Panels do not pass judgment on member governments' failure to enforce their own national laws and policies where these laws and policies are not germane to specific WTO obligations.[21] For a panel to do so in the case of competition policy would not only set a new precedent, it would be a precedent that member governments would almost surely not accept.

These two considerations suggest that the way forward is for the WTO member nations to consider explicitly undoing the 1960 Working Party recommendation and to negotiate criteria under which Article XXIIIc could be invoked in situations involving private business practices. Adoption of Fox's proposals would be a sensible step in this direction.

It is worth the effort to create an agreement on TRAMs along the lines proposed by Fox. Her approach—concentrate on those specific areas of competition policy that pertain most closely to problems of market access—would lead negotiators into territory where different nations have different substantive standards. But this excursion into difficult territory would be truncated. Negotiators would not be forced to attempt to harmonize all of competition law, but only a portion of it. Furthermore, with respect to at least one issue (cartels with boycotts), there is the possibility of fairly ready agreement on standards. Indeed, an agreement on only this one issue would be worthwhile. With respect to the other two issues (vertical arrangements impeding market access, and discrimination and exclusion by monopolistic firms), negotiations would be more thorny. The contentious terrain involves what exceptions would be allowed, including whether a general exception based on an efficiency defense would be allowed. Agreement on common standards might or might not be achievable. Whatever the outcome, it certainly would be worth a try.

CONCLUSIONS

At the 1996 Singapore ministerial meeting of the WTO, trade and competition policy and trade and investment policy were among the most contentious issues. The decisions to form working parties to study these issues and to make recommendations to the WTO ministers at a future time reflected a lack of consensus as to what action, if any, is needed. But these same decisions also represented a consensus that the issues are important.

To make markets more contestable internationally, action on these issues is necessary. There is, however, no single course of action. Rather, there is need for an international debate. The debate has the potential to be rich, and the 1996 decisions of the WTO ministers ensure that the debate will proceed.

Great progress has been made in improving the architecture of the world trading system with the completion of the Uruguay Round. However, this very progress has served to reveal gaps. Satisfactory agreements on trade and investment policy and trade and competition policy are important components toward creating a complete architecture. The working parties created by the ministers in Singapore represent opportunities to move forward on these important issues. These opportunities must not be lost.

NOTES

1. For Kodak's account, see Dewey Ballantine, "Japanese Market Barriers in Consumer Photographic Film and Paper," Washington, DC, 1995. For Fuji's account, see Willkie, Farr, and Gallagher, "Rewriting History: Kodak's Revisionist Account of the Japanese Consumer Photographic Market." Submitted to the United States Trade Representative, July 31, 1995, chapter 6.

2. This requirement is unlikely if the network is a government-owned monopoly. Thus, for example, the United States Federal Communications Commission (FCC) believes that publicly owned telecommunications monopolies in a number of countries overcharge access by overseas callers to local networks. The costs to U.S. callers are estimated to be $3 billion to $4 billion a year. See Ben Petrazzini, "Global Telecom Talks: A Trillion-Dollar Deal," *Policy Analyses in International Economics* 44 (Washington, DC: Institute for International Economics, 1996).

3. Geza Feketekuty and Robert A. Rogowsky, "The Scope, Implications, and Economic Rationale of a Competition-Oriented Approach to Future Multilateral Trade Negotiations," *The World Economy* (Supplementary

Issue: *Global Trade Policy 1996*) (1996), pp. 167–182; Edward M. Graham and Robert Z. Lawrence, "Measuring the International Contestability of Markets," *Journal of World Trade* 30, no. 5 (1996), pp. 5–20; Americo Beviglia Zampetti and Pierre Sauvé, "Onwards to Singapore: The International Contestability of Markets and the New Trade Agenda," *The World Economy* 19, no. 3 (1996), pp. 333–334.

4. Competition policy is often termed "antimonopolies" or "antitrust" policy.

5. Competition policy sometimes allows an "efficiency defense" where market concentration is high or where business practices result in some sort of exclusion. To establish an efficiency defense, the firms holding large market share or using a "restrictive business practice" (RBP) must demonstrate greater producer efficiency than would be the case if the market were less concentrated or the RBP did not exist and, in addition, demonstrate that the efficiency results also in greater output and lower prices to consumers than would otherwise prevail. In these situations, the efficiency itself can create an entry barrier and hence be at variance with the goal of increasing contestability. Natural monopoly is an example of a situation where high seller concentration results in efficiency. One dilemma of competition policy is assessing the correct trade-off between increased efficiency and decreased contestability.

6. The goals of competition policy and trade policy are not identical, however. In some cases, there might be overriding reasons to prevent a market from being internationally contestable (a reason might be national security), yet the goal of competition policy might still be to maintain a high degree of domestic contestability. Also, in some cases, foreign firms might achieve such high degrees of efficiency as to exclude domestic firms; it then might be argued that international contestability of the market is inconsistent with domestic contestability.

7. Petrazzini, "Global Telecom Talks."

8. The term "globalization," when applied to a market or an industry, is somewhat ill-defined, but the essence is that demand in any national market in such an industry can be met by producers based anywhere in the world. Demand can be met by exportation, by local production enabled by FDI, or some combination of the two. Increasingly, indeed, "global" firms combine trade and local production as a means of supplying markets all over the world. Edward M. Graham, *Global Corporations and National Governments* (Washington, DC: Institute for International Economics, 1996).

9. In some instances Japanese firms were able to sell their products through established dealers already carrying U.S.-made autos. During the 1950s, the then-common practice of U.S. automakers requiring that dealers exclusively carry their product had been ruled illegal under U.S. antitrust laws, and Japanese firms were able to benefit from this ruling.

10. See David D. Hale, "The Post-Chicago Era in American Economic Policy," *The Marcus Wallenberg Papers on International Finance* 2, no. 3. (1988), pp. 25–36.

11. See United Nations Conference on Trade and Development (UNCTAD), *World Investment Report 1994* (Geneva: United Nations, 1994).

12. In most cases, the "investment" would be a local business firm under the control of a foreign-owned multinational firm.

13. Under the existing WTO Agreement on Subsidies and Countervailing Measures, subsidies to foreign investors used in conjunction with prohibited TRIMs are prohibited. It has been argued by legal experts (consulted by this author) that a wide variety of investment incentives might be challengable under this agreement. However, for one reason or another, governments have been unwilling to bring cases before the WTO. A future agreement might therefore serve to clarify the scope of the existing agreement (rather than to create an entirely new set of rules) by specifying exactly what types of subsidies or subsidy-like measures granted to foreign investors should be considered either prohibited or actionable under existing rules.

14. Various aspects of the inconsistencies are discussed in Graham, *Global Corporations and National Governments,* and in Edward M. Graham and Pierre Sauvé, "Towards a Rule-based Regime for Investment: Issues and Challenges," in Pierre Sauvé and Daniel Schwanen, eds., *Investment Rules for the Global Economy,* Policy Study 28 (Toronto: C. D. Howe Institute, 1996). The latter in particular discusses inconsistencies with WTO obligations that could arise as a result of accession to a future OECD MAI.

15. Even assuming that it is true that higher standards can be agreed within the OECD group, why not seek a plurilateral agreement in the WTO at the same time? (A plurilateral agreement is one that only a subgroup of WTO member nations sign.) Plurilateral agreements currently exist within the WTO—for example, the Agreement on Government Procurement. Such an arrangement might more readily be made consistent with other WTO agreements. In particular, a WTO plurilateral agreement might make use of the existing Dispute Settlement Understanding, appropriately modified so as to create a means by which firms would have limited standing to bring disputes to the WTO. Also, a WTO plurilateral agreement might gain more adherents over a decade than an OECD agreement.

16. See UNCTAD, *World Investment Report 1996* (Geneva: United Nations, 1996), appendix tables 5 and 6.

17. Thus, for example, there is little argument among advocates of international contestability that all nations should have competition laws that are adequately enforced.

18. The latter is true both at the national level and the level of the European Union. Competition law within the European Union is enabled by Treaty of Rome articles 85, 88, 92, 93, and 97 and by the Mergers Regulation. Directorate General IV of the European Commission enforces competition law at the EU level and, indeed, has certain rather extraordinary powers not possessed by other agencies of the European Union. For an analysis of EU competition policy, see Raymond Vernon and Kalypso Nicholaidis, "Competition Policy in the European Union," in Edward M. Graham and J. David Richardson, eds., *Global Competition Policies* (Washington, DC: Institute for International Economics, forthcoming).

For a comparison of U.S. and EU law and policy, see Eleanor Fox and Robert G. Pitofsky, "U.S. and the EU: Prospects for Cooperation and Harmonization of Competition Law," in Graham and Richardson, *Global Competition Policies.*

19. However, the ability of these agencies to conclude "consent decrees" does give them some quasi-judiciary powers.

20. Eleanor Fox, "Towards World Antitrust and Market Access," *American Journal of International Law* 91, no. 1 (1997), pp. 1–25.

21. Failure of a government to enforce its own law where this law reflected a WTO obligation would, of course, be considered by a WTO panel.

Chapter 12

Anticorruption as an International Policy Issue: Its Origins and Implications

R. Michael Gadbaw and Timothy J. Richards

If *Time* magazine designated a "policy issue of the year," "anti-corruption" would almost certainly have graced its front cover in December 1996. Thanks to the significance given the issue in the addresses of both Michel Camdessus, the head of the International Monetary Fund (IMF), and James Wolfensohn, the leader of the World Bank, the international implications of corruption became the most talked about new issue at the annual meetings of the IMF and World Bank. Then at their meeting in Singapore in December, the world's trade ministers placed anticorruption on the agenda of the World Trade Organization (WTO) as that institution charted its course into the next century. This attention from the IMF, the World Bank, and the WTO comes in the wake of impressive progress in the Organization for Economic Cooperation and Development (OECD) and the Organization of American States (OAS) in identifying international initiatives to tackle the corruption problem. These initiatives amazed those who warned that governments would not acknowledge an issue that reflects so directly on their own governance. Indeed, the current attention paid to fighting corruption is remarkable given the suddenness of its ascent on the policy scene, prompting some cynics to ask what makes this issue so important, whether it deserves the preeminent role it is being accorded, and if all this interest will have any lasting impact on the root causes of corruption, which are as old as civilized society itself.

Journalists, editorial writers, authors, and academics are rushing into print with their own personal analyses of the issue and policy prescriptions. Some press the point that, like poverty, corruption will always be with us. Others insist that the world in fact is changing in ways that will have a permanent impact on this problem. What is remarkable is how every week brings fresh material to illustrate the pervasiveness and significance of corruption. No country or region or form of government seems immune. In India, the world's largest democracy, corruption was a major factor in the electoral overthrow of the Congress Party. In Japan, corruption scandals helped bring an end to the Liberal Democratic Party's decades-old rule. And similar concerns are eating at the roots of the ruling party's domination of Mexican politics. President Jiang Zemin has launched a major anticorruption initiative in China, citing Mao's warning that corruption can threaten the Communist Party's rule like no other problem. The former rulers of Korea were imprisoned for their violations of the public trust. Waves of prosecutions have swept the traditional democracies of Europe and the United States, raising the stakes for chief executive officers and government officials who engage in illicit practices.

It is impossible to understand the significance of these developments without recognizing two historical forces that have converged to give impetus and direction to the anticorruption movement. Internally, the forces of political accountability are demanding that governments take responsibility for illicit practices, while externally, the forces of globalization are pressing for reforms to remove the barriers that corruption places in the way of global trade and investment. These forces have transformed the corruption issue from one primarily of ethics and human behavior to one that, at its core, relates to international economic development, the effective operation of markets, good governance, and competitiveness. They also have led many countries and institutions to give priority to the fight against large-scale corruption, thereby avoiding the pitfalls of cultural relativism that inevitably pervade debates over bureaucratic or petty corruption.

As corruption is a global issue, only international cooperation can address it effectively, a fact that is demonstrated by a review of the recent activities in the OECD, OAS, the Asian Development Bank (ADB), and the WTO. Moreover, the very breadth of this response is essential to the effectiveness of the overall effort. An analysis of the various policy options indicates that only an international and integrated approach that attacks the root causes of corruption from many different but reinforcing directions has any prospect of making a lasting impact on the problem.

THE CONVERGING FORCES OF POLITICAL ACCOUNTABILITY AND GLOBALIZATION

Concern about corruption is not a new phenomenon; what is new is that corruption has taken center stage in the political arena. Interestingly, the general public is way ahead of academics and policy analysts on this issue. The scholarly literature is filled with works that struggle to find a theoretical basis other than ethical concerns for challenging corruption. Indeed, in the past some economists argued the merits of corruption, describing the practice as a means of greasing the wheels of bureaucracy or mitigating the distorting effects of overregulation. Even corruption on a grand scale was seen as simply a matter of shifting monopoly rents from one group to another.

The effort to address corruption as an ethical issue raises a number of quandaries. What is the line between customary gift giving and bribery? How can different cultural attitudes be reconciled? What about societies where government service is an accepted form of entitlement to self-enrichment or where bribes are simply a form of user fee, used to supplement the incomes of intentionally underpaid civil servants? After all, what is a bribe? Even the U.S. Foreign Corrupt Practices Act (FCPA) seems to struggle with the distinction between a "facilitating payment" as a subset of bribes that are not illegal under the FCPA and the bribes that constitute a criminal offense. In the end, isn't bribery so susceptible to the vagaries of cultural relativism as to render trying to challenge it in a systematic way pointless—or even counterproductive?

But in recent years, in country after country, in all regions and all major cultures of the world, this cynicism seems to have been swept away—by magistrates in Italy and France; prosecutors in Germany, the United States, and Japan; and voters in India, Mexico, Korea, and a host of other countries. If one looks into the facts behind these developments, it is clear that the magnitude and scope of the practices for which government and corporate officials are being held accountable have simply overwhelmed the notions of the cultural relativists. The practices being challenged involve millions, tens of millions, and hundreds of millions of dollars paid to obtain a deal or influence a decision. Illicit payments typically are going toward the personal enrichment of individual officials, not into government coffers, and the government decisions bought by the corruption clearly do not serve the public's overall interest.

Politics is propelling corruption into the limelight in amazingly similar patterns across a range of countries. As journalists break through taboos that once prevented informed reporting of juicy details, and, as electronic communications allow the widespread distribution of information free of government control, political and corporate icons are finding themselves facing removal from office and criminal prosecution. The demand for accountability is part of the broader shift to economic performance as a primary determinant of government legitimacy. The end of the Cold War also may have helped countries confront corruption among political leaders without fear that scandals would weaken their nation's ability to resist the paramount external threat.

Globalization also is having a profound effect on both the nature of corruption and the means available to address its underlying causes. The magnitude of international transactions and the major scandals too often associated with them spotlight the distorting effects of illicit payments on government decisions and economic growth. While the complexity of international deals and the technology that allows the instantaneous movement of funds make the detection of illicit practices more difficult, the greater transparency and oversight that comes when economies are exposed to international markets also brings more intensive scrutiny. All countries, especially emerging markets, are sensitive to the impact that a country's image for fairness and consistency can have on its ability to attract investment and financing. Moreover, the involvement of a community of international developers, traders, financiers, and service providers in increasingly multilateralized deals is driving the structure of major investments and projects toward an international standard in order to mitigate risk and lower transactions costs.

Some see the forces of globalization—economic integration, elimination of barriers to trade and investment, privatization, and decentralization—as creating opportunities for corruption on a new and grander scale. They argue that privatization creates fertile ground for rent seeking and that global networks of communications and finance make monitoring and controlling corruption more difficult. They argue that only in the long run will other aspects of globalization bring relief.

While clearly globalization has changed the nature of corruption, its more salient impact has been in bringing to bear forces that will curtail and ultimately control the most destructive manifestations of the problem. Much of the economic analysis of corruption dates from the 1960s and 1970s, when the forces of globalization were only beginning to open markets and transform economies away from autarkic, central planning. In the environment of the 1990s, corruption has a more direct impact on economic growth because other negative factors have been cleared away, leaving this issue as one of the big remaining barriers.

While the linkages between corruption and economic growth are not fully understood, it is increasingly clear that corruption has a direct and adverse impact on the effective operation of markets, domestic support for economic liberalization, successful privatization initiatives, and the availability of resources for education and other infrastructure policies—all of which facilitate faster growth.[1] In other words, analysis is catching up to the instincts already being expressed in the political arena.

The experience of companies engaged in international trade and investment confirms this message. For international companies, corruption heightens the importance of a rule-based system at both the national and the international level. China provides a case in point. Chinese officials argue that the United States is being too aggressive in pressing for market opening measures because China's market is already open in substance, if not in form. For example, senior Chinese trade officials argue that around 1995 the nominal average tariff on China's imports was 42 percent while the effective average rate was only 4 percent. The difference is due largely to the fact that many products enter China illegally, without appropriate import duties being paid. For China this is evidence that the Chinese market is more open than the United States is prepared to recognize. This line of argument, however, ignores the fact that companies unwilling to engage in illicit practices face discrimination.

This discrimination is potentially just as damaging to the interests of the host country, as it harms companies that prefer to play by the rules. If customs duties or taxes are evaded routinely, the state loses revenue along with its legitimacy. China needs law-abiding companies as much as companies in China need the rule of law.

The key mechanism that makes the process of globalization incompatible with corruption is the international competition for infrastructure projects. Policies that increasingly open up the infrastructure market have sparked an explosion in the number of companies involved in all aspects of infrastructure projects—from developers to engineers, equipment suppliers, service providers, and financiers. For example, in the first independent power project tendered by the Egyptian government, some 54 bidders sought to be qualified; from that group, some 34 moved to the next stage. With this degree of competition, and with the increasing use of transparent bidding systems, comes pressure on prices that ultimately eliminates monopoly rents and curtails the scope for corruption, all to the benefit of the host country.

Another dimension of infrastructure competition that is forcing change is the tendency to diversify risk by involving a mix of companies with different national affiliations. This situation increasingly means that an international standard is emerging and that wherever an American company is involved, that standard includes ethical business practices because of the FCPA.

As globalization is forcing internationalization of the issue of corruption, domestic politics are beginning to resonate off international concerns, driven by the rapid flow of information and sensitivity of national governments to international investors. For example, the French supported the groundbreaking OECD anti-corruption initiative in 1994 because domestically they could not appear soft on corruption at a time when politically charged scandals were playing out in Italy and Germany and notorious corruption scandals involving French parties were starting to break. At the same time, Latin American countries felt the need to change international attitudes about the commitment of their governments to good governance and pressed for a treaty on corruption as good public relations as well as good substance.

In short, domestic politics lead governments to compete for international investment. The market forces (and frequently the legal requirements) that accompany competitive international investment then can reduce opportunities for and the level of corrupt activity. At the same time, globalization can give national politicians the cover they need to take actions they know are right.

PRIORITIES: GRAND CORRUPTION VERSUS PETTY CORRUPTION

The focus of political accountability and globalization on examples of grand corruption suggests a direction and priority for policy initiatives. International attention and political accountability is focusing attention on grand corruption because that is where the problem has its greatest impact, politically and economically. The magnitude of the issue is suggested by a U.S. government study that found that between April 1994 and September 1996, U.S. companies encountered bribery by their competitors on at least $64 billion worth of transactions.[2] All of these instances of bribery fall into the category of grand corruption. By turning attention to cases where large payoffs are being made to obtain big international deals, the international community avoids divisive debates over whether a "bribe" actually was involved or whether cultural norms suggest a different approach in different countries.

A priority focus on the problem of grand corruption is also key to making progress on the much more complicated and intractable problems of bureaucratic and petty corruption that plague many countries.[3] The linkage is a direct one. Where corruption on a grand scale is tolerated by the leadership of a country, there is a corrosive effect on the society as a whole. A kind of "culture of corruption" emerges in which people feel justified in getting their piece of the action by illicit means. Where this mentality takes hold, governance becomes impossible.[4] The civil authorities lack the moral authority to enforce their own laws, and the basic rules of society break down: Bribes are necessary to obtain even the most modest government services. Inevitably this kind of breakdown has an impact on the prospects for economic growth.

INTERNATIONAL POLICY INITIATIVES

With this background, it is helpful to review some of the most important policy initiatives at the international level, not for the purposes of providing a comprehensive catalogue but rather to emphasize the breadth of the international response to corruption during the 1990s.

The Organization for Economic Cooperation and Development

The most important action yet undertaken against bribery and corruption has occurred in the OECD. Its actions in this area began with its 1994 approval of the "Recommendation on Bribery of Foreign Public Officials in International Business Transactions." Unable to forge a consensus at that time on what specific measures the parties should take, the negotiators agreed to include a menu of items and to call upon members to draw from that menu in their individual action programs. The recommendation provided a basis to keep working on the issue and allowed OECD members to mutually reinforce one another's actions through periodic reviews. It also opened the door for further OECD measures by proposing that members "take concrete and meaningful steps, including examining tax legislation, regulation and practices insofar as they may indirectly favor bribery."[5] This statement was significant because most developed countries currently allow bribes paid overseas to be deducted as a legitimate business expense.[6] The 1994 OECD recommendation subsequently was supported by the Transatlantic Business Dialogue, a forum through which business executives in the United States and the European Union make policy recommendations to their governments.

Spurred by the 1994 recommendation, the OECD Committee on Fiscal Affairs reviewed the tax policies of OECD members and recommended that "those Member countries that do not disallow the deductibility of bribes to foreign public officials reexamine such treatment with the intention of denying this deductibility."[7] The OECD Ministerial Council approved this recommendation on April 12, 1996. Individual OECD members will now decide how they will implement it. Ensuring full implementation is extremely important because some countries already have suggested that the recommendation will be implemented in a half-hearted way.

The OECD recommendation on tax deductibility is intended to eliminate a government incentive that encourages bribery of foreign officials. When fully implemented, the tax deductibility recommendation will move governments toward a neutral stance on the question of foreign illicit payments. For some OECD members, particularly the United States, neutrality on the issue of bribery, while a step in the right direction, was insufficient. As a result, the OECD is working on the additional step of placing itself squarely in opposition to bribery in international transactions.

In 1995 the OECD Committee on International Investment and Multinational Enterprises (CIME) asked a Working Group on Bribery to consider criminalizing the payment of bribes to foreign public officials as well as making appropriate changes to accounting and auditing procedures. In late fall 1997, this work culminated in a convention that calls for the criminalization of bribery and is expected to be signed by all OECD countries and five non-OECD members. Adoption, implementation, and full enforcement of an OECD recommendation in this area would constitute another significant "hard" step toward addressing the issue of illicit payments between government officials and foreign companies.

In addition to the direct impact they may have eventually, the OECD actions have increased the visibility of corruption as an issue and have led to the adoption of anticorruption measures by other international institutions. The North American Development Bank, created in conjunction with the North American Free Trade Agreement (NAFTA), for instance, included in its eligibility guidelines a prohibition on bribery related to bank activities.

World Trade Organization

As demonstrated by the U.S. government's statistic that bribery has been encountered by U.S. firms on at least $64 billion worth of projects over an 18-month period, corruption exerts a powerful influence on international trade flows, often offsetting the market forces that the WTO agreements bring to bear on international transactions. This fact argues strongly for a WTO role in ensuring that corruption does not undercut its disciplines. The question, however, is what sort of role is appropriate for the WTO. In the immediate future, pressing for explicit new WTO rules on corruption as a stand-alone issue is likely to be counterproductive. The consensual basis on which the WTO operates means that new issues must be developed over a period of years before they can be addressed effectively. Moreover, many countries that recognize they have an internal problem with corruption would not wish to be dragged before a WTO panel.

The most effective and practical approach to addressing corruption within the WTO lies, therefore, not in enacting new anticorruption rules per se but in applying, and where necessary expanding and improving, existing WTO rules and principles that deter corruption. Nowhere is this more appropriate than in the core WTO principle of transparency. Among its many beneficial aspects, transparency in the development and administration of laws and regulations applied to international trade eliminates the conditions under which corruption can flourish. Article X of the General Agreement on Tariffs and Trade (GATT) already addresses this general issue. Where corruption undermines a country's ability to carry out the obligations of Article X, WTO members should consider addressing that matter under the existing WTO consultation, trade policy review mechanism, and dispute settlement procedures. Where there exists a pattern and practice of corruption that undermines one country's ability to trade with another in particular product areas, aggrieved parties also could consider addressing the issue under existing WTO rules as a case in which tariff concessions have been nullified or impaired by the presence of corruption. As a practical matter, however, given the current level of political sensitivity to corruption issues in most countries, use of Article X or even the trade policy review mechanism to challenge corruption in a WTO member would be widely perceived as introducing an entirely new and largely unwelcome level of politicization into the WTO. For this reason WTO and GATT rules have never been used to address corruption.

Among existing WTO agreements, the Government Procurement Agreement (GPA) provides one of the best mechanisms by which to make transparency itself, and not corruption, the issue in a dispute. This focus has the further advantage of sidestepping difficult issues of proof; usually it is much harder to prove corrupt bids than to prove that the bidding system is nontransparent. There is, however, a major gap in the GPA coverage: It is optional for WTO members, and most WTO members will not join the current agreement because it entails an all-or-nothing approach to the elimination of domestic preferences. This means that government procurement in most countries is not subject to effective transparency provisions. The low level of international discipline on government procurement is a serious problem for the WTO system because government procurement represents such a high percentage of economic activity in many current and prospective WTO members .[8] In fact, government procurement carried out without transparency is one of the forms of economic activity most likely to generate corruption.

Recognizing the need to bring government procurement fully into the WTO system and the impossibility of doing that with the current GPA, the United States proposed in 1996 that WTO members negotiate a new agreement on transparency, openness, and due process in government procurement. The initiative was supported by the members of the GPA and nominally, at least, by the members of the Asia Pacific Economic Cooperation forum.

The objective of the GPA members was to launch negotiations at the December 1996 WTO Ministerial Meeting held in Singapore. This objective was frustrated by a group of approximately ten developing countries led by Malaysia and including Uganda, Cuba, Zimbabwe, and Malawi. These opponents expressed skepticism that the proposed agreement would yield any benefits for their economies and effectively blocked the effort to launch negotiations. Instead the WTO ministers established a working group to study the issue and make recommendations about elements to include in an agreement, "taking into account national policies." This step, while short of what backers of the agreement had sought, represents a substantial move toward expanding the use of procurement disciplines that can reduce corruption.

Substantively, the initiative finally will address, in a realistic manner, the age-old problem of procurement reform. Procurement reform is to trade policy what the sound barrier has been to commercial aircraft: the barrier that has proven too difficult to penetrate on a commercially viable basis. When GATT was adopted in 1947, public procurement was allowed to be a major loophole in the nondiscrimination provisions of Article III (national treatment). This loophole continued until the Tokyo Round attempted to close it by the elaboration of the Public Procurement Agreement of 1979.

A similar fate befell procurement in the 1957 Treaty of Rome that created the European Community. The Europeans found it impossible to address procurement until some 30 years later, when a series of directives were promulgated to open procurement within the Community. While the 1992 Single Market Initiative gave impetus to this effort, progress in implementing the directives has been slow. No less a player than Germany is now subject to an enforcement proceeding in the European Court of Justice for its failure to implement properly the remedial measures for addressing violations of European Union procurement rules.

Statistics on government procurement from foreign sources—even among nations of the European Union—demonstrate that initiatives undertaken to date have been largely ineffective in opening procurement regimes.[9] What is needed is an admission that the approach the WTO has taken in this important area has been a failure. The reason for this failure is precisely because the GPA involves an all-or-nothing commitment—either free trade in procurement or no commitments at all. Naturally, most countries are unwilling to make such a quantitative change in a regime that is a major source of political patronage.

The story of the new transparency agreement sheds light on the extent of the opposition to membership in the GPA. The supporters of the transparency agreement originally described it as an "interim" agreement, with the thought that it ultimately would lead to full participation in the existing GPA. The concept of this linkage was so controversial that the supporters of the new agreement have quietly dropped the word "interim" from the agreement's name. In fact, a better approach may be to reverse the original concept entirely and look instead to how the new agreement can form the basis for eventually supplanting the existing GPA.

The greatest advantage of the proposed new alternative is that it offers a practical approach to achieving the ultimate elimination of buy-national procurement preferences. By starting with a commitment to transparency and the identification of existing restrictions, it represents a first step toward following the same sensible approach that was taken to tariffs. Later these restrictions can be translated into the equivalent of a tariff, namely a price preference, and the margin of preference can be included in a schedule of concessions that are then subject to negotiated reduction over time.

This simple formula offers the potential for penetrating the procurement sound barrier. In turn, an important step in tackling corruption will be taken.

Regional Initiatives: OAS and the Asian Development Bank

The InterAmerican Convention Against Corruption was adopted on March 29, 1996, by the Organization of American States. As of January 1997, 31 nations of the hemisphere had signed the convention, and it had been ratified by Paraguay, Bolivia, Argentina, and Mexico. This convention, when fully ratified, will require its signatories to criminalize making or receiving bribes. The convention also establishes requirements for state-to-state cooperation in investigations of corrupt behavior and includes provisions for extradition. Furthermore, it commits the nations of the hemisphere to take a leadership role in seeking similar commitments around the world.

The explicit cooperation between the countries of the Americas in addressing the criminal aspects of illicit practices stands in dramatic contrast to that of the Asian countries. While the negative initial reaction of some Asian countries to the U.S. initiatives in the WTO has been seen as a refusal to recognize the extent of corruption in their economies, this conclusion shows an insensitivity to Asian values. In fact, the Asian Development Bank was the first international financial institution to incorporate in its lending policies an explicit policy to address "good governance." When examined carefully, it is clear that this policy approach goes to the core issues underlying corruption in Asia in a way that may be more effective in building support for remedial action there than the higher-profile efforts of the West.

The ADB's approach incorporates into the bank's lending framework an explicit consideration of the impact of a funded project on the quality of governance in the recipient country. This review in the context of a lending program promotes transparency, accountability, open competition, and rule-based decision-making and provides a potentially effective means of introducing reforms in a positive and reinforcing setting. The bank's experience with this policy approach has much to offer to other international financial institutions as they address this issue.

International Financial Institutions

The 1996 annual meetings of the World Bank and the IMF marked a turning point for the involvement of the premier international financial institutions in addressing corruption. Their attention is a reminder that international initiatives against corruption are driven not solely by moral or ethical considerations but by a hard-nosed recognition that corruption stands in the way of other policy objectives, particularly economic growth and the efficient operation of international markets.

The resources these institutions can bring to bear in understanding the linkages between corruption and economic development are making the case for international cooperation. Studies to date find a correlation between corruption and the lack of adequate spending on education, which—as a recent World Bank study of East Asian economies demonstrated—is one of the key factors in that region's strong growth patterns. More recent studies by World Bank and IMF economists show conclusively that in countries that are moving down the path toward liberalization and economic openness, anticorruption initiatives are an essential part of effective economic growth strategies.

In addition to providing sound analytical foundations for anticorruption initiatives, the international financial institutions are addressing the problem in two other dimensions: lending conditionality and procurement reform. The World Bank has launched a program on both these fronts, with particular emphasis on procurement reform. It is certain to have an impact, given the importance of World Bank lending in the emerging markets of the world and its engagement with the major players on the supply side of the equation.

PRIVATE SECTOR INITIATIVES

One of the most effective ways to address grand corruption is through voluntary efforts within the business community. By adopting and faithfully implementing serious corporate policies against corruption, companies themselves can cut back the supply side of the grand corruption equation. During 1996 the International Chamber of Commerce (ICC) "invited companies worldwide to adopt rules of conduct designed to combat extortion and bribery in international trade."[10] In adopting this position, the ICC also published a model corporate policy.

Recognizing the value of this approach, the U.S. government has begun to condition the availability of its programs on the maintenance of corporate anticorruption policies. The first instance of this new approach was announced in the National Export Strategy published in October 1996 by the Department of Commerce. U.S. Advocacy Guidelines now require more than simple compliance with the FCPA; rather, beneficiaries of U.S. government advocacy are now required to maintain and enforce policies against corruption in their worldwide operations. Initial steps in this direction also were taken for programs supported by the Export-Import Bank of the United States (EXIM) and the Overseas Private Investment Corporation (OPIC).

As a complement to the ICC effort, other business groups, such as the European-American Industrial Council, have taken the initiative in publicly calling for stronger national and EU policies to address bribery and corruption. One litmus test of business support for a real anticorruption crusade will be the ability of the Transatlantic Business Dialogue to reach a consensus.

A FORMULA FOR SUCCESS

The fact that the many initiatives just described have been undertaken indicates that anticorruption is likely to remain a major issue on the international policy agenda. There is, however, always the risk that some new and misguided policy initiatives could alienate potential allies in the anticorruption initiative or that a diffusion of effort could dilute the most meaningful exercises and ultimately bring back the sense of futility that dominated much of the last half century. Consequently, there is a need to fit all anticorruption efforts into a clear overall context and to maintain a sense of priority.

Level Up, Not Down

For many years after the passage of the Foreign Corrupt Practices Act, debate in the United States centered around whether the act should be repealed. Critics of the FCPA saw it as an unnecessary burden on the competitiveness of American business that had no realistic chance of actually influencing either the supply of or demand for bribes. As American companies came to learn that bribery and success in international markets did not go hand in hand, they began to change their attitudes; now a clear majority of U.S. companies operating internationally see the FCPA not as part of the problem but as part of the solution. Most U.S. companies operating abroad have strong anticorruption policies, which they support with programs for training, counseling, and crisis management. Moreover, they see the advantages of operating on a purely commercial basis without the distortions of bribery and the culture that accompanies it.

Criminalization of foreign bribery along with the creation of effective corporate anticorruption policies should be the first objective of anticorruption initiatives. This approach allows countries to go after the supply side, recognizing that, in virtually every country of the world, bribery is already illegal at the national level. Criminalization of transnational bribes is thus a central element of the OAS anticorruption treaty and has been supported by the OECD. At present, however, beyond the United States, only Sweden and the United Kingdom claim to have laws that penalize foreign bribery.[11] As the world becomes more integrated, the notion of a double standard that allows bribes if they take place across a border but makes them illegal if paid domestically is irrational and impossible to maintain. Toleration of corruption in international dealings inevitably comes back to corrupt the culture in domestic dealings.

As the success of the private sector group Transparency International has shown, this orientation toward leveling up, not down, is becoming more and more the international norm, putting business in line with the general public in demanding transparency and accountability. Private sector support was key in the progress made in the OECD, the World Bank, and the OAS. Ultimately, progress will depend on public support for implementation of the measures agreed to internationally.

The United States will continue to play a pivotal role in this effort. But equally important is that leadership be driven as much by actions as by rhetoric. The United States is constantly reminded of the need to keep its own house in order, and the difficulty Americans have in attacking such sensitive subjects as campaign finance reform illustrates the difficulties facing all countries in moving their politicians toward meaningful reform.

Stop Subsidizing Bribery, Start Incentivizing Ethical Practices

An important complement to this effort to level up international legal standards is to recognize that important incentives exist that tolerate or even encourage international corruption. Most egregious is the fact that in a number of developed countries, bribes are tax deductible, effectively providing a government subsidy for corruption. Hence the need to insist on full implementation of the recommendation to deny tax deductibility as proposed in the OECD. This rule should apply to all domestic bribes and foreign bribes, not just bribes for which a conviction has been secured.

In its recommendation, the OECD called on governments to review their programs to identify opportunities for requiring ethical practices. All governments should scrutinize their own policies that come close to subsidizing bribery. They should adopt a general requirement that companies and all of their parents and affiliates must adhere to policies against corruption in their international operations as a condition for participating in any government program that provides them benefits. In the United States, where the FCPA already addresses the corruption issue for U.S. companies, the focus should be on policies that provide support to U.S. subsidiaries of foreign companies. Where these subsidiaries receive U.S. government benefits, their entire corporate control group should maintain an effective anticorruption policy. In this regard, the valuable steps already taken on advocacy by EXIM and OPIC should be reviewed further to ensure that they are as effective as possible. The advocacy guidelines, for instance, should clearly require company antibribery policies to encompass agents and joint venture partners as well as all companies in the same corporate family.

The practices of other agencies also should be reviewed. Consideration should be given to whether foreign companies should continue to get an unqualified exemption from the FCPA when their securities are marketed in the form of American Depository Receipts (ADRs). Again, the Securities and Exchange Commission (SEC) recently has taken initial steps in this direction by prosecuting Montedison Company for falsifying its report of a bribe. The SEC did not, however, propose to require those who market ADRs on U.S. securities markets to abide by the FCPA. Alternatively, the SEC should condition the existing exemption from the FCPA on company commitments to maintain and enforce corporate policies against bribery or on company disclosure of bribes that are paid in its international operations. At a minimum, ADR purchasers have a right to know how their companies are managed.

Get the Bureaucrats Out of Business

The market is the best discipline against corruption. With market forces come transparency, accountability, and incentives to find the best combination of price and performance from suppliers. Private companies operating in a competitive environment have every incentive to make their purchasing and other decisions solely on the basis of price and conformity to required specifications. Privatization and the promotion of competition are thus the two most important policies governments and international institutions can pursue to control the demand side of bribery. Moreover, these policies also will contribute significantly on the supply side as shareholders of private companies use their influence to avoid having their company associated with bribery scandals.

By contrast, where government bureaucrats act in a commercial role and political decision-making governs public tenders, there exists an atmosphere that is ripe for corruption. Governments should be relegated to an appropriate regulatory role in the economy where they can effectively counter rather than contribute to corruption.

Governments should begin the process of promoting transparency by adopting a WTO agreement on transparency in procurement. A related mechanism for reducing corruption is to establish regulatory environments that minimize both the number of regulations and the scope for discretion accorded to government officials. By reducing the number of "choke points" at which regulatory approval is required and by applying regulations in a predictable manner, governments will create fewer opportunities for corruption. An OECD initiative in the area of regulatory reform may provide a model for regulatory regimes that minimize the number of opportunities for corrupt activities.[12]

Finally, transparency and good governance should have the same priority as other international economic policies, taking their rightful place along with most-favored-nation (MFN) treatment, national treatment, fiscal integrity, foreign exchange stability, and sustainable economic development. In all future trade agreements, transparency should be included in Article I of the accord to demonstrate the importance of this issue. At the same time, multilateral development banks should all make good governance a criteria in loan evaluations and should adopt procurement rules that incentivize ethical policies rather than underwrite illicit payments. Finally, the private sector can promote the formation of local chapters of Transparency International to support grass-roots action against corruption at the national level.

CONCLUSION

The historical forces of political accountability and globalization are exerting steady pressure on government handling of corruption. The pressures built unrecognized for long periods of time, only to express themselves today in dramatic realignments as governments, companies, and institutions around the world move to address the issue that they tried to ignore for so long.

There is also a human dimension to this issue. The forces of history are recognized primarily by a new generation of leaders who do not accept corruption as an inherent element of economic life, see the harm corruption causes, and are prepared to take action against it. Although national and international policies on the issue have changed fundamentally in only a few years, corruption will not be eliminated tomorrow. The first major shift in response to political accountability and globalization—adoption of international policy initiatives to counter corruption—is well under way. The second phase of that process, in which the new policies and new attitudes begin to have their desired impact, will take additional time and the continued commitment of new leaders. Over time, however, the initiatives described in this chapter, together with many others around the globe, will alter fundamentally the way people perceive and deal with corruption and its consequences.

NOTES

1. See Paulo Mauro, "Corruption and Growth," *Quarterly Journal of Economics* (August 1995): 681–712; and *From Plan to Market*, World Bank Development Report (New York: Oxford University Press, 1996), p. 95. A compendium of additional academic work reaching similar conclusions will soon be published by the Institute for International Economics.
2. *The National Export Strategy*, Fourth Annual Report to Congress by the Secretary of Commerce (October 1996), p. 113.
3. The difficulty of taking on petty corruption is greatly increased by the fact that, in many countries, thousands of clerks and bureaucrats are woefully underpaid and use bribes to make up for it. To eliminate this well-established system would mean laying off huge numbers of people and facing a serious political backlash or driving overburdened government budgets further into deficit.
4. See Vito Tanzi, "Corruption, Governmental Activities, and Markets," IMF Working Paper WP/94/99, August 1994, p. iii.
5. OECD, "Draft Recommendation on the Tax Deductibility of Bribes to Foreign Public Officials," February 1996, document C(96)27, p. 2.
6. To varying extents the following OECD members allowed tax deductibility of bribes as of mid-1996: Austria, Australia, Belgium, Canada, Denmark, Finland, France, Germany, Greece, Ireland, Italy, Luxembourg, the Netherlands, New Zealand, Norway, Portugal, Spain, Sweden, and Switzerland.
7. "Draft Recommendation on the Tax Deductibility of Bribes to Foreign Public Officials."
8. Without a universally applied procurement agreement, Russia and China, when they join the WTO, will enjoy a tremendous loophole for all activity that takes place in a government procurement environment. The

World Bank has analyzed the state-owned enterprises that are engaged in commercial activities in emerging markets and has found that, cumulatively, they account for up to 20 percent of their gross domestic products, which means that the procurement loophole covers a major part of some of the most important markets in the world.

9,   The European Union's 1996 Green Paper "Public Procurement in the European Union—Exploring the Way Forward" (November) makes clear that its government procurement directives have had little identifiable impact on increasing cross-border procurements within Europe and seeks to initiate a dialogue on ways to achieve truly open procurement markets in the EU member states.

10.   International Chamber of Commerce, "Business Adopts Its Own Rules Against Extortion and Bribery," press release, Paris, March 27, 1996.

11.   The Japanese government also has decided to propose legislation criminalizing foreign bribery. Nikkei Fax, Nihon Keizai Shimbun, Inc., 5, no. 942 (February 26, 1997).

12.   See World Bank, *Bureaucrats in Business: The Economics and Politics of Government Ownership,* (Oxford: Oxford University Press, 1996).

Chapter 13

Regulatory Reform and Trade Liberalization

Claude Barfield

As tariff and other border barriers have fallen over the past several decades, national regulatory systems—particularly for services, investment, and energy—have assumed greater importance in trade negotiations. This is because, depending on how they are structured, national regulatory systems can create formidable barriers to the operation of truly "contestable markets" for both domestic and foreign firms. Thus national efforts to introduce more market-based domestic regulatory systems have important implications for the multilateral trading system.

Regulatory reform encompasses a spectrum of policy changes, ranging from the breakup of public and private monopolies and oligopolies to more efficient and focused regulation and even in some cases complete deregulation. Trade liberalization reinforces and extends domestic regulatory reform by allowing the introduction of more competition in national markets and by providing the opportunity for domestic firms to expand into other national markets. In addition, trade negotiating principles can serve as guidelines for more open domestic regulatory regimes. Among the most important of multilateral principles are *national treatment*, or the commitment to equal treatment for both foreign and domestic firms, and *due process*, meaning full consultation before the promulgation of regulations and a fair and expeditious adjudication process.

WHAT IS REGULATORY REFORM?

Led by the United States, most industrial nations have undertaken extensive programs of regulatory reform over the past two decades. Particularly since the late 1980s, both the new industrial economies (NIEs) of East Asia and Latin America and the formerly command-and-control states of Eastern Europe and the Soviet Union have joined the movement. Given the diverse history and nature of these countries, it is no surprise that regulatory reform has taken different forms and meanings.

In its broadest reach, the concept of regulatory reform has the goal of introducing more efficient methods of public intervention into national market economies—assuming that such intervention is necessary at all. Within this broad definition are core goals that aim to increase the efficiency of rules governing market entry, production methods, transactions between producers and suppliers, and firm responses to competition.

Regulatory reform encompasses a spectrum of public policy changes, from privatization of public monopolies, particularly in the NIEs and former communist states, but also in some industrial economies, such as the telecommunications monopolies in Germany and France; the breakup of private monopolies, such as AT&T in the United States; more efficient and focused regulation of an existing private market, such as airline deregulation in the United States and in the European Union (EU); and virtually complete deregulation, such as the United States has done in trucking and railroads, including abolition of the Interstate Commerce Commission.

In most such cases, regulatory reform has not resulted in the complete withdrawal of government oversight. Even after sweeping sectoral deregulation, firms are still subject to national competition and antimonopoly laws and regulations. The fact that complete laissez-faire is not the endpoint of most regulatory reform has led some observers—implicit skeptics of the whole process—to introduce the term "reregulation" to describe much that is taking place.[1] Use of this term is flawed on several counts: First, proponents of regulatory reform do not deny the necessity for government oversight in some situations: They just want less intrusive and distortive intervention. Second, characterizing the result of many national economic deregulatory efforts as reregulation inaccurately describes the thrust and direction of what is taking place. In all cases, the movement has been from either total monopoly or tight oligopoly, combined with public regulations that aid collusion, to a more truly competitive market, accompanied by less regulatory oversight.

Unfortunately, when government has been a "pervasive participant" in strategic sectors, rent-seeking by firms and individuals is also "pervasive," and thus the path to regulatory reform is strewn with pitfalls. Specifically, economist Robert Rogowsky has written, "rather than directing energy toward improved products and distributional efficiency, [firms have directed] their resources toward maintaining their politically favored or protected position."[2]

BENEFITS OF REGULATORY REFORM

Despite uneven progress, the overwhelmingly positive results have created a strong consensus for wide-ranging national regulatory reform programs. These results span differing political regimes, national levels of development, and regional boundaries. Thus in the United States, estimates of the welfare gains to consumers from regulatory reform in the airline, trucking, and gas industries were $5 billion, $8 billion, and $3 billion respectively.[3] A study of privatization in the telecommunications sectors of Chile and Mexico found economy-wide efficiency gains of 50 percent for Telmex and 155 percent for Chile Telecom. A similar study found gains of 12 percent for British Telecom after privatization. In New Zealand, the cost of long-distance calls has declined almost 11 percent each year since telecommunications reform was completed in 1988, and over $4 billion has been invested in capital improvements by the main competing firms.[4]

The list could go on at some length, but the central point is that there is now little dissent from the proposition that domestic regulatory reform boosts national economic growth and welfare. Extending these benefits to foreign firms engaged in international trade and investment, however, presents a separate set of challenges.

THE LINK BETWEEN REGULATORY REFORM AND TRADE LIBERALIZATION

Trade liberalization complements and reinforces domestic regulatory reform: Both aim for the achievement of truly "contestable markets." Unfortunately, in many instances domestic regulatory rules and apparatus have the effect of thwarting competition and market entry by more innovative firms both domestic and foreign, often in the name of protecting employment. Because inefficient regulation can harm the performance of domestic firms, firms are likely to enlist strong sympathy from elected officials when they seek protection from foreign competitors.

Further, each sector presents a complex set of issues and delicate questions of timing as public regulatory bodies construct strategies to introduce more competition. At many junctures, there is the danger that foreign competitors will be thwarted by both the method and the content of reforms instituted in the name of deregulation.

An excellent example of the potentially negative consequences of mismanaged or rigged deregulation is now unfolding in the Japanese insurance market.[5] This $400 billion market is one of the most tightly regulated in the world, with rules forbidding price and product competition that include restraints on innovative marketing and distribution practices. Foreign firms have been able to establish a presence only in the so-called Third Sector, consisting of niche products such as personal accident and cancer insurance and long-term disability. This sector comprises only 3 percent of the total Japanese insurance market.

In 1994 the Japanese Ministry of Finance agreed not to introduce new competition into the Third Sector until the much larger life and nonlife insurance sectors were opened up to competition. Since then the ministry has taken no significant steps to accomplish this goal. Despite this failure, in early 1996 it announced plans to allow the huge, domestic Japanese insurance firms to compete in the niche markets. Without real regulatory reform across the entire insurance sector, these firms will almost certainly wipe out the foreign presence in the Third Sector.

The United States and other nations vigorously opposed this manipulation of market liberalization to favor domestic firms, and ultimately the Ministry of Finance backed down. Ironically, by refusing to distinguish between private restrictive practices (in automobiles and semiconductors) and public regulatory actions (in insurance and other financial services), the United States has clouded its own case for strong retaliatory measures. At this juncture of World Trade Organization (WTO) jurisprudence, public actions are far more likely to be found inconsistent with multilateral trading rules than private actions.

ANALYZING REGULATORY REFORM

As tariff and other border trade barriers have fallen over the past several decades, national regulatory systems—particularly for the service sectors, but also importantly for energy—have assumed a greater importance in trade negotiations, not the least because they now represent the greatest impediments to the free flow of trade and investment.

In effect, service, investment, and energy trade negotiations represent negotiations between competing regulatory systems, and these systems can be analyzed in ways similar to standard microeconomic analysis of competition among firms. The economic analysis of the efficiency of regulatory systems focuses both on market failure—such as market power, externalities, and imperfect competition—and on government failure.

Market Power

Market power refers to situations in which one or a few sellers control the market, with the result that the quantity of goods sold is smaller and the price greatly exceeds production costs. Market power can arise through explicit or implicit collusion among producers, through mergers, or even through government restrictions that prevent or impede market entry.

Examples of market power have abounded in key traded sectors such as financial services and telecommunications. In financial services, often in the name of consumer safety and protection, firms were protected by geographic restrictions such as on the number of branches, by limits on rates of interest paid on savings accounts and charged on loans, and by restrictions on technology that could expand the range of competition (e.g., automated teller machines). More recently, rapid advances in technology have enabled individual firms to increase their scope vastly. Thus in almost all countries, including the United States, despite the arcane limitations of the Glass-Steagall Act, there has been a merging of the separate banking, securities, and insurance sectors.

In a number of sectors, the issue of regulation has been complicated by historic arguments that a monopoly is "natural"; that is, the technological and economic underpinning of the sector is such that only one company can serve the market. Natural monopoly conditions have been asserted in energy, petroleum extraction and distribution, electric and gas utilities, and telecommunication, among others, as a rationale for economic regulation that supported regulated or nationalized monopolies. Over the past decade, economic research has undercut the basic premise of many "natural" monopolies, demonstrating that there is little evidence for the economies of scale necessary to justify continued monopoly. Moreover, nations that have introduced competition and less restrictive regulation have experienced lower prices and higher productivity. In the United States, for example, more efficient regulation in telecommunications and railroads saves consumers an estimated $2 billion annually.[6]

On both the domestic and the international fronts, however, the most significant recent activity in regulatory reform has been the attempt to manage relations between regulated public and private monopolies and potential new market entrants. The aim is to construct rules that will constrain the market power of the monopolies. For instance, in the telecommunications area, key areas for reform include equipment sales to regulated monopolies and conditions of entry for competing service providers. Specifically, policy reforms aim to achieve nondiscriminatory access to communications networks, reasonable rates for leased lines for new service providers, and transparent, open bidding for equipment suppliers to national monopolies.[7]

Externalities (Spillover Effects)

Positive and negative externalities occur when the consequences of one entity's production or consumption decisions result in uncompensated effects on others. Of particular concern are the consequences of negative externalities in areas such as the environment, where the result will be too much of a good or service, at too low a price, and with too few resources being devoted to reducing or correcting the negative externality, such as increased pollution.

The World Trade Organization is now moving to place environmental issues on the multilateral trade agenda; therefore national environmental regulatory systems will come under increasing scrutiny. The major challenge is to move toward a consensus on procedures and methods of regulating the environment by means of flexible, market-based policies.

The move toward multilateral trade discussions on the environment comes at a time when many nations are rethinking their approaches to pollution regulation, although real changes are still sporadic. For most nations, the traditional means of environmental regulation entails setting rigid technical standards that prescribe specific allowances by source or mandating particular technologies, such as particular kinds of wastewater treatment plants. These standards almost always introduce distortions by discriminating between old and new plants and between different industries.

As the costs of such regulation have become more evident and the lack of progress more glaring, some nations have begun to experiment with more economically productive alternatives, including incentives and taxes. The two main experiments to achieve greater economic efficiency have been the use of emissions trading and effluent fees.

The United States has experimented with emissions trading since the late 1970s, although often the process has been burdened with cumbersome constraints. The first major experiment in the early 1980s consisted of trading options for six air pollutants whereby two or more companies that were the sources of a particular pollutant could propose regulations to reallocate pollution among themselves. More recently the United States and Singapore both have used emission trading to meet the requirements to reduce fluorocarbons under the Montreal Protocols.

Effluent fees or taxes have been used more extensively, with mixed results. The challenge is to set the tax high enough both to cover the cost of the potential environmental damage and to create an incentive for polluters to minimize damage. While political pressures often have thwarted this result, more and more nations are adopting the principle behind it: The polluter pays.

The principle of "polluter pays" is the entering point for international negotiations on trade and the environment, for in a number of areas environmental pollution transcends national boundaries and externalities necessarily become subjects of international concern.

Negative externalities also can be found in the financial ser-

vices area.[8] For banks, a depositor run represents a major negative externality. Depositors either fear that their bank is really insolvent or fear that other depositors fear that the bank is insolvent—and
either fear can cause depositors to withdraw their deposits. For
international negotiators, there is also the fear of "systemic risk";
that is, that the failure of a large bank or the entire banking system of one country will have negative effects on the entire international banking structure. Recent research has underscored that
such fears should not cause elaborate financial regulation at either
the national or international levels but that a few basic regulatory requirements, such as adequate capital levels and limitations on
a bank's exposure to one or a few borrowers, will suffice to maintain the safety and integrity of the system.[9]

A second key factor in warding off systemic risks is full and
timely information about the structure and operations of banking firms in the system—and this leads to the third potential cause
of market failure: asymmetric or inadequate information.

Information Requirements

Problems of "asymmetric information" arise when a party on one
side of a transaction has information that a party on the other side
does not possess. For instance, a borrower may know more about
his or her ability to repay a loan than the lender; a manufacturer
of a product will know more about the safety of the product than
the consumer; and a drug manufacturer will know more about the
efficacy of a drug than either a doctor or a patient.

Remedies for this type of market failure include various disclosure requirements as well as protective standards. In both
cases, costs will be incurred, and the challenge to regulators is to
find the most effective and least costly alternatives among competing regulatory options. Mandatory product standards, for
instance, run the dangers of thwarting technological change by fixing on a particular design or product and of preventing flexible
responses to differing local problems. Of equal concern from a trade
policy perspective is their vulnerability to capture by local firms
and interests that tailor the specifications to local advantage and
exclude foreign competition.

Several alternative public interventions offer more market-oriented solutions, less vulnerable to capture. First is the shift from
product to performance standards that do not mandate specific technologies or designs and instead lend themselves to open compe-

tition. More important are steps to ensure full disclosure to all participants in the process, including foreigners. With each participant able to have a voice in setting standards, routine market bargaining can determine the outcome.

Finally, of particular importance for international transactions, some progress has been made toward the internationalization of standards and product certification. The most important and advanced efforts are being pushed by the business sectors in Europe and the United States, but the members of the Asia Pacific Economic Cooperation forum (APEC) also are holding a series of consultations with the aim of mutual recognition agreements (MRAs) and possible harmonization of some aspects of the standards-setting process. Among the barriers they are addressing are: testing and certification requirements that are higher for imports than for domestic goods and services; discriminatory product labeling rules; manipulation of domestic laboratory accreditation to block imports; and mandatory compliance with quality system registration schemes.

In June 1997, pursuant to the much-publicized "New Transatlantic Agenda," agreed to by European Union and U.S. corporate groups, the United States and the European Union negotiated mutual recognition agreements for five sectors: pharmaceuticals, electrical equipment, medical devices, telecommunications equipment, and marine recreational craft. The products covered involve about $50 billion in U.S.-EU trade.

GOVERNMENT FAILURE

The case for public intervention to remedy the consequences of market failure must be balanced against the equal potential for government failure. While government regulation can increase the efficiency of imperfect markets, governments also can fail to meet their goals and intervention can worsen the efficiency of already imperfect markets.

While a number of factors can cause government failure, four problems are particularly relevant.

Conflicting Goals

Often legislatures and political leaders mandate vague and even conflicting goals to regulators, making it difficult to establish and carry out clear programs. For instance, regulators may be required simultaneously to protect the environment, enhance economic growth, advance goals of racial diversity, and guard consumer interests—with little guidance as to priorities or methods of achieving balance. This can lead to disguised protection, as was the case when the U.S. Environmental Protection Agency, in the name of safekeeping the environment, discriminated against non-U.S. oil refineries in regulating emissions, and when Congress, in creating fuel economy standards for motor vehicles, clearly favored the Big Three U.S. automakers.

Asymmetric Information

Even with able personnel, government agencies have difficulty obtaining and utilizing the information necessary to understand market developments in complex sectors such as telecommunications and financial services. The problem of inadequate information is likely to lead to the same problems encountered by private sector entities in overcoming market failures.

Income Distribution

Domestic regulatory agencies often are asked to ameliorate perceived inequities in a nation's income distribution. More efficient methods of addressing inequities would entail taxes and subsidies, but regulation is often the preferred policy choice, particularly through the use of cross-subsidies. Examples of the inefficiencies introduced for such purposes are "must-serve" mandates to insurance companies and the similar mandate for banks to establish branches in poor districts set forth in the U.S. Community Reinvestment Act. In Europe, the "must-serve" mandates have been used as a means of slowing down and blocking the opening of telecommunications markets to non-EU firms.

Rent-Seeking and Capture

Finally, the greatest threat to both efficient and equitable public regulation stems from the lobbying activity of affected individuals and firms that will expend considerable resources to bend policies and regulations in their favor. In many countries the history of economic and health and safety regulation has seen the gradual capture of the regulatory authority by the producers and groups at whom the regulations were originally aimed.

After analyzing the dynamics of both market and government

failure, a recent study concluded:

> [t]he real world imperfections of government have yielded numerous instances of the regulatory processes being used for abusive purposes and reaching inefficient outcomes. Indeed the deregulation movement of the late 1970s and 1980s was a reaction to these abusive purposes and inefficient outcomes. These abuses need not lead to the conclusion that all governmental regulation should be forsaken. But they do point toward constant caution in embracing new regulation—national or international—and toward the value of frequent reassessments of the motives, methods, and outcomes of existing regimes.[10]

HARNESSING REGULATORY REFORM TO TRADE LIBERALIZATION

Despite the warning message of recent Japanese experience with insurance reform, the goal of harnessing domestic regulatory reform to trade liberalization will be attainable over time. Given the myriad of regulatory regimes, political traditions, levels of economic development—and the very particular technological and competitive challenges that each sector represents—progress will be varied and programs will have to be tailored to national priorities.

As they move in future years to revise their regulatory systems, individual national regulatory systems and national policymakers should keep their eyes on the following guidelines: WTO procedural principles and mutual recognition agreements.

WTO Procedural Principles

Because virtually all nations belong to, or soon will belong to, the World Trade Organization, a sensible beginning to the linkage of regulatory reform to trade liberalization would be a commitment to apply certain multilateral principles in reconstructing national regulatory systems. Among these would be the following.

Transparency. This includes the commitment to publish all rules governing sectoral regulation and to see to it that all affected parties—both domestic and foreign—have access to these rules.

National Treatment. This involves the commitment that foreign and domestic firms be treated equally in the construction and application of regulatory regimes.

Minimal Distortion of Trade. This is a commitment to observe the WTO requirement that governments will adopt the method or policy that is the least trade distorting to achieve a social, economic, or political objective.

To these basic WTO rules, the following procedural safeguards should be added:

Due Process. Governments should commit to full consultation with all interested parties—both domestic and foreign—before proposed standards or regulations are put in place. Provision also should be made for an open and expeditious appeals process when affected parties feel that unwarranted economic burdens will result from new or revised regulations.

Mutual Recognition Agreements

Moving beyond general principles, a number of plurilateral negotiations are taking place that aim for a series of MRAs that will enhance regulatory reform. Indeed, one recent study predicted that "MRAs will likely be at the heart of trade diplomacy in the coming decade."[11] The high interest in MRAs stems from the continuing drive to reduce trade barriers and the recognition that there exist wide and deeply rooted differences in national regulatory systems based on social preference, level of development, income distribution, tolerance of risk, geography, and government-societal relationships.

As a way station to harmonization, mutual recognition is based on a principle of "equivalence" or at least "acceptability" of each nation's regulatory systems. From this flows the rule that if a product or service is sold (or tested) lawfully in one jurisdiction, it can be sold (or tested) in all member jurisdictions without meeting separate standards or undergoing additional testing. Mutual recognition has been called an extreme form of national treatment: It restricts the regulatory authority of member nations, but it does not involve a transfer of power to the supranational level. (The European Union in its present form blends mutual recognition in some areas with complete harmonization in others. The Maastricht Treaty, and likely the results of the recent Intergovernmental Conference, will move the European Union toward greater harmonization.)

MRAs also can be powerful tools to increase market contestability. They inevitably introduce competition between regulatory systems while also introducing the possibility of a single rule toward which all producers of a product or service will trend. It is for this reason that national regulators remain chary and even skeptical of MRAs in strategic sectors such as financial services and telecommunications.

The two most important specific principles that governments can adopt in the furtherance of mutual recognition are mutual recognition of testing results and the mutual recognition of trade- and investment-related standards. Obviously, each nation still must decide which of its health, safety, and environmental standards are too sensitive or critical for inclusion in MRAs.

Mutual Recognition of Testing. It is universally recognized that there are high costs associated with the duplication of test results that are necessary to certify that various products, production processes, and services meet individual national standards. Commerce is also impeded when professionals—lawyers, accountants, and the like—working for multinational companies are blocked from practicing their professions because of differing educational and professional accrediting organizations. In order to remove these roadblocks, governments, through MRAs, can establish procedures and joint bodies to achieve mutual recognition of both testing and professional certification.

As an important part of the transatlantic business dialogue (TABD), the United States and the European Union negotiated an MRA for pharmaceutical testing. This groundbreaking negotiation focused attention on both the possibilities and the problems inherent in melding different regulatory systems. Among generic problems the negotiators had to overcome were: different definitions of what constitutes the industry—the United States wanted to include medical devices, the European Union did not; level of detail in testing—the U.S. Food and Drug Administration demanded copies of all relevant documents; criteria for judgment—the United States wanted only health and safety, the European Union wanted some economic judgment; and competing bureaucratic perspectives—in both the United States and the European Union, trade and commerce bureaucracies often are at odds with drug regulators.[12]

Mutual Recognition of Trade and Investment-Related Standards.
Mutual recognition of actual substantive standards presents somewhat more sensitive issues, particularly when political and social
as well as economic objectives are intermixed in regulatory regimes.
But as with testing and certification, the costs of differing levels
and means of regulation constitute major impediments to trade and
investment. The aim of the negotiations is first to induce governments to review their regulatory system to determine elements of
criticality and noncriticality in the achievement of fundamental social
and political goals. Rules not deemed central to these goals should
become candidates for mutual recognition, relieving producers,
exporters, and importers of substantial costs—and ultimately
resulting in more varied goods and services at less cost for national consumers.

Harmonization: Negotiated Multilateral Rules. The highest level
of integration would be achieved by international negotiations to
create some form of multilateral code of regulatory rules. This goal
is far down the road, but there are precedents in previous multilateral negotiations and in the current rules governing the WTO.
Indeed, it can be argued that all of the nontariff codes (now binding obligations) established during the Tokyo and Uruguay Rounds
are precedents for a more wide-ranging code for regulatory
actions. These would include, for example, existing rules for subsidy, government procurement, and the new multilateral regimes
for services and intellectual property.

At the moment, the most important work linking regulatory
reform to trade liberalization has been undertaken by the Organization for Economic Cooperation and Development (OECD). In March
1995 the OECD issued a preliminary set of guidelines for member
governments to consider before establishing new domestic regulations entitled "Recommendations on Improving the Quality of
Government Regulation." The guidelines consist of a series of
questions governments should ask when considering new regulations. The questions include such issues as: Is government action justified? Is regulation the best form of government action? What is
the appropriate level of government for this action? Do the benefits justify the costs? Are the distribution effects across society
transparent? How will compliance be achieved?

Also in 1995, Japan proposed that a number of existing
OECD committees should analyze issues presented by domestic

regulatory systems with the goal of distilling a set of core principles to guide governments in the future and to minimize barriers to trade. Work is under way in several OECD committees, although as yet no results have been published.

If some consensus can be reached regarding overall principles, the OECD guidelines could very well provide great assistance to ongoing negotiations for specific WTO service sector agreements and for what are likely to be quite difficult and complicated negotiations in the areas of competition policy and the environment.

It also should be noted that regional negotiations in both APEC and through the transatlantic business dialogue are proceeding simultaneously; and if negotiations begin again in the next few years for a Free Trade Area of the Americas, the issue of regulatory reform with at least some attempt at mutual recognition will almost certainly be high on the agenda.

WTO Role. Any future multilateral code for regulatory activity would build on and incorporate the principles and rules for mutual recognition.

Thus existing WTO principles regarding transparency, national treatment, minimum distortion of trade, and due process would form a bedrock set of safeguards. In addition, the WTO could provide the framework for future negotiations to achieve mutual recognition of testing results and standards in an increasing number of substantive areas. These negotiations likely would consist of agreement not only among individual WTO members but also between regional trading groups, if the regional groups reach agreement earlier.

Finally, in some areas—services and investment are key examples—WTO negotiations will involve the establishment of minimum substantive standards. For instance, in the telecommunications sector, questions relating to specific rules for competition between public and private monopolies and outside competitors, and rules for interconnection and equipment procurement necessarily will be included in any multilateral agreement. It should be noted that with regard to both services and investment rules—as well as potential agreements in high-technology sectors—many developing countries will need assistance and competence-building aid because they currently lack the ability to create and maintain sophisticated regulatory systems.

This point leads to a final caveat: Whether through bilateral, regional, or multilateral negotiations, it should be understood that the substantive issues raised by changes in national regulatory systems reflect social, political, and economic beliefs and practices that often are deeply embedded in particular national histories and experiences. Thus, despite sweeping technological changes that are driving pressure for reform and harmonization, progress is not likely to be swift. And to be successful, any proposals for systemic reform will have to accept the necessity for wide variations in approach and substantial leeway for national idiosyncrasies.

NOTES

1. Jonah Levy, "Globalization and National Systems" (BRIE Working Meeting on Globalization, University of California, Berkeley, March 1996, photocopy); Steven K. Vogel, "The Bureaucratic Approach to Financial Revolution: Japan's Ministry of Finance and Financial System Reform," *Governance: An International Journal of Policy and Administration* 7, no. 3 (July 1994), pp. 35–36.
2. Robert Rogowsky, "The Benefits of Regulatory Reform" (OECD Symposium on Regulatory Reform and International Market Openness, Paris, July 1996, photocopy).
3. Clifford Winston, "Economic Deregulation: Days of Reckoning for Microeconomists," *Journal of Economic Literature* 31, no. 3 (September 1993), pp. 1420–61.
4. Ahmad Galal, Leroy Jones, Pankaj Tandon, and Ingo Vogelsang, *Welfare Consequences of Selling Public Enterprise: An Empirical Analysis* (New York: Oxford University Press, 1994).
5. Claude Barfield, "Principles Needed in U.S. Japan Trade," *Journal of Commerce* (September 5, 1996).
6. Winston, "Economic Deregulation."
7. Greg Sidak, *International Competition in Telecommunications* (Washington, DC: AEI Press, 1997).
8. Lawrence White, "Competition vs. Harmonization: An Overview of International Regulation of Financial Services," in Claude E. Barfield, ed., *International Financial Markets: Harmonization vs. Competition* (Washington, DC: AEI Press, 1996), pp. 5–18.
9. Jean Dermine, "International Trade in Banking," pp. 49–83, and Ingo Walter, "Global Competition and Market Access in the Securities Industry," pp. 84–150, in Barfield, *International Financial Markets.*
10. White, "Competition vs. Harmonization," pp. 23–24.
11. Kalypso Nicolaidis, "Mutual Recognition of Regulatory Regimes: Some Lessons and Prospects" (OECD Symposium on Regulatory Reform and International Market Openness, Paris, July 1996, photocopy).
12. *FDA Week*, November 8, 1996 (Washington, DC: Bureau of National Affairs).

Chapter 14

A Question of Fairness: The Global Trade Regime, Labor Standards, and the Contestability of Markets

Michael Hart

Proponents of embedding international fair labor standards into the fabric of the World Trade Organization (WTO) appear to have suffered a major setback at the WTO's first ministerial conference in Singapore in December 1996. Ministers took an unequivocal stand against using trade discipline to strengthen international observance of fair labor standards. More to the point, in summarizing ministerial consideration of the issue, the chairman of the conference went out of his way to stress his understanding that ministers had precluded further consideration of labor standards by the WTO. He stressed that "some delegations had expressed the concern that this text may lead the WTO to acquire a competence to undertake further work in the relationship between trade and core labor standards. I want to assure these delegations that this text will not permit such a development."[1]

The debate over the proper relationship between trade and labor involved protracted and difficult discussions but led to stalemate. Proposals by the United States, the European Union (EU), and Norway to inscribe the issue of labor standards on the WTO's future work agenda met stiff resistance from developing countries. In the end, the United States and other proponents decided to put the issue off for reconsideration at a later time and agreed to an anodyne paragraph in the final communiqué that in effect seems to have buried the issue for the time being.

Nevertheless, the fact that ministers issued a statement on the nexus between trade and labor standards at the very first conference of the WTO suggests that the issue may not be as deeply buried as some of its critics might wish. Ministers have now reiterated what their predecessors had stated at the founding of both the International Labor Organization (ILO) and the General Agreement on Tariffs and Trade (GATT),[2] that there is a relationship between the pursuit of prosperity through trade and the observance of internationally recognized labor standards. The burden of proof now may lie with those who want to introduce labor standards into trade agreements. But as the globalization of trade and investment deepens, the values and preferences of civil society and the burden of proof will shift. That shift is now closer than many trade officials are prepared to admit. It thus behooves all those concerned with the preservation of the benefits of free and open markets to begin considering means to achieve the objectives of those concerned about labor standards in ways that will not undermine the continuation of an open global economy.

To make the next stage of trade and labor discussions more than a sterile confrontation between industrial and developing countries, proponents will need to analyze the issues more carefully. They will have to demonstrate, for example, that the issue of wage levels is not part of the discussion. Similarly, proponents in the United States and the EU must accept that coercive and unilateral approaches cannot be the goal of the exercise if they are to win converts to their cause. Developing countries, on the other hand, will need to exhibit a less defensive attitude about exploitive labor practices. Core labor standards are not a matter of Eurocentric values but of widely recognized human rights. The solution does not lie in the single-minded pursuit of one perspective or the other but in a strategy that recognizes the legitimacy of both objectives.

The ability of governments of the Organization for Economic Cooperation and Development (OECD) to maintain support for an open, expanding multilateral trading system depends importantly on their ability to convince a wider public that the trading regime is responsive to sensitive social issues such as protection of the environment and the promotion of human rights at the international level. To this end, international fair labor standards must be incorporated in WTO disciplines. This can be done without impairing either the objectives of the WTO or the legitimate aspirations of developing countries.[3]

To bridge the gap between broad acceptance and actual enforcement of core labor standards, governments need to include a commitment to guarantee the right to collective bargaining as part of wider WTO consideration of rules on the contestability of markets. (Contestability rules govern the full range of impediments to market access that may arise as a result of either public policy or private behavior.) Such a guarantee would ensure that all core labor standards could be realized on a democratic basis. This guarantee would furnish a cooperative basis for the WTO and the ILO to promote greater observance of core labor standards on a global basis.

NATURE OF THE TRADE/SOCIAL LINK

Interaction between trade and social matters is, of course, not at issue. Trade takes place within a social and political institutional setting—domestic and international—that influences who trades what with whom. Trade policy decisions can affect social policy decisions and vice versa. Government decisions about social programs, for example, will influence production costs and firm investment behavior, affecting profits and future trade and investment flows. Social policies such as labor market regulations, training programs, environmental protection laws, health care systems, or income support programs all influence a society's capacity to respond to structural changes. The pressure of structural changes will in turn affect the design and delivery of such programs and policies.[4]

There has long been a complex interplay between social issues and trade issues. What is new are the extent and intensity of international transactions and their capacity to influence matters that traditionally were addressed wholly within the confines of the nation-state.

Globalization is the key to the new urgency in discussions about trade and social issues. Narrowly defined, globalization involves a major shift toward the internationalization of production, distribution, and marketing of goods and services. More loosely understood, it invokes a wide variety of cultural, political, soci-

ological, environmental, and economic trends based on the processes that bring people and places together in more frequent, more
sustained, and more varied contact.

For many firms, the organizational breakthrough that has made
globalization possible is the ability to disperse economic activity
geographically and bring it together electronically. Globalization
realization has led to spectacular growth in the internationalization of services, particularly financial services, and to the further
disaggregation of manufacturing. By adopting computer-based manufacturing and management systems, firms can increase the productivity of workers, managers, and administrative support
personnel; decrease the cost of labor, materials, waste disposal, service, and sales; enhance the quality of products and after-market
service; improve the control of production through tighter inven-
tory and waste management; and add to customer satisfaction through
better-quality products and a wider variety of services. These
developments are leading to fundamental changes in the nature of
work and the structure of wages and income distribution and are
placing a premium on the value of specialized education. Unskilled
labor is now in oversupply on a global basis, and skilled, knowledge-intensive labor is in short supply. Human resource development is thus one key to success in the new economy.

The restructuring of global and domestic economies has generated pressures for change that run against the grain of many public preferences. This is leading to two contradictory developments:
a pressure to redistribute income to reduce the adjustment costs
borne by economically weak but numerically and thus politically strong members of society; and a need to reconfigure the social
welfare system and bring it more into line with fiscal reality. In effect,
globalization is adding to the cost of social programs while simultaneously constraining government's ability to generate revenues.
Cost-conscious firms are pursuing location and investment strategies that minimize their tax exposure at the same time as displaced
workers are calling for more retraining and income-support programs. In virtually every OECD country, the share of government
revenue derived from the corporate sector is declining while the
share of government expenditure devoted to social programs is
rising.

Globalization also is leading to increased pressures in virtually every industrial country to level the playing field at the international level. The goal is to make all countries observe the same

basic social standards, ensuring that no firm or country can benefit from the perceived cost advantages of lower social standards and that no government can use lower standards to attract new investment. The increasing integration of the global economy and the prosperity that can be derived from this integration should provide new impetus to efforts to raise social and other standards around the world.

The convergence of popular culture, the globalization of commerce, and the pressure to level the social playing field all point to the need to develop new norms for interstate relations governing social regulation and trade. These norms would consist of a set of rules that recognizes that production, exchange, and consumption have largely escaped from the effective regulation of the territorial nation-state while the people who make up that state remain largely attached to it. National regulatory structures so painfully built up over the past century are now as likely to lead to conflict as to harmony. Developing global institutions to deal with frictions in the international economy may entail elements of global governance, leading to significant adjustments in the amount of political authority exercised by national governments and a realignment in the authority exercised by or through extranational rules and institutions. Trade and social issues form an integral part of this new challenge to recapture democratic control over the market in a manner geared to the emerging reality of an integrated global economy rather than to that of interdependent national economies. The focus for much of this discussion will be the World Trade Organization, since it provides the most advanced set of rules capable of being enforced among a large number of nations.

THE APPEAL OF THE WTO

The initial success of GATT—now the WTO—derived from its single-minded pursuit of a simple goal: the development of a universal framework of rules and procedures dedicated to liberalization and nondiscrimination enforced through mutual respect of its members for the rule of law. Its success is demonstrated by growing membership, steady progress in widening and deepening liberalization, and stronger rules and procedures to back up national commitments. The Uruguay Round marked but the latest in a sequence of successful efforts to make the system work to the mutual benefit of its member states. With the entry into force of the WTO, the trading system achieved a new level for ensuring compliance. Decisions on the interpretation and effective implementation of the agreements covered by the WTO are now binding on all member states.[5] Moreover, the more robust dispute settlement procedures make credible the breakthroughs in new, deeper, broader, and tighter obligations.

The Understanding on Dispute Settlement enshrines a number of critically important principles and procedures in the WTO, including:

- The right of every member to have its complaints addressed by a panel of experts,

- The promise that the panel will act expeditiously and independently on the basis of clear rules and procedures,

- The commitment that panel reports will be adopted by the WTO unless an objecting member is successful in organizing a consensus to block adoption,

- The right to have the decisions and reasoning of panels subjected to review by a permanent appellate body,

- The obligation of members to implement adopted panel findings by taking action to remove the basis of the complaint; the right to compensation or to authorized retaliation, while possible in order to give teeth to this obligation, does not let the offending member off the hook,

- The promise that panels will have the assistance of a qualified, capable, independent group of officials with legal training in analyzing the issues and reaching decisions,

- The expectation that decisions gradually will accumulate into a body of precedent that will further strengthen the rule of law in international trade and trade-related activities.

Taken together, these developments embody a powerful set of provisions that give governments, traders, and investors the basis for confidence in the rules and procedures of the international trade regime. Governments now have agreed to a consequential degree of potential intervention in their internal affairs by other member governments through the dispute settlement and trade policy review procedures. Even a cursory examination of the WTO

Agreements on Agriculture, Technical Barriers to Trade, Subsidies and Countervailing Measures, and Trade-Related Intellectual Property Rights supports this conclusion. Both the early record of dispute settlement cases and the emerging agenda for future negotiations suggest this trend is irreversible. They also underscore why the trade regime is now well ahead of any other international regime in terms of both enforceability and credibility.

It is the very success of the WTO rules-based system that has convinced its critics—many of whom do not share the WTO's dedication to further economic liberalization and nondiscrimination—that the solutions to a range of nontraditional trade problems lie within its purview. The idea of negotiations leading to mutually agreed, enforceable rules acts as a powerful magnet to those seeking solutions to a wider range of problems that now transcend national solutions, including the desire to establish enforceable international fair labor standards.

NOT A NEW QUESTION

That there should be a link between trade rules and labor standards is, of course, not a new question. The problem is that this link has never been implemented successfully at the international level. If anything, efforts to make the link operational have become steadily more controversial over the years. This is a matter of some regret and one that critics of GATT, and now the WTO, have found particularly offensive. They point to the considerable energy and political capital governments have devoted to the progressive liberalization of the exchange of goods, services, capital, and technology and the relatively little attention they have extended to the international advancement of social, humanitarian, and similar values. While this charge may be somewhat unfair, given the substantial aid and other efforts committed to raising living standards and health conditions in developing countries, it is true that the success of the multilateral trading system stands in sharp contrast to the gap between rhetoric and reality in the pursuit of the ILO's objectives.

Thousands of standards have been elaborated in ILO conventions. Many have been implemented by industrial countries. But in developing countries, most of these conventions serve more as political statements than as enforceable or contractual commitments. What has been missing has been either a willingness or a capacity to translate this recognition into widely applied and enforceable policies at the international level. The complexity of this task, however, can be appreciated by a cursory examination of the long struggle required to make this link operational in most OECD countries.

Within most industrial societies today, there is broad consensus on the need to strike a balance between the demands of allocative efficiency and those of distributive justice.[6] Regulatory structures have been developed over the years to govern the operation of the market, to deal with anticompetitive behavior, and to address market failures.[7] Markets thus operate within a framework of laws and regulations that address not only narrow issues of commercial policy but also broader concerns related to social, humanitarian, environmental, and other considerations. The balance between allocative efficiency and distributive justice may vary from country to country, but among the major industrial countries substantial convergence in regulatory goals and methods has now been achieved—thanks in part to cooperative efforts under GATT and other international instruments—to allow for a high level of relatively smooth economic interaction and integration.

Most developing countries, however, lack the economic capacity and political will to achieve a reasonable balance between market performance and income distribution. Indeed, the common experience has been that a combination of government policy and private market behavior has frustrated the achievement of distributive justice. The slow progress of many developing countries in simultaneously pursuing both goals of modern governance lies behind current demands on the trading system.

The issue has become more acute over the past few decades because a number of developing countries—particularly in East Asia—have made considerable progress in their pursuit of allocative efficiency. Firms located there have proven adept at taking full advantage of modern process and product technologies to make highly sophisticated and competitive products. In many ways, these firms now fashion goods and services fully competitive with those produced in Europe, Japan, and North America. In the view of many social activists, however, this progress has been made in part by ignoring the demands of distributive justice. Labor and other social standards and conditions in Asia and Latin America remain at levels far below those of industrial nations, providing fuel for those frustrated by low-cost competition as well as for those fired by humanitarian concerns. Both groups are advocating a more activist international approach.

From the perspective of the governments of Asian countries and of those seeking to replicate their success, however, insistence that developing countries achieve a level of distributive justice achieved only over many decades in industrial countries smacks either of paternalism or of opportunistic protectionist concerns dressed up in humanitarian garb. At the same time, the insistence that Asian values and preferences are sufficiently different from those prevalent in Europe and North America to justify a different appreciation of human rights and social norms also can be interpreted as offensive opportunism.[8] Neither sentiment is conducive to discussions that are likely to prove satisfactory.

While the basis for the multilateral trading system always has resided in economic and commercial factors—in the economic benefits to be derived from freer trade and in the commercial benefits that flow from rule stability and predictability—its political support often has flowed from noneconomic factors. The geopolitical basis for broad support of this system disappeared with the end of the Cold War. Political leaders in industrial nations are finding it increasingly difficult to respond to critics of an open system. Appealing to the aggregate benefits that accrue to a more open, competitive economy is unlikely to dull the anger of a worker displaced by more competitive imports, restructuring, or outsourcing, or to appease the concern of an industrialist reeling under the onslaught of a foreign competitor benefiting from lower labor costs and less stringent environmental requirements.

Without progress on some of the more sensitive issues, such as labor and environmental standards, it will become difficult to maintain broad support for the system in the United States and the European Union and, at the same time, to respond to the legitimate needs of developing countries. As Sir Leon Brittan, vice president of the European Union, notes, " . . . the WTO will survive and prosper only if we are seen to be responding to the concerns of our citizens. . . . If the open trading system is not seen to be actively contributing to a solution to that [child labor] problem, it will too readily be assumed that open trade is part of the problem. The same is true of the trade-environment link."[9]

Finding a cooperative and collective approach in the WTO is infinitely better than proceeding unilaterally. The United States, for example, already has in place a range of legislative mandates

that tie access to its market to satisfactory performance by the exporting nation on U.S. definitions of worker rights. These laws have
had ambiguous results. Continued frustration, however, of legitimate U.S. concerns about labor standards will only fuel demand
for further unilateralism and undermine achievement of other
multilateral trade and economic objectives as other nations react
to heavy-handed U.S. measures.[10]

U.S. commitment to liberalized trade is now deeply embedded, with ideas, interests, and institutions all in place to reinforce
this basic ideological orientation.[11] Nevertheless, ideological commitment does not translate automatically into freer trade and
investment conditions. Achieving specific objectives still requires
a political coalition prepared to offset the influence of coalitions
with contrary views. Thus while the United States is not about to
slide back into full-scale protectionism, the coalition of interests
committed to future market-opening decisions and negotiations
is paper thin.[12] That coalition can be strengthened by bringing in
those moderate voices interested in strengthening protection of the
environment and in promoting human rights through trade agreements. Notes labor economist Ronald Ehrenberg: " . . . economic integration can take place between nations with very different
levels of labor market standards and policies. However, to be unam-
biguously judged as desirable, and to win political support, proposals for increased economic integration may require adjustment
policies both within and across nations as well as the convergence
of labor standards."[13]

COMPETING APPROACHES

Forging an operational link between trade rules and labor standards is complicated by the deep divisions about these matters not
only between industrial and developing countries but also within industrial nations, in which there are two distinct, opposing
approaches. On one side of the question stand traditional trade
purists who shudder at the thought of complicating the effective
functioning of the trading system by adding rules and procedures
that are only indirectly related to the flow of goods and services.
On the other side stand those who insist that without rules governing the broader social impact of trade and investment, the system is both morally bankrupt and in danger of becoming irrelevant

to the real concerns of many citizens. The difficulty is that both sides are able to marshal intellectually potent arguments to make their case while in effect talking past one another. Reconciling these two solitudes will not be an easy task.[14]

Trade purists are willing to concede that there may be more complementarity between commercial and social goals than they have previously been prepared to admit, but they express these in terms of the capacity of an open, fixed-rule trade regime to generate the resources to solve new problems. Notes WTO Secretariat official Richard Eglin, "Trade liberalization generates the economic resources that allow more ambitious and costly environmental and social policies to be put in place. Those policies in turn foster a more favourable climate for countries to sustain their commercial competitiveness and to participate more effectively in the international trading system."[15] Additionally, trade purists suggest that the WTO's focus on nondiscrimination and the removal of trade-distorting practices can act as a cogent incentive to address a wide range of problems with the most appropriate instruments. It helps governments to avoid using instruments that either discriminate on the basis of national origin or impose restrictions that are unlikely to have their intended effect.

Trade purists argue that using trade measures in one country to address problems in another is likely to yield ambiguous results. Such measures may, or may not, hit the target problem but are also likely to lead to secondary, unintended problems. Again, in the words of Richard Eglin:

> [t]he primary role of the WTO is to avoid trade disputes, not to encourage them. A trade dispute reflects the failure of the underlying system of voluntary cooperation and coordination, and repeated disputes over the same or similar issues suggest the need to correct through renegotiation the basis of that cooperation. . . . The role assigned to dispute settlement in the WTO therefore sits uncomfortably alongside demands that it should be used to correct forcibly the behaviour of those countries whom it has not proved possible to persuade to cooperate voluntarily through negotiations conducted in other intergovernmental organizations.[16]

Thus, in Eglin's view, trade measures applied to nontraditional trade problems are likely to inflict unintended collateral damage.

Social activists find these arguments hypocritical. In their view, trade purists are fully prepared to accept WTO rules that deal with fair competition relating to price discrimination (antidumping duties), subsidies (countervailing duties), and intellectual property rights but are unprepared to extend the same concept to workers' rights and other social and humanitarian issues. To social activists, what is at stake is not a matter of imposing the full range of industrial country standards on the rest of the world but of ensuring compliance with broadly agreed principles and standards, such as the core conventions of the ILO. In their view, virtually all governments already have agreed to these standards; it is just a matter of ensuring compliance. For example, human rights activist Christine Elwell maintains that "if the new WTO is to attain true status as an international organization, it must begin the difficult process of integrating the third pillar of sustainable development into its mandate—social justice through social progress."[17] Elwell characterizes a "social clause in trade agreements . . . [as] a mechanism for ensuring that social progress keeps pace with economic development, based on international labor standards."[18]

Social activists also have little patience with arguments about whether the WTO or the ILO is the proper place to pursue social policy issues. In their view, these issues should be pursued in both organizations and the necessary linkages developed to make sure that standards and compliance/enforcement mechanisms are developed cooperatively so that they actually work. For example, the ILO's chief economist, Gijsbert van Liemt, recently noted that "globalization is frequently defined as the declining relevance of national structures and equated with a weakening of the power of national governments. . . . Almost by implication, there is a search for new or reinforced supranational structures. It is no coincidence . . . that the new WTO will have a mandate that is both much broader . . . and much deeper . . . than that of the old GATT. There is no reason why concern about minimum labor standards should not be part of this discussion."[19]

Social activists further reject the argument that requiring compliance with basic social, humanitarian, and environmental provisions would deny developing countries their comparative advantage. They note that compliance with stringent standards has, as often as not, stimulated firms to adopt better, more competitive production processes.[20] In Elwell's view, for example: "The absence of minimum international labor standards would place workers in a potentially disastrous competition against each other . . . [leading] to a destructive downward spiral in the conditions of work and life of working people around the world. . . . Including labor standards in the mandate of the WTO would encourage producers to internalize social costs into profits or prices."[21]

Finally, social activists are not convinced of an inevitable positive correlation between rising incomes and improvements in living, environmental, and social conditions. Without regulatory protection of workers' rights and other social goals, improvements in productivity and incomes are as likely to accrue to transnational firms as to workers in countries with low standards. Insists former U.S. Labor Secretary Ray Marshall: " . . . markets must operate within the framework of rules, especially those that protect basic labor standards. Such standards promote human resource development and force companies to compete by becoming more efficient, not by reducing basic labor standards. In a global economy, however, labor standards must now be part of international trade rules."[22]

Trade purists, while admitting the moral force of some of the points raised by social activists, are concerned that such arguments are too easily captured by protectionist forces. In the hands of protectionists, the goal becomes less one of advancing the needs of exploited workers in developing countries and more one of protecting workers and employers alike in import-sensitive industries in developed countries. The result would be perverse, denying such countries the opportunity to better their lot by pursuing their comparative advantage of abundant low-skilled labor in standard-technology industries. Stanford University economist Anne Krueger puts it this way: "It is vitally important for world economic growth that legitimate concerns with labor standards be clearly separated from the calls for enforcing measures that would deny developing countries their comparative advantage."[23]

THE POLITICAL CONTEXT

The arguments being advanced by both social activists and trade purists are serious ones born out of strong conviction and careful consideration. Discussion between these competing approaches, however, has been muddied by the assertions of demagogues like Ross Perot in North America and the late Sir James Goldsmith in Europe. They have succeeded in tapping a wellspring of fear and anxiety arising from low-cost competition, arguing that it is not possible for an industrial country to compete head-to-head with a low-cost developing country. Industrial countries should trade only among themselves and protect themselves from developing country competitors until those competitors have established the full panoply of social and other conditions that are an integral part of the social contract in industrial countries.[24] There is no shortage of well-constructed arguments to counter what is essentially an emotional and illogical case.[25] But those who find the Perot-Goldsmith case convincing are not likely to be swayed by well-constructed arguments. Their case is political and can only be rebutted politically. Competition from low-cost, low-standard labor countries may not cause rising unemployment or widening income disparity in advanced industrial economies. But that charge is more difficult to refute in the face of deliberate efforts to prevent workers in some developing countries from taking steps to better their lot, such as exercising their basic human right of freedom of association.

Among policies and practices in Asia that are ripe for closer scrutiny are the willingness of some governments to relax regulatory requirements and enforcement in export processing zones (EPZs) in order to attract investment, the benign neglect of regulatory abuses in the informal sector, and the denial of basic rights to migrant workers. In all three cases, the opportunity for unscrupulous practices is enhanced and the charge of unfair competition easy to document. The fact that not all governments feel compelled to pursue this route indicates some differentiation in policy that can be addressed through international rules and procedures. The informal sector is the main source of employment for street kids and prostitutes throughout Asia and Latin America; often this sector involves some of the worst labor practices in the world. In some jurisdictions, an attitude of benign neglect causes such practices to proliferate. Finally, in Asia the high level of migration by unskilled labor, much of it illegal, leads to very exploitive working conditions.[26]

It is more difficult to dismiss the argument that imposing tougher standards on developing countries may prove counterproductive; rather than helping those exploited by low standards, tougher standards will drive away industries that provide income to people who would otherwise be destitute. Various studies by the OECD and others, however, suggest that such links are weak. One OECD study concludes "that concerns expressed by certain developing countries that core standards would negatively affect their economic performance or their international competitive position are unfounded."[27] Even where there may be more correlation than studies have proven, rules and disciplines that destroy industries without providing alternatives are not the way to go. What is needed are serious analysis and widely based discussion of what kinds of rules and procedures are appropriate to what circumstances and to what time frame.

On the other hand, it is hard to take too seriously the charge that imposing labor standards on developing countries amounts to cultural imperialism. As noted earlier, virtually all developing countries are parties to ILO and U.N. international agreements and conventions that promote a multitude of labor and other social rights and standards. The problem is making these widely shared instruments operational; consensus on what constitutes a basic set of human rights, including those related to labor standards, exists. More fundamentally, there is now broad acceptance that markets provide the most efficient way to create wealth, including a consensus on how to make this ideology operational through a variety of international agreements. What is needed is to make the distributive justice part of the consensus, as it has operated in industrial countries for more than half a century, effective at the international level. As noted by WTO Director-General Renato Ruggiero: "No one can deny the importance of core labor standards. . . . The issue is now about the extent of the relationship with trade and the best forum for discussion."[28]

The real issue, therefore, is not whether governments will negotiate about these issues but when, where, and to what effect. The pressure to act is already there. Effective lobbying by a broad coalition of environmental, labor, human rights, religious, and citizens' groups concerned about job loss and erosion of regulatory standards already has made the political case that there is a relationship among trade liberalizing, fixed-rule agreements, and social and environmental degradation. Part of the case, of course, is pure strategic opportunism: Interest groups are able to hold a politically important trade issue, such as the passage of the North American Free Trade Agreement (NAFTA), hostage to demands to meet their own agenda—tougher labor regulation and enforcement. Additionally, however, symbolic politics are involved. To many political activists, the GATT, NAFTA, WTO, and other trade agreements have come to symbolize environmental rape, corporate exploitation, a social race to the bottom, and other broad social problems flowing from a much more complex set of factors. Governments will respond to such claims either unilaterally or cooperatively.

The question, therefore, is the extent to which governments, and the people they represent, are prepared to tolerate differences in regulatory standards, values, and national priorities within a more open global economy. John Jackson of the University of Michigan has argued that dumping and countervailing duties and safeguard measures were necessary to lubricate the tensions that arise from such systems friction.[29] As the scope of systems friction widens, the need to enlarge the role of these lubricating measures similarly needs to expand.

TRANSPARENCY AND OTHER MARKET SOLUTIONS

Various authors have provided a catalogue of ways in which private firms and citizens as well as governments can work to promote labor standards on a global basis.[30] They make a convincing case that market-based solutions alone are not enough. There are too many problems arising from free riders and the provision of public goods to rely wholly on market-based disciplines. At the same time, they clearly demonstrate that a range of market-based solutions, reinforced where necessary by government regulations in the consuming country, could make a useful contribution to raising labor standards around the world.

Private sector labeling and codes of conduct, for example, would improve consumer knowledge and have an effect on investment and other decisions. Similarly, technical assistance to the governments of developing countries could strengthen their competence to deal with labor standards issues, while efforts to strengthen the competence of home-grown nongovernmental organizations devoted to social issues would increase domestic pressures to address these issues.

In recognition of the potential benefits of transparency and widely agreed process standards, the International Standards Organization (ISO) has initiated work to develop a series of standards related to labor practices similar in scope and intent to those related to environmental practices. The ISO's success with its ISO 9000 series related to quality standards may well be replicated with its proposed ISO 14000 and ISO 25000 series related to environmental and labor standards. The extent to which the ISO's work succeeds may well obviate the need for efforts to forge a stronger link between labor standards and international trade agreements.[31]

Many of the proposals along these lines can be implemented now at the national level and would not contravene any international trade obligations. For some commentators, such private sector solutions will in the long run prove the most productive. There is little empirical evidence to support the fear that large, global corporations seek out jurisdictions with lower labor standards and costs to pursue labor-intensive production processes. The pressures of global competition do force firms—whether large or small, global or local—to search out the most cost-effective way to produce their products and bring them to markets. But there is little evidence that a strategy of locating in jurisdictions that abuse human rights and tolerate egregious labor conditions pays long-term dividends. Modern production methods are not only more efficient and lead to higher quality outputs but also require a better-educated labor force. More typically, therefore, globally active firms tend to pay among the highest wages in developing countries and to pursue labor practices that are well above those of locally based firms. Pursuing the issue by promoting good corporate practice by globally active firms, through labeling and other transparency measures, will go a long way toward mitigating the fundamental problems of human rights abuses and unacceptable labor practices. They will not, however, deal with the political pressures to address the issue more immediately through a social clause or similar mechanism in trade agreements. That will require a political response, preferably one that complements these market-based approaches.

A ROLE FOR THE WTO

The debate between trade purists and social activists suggests that arguments for and against a social clause in trade agreements are unlikely to reach a conclusion satisfactory to either side as long as the issue is treated in isolation. Similarly, there is unlikely to be closure on the issue of linking trade and environmental obligations strictly within the confines of that debate. If one enduring lesson has been learned during the past 50 years of multilateral and regional trade negotiations, it is that few politically difficult issues are resolved on their merits and in isolation.

The politically sensitive issues of trade in agriculture and trade in textiles and clothing, for example, when dealt with in isolation (as they were throughout most of the past 40 years) either led to agreement to disagree or to agreements that appealed to narrow rather than broad interests. They did not lead to more open markets. They did not solve problems: At best, they isolated them; at worst, they deepened them. The lesson from this experience is that, in order to make progress on politically sensitive issues, they must be incorporated within broader frameworks that allow sufficient scope for the kind of extensive trade-offs that may be necessary.

It is unlikely, therefore, that the links between trade and labor and other social issues will or can be addressed successfully unless they form part of a broader agenda that allows for the development of politically persuasive coalitions at both the national and international level. Such an agenda appears to be emerging in ongoing efforts at the OECD and elsewhere to define the terms and conditions of open market access in a globally integrated economy. Borrowing from concepts developed in the context of industrial organization theory and competition policy, proponents of this new approach are advocating the development of a global regime that addresses the ability of any firm located anywhere on the globe to contest markets anywhere else.[32]

Contestability involves the embrace of a much broader approach to market access than that which prevailed even as recently as the Uruguay Round. It straddles the continuum of trade, investment, and competition policy. It emphasizes the need to stem anticompetitive practices that may impede the ability of producers to contest a market, whether such practices flow from public policy or private behavior. It requires that effective market access and presence not be unduly impeded by border restrictions, investment restrictions, regulatory obstacles, or structural barriers. It should provide private traders and investors with the assurance of fair, nondiscriminatory treatment and governments with some capacity to address behavioral problems that may lie beyond the reach of national regulators. Governments will need to develop a seamless set of trade and investment disciplines with which to govern both private actions and public policies affecting the ability of internationally active firms to contest markets anywhere in the world.

It is within this context that scope may be found to address the nexus between trade and social issues. Governments are likely to see some benefit in the negotiation of a series of codes setting out minimum standards in such areas as labor practices and environmental protection, in the context of a larger package addressing the full range of contestability issues. Given the wide variety of social and political values and experiences around the globe, such codes would need to begin cautiously and develop incrementally. Initially they should be more descriptive than prescriptive and build on positive experience in the ILO and other multilateral institutions. In effect, they would constitute a bridge between the ILO and the WTO.

An important consideration, of course, is "which" labor standards. Extreme proponents and opponents of using the international trading system both complicate the issue by insisting that it involves the full panoply of labor legislation as it has developed in the most industrialized parts of Western Europe or North America. Such an approach serves only to cut off debate. The widely shared concept of core labor standards really involves basic human rights, such as freedom of association, the right to organize and bargain collectively, the prohibition of forced or compulsory labor, a minimum age for the employment of children, and a guarantee of safe working conditions. On closer examination, the issue can be reduced to a single core standard: the right to organize and bargain collectively. It assumes the prior right of freedom of association, while its observance should, in most instances, provide workers with the capacity to bargain and pursue the next level of rights, including wages and conditions of work. The work of the ILO then would serve the useful purpose of providing guidance to workers in bargaining for more detailed rights and working conditions.[33]

Given a consensus on what constitutes core labor standards, appropriate institutional provisions will have to be developed to encourage observance of those standards. Institutional provisions are more likely to garner broad support if they lean toward cooperative rather than coercive solutions.[34] One of the weaknesses in the case being made by social activists is the eagerness with which they are prepared to use coercive measures such as trade sanctions and countervailing duties. Instead, the focus needs to be on a range of noncoercive measures that can be applied to help countries comply with more stringent requirements, including reporting requirements, multilateral scrutiny, assessment, and consultation procedures as well as publication and other transparency provisions.

At least initially, the proposal to promote basic labor standards through the international trading system can be boiled down to the very simple proposition that members of the World Trade Organization accept a contractual obligation to guarantee the fundamental right of collective bargaining and to promote, through collective bargaining and regulation, a code of good labor practices. Implementation of these twin obligations would be monitored through the Trade Policy Review Mechanism. Public criticism would arise only in instances in which a process of consultations and fact-finding has established that there exists a pattern of persistent denial of these obligations, that the member state is unwilling to take remedial action, and that other members agree that the pattern is sufficiently flagrant to warrant public reproach.[35] Proceeding this way also underlines the point that the issue is less one of rule making and more one of finding the means to encourage the implementation of widely accepted standards. To make the case more credible, it is important that developed countries lead by example by completing their ratification of ILO core labor conventions. The U.S. record in this regard is less than stellar: It has ratified only a handful of conventions, and has not ratified some of the conventions widely regarded as guaranteeing the six core labor standards.[36]

The virtue of such an approach is that, in most instances, the threat of collective opprobrium and the spotlight of negative publicity is the primary stimulus to corrective action. Over time, as experience is gained with the impact of public scrutiny and with the extent of exploitive conditions, reconsidering the need for sanctions may be useful. Even then sanctions would have to be approached with the greatest of care and be limited to those rare circumstances for which there is broad consensus that the country persistently disregards an agreed standard of behavior. Under no circumstances should it be possible for such sanctions to be captured by narrow protectionist interests, nor should it be possible for one state unilaterally to determine when there has been a breach of the obligation to allow workers to organize and pursue their interests collectively.

With the development of an increasingly global social and economic order, political structures to defend freedom in that order must, where necessary, assume a global dimension. The concept of contestability in all its richness can ensure the establishment of a framework of rules capable of preserving not only property rights but also human rights.

The development of a regime to promote global contestability fits part of a pattern of efforts to adapt rules and institutions first devised to govern national social and economic orders to the emerging global social and economic order. It would ensure that clear rules and procedures govern the kinds of actions both governments and private firms can take to impede market-based outcomes. It would recognize the extent to which labor, trade, investment, and technology are complementary means to contest markets and thus can no longer be treated as separate issues. It also would provide a policy and negotiating context within which to address the more politically sensitive issues that now create frictions between and among governments and that require solutions transcending the authority of individual governments.

Only by pursuing an agenda that addresses questions of both allocative efficiency and distributive justice at the global level, in a manner that would make pursuit of these goals mutually reinforcing and complementary, is there likely to be much progress on either front. As Gary Fields concludes: "In order to raise people's material living standards, countries should seek economic growth, using trade and labor market policies as appropriate means to an end. Labor standards and international trade can be complementary. Such complementarities should be sought by countries and by companies and fostered by the international community."[37]

NOTES

1. Concluding remarks by H.E. Mr. Yeo Cheow Tong, chairman of the Ministerial Conference, Minister for Trade and Industry of Singapore, December 13, 1996. He added that ministers had "agreed on a text which sets out a balanced framework for how this matter should be dealt with. The text embodies the following important elements: First, it recognises that the ILO is the competent body to set and deal with labour standards. Second, it rejects the use of labour standards for protectionist purposes. This is a very important safeguard for the multilateral trading system, and in particular for developing countries. Third, it agrees that the comparative advantage of countries, particularly low-wage developing countries, must in no way be put into question. Fourth, it does not inscribe the relationship between trade and core labour standards on the WTO agen-

da. Fifth, there is no authorization in the text for any new work on this issue. Sixth, we note that the WTO and the ILO Secretariats will continue their existing collaboration, as with many other intergovernmental organisations. The collaboration respects fully the respective and separate mandates of the two organisations."

2. In 1919 the Versailles Treaty that established the ILO called on governments to endeavor to secure humane conditions for labor at home and "in all countries to which their commercial and industrial relations extended." Similarly, the 1948 Havana Charter for an International Trade Organization—whose Commercial Policy chapter provided the basis for GATT—recognized "that unfair labor conditions, particularly in production for export, create difficulties in international trade, and, accordingly, each member shall take whatever action may be appropriate and feasible to eliminate such conditions within its territory" (Article 7). See Steve Charnovitz, "Promoting Higher Labor Standards," *Washington Quarterly* 18, no. 3 (1995), p. 169.

3. I carefully avoid calling the demand for labor standards in international trade agreements a "nontrade" issue, as many critics of the issue are wont to do. Given the potential influence of labor standards on trade and investment decisions and vice versa, it is difficult to argue that labor standards are more of a nontrade issue than technical standards or the protection of intellectual property. It is important to recognize that the issue really is about human rights rather than protectionism. Most activists seeking to advance labor, environmental, and other social issues at the international level are primarily interested in those issues. At the same time, it is also true that the enforcement of high international standards of any kind can be exploited effectively by those who want to protect specific industries and jobs from international competition. The fact, however, that noble objectives can be perverted by less noble ones does not invalidate the noble objectives. Rather, it means that some care will need to be exercised in the means chosen to meet the noble objectives.

4. For a full discussion of the interaction between trade and labor issues, see Ronald Ehrenberg, *Labor Markets and Integrating National Economies* (Washington, DC: Brookings Institution, 1994).

5. See the two-volume collection of papers edited by Jagdish Bhagwati and Robert Hudec, *Fair Trade and Harmonization* (Cambridge, MA: MIT Press, 1996), for an early appreciation of the extent of WTO members' obligations regarding traditional domestic regulatory structures.

6. See Arthur M. Okun, *Equality and Efficiency: The Big Tradeoff* (Washington, DC: Brookings Institution, 1975), for a classic statement of the trade-offs between the demands of allocative efficiency and those of distributive justice.

7. International fair labor standards (ILFS) are more than a matter of distributive justice; they also can involve a large measure of allocative efficiency. The denial of workers' rights, particularly the right to organize and bargain collectively, is anticompetitive. It can lead to a misallocation of resources by underpricing labor. Thus IFLS can correct an existing distortion of the market arising from political conditions that give employers rights

to pursue exploitive conditions. Ensuring that workers have the right to bargain for their wages and other working conditions is thus a promarket, procompetitive solution. Labor proponents of IFLS might note, however, that the closed shop that has become an integral part of the North American labor scene also can distort labor markets.

8. A strong case can be made that in many instances so-called Asian values are little more than a smokescreen to hide rent-seeking by ruling elites: They are arguments designed to preserve an exploitive status quo that preys on vulnerable workers. Interpreted this way, "Asian values" differ little from the self-serving arguments of firms and workers in import-sensitive sectors seeking protection from products benefiting from lower wages and less rigorous regulatory standards.

9. Speech to the Graduate Institute of International Studies, Geneva, April 1, 1996, p. 6.

10. Jorge F. Perez-Lopez provides an overview of U.S. unilateral efforts to use U.S. trade laws to condition the implementation and enforcement of labor standards in "Conditioning Trade on Foreign Labor Law: The U.S. Approach," *Comparative Labor Law Journal* 9, no. 2 (Winter 1988). Philip Alston, "Labor Rights Provisions in U.S. Trade Law: 'Aggressive Unilateralism'?" *Human Rights Quarterly* 15 (1993), subjects the same provisions to a rigorous analysis and finds that U.S. practice is neither efficacious in promoting the observance of human rights nor conducive to greater respect for international law.

11. See Judith Goldstein, *Ideas, Interests, and American Trade Policy* (Ithaca, NY: Cornell University Press, 1993), for a discussion of the change from embedded protectionism in the 19th century to embedded liberalism in the second half of the 20th century.

12. See Chapter 4 for a discussion of the political context. See also I. M. Destler, "American Trade Politics in the Wake of the Uruguay Round," in Jeffrey J. Schott, ed., *The World Trading System: Challenges Ahead* (Washington, DC: Institute for International Economics, 1996), pp. 115–24.

13. Ehrenberg, *Labor Markets and Integrating National Economies*, p. 3.

14. For a discussion of these two perspectives in the context of labor standards, see Stephen A. Herzenberg, Jorge F. Perez-Lopez, and Stuart K. Tucker, "Introduction," in Herzenberg and Perez-Lopez, eds., *Labor Standards and Development in the Global Economy* (Washington, DC: U.S. Department of Labor, 1990).

15. "Environment, Labour, and Human Rights Concerns and the International Trading System" (speech to the Conference on Globalization, Trade and Human Rights, Toronto, February 22, 1996), p. 2.

16. Ibid., p. 4.

17. Christine Elwell, *Human Rights, Labour Standards, and the New WTO: Opportunities for a Linkage* (Montreal: International Centre for Human Rights and Democratic Development, 1995), p. 32.

18. Ibid., p. 24.

19. Gijsbert van Liemt, "The Multilateral Social Clause in 1994" (draft discussion paper, International Coalition for Development Action, August 1994), p. 8.

20. The work of Harvard business economist Michael Porter often is invoked in support of this thesis. See his *The Competitive Advantage of Nations* (New York: Free Press, 1990), pp. 647–649.

21. Elwell, *Human Rights, Labour Standards, and the New WTO*, p. 31.

22. Ray Marshall, "Labor in a Global Economy," in Steven Hecker and Margaret Hallock, eds., *Labor in a Global Economy: Perspectives from the U.S. and Canada* (Eugene, OR: Labor Education and Research Center, University of Oregon, 1991), p. 21.

23. Anne Kreuger, *American Trade Policy: A Tragedy in the Making* (Washington, DC: American Enterprise Institute, 1995), p. 123.

24. See, for example, Sir James Goldsmith, *The Trap* (New York: Carroll and Graf, 1993), and *The Response: GATT and Global Free Trade* (New York: Carroll and Graf, 1993). For those interested in other populist criticisms of globalization and free trade, see Jerry Mander and Edward Goldsmith, eds., *The Case Against the Global Economy and for a Turn Toward the Local* (San Francisco: Sierra Club Books, 1996).

25. See, for example, Robert Lawrence and M. Slaughter, "International Trade and American Wages in the 1980s: Giant Sucking Sound or Small Hiccup," *Brookings Papers on Economic Activity, Microeconomics* no. 2 (1993).

26. Some of these exploitive strategies are documented in Ozay Mehmet, "Tigers, Asian Values, and Labour Standards: Promoting a Fairer Global Trade," in Maureen Molot, Martin Rudner, and Fen Hampson, eds., *Canada Among Nations 1997* (Ottawa: Carleton University Press, forthcoming).

27. "Trade and Labour Standards," Document COM/DEELSA/TD (96)8REV1, April 18–19, 1996, p. 7.

28. Renato Ruggerio, "The Road Ahead: International Trade Policy in the Era of the WTO" (Fourth Annual Sylvia Ostry Lecture, Ottawa, May 28, 1996).

29. John Jackson, "Achieving a Balance in International Trade," *International Business Lawyer* 2 (April 1986), pp. 123–128.

30. See Charnovitz, "Promoting Higher Labor Standards"; Steve Charnovitz, "Environmental and Labour Standards in Trade," *The World Economy* 15, no. 3 (May 1992); and Steve Charnovitz, "The Influence of International Labour Standards on the World Trading Regime: A Historical Overview," *International Labour Review* 126, no. 5 (1987). Also see Richard Freeman, "International Labor Standards and World Trade: Friends or Foes?" in Schott, *World Trading System*; pp. 87–114; Richard Fleeman, "A Hard-Headed Look at Labor Standards," *International Labor Standards and Global Economic Integration,* proceedings of a symposium (Washington, DC: U.S. Department of Labor, July 1994); Gary Fields, "Labor Standards and International Trade" paper prepared for an Informal OECD Trade Committee Meeting on Trade and Labour Standards (The Hague, September 19–20, 1994); and Gary Fields, "Labor Standards, Economic Development, and International Trade," in Herzenberg and Perez-Lopez, *Labor Standards and Development in the Global Economy.*

31. See National Research Council, *Standards, Conformity Assessment, and Trade into the 21st Century* (Washington, DC: National Academy Press, 1995); and Alan O. Sykes, *Product Standards for Internationally Integrated*

Goods Markets (Washington, DC: Brookings Institution, 1995) for discussion of ongoing efforts to strengthen international standardization efforts.

32. See Geza Feketekuty, "The New Trade Agenda," (Group of Thirty, Washington, DC, January 1992); and Americo Beviglia Zampetti and Pierre Sauvé, "Onwards to Singapore: The International Contestability of Markets and the New Trade Agenda," *The World Economy* 15, no. 3 (May 1992). For a fuller discussion of concepts related to the contestability of markets, see the chapters by Sylvia Ostry and Patrick Low in OECD, *New Dimensions of Market Access in a Globalising World Economy* (Paris: OECD, 1995).

33. Richard Freeman, in "International Labor Standards and World Trade," p. 106, notes "Effective trade union movements in developing countries would go a long way to alleviating world concerns over standards. If employees have freedom of association, they ought to be able to gain other standards as well, and increase compliance in their country. This strategy makes freedom of association central to any effort to rely on private parties to improve enforcement of standards." To encourage achievement of the next level of standards, it would be useful for the WTO, in consultation with the ILO, to adopt a code of good labor practices. Such a code would involve two elements: a set of guidelines aimed at the behavior of firms and a set of guidelines aimed at the regulatory practices of governments. The implementation of such guidelines would not be contractual but voluntary.

34. Gary Fields suggests that core labor standards should be couched in positive language. He suggests, for example, that this central right be couched as "every person has the right to freedom of association in the workplace and the right to organize and bargain collectively with employers." "Labor Standards and International Trade," p. 7.

35. It is worth noting that this proposal falls considerably short of the NAFTA side agreement in that it does not contemplate a complaints procedure triggered by private interests or a dispute settlement process that can ultimately lead to multimillion-dollar fines. While the NAFTA side agreement may have proven acceptable to Mexico, its provisions would not appear to be negotiable in a wider context.

36. See Efrén Córdova, "Some Reflections on the Overproduction of International Labor Standards," *Comparative Labor Law Journal* 14 (1993), p. 158.

37. Fields, "Labor Standards and International Trade," p. 17.

Chapter 15

Trade and the Environment

Robert J. Morris

Over the past several decades, trade and environmental issues have become increasingly intertwined. Interest groups and governments are more and more concerned with environmental protection, partially in response to negative environmental effects that they perceive to be associated with the globalization of production and markets. Many environmentalists have come to see trade measures as a means to enforce internationally agreed environmental standards. Some would even like to use the threat of trade sanctions to pressure foreign governments to adopt stricter environmental standards.

Trade policymakers, however, generally have resisted the use of trade measures to achieve environmental objectives. Even in situations where such measures might be appropriate, trade policymakers fear that, if allowed, environmental concerns would further complicate and might even overwhelm the rule-based regimes that govern the international trading system. In many instances, the use of trade measures for environmental purposes already distorts competition and provides avenues for disguised protection of domestic industries. More of the same could happen in the future.

The issue is not which policy—environment protection, or trade—should take priority; governments are agreed that both are legitimate expressions of national interests. The challenge for trade policy is to manage the conflicts between trade and environmental policies in ways that protect the integrity of a rule-based, open trading system while also permitting governments to address national and international environmental concerns. In other words, the task is to reach international agreement on the appropriate use of trade measures for the pursuit of environmental goals. Without such agreement, governments will find themselves caught between public pressure for unilateral action to protect an environmental goal and opposition from both business and foreign governments to any adverse commercial impact of such actions. Where governments either find it impossible or undesirable to resist the pressure for unilateral action, trade conflicts will result.

Some forward progress has been made toward reconciling trade and environmental concerns. At the 1992 Rio Conference of the United Nations on Environment and Development, governments reached general agreement (Principle 12) on how states should deal with the trade aspects of environmental policies.[1] The key elements of the principle are: (1) environmental measures dealing with transboundary or global problems should be based on international agreements; (2) unilateral action to deal with such problems "should be avoided"; and (3) trade measures should not be arbitrarily or unjustifiably discriminatory or a disguised restriction on trade.

Two years after Rio in 1994, the World Trade Organization (WTO) established a Committee on Trade and Environment (CTE). In addition, the issue has received considerable attention in the Organization for Economic Cooperation and Development (OECD). The CTE has focused on translating Principle 12 into operational guidance for the WTO system, and the OECD countries issued a set of basic principles to guide policymakers.[2] Unfortunately, at the 1996 WTO Ministerial meeting in Singapore, the most that governments could agree upon was that the mandate of the CTE and its work program should be continued. Indeed, despite some forward progress in sorting out trade and environment issues, it seems unlikely that the international trade community will be able to move to a consensus on this issue in the near term.

GREEN TRADE MEASURES

Three general categories of trade measures have been used to address environmental concerns. A clear understanding of the differences between these categories is essential to agreement on what, if anything, the WTO needs to do about the issue.

1. *Trade measures that ban imports of products which do not meet the importing country's environmental (mainly health) standards.* Trade rules embodied in the General Agreement on Tariffs and Trade (GATT) permit such import restrictions if a product does not meet the importing country's environmental standards. This includes consideration of both the use and disposal of the product. Current WTO rules are clear and adequate on this issue. No further rules are necessary. However, to the extent that countries can agree on harmonized product standards, such as the Codex Alimentarius that sets standards for agricultural products, the potential for trade distortion will be reduced.

2. *Trade measures against imports in which the undesirable environmental effect is not conveyed directly in the product.* GATT rules do not permit import restrictions based on the undesirable effects of a production process unless the effects of that process somehow render a product unfit for use. In other words, GATT rules allow import restrictions only when a product itself will have an undesirable effect within the importing country. Import restrictions are not warranted by the fact that the product's production process has negative environmental effects in the producing (exporting) country.

    There are, however, a growing number of cases, such as the Montreal Protocol, in which multilateral environmental agreements (MEAs) call for import restrictions on products, when the MEA signatories deem the production process environmentally unsound. GATT rules are silent on this aspect of import restriction. The problem, of course, arises when a WTO member state, which is not a party to the governing MEA, wishes to export a banned product to a country that is a member of the MEA. In this case, there is likely to be a conflict between the terms of the MEA and GATT rules.

3. *Trade measures used as sanctions to penalize a country for behavior regarded as contrary to either a national environmental law or an international environmental agreement.* Some countries and most environmental activists claim the right to use such sanctions. The sanctions target products (or services) that are not specified in an MEA and do not directly cause environmental harm. For example, a few years ago the

United States imposed tariff increases on a wide variety of imports from Taiwan to punish it for alleged violations of the Convention on International Trade in Endangered Species (CITES).

These categories and the distinctions between them suggest two fundamental questions. First, should GATT rules be changed to deal with problems raised by the use of trade measures against imports when the environmental effect is not conveyed in the product? Second, what role, if any, should trade rules or agreements play in sanctioning another country for environmentally destructive behavior not directly related to commercial policy concerns? No existing MEA authorizes trade measures specifically to punish another country. Many do, however, authorize or require trade measures as an integral component of the regulatory regime created by the agreement. For example, the CITES agreement authorizes countries to ban imports of listed species but contains no explicit authorization for countries to take defined actions against other, unlisted products from a country that defaults on its CITES obligations.

TRADE MEASURES IN MULTILATERAL ENVIRONMENTAL AGREEMENTS

Trade policymakers have advocated a multilaterally agreed-on approach to international environmental problems.[3] They see such an approach as the only effective alternative to the chaos that could ensue if nations with the power to do so increasingly decide to take unilateral measures to promote their own environmental protection goals. U.S. law requires such action in several areas, and the European Union (EU) is moving more aggressively in that direction. This is a serious source of concern for business. International commercial activities are exposed to greater risks of disruption or retaliation when powerful countries act unilaterally. Such actions raise costs unnecessarily and impair the integrity of the open trade system. Moreover, many argue that unilateral actions are not an efficient means of achieving important transboundary or global environmental goals.[4]

Thus many trade policymakers advocate the development of

an arrangement within the WTO whereby trade measures included in an MEA that meet certain agreed-on criteria would be exempt from other international rules. These criteria would have to address the two main exemption requirements set forth in current trade rules. In order to be exempted from GATT rules, a measure (1) must qualify as necessary to protect life or health, or relate to the conservation of natural resources, and (2) must not be applied in an arbitrary or unjustifiably discriminatory manner, or act as a disguised restriction on trade.

The WTO Committee on Trade and Environment currently has before it several proposals for meeting these requirements, the two main ones from the European Union and New Zealand. Another fairly detailed proposal for judging whether an MEA is within the bounds of the GATT or not has been advanced by the U.S. business community (at least that portion represented by the U.S. Council for International Business). The crucial recommendations are:

• The MEA must define precisely what trade measures are authorized or required,

• The measures must be directly related to the achievement of the environmental objective identified in the MEA,

• Trade measures should not be used simply to punish or "sanction" another country for failure to meet the MEA's obligations or for actions considered inconsistent with those set forth in the MEA,

• The trade measures should not be unnecessarily restrictive of trade. To make that determination, a form of proportionality test should be used (as, for example, is now required by U.S. courts when determining whether a state environmental regulation is consistent with the interstate commerce clause of the U.S. Constitution).[5]

A proposal along these lines involves minimal interference in the sovereign right of nations to negotiate any kind of MEA they wish and to include in their MEAs any kind of trade measure they deem necessary. However, the proposal also does two things that are very important for the integrity of a trade system based on the mutual exchange of contractual commitments among nations: It protects the rights of all WTO members, specifically the right of each to be compensated in the event that others take actions that are contrary to the rules; and it gives guidance to MEA negotiators about the kind of agreements and trade measures that will be accepted as GATT-consistent—guidance that they remain free to follow or reject as they see fit.

The proposed understanding would be especially useful in clarifying the role of the WTO process with regard to disputes between MEA parties and between a party and a nonparty. For example, the Basel Convention on trade in hazardous wastes contains provisions that discriminate between parties and nonparties. The United States is not a party to this agreement and retains its rights to contest in the WTO discriminatory trade measures taken as a result of the convention.

In general, future MEAs should contain provisions for disputes between MEA parties. The WTO role, if any, should be limited strictly to the question of whether a specific implementing action is consistent with GATT rules. A party should not use the WTO to contest either the validity of the trade measure sanctioned within an MEA or the validity of the MEA itself. Parties to an MEA should be presumed to have consensually waived their GATT/WTO rights regarding measures specified in the agreement. Nonparties should be able to bring a dispute with an MEA party to the WTO, but the MEA party would benefit from a presumption that the trade measure is consistent with WTO rules if it met the criteria set forth above.

Until a proposal like this is accepted, WTO panels will proceed as they do now. Specifically, they will have no agreed criteria with which to judge trade measures embedded in MEAs. Indeed, panels are free to make judgments independent of previous decisions, and neither trade advocates nor environmentalists can have any confidence about how a panel will decide a specific case.

The WTO has a crucial interest in coming to closure on this problem. Failure to do so will leave the field open to those countries favoring strict and discriminatory environmental agreements with less than full international acceptance. Such failure also could jeopardize the effort of finding an acceptable modus vivendi among trade and environment policy goals. However, this is not the only problem that must be resolved if a coherent approach to transboundary environmental problems is to be realized.

THE UNILATERAL USE OF TRADE MEASURES

For all practical purposes, only those countries that can claim significant market power can resort to unilateral measures. Nevertheless, unilateral measures are now becoming increasingly problematic.

All countries use trade measures to ensure that imported products comply with national standards or technical regulations. Some also use them to enforce national laws or policies regarding the methods by which certain products are produced, called production and processing method requirements, or PPMs. These often go beyond what is internationally authorized to render a product "fit for use." Such measures include U.S. requirements forbidding the use of purse seine nets to catch tuna in the eastern tropical Pacific and proposed EU restrictions on imports of skins from animals caught by leghold traps.

Environmentalists argue, with considerable justification, that often the only effective stimulus to countries to come to the table to negotiate a multilateral solution to an environmental problem is when a country with real market power takes action unilaterally. In both cases just cited, multilateral solutions were either agreed to (the La Jolla and Panama Declarations on tuna) or sought (EU/U.S./Canada/Russia talks on humane trapping) only after the trade actions were taken or threatened.

The situation is analogous to that which developed during the last two decades over the safeguard system under GATT. Seeking to avoid the rigors of the GATT-authorized system for getting temporary relief from import competition, some governments increasingly made use of voluntary export restraints (VERs) by countries thought to be the main source of the competitive pressure. To remedy this undesirable situation, the Uruguay Round negotiated a revision of the GATT Article XIX safeguard regime. Under it a country can impose import restrictions for a limited period in order to gain temporary relief from competitive imports. As long as this restrictive action meets certain conditions, the country is exempt from the requirement to pay compensation or accept retaliation for up to three years while the restrictions are phased out.

The revised safeguard rules provide a model for addressing import restrictions imposed to enforce national PPM requirements. The WTO should consider permitting countries to address an environmental harm with unilaterally imposed trade measures when the need is so urgent as to require action before a multilateral solution can be worked out.[6]

The amended rule, however, should be available only to deal with direct threats to living organisms. While other environmental harms may be more dangerous, such as air or water pollution, climate change, and so forth, these threats are rarely so imminent as to justify action before an international consensus is developed. Further, action taken under this arrangement should be required to be nondiscriminatory and should not restrict trade more than necessary.

An arrangement along these lines would not just minimize the potential for trade disruption. It also contains incentives for all affected parties to begin serious negotiations to see if a multilateral solution is possible.

Together, an environmental "safeguard" arrangement coupled with an agreement on criteria for WTO exemption of MEA-sanctioned trade measures provides a workable system for considering environmental interests within the WTO context. Moreover, the two proposals together satisfy the general principles agreed to at the United Nations' 1992 Rio conference.

One other case of unilateral action for environmental purposes also needs international attention. Although not usually thought of as "unilateral," the fact is that multicriteria ecolabeling schemes can effectively be unilateral, even if administered privately on a voluntary basis. In contrast to labeling programs that convey clearly specified information to consumers about specific or health-related aspects of a product, such as the nutrients in a serving of cereal, multicriteria schemes purport to evaluate products through their full "life cycle." For example, Germany's Blue Angel and Scandinavia's White Swan programs give their seals to products that meet a variety of criteria ranging from manufacturing, packaging, and disposal requirements.

However, there is no internationally agreed-on methodology for assessing the environmental effects of a product through its life cycle. Thus national schemes that claim to do so may in fact be expressions of unilaterally determined preferences that may or may not be environmentally or scientifically sound. They seek to persuade consumers that products that carry the approved "seal" are better in some undefined sense for the environment. Imported products may be subject to different regulatory requirements in their country of origin or be considered environmentally acceptable under a different set of life cycle criteria. However, if they cannot meet the specific criteria of the importing country's scheme, they may well face effective discrimination in that market. Such schemes are, in effect, unilaterally determined requirements imposed extraterritorially on foreign products.

The best way to deal with this problem may be through the development of criteria in the International Standards Organization (ISO) that all ecolabeling programs should meet. Such criteria would be helpful in preventing new barriers to trade arising from ecolabeling programs. They also would help provide usable information to consumers. Governments would do well to encourage voluntary industry initiatives of this kind on an international basis as an alternative to even inadvertent unilateralism. Failure to do so inevitably will generate WTO complaints that a particular multicriteria labeling scheme is discriminatory.

THE ROLE OF THE ENVIRONMENT IN TRADE AGREEMENTS

Those who argue that trade agreements need to contain specific provisions addressing environmental concerns are in effect proposing that trade agreements should become a primary instrument for advancing the environmental policy objectives of the parties. To the extent that the parties are of more or less equivalent economic power or stage of development, and provided that the measures they agree on do not impact the commercial interests of nonparties, there is no reason of principle why such agreements could not contain such provisions. The European Union's Single European Act of 1987 is a case in point.

But if the agreement is among countries of significantly different levels of economic power, such provisions begin to look like means of coercing the less powerful. It is begging the question to say that such provisions are freely agreed on by all parties when the less powerful are, in effect, required to accept them as a price for getting the market access advantage that is the main attraction of the agreement.

This was certainly true during the 1993 North American Free Trade Agreement (NAFTA) negotiations, when the United States pressured Mexico and Canada to accept the NAFTA environmental "side agreement." Ottawa and Mexico City did not object to the concept of increased cooperation or the mechanisms established to achieve it. They, and the American business community, objected to the coercive features of the agreement whereby governments found to be violating their own laws could be penalized by the imposition of fines or restrictive trade measures by the other NAFTA parties. Although these provisions were considerably changed in the final version from those the United States originally proposed, they remain a source of future concern as an undesirable precedent. They are, for example, already a prior condition for accession of other countries to NAFTA. Whether such coercive provisions are either sensible or necessary in the efforts to extend free trade to other nations in the hemisphere is open to serious question.

Considerations about the use of trade measures to promote social policy objectives are not, of course, unique to the trade and environment debate. Nor are they confined to the issue of how appropriate or desirable it is to use trade agreements to coerce changes in the standards of behavior of the less powerful parties in a variety of "noncommercial" policy areas. Powerful states often use trade agreements as vehicles to insist that their partners implement a whole series of policies that are well beyond the usual parameters of a "trade" agreement. Thus NAFTA, for example, contains provisions on investment, services, government procurement, and intellectual property that many have argued constitute a precedent for insisting that future trade agreements also cover environment, workers rights, or provisions to combat drug trafficking or to promote democratic institution building. The real questions remain: Is there a meaningful difference between what is and is not a legitimate subject for a trade agreement? And, if not, are there any limits to the noncommercial interests that can reasonably be promoted by a trade agreement?

Many in the trade community would argue that there are indeed clear lines to be drawn on what should and should not be in a trade agreement. The Uruguay Round incorporated agreements on trade in services, intellectual property rights, and trade-related aspects of investment. Most trade policymakers argue that "trade" agreements of the future will have to deal with all aspects of policies that have a direct affect on the conditions under which governments will permit commercial transactions to occur between their nationals and those of other states. In this perspective, even the Uruguay Round extensions of the idea of "commerce" were too limited.

The rationale for this broader definition of "commerce" lies in the immense acceleration of the movement toward globalization of markets. Not that all markets are becoming one in the global economy; rather, participation by individuals and companies in a given national market increasingly depends on governments applying substantially the same rules to all players. Thus a pharmaceutical manufacturer holding a patent on a particular medicine cannot effectively enter a foreign market to sell that product, even at a zero tariff, if the intellectual property defined in its patent is not protected and enforced in that market. The reason is that some other company simply will enter the same market with knockoff copies sold at a far lower price. Similar linkages among right-of-establishment and regulatory and tax policies define the ability of firms to "trade" in a wide variety of goods and services in today's world.

No such inherent linkages exist between commercial activities and environmental policies. Clearly, anyone doing business as either a trader or investor in another country is required to observe the environmental protection laws applicable in that country. But the environmental laws, regulations, or priorities of the exporting country are, with very limited exceptions, not relevant to the ability of the exporter to engage in a commercial activity in the importing country. Establishing such a requirement in an agreement designed to regulate the conditions of access to the market of the importing country would take the arrangement well beyond the subject of a "commercial" agreement.

Most participants in the environmental movement, and others promoting civil or human rights internationally, would take strong exception to this argument. To them, a globalizing economy cannot be sustained in a social policy vacuum. As business grows beyond political frontiers, social activists are concerned that the ability of national governments to protect the economic benefits and social welfare preferences of their citizens, including their environmental preferences, will be eroded. Many fear that the political consensus upon which tolerance for an open trade system depends could be undermined by ignoring these concerns.

Governments need to take meaningful action to counter these fears and the nationalist and protectionist sentiments found in virtually every society. In fact, this is the motivating force behind the relevant principles of the Rio Declaration. Stressing the need for international cooperation to address environmental problems, and specifically those of transboundary or global concern, is at the heart of that consensus.

There is another group within the environmental movement for whom such measures will never be adequate. This group believes that some authority is needed to impose order and control over a globalized economy to achieve the environmental policy objectives that the most advanced societies have defined as priorities. Lacking a supranational institution for that purpose, they seek to transform the WTO into such an instrument. Within a "reformed" WTO, the socially advanced countries can coerce the less advanced ones to adhere to their priorities through the power of their markets. Collective action would be preferable, but states should act unilaterally if necessary. Although these arguments for linkage among commercial and social policy objectives have some political appeal, the real issue is whether the linkage should be expressed contractually.

For those in the trade community, the answer must be no. It cannot be emphasized too strongly that the WTO is not a world government institution with attendant policing and enforcement powers. It is essentially a contract among governments defining the conditions under which each will permit commercial activities to take place between their nationals and those of the other contracting governments. Like most other contracts, this one also contains provisions under which disputes will be resolved and penalties for violations will be assessed. Unlike the U.N. Charter, the WTO contains no provisions for collective enforcement. Further, it does not recognize the jurisdiction of any outside authority to nullify any aspect of the contract or to require any kind of collective action by contract participants.

Agreement among governments on the conditions necessary to permit international commercial transactions to occur with anything like the efficiency of domestic transactions has proven over the centuries to be enormously complex. In our time, the GATT system has taken 50 years to evolve to the point where agreement on some policies or practices, going beyond barriers at the border to trade in goods, has been possible. To require either the WTO system or regional agreements to use trade to change behavior in the domestic social or foreign policies of individual states is simply loading too much responsibility on an instrument that exists more by the sufferance than the conviction of national governments.

Clearly, some aspects of environmental policy can be addressed in a trade agreement. NAFTA, for example, contains provisions requiring that imports from other NAFTA partners must meet the product standards of the importing state. NAFTA also set a precedent by addressing environmental aspects of inward investment and records the view of the parties that "it is inappropriate to encourage investment by relaxing domestic health, safety, or environmental measures." It is entirely appropriate for commercial agreements to clarify the domestic legal and regulatory conditions under which the parties will permit business to take place and to specify actions that the parties agree to apply or avoid in facilitating commercial transactions.

There also could be a role for trade measures in the limited case of intergovernmental programs to control transboundary air or water quality among states or localities sharing a common catchment area. Assume that one state regulates gas or effluent emissions from enterprises on its territory and has the authority to force those that do not meet the standards to stop production. It would arguably be consistent with the principle of national treatment to require that establishments on the other side of its border that contribute emissions to the common air or water basins be held to comparable standards. If such enterprises failed to meet those requirements, some would urge that their products not be allowed to be sold in the other country.

Whether unilateral action of this kind would be consistent with current GATT rules would be for a WTO panel to decide. However, the states commonly affected could negotiate an agreement containing such provisions, and the agreement certainly would not offend the WTO. The parties would have consensually waived their WTO rights in favor of what they agree is an overriding objective. However, care must be taken both to limit such agreements to countries that share genuinely common air and water basins and to guard against the temptation of a powerful state to coerce a less powerful one to adopt its standards, whether environmentally sound or not.

CONCLUSIONS

The following principles and recommendations are set forth in order to help guide trade and environment policymakers in their efforts to reconcile successfully legitimate, although sometimes divergent, goals.

- Environmental agreements should be used to achieve environmental objectives, and trade agreements should be used to achieve commercial objectives.

- To the extent that trade measures are deemed necessary to achieve an environmental objective, they should be used only within the context of an MEA and only when directly related to achieving that objective. They should not be used as sanctions to penalize another country for behavior that a trading partner might find objectionable.

- If collective sanctions are deemed necessary, they should be taken only pursuant to the procedures specified in the U.N. Charter and should be applied by all parties to the charter.

- International trade rules should be amended to clarify the conditions under which MEAs requiring the use of trade measures would be deemed consistent with current WTO rules.

- Both to deal with real-world pressures to take unilateral action to promote environmental objectives and to stimulate governments to negotiate multilateral agreements to deal with transboundary or global environmental problems, the WTO should amend the international trade rules to establish renewed discipline and incentives to meet both objectives.

NOTES

1. Report of the United Nations Conference on Environment and Development, Resolutions Adopted by the Conference, Annex I (Declaration on Environment and Development), Rio de Janeiro, June 3–14, 1992.
2. Report on Trade and Environment to the OECD Council at Ministerial Level, OECD/GD/(95)63 (Paris: OECD, 1995).
3. The viewpoints and specific proposals developed in the rest of this chapter are drawn from the author's work and experience with the U.S. Council for International Business. However, unless specifically identified as those of the U.S. Council, the views expressed are those of the author and not necessarily those of the U.S. Council.

4. See, for example, OECD Report, p. 22, par. 42. For similar views from business sources, see The Business Roundtable, "Protecting the Global Environment and Promoting International Trade" (March 1993), Washington, DC; and U.S. Council for International Business, "Policy Statement on an Integrated Approach to the Environment and Trade Issues and the GATT," New York, May 1, 1992.

5. United States Council for International Business, "Policy Statement on International Environmental Agreements and the Use of Trade Measures to Achieve Their Objectives," New York, December 1993.

6. The concept of this approach was originally put forward in an article by Kenneth Berlin and Jeffrey Lang, "Trade and Environment," *The Washington Quarterly* (Autumn 1993). The specific proposals that follow are summarized from the United States Council for International Business, "Policy Statement on Constraints on the Unilateral Use of Trade Measures to Enforce Environmental Policies," New York, April 1994.

Chapter 16

The Trade Remedies: A U.S. Perspective

Thomas R. Howell

Trade remedies exist as an integral part of the multilateral trading system and the laws of major open economies. They form a foundation of the international trading system as well as national trade regulation. These laws have provided the political and intellectual base that has allowed the major General Agreement on Tariffs and Trade (GATT) contracting parties and subsequently World Trade Organization (WTO) member countries to join in elimination of high, standing tariffs and other protective border measures. The logic of these trade remedies is straightforward: Permanent protection will be eliminated, but if certain defined trade-distorting practices that cause economic harm exist, then the importing country can employ offsetting duties.

The rules of the multilateral trading system condemn dumping and seek to limit trade-distorting subsidies. Dumping, a private practice, is the selling of goods abroad for less than fair value, which may consist of price discrimination (selling abroad for less than at home) or selling below the average cost of production. Government aids are not condemned in blanket fashion but are divided by purpose into those that are likely to cause the least damage, such as environmental aids, and are nonactionable, and those that may cause the most harm, such as export subsidies, and are prohibited. Before offsetting measures may be imposed, actual harm must have been demonstrated—that is, an injury test is applied. National trade remedy decisions are reviewable by WTO dispute settlement panels.

The principal trade remedies, antidumping (AD) and countervailing duties (CVD), invoked by the petition of an injured industry, have been utilized almost exclusively by large, open market economies, where trade is regulated in a transparent manner. These are the European Union (EU), the United States, Canada, and Australia. In addition, countries that are emerging from systems of permanent, high import barriers, such as Brazil and Mexico, are beginning to employ antidumping, with varying degrees of success in adhering to the WTO rules. Where trade is regulated by nontransparent means, such as in Japan, these trade remedies almost never have been employed.

Another form of trade remedy that is part of the U.S. trade law scheme is directed primarily at opening foreign markets. Section 301 of the Trade Act of 1974 is the means by which a domestic industry can formally ask the U.S. government to bring a matter to international dispute settlement. It also gives authority to the president and the office of the United States Trade Representative (USTR) to retaliate against foreign goods or services if market opening activities ultimately are unsuccessful. Only foreign governmental practices can be addressed, and private restraints of trade can be the subject of complaint only if the foreign government tolerates these anticompetitive practices. A major element of the Uruguay Round agreement was the establishment of significant new limits on the ability of the United States to use Section 301 as leverage to open foreign markets other than through bringing a dispute settlement case.

Other trade remedies include the highly specialized Section 337 of the Tariff Act of 1930, which bars entry of goods that violate intellectual property rights, and Section 201ff. of the Trade Act of 1974, which allows for import relief when serious injury is caused, regardless of the kind of trade practices involved. For a variety of reasons, the import relief remedy has fallen completely into disuse. This leaves antidumping and countervailing duties as the principal remaining WTO-authorized trade regulatory instruments. Of these, countervailing duties attract only the enmity of those whose governments heavily subsidize export industries. Since subsidies are widely condemned, there is little general debate in the trade community or academia about the merits of applying countervailing duties. The current debate over trade remedies thus focuses on a single remedy with respect to imports—antidumping duties—and a single remedy with respect to access abroad for exports—Section 301. These are almost universally condemned by academic economists; by countries whose goods are found to be dumped most often, such as Japan; and by countries that limit access to their own markets. It is not surprising that China, the largest nonmarket economy in the world, on seeking WTO accession is trying to curb the use of antidumping duties.

It is useful to consider whether the current intellectual trend, apparently running against the use of national trade remedies, is healthy. Should the remedies gradually be eroded through a combination of international negotiation, administrative inhibition, and legislative change pursued by importers—all in the name of "free trade"—as many in the trade debate now appear to desire? Or do these laws serve a necessary function, not only in promoting U.S. commercial interests but in maintaining an open world trading system? And if retention of a system of trade remedies is necessary, are the current ones adequate to the tasks that are assigned to them? If not, can they be modified, particularly within the scope of an international legal framework that now places severe constraints on the application of unilateral measures?

Trade remedies play a necessary role in U.S. trade strategy. They assist in maintaining the openness of the U.S. market and in public support for a liberal world trading order. They are, in short, essential to the nation's commercial and strategic interests. It is true the remedies are not always adequate to address international market distortions of increasing complexity, nor is their application beyond criticism. But that does not mean they should be abolished. To the contrary, they should be refined and strengthened, consistent with existing U.S. commitments, to the extent necessary to offset market-distorting policies and practices. Much of this needed reform can be accomplished through a combination of administrative actions within the current legal framework, new legislation, and, if necessary, renegotiation of some of the existing but temporary WTO provisions. Concurrently, the U.S. government needs to devote a greater effort to developing its information base about foreign policies and practices that make trade remedies necessary.

WHY TRADE REMEDIES MATTER

The current call for limitation of national trade remedies is weakening one of the pillars supporting the multilateral trading system.

Simply put, the global open trade system was created because of an abiding political consensus within the United States and the EU that their respective domestic markets should be kept relatively open to the rest of the world. The trade remedies—which offset the most disruptive effects of market-distorting practices abroad—were necessary for the creation of that consensus both in the United States and in Europe and remain essential to its survival.

Now and in the future, the WTO system is increasingly important to the interests of many medium-size trading countries, such as Mexico and Brazil. Their economies are undergoing substantial liberalization, and trade remedies will become ever more important to the political balance necessary for their full participation in the liberal world trading system. Domestic support for free trade is not immutable in great industrial powers. It collapsed with astonishing suddenness in 1930 to 1932 in Britain, the original exponent of the doctrine. An important element in Britain's abrupt abandonment of open markets in favor of GATT was the loss of support for free trade within the business community, an erosion that had been under way for years prior to the actual event.[1] British business complained that foreign markets were closed to British exports while dumped and subsidized foreign products freely flowed into the empire. The perception that the government was taking action against these structural problems might have altered business attitudes, but successive British governments proved utterly unable to develop a policy response. The creation of trade remedies selectively targeted against specific foreign mercantilist practices was debated, but workable remedies were never created.[2] When the depression came, much of the business support for free trade that might have countered surging protectionist sentiment was already gone.[3] It can, of course, be argued that Britain's abandonment of free trade reflected nothing more than the particular circumstances of the country and the time—the tangle of intractable cultural and economic problems sometimes referred to as the "British disease," the depression, efforts to protect the pound sterling, and so on—and thus offers no lessons for us today. But the history of trade remedies as they have evolved in many countries during this century demonstrates a natural nexus between their existence and the maintenance of an open market.[4]

Trade remedies, however, are more than just a means to try to keep narrow industrial interests from opposing further trade liberalization. They are themselves an important form of discipline on market-distorting practices in the world economy. Without them, competitive outcomes would be determined much more frequently by factors other than the relative efficiency and competitiveness of individual producers. The use of trade remedies by a few large, relatively open economies, such as the United States, the EU, Canada, and Australia, has proven more effective at combating specific distortions than any multilateral mechanism yet devised, for the simple reason that many foreign countries and companies will opt to modify their behavior rather than lose access to such large markets.[5]

Apart from the positive role trade remedies play within the current liberal trading system, the United States has a legitimate national interest in regulating the extent to which market distortions that occur abroad are allowed to shape the American economy. It has chosen to do this largely through the use of the trade remedies—that is, quasi-adjudicative legal procedures that are relatively transparent, that offer interested parties an opportunity to be heard—and that provide a panoply of procedural safeguards and protections. These proceedings are highly visible, subject to detailed public scrutiny, and involve the rendering of published judgments by U.S. authorities. All these procedures tend to highlight U.S. actions and expose the United States to international disapproval. Making the measures less transparent, as they are in some other countries, would hardly be a step forward for the international trading system.

But if the trade remedies are worth saving and reinforcing, what needs to be done, and how to do it? At the outset, a frank assessment is needed as to whether the remedies that now exist still work to offset the major market distortions abroad that are most problematic for U.S. industries.[6] A particular area of concern is private restraints of trade and the murky subject of covert government support for private restraints. Another problem is official corruption, which often is linked to restrictive anticompetitive private acts.[7] A comprehensive survey of the market-distorting practices currently confronting U.S. industries abroad would no doubt yield many other examples of real problems for which trade remedies offer little or no answer. The United States should mount a serious effort to identify areas of weakness in the current system of remedies, and then seek to improve and adapt them to the competitive realities its industries will confront in the next century. Such reforms should take place within the current WTO framework and should be designed to support, not undercut, WTO disciplines.

ANTIDUMPING

The U.S. antidumping law emerged from the Uruguay Round with relatively few additional constraints on its operation. There were, however, a number of technical changes introduced into the Antidumping Agreement that will work to the advantage of companies subject to antidumping action.[8] Nonetheless, antidumping measures are currently the subject of constant criticism, if not censure, from a significant part of the business press in the United States and Britain, from trade policy officials in a number of countries, and from a large number of academics. Antidumping duties, it is said, hurt consumers and industries that use "dumped" imports as inputs; they are inherently unfair, or at least administered in a way that is unfair; and most significantly, it is said, whatever its original purpose may have been, the antidumping remedy today is being abused by private interests to advance unworthy objectives, including "harassment" of commercial rivals, "rent seeking," and outright cartelization. These are serious charges, leveled by individuals and institutions that command considerable respect in the realm of economic policymaking.[9] Over the longer term, if not addressed, such criticism will lead to the weakening of the remedy itself, whether through administrative inhibition, adverse panel decisions, legislation, or a combination of all of these.

The antidumping laws serve a necessary function, both in U.S. trade policy and in the world trading system. For whatever reason, they have attracted few articulate defenders since Professor Jacob Viner published his seminal work on the subject in 1923.[10] Conversely, a large number of books and articles have been published in the past 20 years, many of them by respected academics, that are highly critical of antidumping measures.[11]

But there is a case for antidumping. Dumping erodes and sometimes destroys industries in markets where dumping is occurring. This phenomenon is more than a function of the short-run lost sales and price suppression that dumping causes and that many argue is simply a manifestation of healthy competition. More important, the ability to dump is a long-run competitive advantage enjoyed by the firm that does the dumping and it is a product of a market distortion, generally a protected home market and some degree of monopoly power within that market, which can alter the long-run competitive balance between national industries. In effect, dumping places firms that operate in a laissez-faire milieu at a continuing long-term disadvantage relative to competitors operating from a protected sanctuary. There are at least two reasons for this.

One is unit cost differential. Dumping firms tend to enjoy lower unit costs than firms based in markets where dumping is occurring, other factors being equal, because dumping enables them to operate their facilities at a higher rate. In capital-intensive industries, the utilization rate often has a greater impact on costs than any other element of a company's operation. The disparity in operating rates leads to a progressive loss of competitiveness by firms based in the market where dumped goods are sold.

The second is investment deterrence. Over time, dumping functions as an incentive to disinvestment in markets where dumping is occurring and, conversely, encourages intensive, even excessive investments in the protected countries from which dumping is taking place. This phenomenon, too, leads to a progressive loss of competitiveness by the former relative to the latter.

Why should this matter? Dumping benefits consumers of dumped products, at least in the short run, and in most cases a country will regard dumping as problematic only if its own industries make a dumped product or would like to do so. But it is necessary to balance short-run consumer benefits, which often are highly dispersed and minimally felt, against the fact that dumping permits less efficient firms to prevail over more efficient ones, and the fact that effects tend to be highly concentrated in specific sectors. From a policy perspective, the shape of a country's economy should be determined by the competitiveness of its industries, not the maneuverings of anticompetitive business groups abroad.

Despite the sheer tonnage of published criticism of antidumping, a solid case for the curtailment of the antidumping remedy has not yet been made. The basic flaw that unites these works is that they examine the remedy, antidumping, in isolation, without an informed analysis of the problem the remedy is designed to address. Not one of the dozens of contemporary articles and books that attack antidumping examines a single case of dumping in detail; the phenomenon of dumping itself usually is simply brushed aside as not worthy of serious examination.[12] Even more striking, given the sheer number of academics and journalists who have examined the issue, is the precariously small empirical base on which their body of work rests. The case against antidumping has been developed primarily through use of abstract mathematical models,[13] application of laissez-faire ideological doctrine, and rhetorical blasts at "protectionists," "vested interests," and other unholy influences, not an examination of the factual record.

To be sure, as is the case with respect to any major regulatory regime, antidumping enforcement produces some results that are not defensible. Small companies charged with dumping may find it difficult and costly to respond to lengthy information requests from administering authorities and may simply exit the market before a decision is rendered—hardly an equitable outcome. There is little reason to doubt the charge that nonmeritorious cases sometimes are brought for nuisance or harassment effect, a phenomenon that can occur with respect to any form of litigation and that constitutes an abuse wherever it occurs, be it torts or trade. Critics argue that antidumping penalizes some types of normally accepted commercial activity, a charge that is highly debatable in many cases but clearly accurate in at least a few. For example, an exporting firm that has been selling its product at an equal price in domestic and foreign markets may be thrown into a position in which it is technically "selling at less than fair value" merely through a realignment of exchange rates, even with no change in the actual domestic or export price. But it is not likely to be found to have been "dumping" because a finding that injury is taking place or is likely to take place is necessary before antidumping duties can be imposed. Where anomalies occur and dumping duties are imposed where there is no clear harm, the problem should be rectified through incremental legislative and administrative reforms. Anomalies should not be confused with systemic weaknesses, and they do not provide the basis for a broad indictment of the entire regime.

A more serious criticism of the antidumping law is that the remedy it provides—a duty at the border—is wholly inadequate to the complex task that it has been assigned by default, to compensate for the imbalance in antitrust enforcement that exists between national markets. Antidumping cannot break up cartels in foreign markets when foreign antitrust authorities fail to act, nor can it open "sanctuary" markets protected by restrictive private practices and arrangements. It does not follow, however, that the antidumping remedy should be repealed in anticipation of either increased antitrust enforcement by foreign authorities or enforceable and effective multilateral competition rules. Neither of these alternatives will occur in the foreseeable future. A vast gulf in national economic traditions has frustrated every attempt at international consensus on this subject since the birth of GATT.[14] For the time being, antidumping measures must function as a crude buffering measure between economies organized under fundamentally different rules, a "poor but necessary substitute for enforceable multilateral competition policies."[15]

Before the antidumping law is weakened or eliminated in response to the growing chorus of criticism, U.S. policymakers should satisfy themselves that the restrictive private practices that foster dumping have been largely eradicated in world commerce. Such an assessment is literally impossible at present simply because the once-formidable body of knowledge that existed on this subject a generation ago has been allowed to decay.[16] Empirical study of actual anticompetitive regimes has been supplanted almost entirely by abstract mathematical modeling exercises that, simply put, do not provide an adequate basis for the actual formulation of policy.[17] Admitedly, amassing a comprehensive picture of actual anticompetitive practices in the world market is a difficult task, not only because fact-based study of the subject has been extremely thin, but also because foreign governments and industries are not eager to advertise the various ways in which they limit competition. However, the U.S. government already has demonstrated that it is capable of developing a comprehensive information base on this subject,[18] and it should find the resources and the resolve to do so once again.[19]

COUNTERVAILING DUTIES

While all nations, including the United States, provide subsidies to various industries, the notion that subsidies that injure industries should be offset has been enshrined in GATT since its inception. Some economists argue that importing nations should gladly absorb subsidized products from abroad as a consumer benefit financed by foreign treasuries. But this view has never enjoyed much support in the United States. The extraordinary political turmoil and economic dislocation caused by subsidies in the European Union as internal barriers have fallen—in effect, putting the economists' theory to the test—should dispel any notion that simply ignoring subsidies is economically prudent, much less politically sustainable.[20]

U.S. trade policy consistently has sought to strengthen disciplines on injurious subsidies, through both negotiation of multilateral disciplines and the continuing refinement of the U.S. countervailing duty (CVD) law. In the Uruguay Round, the United States placed a high priority on securing increased disciplines on subsidies. The outcome, regrettably, can hardly be regarded as a success. While subsidy disciplines on an international level were strengthened in some areas with the adoption of the Agreement on Subsidies and Countervailing Measures (SCM Agreement), they were reduced in other areas, arguably with little net material improvement. At the same time, the U.S. CVD law—historically the only effective mechanism for offsetting the injurious effects of subsidies—has been clearly weakened as a result of the round.[21] This outcome reflects the fact that U.S. negotiators confronted a fundamental disagreement at the international level on the subject of subsidies. While the United States regarded subsidies as a problem to be brought under discipline, many key countries regarded U.S. efforts to offset their subsidies through the application of countervailing duties as the principal problem to be addressed in a new agreement. This stark division in outlook was straddled through an agreement that created the potential for some new multilateral discipline but at the same time opened sizable holes in the countervailing duty remedy.

The challenge facing U.S. policymakers on the subsidies front is thus primarily one of damage control. Two steps should be taken: The SCM Agreement should be reassessed, and "green light" provisions should be renegotiated.

The United States accepted new constraints on its use of countervailing duties in return for new multilateral norms and procedures governing subsidies. Whenever possible, these should be put to the test by the United States in challenges to specific injurious foreign subsidies. It may be that the new mechanisms will prove highly effective, although there is little international precedent to suggest such a result. But if the SCM proves to be as ineffective a discipline on subsidies as the Tokyo Round Subsidies Code, that fact needs to be established.

Prior to the Uruguay Round, U.S. countervailing duty law provided that a subsidy was countervailable if it caused material injury, regardless of the purpose for which the subsidy was granted. The SCM, however, establishes three categories of "green light" subsidies that cannot be countervailed even if they cause material injury—subsidies given for regional development, environmental compliance, and research and development. The green light provisions arguably open major holes in the countervailing duty regime. The fact is, money is fungible. Allowing subsidies for any purpose, even if they are noble ones, relieves companies of their obligations. This can create trade distortions. Company A in country A and company B in country B compete. Both have pension costs, environmental costs, and research and development costs, which can amount to billions of dollars. If enough public funds can be channeled to company B by country B, it is more than possible that competitive outcomes can be changed to the point where injury to country A's industry will occur. In these instances, the intellectual justification for greenlighting is not that clear, especially since the remedy that is being blocked consists solely of allowing offsetting measures. In anticipation of the renewal negotiations, the U.S. government should closely monitor the greenlighting provisions and study the extent to which green light subsidies granted abroad may be adversely affecting U.S. industries that are no longer able to turn to the countervailing duty law for relief. Based on principle, and informed by this review, the United States should oppose renewal of the green light provisions when they expire.

A WORD ABOUT IMPORT RELIEF

Section 201 of the Trade Act of 1974, which provides for import relief under the GATT "Escape Clause," has fallen into disuse, apparently because of the perceived inability of industries suffering from serious harm due to import competition to obtain relief. Proposals have been advanced for legislation that would make the grant of relief easier or at least lead to more predictable outcomes. While these proposals are worth examining, the fact is that import relief cases tend to be highly politicized—making the pattern of results from case to case rather capricious—and it is not clear that further revision of the statute would cure that defect. Moreover, even a successful revision of Section 201 would not resolve its problems because import relief, even if granted, yields a meaningful result only in select situations.

It is true that in some cases, an industry that has lost international competitiveness can benefit from temporary protection to take adjustment measures—whether to exit the market or to attempt to regain competitiveness through new investment—and reform of the current statute could be of benefit in such instances. In many other situations in which U.S. industries are suffering from import pressure, however, the question faced is, in effect, "Adjust, yes—but to what?" Foreign steel producers receive billions of dollars in subsidies. Many foreign markets for textile fabric are restricted or closed. Cartels distort trade and foster dumping. Section 201 offers no answers to these problems. Apart from a strategy of disinvestment and market exit, the ability of domestic industry to "adjust" in such cases is limited, given that these distortions reflect matters beyond an industry's power to affect through its own efforts and will still confront the domestic industry when the period of temporary protection ends.

SECTION 301 OF THE TRADE ACT OF 1974

Section 301 of the Trade Act of 1974 is the only remedy available to U.S. industries seeking to engage the U.S. government's support in negotiating the elimination of market barriers abroad. It has proven highly effective in specific cases in which bilateral negotiations, backed by the possibility of U.S. sanctions, led to agreements that reduced or eliminated market barriers. However, the Uruguay Round agreement has cast the future role of Section 301 into question, placing significant additional costs on any unilateral imposition of trade measures by the United States outside the procedures of the WTO. U.S. trade measures, imposed as a response to foreign market closure on the part of another WTO member, would be subject to challenge under WTO dispute settlement rules. The United States would face the prospect of not only being found in breach of its international obligations but being subject to WTO-sanctioned retaliatory measures by the complaining party. While the prospect of an adverse GATT ruling was technically already present prior to the Uruguay Round, the United States enjoyed the power to block the adoption of adverse panel decisions. After the round, this is no longer the case, a fact that fundamentally changes the politics of Section 301. The WTO dispute settlement rules thus had the effect of acting as an "equalizer," offsetting the big-country advantage that the United States possessed in terms of its trade leverage. The United States accepted this cost in order to improve its position as a plaintiff in the WTO dispute settlement process. But the advantage to the U.S.-as-plaintiff exists only where another WTO member has transgressed the WTO's substantive rules in closing its market.

Herein lies a problem. The new WTO dispute settlement mechanism creates a conundrum for the United States. WTO rules do not cover what are probably the most significant and pervasive market barriers in the developed world today—restrictive private business practices. At the same time, the new WTO rules significantly impair use of the principal U.S. tool for attacking those practices, Section 301. Japan's behavior toward the United States during much of 1996 and 1997, when it spurned U.S. requests on virtually every major bilateral trade issue pending between the two countries—proclaiming that "the era of bilateralism is over"—is partly attributable to Japan's belief that, with the advent of the WTO, Section 301 can no longer be used effectively. Japanese bureaucrats and business executives appear to believe that Japan's system of import and investment protection, having been "privatized," is impervious to U.S. sanctions. They therefore appear to believe that it is no longer necessary to give serious consideration to U.S. concerns about market access barriers in Japan and, indeed, may no longer feel bound by the various bilateral commitments that have been negotiated between the two countries over the past several decades.[22]

Against the background of these developments, U.S. policymakers are actively mounting legal challenges to market barriers under the new WTO mechanism. At the same time, they have begun casting about for other potential forms of leverage that could be used in Section 301 actions against practices not covered by WTO rules and could be used in ways that do not place the United States in breach of its commitments. The choices are very limited and often impractical.[23]

This dilemma has fostered proposals for legislation that would authorize the imposition of fines on foreign firms that engage in anticompetitive conduct that burdens U.S. commerce. Fines are not trade restrictions and do not, in and of themselves, violate the WTO, as would the unilateral imposition of quotas or tariffs on bound items. While some foreign firms that would be the target of such measures do not have assets in the United States against which fines could be levied and collected, many others do. When the idea of levying fines pursuant to Section 301 first surfaced in Washington toward the end of the Uruguay Round negotiations, a number of legitimate objections were raised, and the practicability and legality of any initiative of this nature pose serious questions. Nevertheless, the concept of fines levied pursuant to Section 301 warrants vetting, if only because alternative forms of leverage suffer even greater defects.

One possible way to implement a proposal to give USTR authority to levy fines would be to vest in USTR authority to issue cease-and-desist orders against certain anticompetitive foreign practices that burden or restrict U.S. commerce. The scope of this authority would be limited to particularly egregious practices that are illegal per se under U.S. antitrust law and that are acknowledged by the laws of most industrial countries as offensive.[24] The order would direct foreign parties to cease and desist from the acts in question or, alternatively, to eliminate the burden on U.S. commerce. The issuance of an order would put parties on notice of USTR's intention to act. If the activity continued in spite of the order, USTR could seek the imposition of a fine through the order of a federal district court. There would be no retroactive penalty for any conduct that occurred prior to the issuance of the order. The fine would not be directed against the conduct itself, only the breach of the order, and would continue to grow as time passed and compliance with the order was not forthcoming. This remedy would be administered in a manner similar to the Federal Trade Commission (FTC) Act, which authorizes the FTC to issue cease-and-desist orders (enforceable by fines in federal court) involving cases of anticompetitive conduct. Indeed, given the fact that the FTC has expertise, staff, and investigatory powers that could be employed to develop the necessary factual and legal base in each case, it may be preferable to amend the Federal Trade Commission Act to provide for a joint role for USTR and the FTC in cases involving certain categories of anticompetitive foreign conduct.

A number of legal objections to this proposal can be anticipated, but they do not appear to be insurmountable.[25] More serious obstacles arise out of bureaucratic and jurisdictional considerations. A major institutional cleavage exists in the federal government between the trade and antitrust policy regimes, each of which is administered by different agencies using entirely separate statutory schemes to achieve objectives that not only differ but sometimes actually conflict. The trade and antitrust agencies report to different committees of Congress, which are protective of their jurisdiction and that of their agencies. Differences in tradition, intellectual outlook, and operational approach contribute to misunderstanding and even hostility between policymakers on opposite sides of the trade/antitrust divide. Such embedded problems, while not insuperable, it is hoped, admittedly would pose formidable hurdles for any initiative aimed at reform. But the institutional fissure between trade and antitrust is itself working to undermine the ability of the United States to deal with new forms of protectionism that jeopardize the world trading system, most notably the "privatization" of market barriers abroad.

The WTO as yet offers no clear answers to this phenomenon. Accordingly, with full recognition of the difficulty involved, a start must be made on the necessary task of reducing the divergences between U.S. trade and antitrust policy and developing a new policy.

What is needed from the point of view of the national commercial interests of the United States is a continuum of tools to deal with the continuum of trade-distorting practices U.S. firms face abroad. If governments subsidize an industry, countervailing duties are applicable. If they clearly order the closing of the market, a WTO case lies ahead. If subsidies or a closed market creates dumping of products in the United States, an antidumping order can be entered. However, if private anticompetitive practices result in market closure, there is no reliable remedy. If these restrictive business practices are informally encouraged or quietly tolerated by a foreign government, the path to an effective remedy is also unclear. This lacuna in the trade remedy laws of the United States needs repair if markets are to be truly open to international trade.

WTO/NAFTA DISPUTE SETTLEMENT

To date there is an insufficient record to determine the effect of WTO and North American Free Trade Agreement (NAFTA) dispute resolution processes on the effectiveness of the trade remedies. Will their dispute resolution panels be inclined against the remedies, at least in some instances? To be sure, U.S. negotiators went to considerable lengths to safeguard against such an outcome. In the U.S.-Canada Free Trade Agreement (FTA), and now NAFTA, the United States tried to write standards of review that limit the extent to which binational panels can permissibly second-guess the decisions of national authorities. The WTO dispute resolution procedures provide for a broader scope of review than those of NAFTA, particularly with respect to countervailing duties, but considerable care was taken to create a system that resembles an adjudicatory appellate process. But it is unclear whether the safeguards in either agreement are adequate.

With respect to the U.S.-Canada FTA (now NAFTA), it is not clear that the limited standards of review negotiated by the United States are being and will be observed by binational dispute resolution panels. In the recent Softwood Lumber case, a binational panel with a majority of Canadian panelists explicitly substituted its own analysis for that of the U.S. Department of Commerce in a CVD decision, notwithstanding the provisions of the FTA itself. U.S. Circuit Judge Malcolm Wilkey's dissent in the Extraordinary Challenge Committee review of this panel action summarized the problem as follows:

> Basically, the Panel opinion attempts to redo, to reevaluate the evidence, to redetermine the technical issues before the administrative agency. The Panel places its own interpretation and makes its own evaluation of the weight of the evidence. In addition, the Panel insists upon its own methodology, thus violating the principle that where there is a gap in the statute, because the Congress has not prescribed precisely the methodology to be used, this is confided to the Agency's expertise and discretion. . . . In summary, I believe that this Binational Panel Majority opinion may violate more principles of agency action than any opinion by a reviewing body which I have ever read.[26]

The binational panel split 3 to 2 along straight national lines, with the Canadian majority unanimously supporting the Canadian challenge to the application of U.S. law. It was subsequently revealed that two of the three Canadian panelists had failed to disclose, among other things, the fact that they belonged to law firms representing Canadian lumber interests with a direct interest in the outcome of the case.[27] The U.S. government sought to overturn the binational panel's ruling based both on its departure from the FTA standard of review and "Material Breach of the Code of Conduct and Serious Conflict of Interest" with respect to the panelists with undisclosed conflicts of interest. The Extraordinary Challenge Committee rejected the U.S. appeal, however, again splitting along straight national lines, with the Canadian majority prevailing 2 to 1.

While Softwood Lumber may prove to be an anomaly, variants on the problems highlighted by this case—biased panelists, disregard for the agreed limits on scope of review, apparent lack of competence by panelists to interpret the laws of another country—are a risk inherent in the current process that could undermine domestic support for the Free Trade Agreement.[28]

The WTO dispute resolution regime differs in many respects from that established under the U.S.-Canada FTA and NAFTA. WTO panels usually will consist of third-country nationals rather than nationals of the parties to a dispute, reducing the risk of bias and conflicts of interest.

The WTO regime more closely resembles a judicial regime of appellate review. In sharp contrast, the NAFTA panelists actually sit in place of national judges and make binding interpretations of domestic statutes. Nevertheless, a significant risk exists that WTO panelists, acting in good faith and in what they believe to be an objective fashion to apply GATT principles, will overturn important aspects of the antidumping and countervailing duty laws. This is because a notion has been put forward in a GATT panel decision that the antidumping and countervailing duty remedies authorized by GATT Article VI are a derogation from GATT itself, so that in disputes arising out of their application, the rules should be narrowly construed against the country applying the measures. This view is wrong as a legal proposition, but if held by prospective panelists, if would be likely to affect their decisions.[29] It is true that the United States succeeded in negotiating language in the Antidumping Code that, on its face, would appear to limit the extent of review by panels of national authorities. But as a legal and practical matter, this language may have little or no effect on panels.[30] Moreover, similar language was not included in the SCM Agreement with respect to review of countervailing duty decisions. While U.S. officials have stated that the two codes are to be administered in the same way, given the absence of standard-of-review language in the SCM that parallels that of the Antidumping Agreement, U.S. countervailing duty decisions could be overturned by WTO panels exercising wide-ranging power of review, quite possibly utilizing a presumption against the application of countervailing duties.

A U.S. domestic consensus favoring NAFTA and the WTO could not have been formed if one of the explicitly stated costs of U.S. accession was the surrender of the ability to use the antidumping and countervailing duty remedies. It is imperative that the same outcome not result from an unintended operation of the dispute settlement process piecemeal over a longer period of time. While events may prove this concern unfounded, policymakers must monitor the operation of the dispute settlement process closely and make sure that it does not undermine support for two institutions, the WTO and NAFTA, that are fundamentally in America's interests.

The United States has not yet put in place a mechanism for achieving an informed assessment of the merits of the WTO's binding dispute resolution procedures. In the debate over the congressional vote to ratify the Uruguay Round, the manner of dispute resolution proved especially controversial. Senate Majority Leader Bob Dole indicated that a precondition for his support was the establishment of procedures for congressional oversight of the WTO dispute resolution process. As a quid pro quo for Senator Dole's support of the implementing bill, President Bill Clinton agreed to support legislation that would establish a commission of federal judges to review WTO dispute resolution decisions.[31] The commission would provide Congress and the president with an informed review of how well the system is working. This, in turn, could provide the basis either for a validation of the system or, if dispute settlement were found to be repeatedly and seriously deficient, for a congressional debate over U.S. withdrawal from the WTO. The review body could mitigate the danger of political backlash in the United States against the WTO system in cases where panels rule against the country but where the review body, consisting of respected, independent U.S. jurists, finds the panel's actions defensible. The proposed legislation, or some variant that achieves the same end, should be enacted.

ACHIEVING MULTILATERAL DISCIPLINES

The WTO gives new opportunities and new tools for opening markets and challenging restrictive policies and practices. Having committed enormous capital to the current WTO regime, the United States must devote a comparable effort to making the system work, using the mechanisms available to attack restrictive policies and practices that it identifies as harmful to U.S. commercial interests.[32] At the same time it must be recognized that dispute settlement panels cannot successfully address practices not governed by substantive WTO obligations, such as private restraints of trade. Three steps must be taken to cure this defect: (1) gain knowledge of the nature and extent of private restraints of trade; (2) adopt effective domestic legal remedies—none exists now—to address these practices; and (3) negotiate multilateral rules that will curb these trade barriers. However, without an effective "unilateral" remedy, progress toward a multilateral discipline is likely to be very slow.

It is essential that the United States act vigorously to prevent the further erosion of trade remedies and move quickly and decisively to strengthen and adapt the remedies to the tasks it will be called upon to address in the 21st century.

NOTES

1. "The speed and completeness with which the remaining free trade support collapsed in 1930 can only be understood in the context of growing disillusion with trade liberalism in the 1920s." *Times* (London) July 10, 1930, cited in Tim Rooth, *British Protectionism and the International Economy: Overseas Commercial Policy in the* 1930s (Cambridge: Cambridge University Press, 1992), p. 70.

2. Pressure from mercantilist foreign practices led Conservative Prime Minister Arthur Balfour (1902–06) to counter growing protectionist sentiment in his own party by advocating the adoption of antidumping remedies and selective retaliatory tariffs as an alternative to across-the-board protection. His party was defeated, however, in the 1906 general election, and his proposals were not implemented. While Britain did enact an antidumping remedy in the 1920s, its unwieldiness (requiring nine procedural stages) rendered it ineffective as a practical tool. See Richard A. Rempel, *Unionists Divided: Arthur Balfour, Joseph Chamberlain and the Unionist Free Traders* (Newton Abbot and Hamden: Archer Books, 1972).

3. In 1930 a prestigious group of British banks—which only a few years before were staunch supporters of free trade—adopted a protectionist manifesto that provided, in part, as follows: "Bitter experience has taught Great Britain that the hopes expressed four years ago in a plea for the removal of the restrictions upon European trade have failed to be realized. The restrictions have been materially increased, and the sale of surplus foreign products in the British market has steadily grown." Rooth, *British Protectionism*, p. 46.

4. The current proliferation of AD and CVD regimes in newly industrializing countries as they scrap systems of administered protection strongly suggests that the availability of such remedies is necessary for the formation of a domestic political base adequate to support a policy of trade liberalization.

5. The imposition of stiff countervailing duties by the United States and the Community in the 1980s was a factor inducing a number of newly industrializing countries to abandon large-scale direct export subsidies. Despite

the opprobrium it bears in many foreign capitals, Section 301 (and the threat of its use) has been effective in opening markets and has probably proven the single most successful policy tool in reducing Japanese trade barriers. Section 301 was also a force driving the Uruguay Round forward, as other countries sought to create multilateral mechanisms as alternatives to U.S. action under Section 301. And although EU policymakers may be reluctant to acknowledge it, the CVD and AD actions brought against the Community's steel industry by the United States in 1980–82 played an important role in prodding some recalcitrant member states into accepting the European Commission's program for stricter disciplines on subsidies. A study published by the Institute for International Economics of Section 301's effect as a market-opening tool concluded as follows: "Careful analysis of 72 cases investigated between 1975 and 1992 leads us to conclude that section 301 was reasonably successful in opening foreign markets, especially after 1985. The analysis challenges the assumptions of 301's critics, concluding that 301 neither triggered major trade wars nor resulted in significant trade diversion. Nor did U.S. aggressive unilateralism in the late 1980s and early 1990s cause the collapse of the Uruguay Round or prevent significant multilateral liberalization and reform of GATT rules. To the contrary, American arm-twisting provided an important incentive for its trading partners to negotiate rules that strengthened the international trading system and discouraged U.S. unilateralism." Thomas O. Bayard and Kimberly Ann Elliott, *Reciprocity and Retaliation in U.S. Trade Policy* (Washington, D.C.: Institute for International Economics, 1994), p. 331.

6. On this point see Office of Technology Assessment, *Competing Economies: America, Europe and the Pacific Rim* (Washington, D.C.: Government Printing Office, 1991).

7. For a case study see Japanese investigative reporting on the relationship between corruption in the Ministry of Construction, "dango" (bid-rigging) in the construction industry, and the exclusion of foreign firms from construction contracts. *Tokyo Shimbun* (February 6, 1989); *Nihon Keizai Shimbun* (May 11, July 6, 1993); *Asahi Shimbun* (December 30, 1989); *Shukan Toyo Keizai* (August 13, 1993).

8. Much of the new Antidumping Agreement is a recitation of American-style procedural protections and transparency obligations assuring equitable and open proceedings. In addition, however, a number of provisions make bringing antidumping cases more difficult and costly (e.g., the standing requirements of Article 5.4) and favor ignoring or understating the degree of dumping (e.g., the averaging presumption of Article 2.4.2 and the "start-up" adjustment sanctioning forward pricing of Article 2.2.1.1).

9. The *Wall Street Journal*, the *Economist*, and the *Financial Times* have published editorials severely critical of the antidumping remedy.

10. Jacob Viner, *Dumping: A Problem in International Trade* (Chicago: University of Chicago Press, 1923). One noteworthy exception is a paper by WTO Economic Affairs Officer Jorge Miranda, "Should Anti-Dumping Laws Be Dumped?" (Centre for Applied Studies in International Negotiations, Brainstorming Conference, Geneva, Switzerland, July 11–12, 1996).

11. See, for example, Brian Hindley and Patrick Messerlin, *Antidumping Industrial Policy: Legalized Protection in the WTO and What to Do About It* (Washington, D.C.: American Enterprise Institute, 1996); J. Michael Finger, ed., *Antidumping: How It Works and Who Gets Hurt* (Ann Arbor: University of Michigan Press, 1993); P. K. M. Tharakan, *Policy Implications of Antidumping Measures* (Antwerp: University of Antwerp, 1991); Richard Boltuck and Robert E. Litan, eds., *Down in the Dumps: Administration of the Unfair Trade Laws* (Washington, D.C.: Brookings Institution, 1991); Richard Dale, *Antidumping Law in a Liberal Trade Order* (New York: St. Martin's Press, 1980); William A. Wares, *The Theory of Dumping and American Commercial Policy* (Lexington, Mass.: Lexington Books, 1992).

12. Michael Finger comments, for example, that "in a practical sense, the word 'dumping' has no meaning other then the one implicit in antidumping regulations. The pragmatic definition of dumping is the following: dumping is whatever you can get the government to act against under the antidumping law." Finger, *Antidumping*, p. viii.

13. A case in point is the U.S. International Trade Commission's 1995 study of the economic effects of AD and CVD, which concluded, based solely on a modeling exercise that was applied in nine sectors, that these remedies had resulted in a net detriment to the U.S. economy. The ITC study examined nine industries subject to AD/CVD orders in 1991. The existence and significance of anticompetitive practices and other market distortions in these industries (and others subject to AD/CVD orders) was not considered. The study focused exclusively on static effects of AD/CVD remedies, and did not take into account the long-term effects of those remedies or the practices which they offset (e.g., the encouragement of investment and technological advances, development of physical and technological infrastructure, and existence of strategic or core industries). The benefit to the U.S. economy of duties paid into the U.S. Treasury was excluded from the model. These limitations led two of the six commissioners to disapprove the study altogether (Newquist: "The estimates provided here are not 'facts' or 'findings' . . . instead they are the theoretical, untested results of certain modeling exercises undertaken by commissioners and economists and should be viewed with that understanding and limitation." Bragg: "Although economic modeling is a useful tool, it cannot substitute for 'real world' experience.") Two others approved the study to enable the commission to meet its deadline but expressed "certain reservations . . . about the adequacy of this report in presenting a balanced and comprehensive discussion of relevant issues." Only two out of six commissioners approved the report without reservations. International Trade Commission, *Economic Effects of Antidumping and Countervailing Duty Orders* (Washington, DC: Government Printing Office, 1995) pp. vii, xi, xiii.

14. Historian Alfred Chandler has observed that the U.S. enactment of antitrust legislation and its institutionalization of the values it reflects "probably marked the most important economic cultural difference between the United States and Germany, Britain and indeed the rest of the world insofar as it affected the evolution of the modern industrial enter-

prise." Alfred D. Chandler, Jr., *Scale and Scope: The Dynamics of Industrial Capitalism* (Cambridge and London: Belknap Press, Harvard University, 1990), p. 73.

15. Laura D'Andrea Tyson, *Who's Bashing Whom? Trade Conflict in High Technology Industries* (Washington, D.C.: Institute for International Economics, 1992), p. 268.

16. World War II removed the veil from the clandestine world of international cartels. Files seized by the Allied Property Custodian, wartime intelligence reports, and the U.S. Treasury's actions to trace blocked bank accounts developed a wealth of specific information about the cartels. The occupation of Japan and Germany, and the partial breakup of the *zaibatsu* and *Konzerne*, provided additional documentary materials. Soon after the war, the Twentieth Century Fund sponsored a massive survey of international cartels. In addition, excellent academic treatment was accorded the subject for a time. Since the 1940s, however, with a very few exceptions, empirical work in this area has virtually come to a halt, with the subject now dominated by modeling exercises and excursions in game theory. See George W. Stocking and Myron W. Watkins, *Cartels or Competition? The Economics of International Cartels by Business and Government* (Chapel Hill: University of North Carolina, 1946). Two noteworthy recent empirical works are Deborah C. Spar's *The Cooperative Edge: The Internal Politics of International Cartels* (Ithaca and London: Cornell University Press, 1994), and Mark Tilton's *Restrained Trade: Cartels in Japan's Basic Materials Industries* (Ithaca and London: Cornell University Press, 1996).

17. "The literature has largely developed around extremely theoretical models where dumping originates in very contrived settings that, generally, have very little to do with the kinds of dumping actually observed. Hence, it is not very helpful for drawing policy prescriptions applicable to real cases." Miranda, "Should Anti-Dumping Laws Be Dumped?" p. 4.

18. In 1916, soon after its formation, the Federal Trade Commission published a massive study of restrictive foreign business practices that affected U.S. exports. This study, which drew on reports from U.S. embassies and consulates and interviews with U.S. and foreign businessmen, was encyclopedic in its scope and depth. It may well still stand as the best comprehensive examination of this subject ever written. Federal Trade Commission, *Report on Cooperation in American Export Trade* (Washington, DC: Government Printing Office, 1916).

19. One subject area that is particularly appropriate for inquiry is that of so-called "sanctuary markets"—protected (and often cartelized) markets from which dumping occurs. At least some critics of antidumping regimes acknowledge that a policy justification exists for countering dumping when the source is an industry based in a sanctuary market. Professor Robert Willig of Princeton speaks of "strategic dumping" from protected markets: "Strategic dumping . . . involves both aggressive, uncomfortably low pricing of exports, together with restraints that protect the home market of the exporter. . . . This kind of dumping, may, in the long run, harm consumers in the country that receives the exports. It certainly harms those seeking to compete with the exporters, because they have this inferior, this

non-economic, inefficient source of competitive disadvantage, which weakens them and creates monopoly power for the exporters." U.S.I.T.C. Investigation No. 332–334, transcript of hearing held September 30, 1994, pp. 418–19. Brian Hindley states that "within the moral tradition of classical liberalism, sanctuary markets are indefensible." Hindley and Messerlin, *Antidumping Industrial Policy*, p. 74. He argues that the opening of such markets is preferable to the imposition of offsetting antidumping duties, a proposition which is likely to meet little argument. The thorny question remains, however, of practical means of opening sanctuary markets. The unanswered factual question—which could benefit from study—is whether the sanctuary phenomenon is relatively rare in world commerce or commonplace.

20. One consequence of the failure to control subsidies in some member states was an escalating "subsidy race"—the grant of offsetting subsidies by countries like Germany that, as a general proposition, share the American perspective that significant limits should be maintained on subsidies.

21. See generally Terry Collins-Williams and Gerry Salambier, "International Disciplines on Subsidies—The GATT, the WTO and the Future Agenda," in *Journal of World Trade* 30, no. 1, (February 1996), p. 12.

22. MITI Vice Minister Yoshihiro Sakamoto stated on March 15, 1996, that "It is no longer relevant to negotiate and have an agreement on issues related to global industries in a limited bilateral context such as between Japan and the U.S. The era of "bilateralism" is over. Let us not allow such disputes to distract us from more pressing global issues such as security, environment, energy, and the strengthening of international rules."

23. It is true that under Section 301 USTR has access to a panoply of remedies other than the imposition of import restrictions, but these actions (suspension of landing rights for foreign commercial aircraft, denial of visas to foreign nationals, intervention in federal and state regulatory proceedings, and other actions within the scope of presidential authority) often yield little direct leverage with respect to the problem at hand and may entail significant political or policy costs.

24. Such practices include price fixing, bid-rigging, joint restraints on output, and some types of boycotts and tying arrangements. The remedy would not extend to the class of activities that U.S. antitrust law subjects to the "rule of reason" (for example, joint manufacturing, joint R&D, and similar activities).

25. The proposed remedy might be attacked as discriminatory and a denial of GATT Article III national treatment, but in fact, it would not subject any foreign firm to liability that U.S. firms do not already face under the Federal Trade Commission Act and other U.S. antitrust statutes—and those laws have not been challenged under GATT. With respect to the charge that foreign firms are being denied due process, they would enjoy the same procedural protections and safeguards as they now do under the Federal Trade Commission Act. Similarly, the act's requirements that the foreign practices at issue have "a direct, substantial, and reasonably foreseeable effect" on U.S. commerce would ensure that USTR would not use this remedy to attack foreign anticompetitive practices unless major U.S. economic

interests were at stake. 15 U.S.C. § 45(a)(3). As a strictly legal proposition, foreign firms are already exposed to such liability under current U.S. antitrust law—as a practical matter, the commission almost never acts against foreign practices. What would change is not the legal exposure of foreign firms, as such, but the priorities of the U.S. government, with the introduction of trade policy considerations into the administration of at least one major U.S. competition law.

26. Extraordinary Challenge Committee Review under United States–Canada Free Trade Agreement, EDD-94-1904-01USA, pp. 35–37. One of the two Canadians expressed the view that binational panels need not feel bound to observe the limited standards of review set forth in their own enabling instrument, the U.S.-Canada FTA itself. "I would like to point out that in reality the replacement of court adjudication by a five member panel of experts in international trade law may very well reduce the amount of deference to the Department in the future. When the Court of International Trade reviews the determinations of Commerce it would be expected to bow to the expertise within the Department. When the parties to the FTA agreed to replace that court with this type of panel they must have realized and intended that a review of the actions of Commerce or of the Canadian agency would be more intense. The panels have been given the right to make a final determination of the matters in dispute between the two countries in a relatively short period of time without any judicial review. Apparently each government felt that this system was more satisfactory than the one which was replaced." Opinion of Justice Gordon L. S. Hart; p. 28.

27. For example, Judge Wilkey found that Canadian panelist Lawson Hunter had failed to disclose the fact that two law firms in which he was a partner represented Canadian lumber companies that were the subject of the U.S. CVD order that was being reviewed by the binational panel on which he served. He was also personally doing legal work for the Canadian government, a party to the proceeding, at the same time that he served on the panel. "As a partner in his two firms, Hunter stood to gain financially from the representation of the lumber companies and the Canadian government." For a complete synopsis of the various conflicts of interest identified by Judge Wilkey, see his dissenting opinion in *Softwood Lumber*, pp. 74–86.

28. The author's law firm, Dewey Ballantine, served as counsel for U.S. softwood lumber producers in this proceeding. Whatever inferences of author's bias the reader might choose to draw from that fact, the Wilkey dissent as well as the majority opinions speak for themselves and on their face are indicative of a fundamental structural defect in the binational panel process. Concerns similar to Wilkey's have been expressed by another U.S. judge who has served on binational Extraordinary Challenge Committees, Federal Judge Charles B. Renfren, in "The American Experience with Alternative Dispute Resolutions," at the Inaugural Symposium on Alternative Dispute Resolution in the Context of Public and Private International Disputes, Legal Center for Inter-American Trade and Com-

merce and Law School Student Council, Monterey Institute of Technology and Advanced Studies (Nov. 15–18, 1995).

29. See, for example, an article by Ernst-Ulrich Petersmann, "International Competition Rules for the GATT-WTO World Trade and Legal System," *Journal of World Trade* 27 (1993), p. 35. Mr. Petersmann served as legal counsel to the GATT Secretariat (1981-90) and has served on several GATT dispute resolution panels.

30. The Antidumping Agreement provides that with respect to questions of law where "the Agreement admits of more than one permissible interpretation, the panel shall find the authorities' measure to be in conformity with the Agreement if it rests upon one of those permissible interpretations" (Article 17.6). That sounds good enough, but as Gary Horlick and Eleanor Shea point out, by its terms the Agreement also requires interpretation in accordance with the Vienna Convention on the Law of Treaties, the language of which may suggest that there is never more than one "permissible interpretation." Thus, "a position that envisions multiple 'permissible' interpretations may conflict with the normal standards of treaty interpretation." Gary Horlick and Eleanor Shea, "The World Trade Organization Antidumping Agreement," *Journal of World Trade* 29 (February 1995), p. 30.

31. See generally Gary N. Horlick, "WTO Dispute Settlement and the Dole Commission," *Journal of World Trade* 29, no. 6 (December 1995), p. 45.

32. USTR's legal and economic staff will need to be expanded. "The problem is not the quality of existing staff, who are extremely competent and hardworking. Rather, there are simply not enough of them. A fairly small increase in analytic staff at the trade agencies can yield huge policy payoffs." Bayard and Elliott, *Reciprocity and Retaliation*, p. 348.

Chapter 17

The Challenge of Deeper
International Integration:
U.S. Trade Policy Options

Robert Z. Lawrence

For much of the postwar era, the United States concentrated on supporting a rules-based, multilateral global system centered on the General Agreement on Tariffs and Trade (GATT). But significant changes in the relationship between the U.S. and the world economy have had dramatic effects on the international economic and trading climate. Increasingly, attention has shifted away from either simply protecting the U.S. market or removing foreign tariff barriers toward changing practices abroad. As the water level of border protection was lowered, the rocks of divergent domestic policies and practices that remain and separate national economies became apparent. The United States has called for international measures involving policies formerly thought of as purely domestic in nature and has supported governance mechanisms that make such measures more credible and binding.

For much of the postwar period, the United States dominated the world economy, but Americans had their economic fate determined at home. The United States was a relatively closed and self-sufficient economy. U.S. policy sought to promote economic growth and free trade abroad, not because the country needed the world economically, but because it was involved in a geopolitical struggle with the Soviet Union. The strength of the American economy allowed it to promote free trade in a multilateral setting, at the same time ignoring the fact that in many countries, government intervention was more extensive and trade barriers higher than those in the United States.

Today, however, the Cold War is over. While the United States is the only political and military superpower, it is much less dominant economically. The U.S. position now is "first among equals." American living standards and productivity remain the world's highest, but the gap between the United States, Europe, and Japan has narrowed markedly. In some industries, the United States no longer leads; in many industries, U.S. firms face tough international competition. The U.S. economy also has become far more open. Trade accounts for twice the share of gross national product than it did two decades ago. The United States has become the largest host country for foreign direct investment and the world's largest net debtor nation. Increasingly, therefore, American producers are concerned about foreign competitors and pressuring their government for assistance.

These pressures can have an important impact. The Constitution of the United States actually gives Congress, rather than the president, the final say in the conduct of U.S. trade policy. And it is a power that Congress jealously guards. As long as there was a strong domestic consensus in support of free trade and trade was relatively unimportant to most Americans, U.S. trade policy could remain relatively focused on global systemic goals and U.S. trade policymaking could be confined to a handful of specialists. However, as trade pressures increased and trade became more salient in the domestic political debate, the conduct of U.S. trade policy has become increasingly constrained by domestic political concerns.

The growing importance of trade issues politically has had powerful effects. First, it has increased the pressure on whatever administration was in power to do something about them. Accordingly, U.S. policy has shifted from relying almost exclusively on time-consuming multilateral approaches through GATT toward a multitrack approach that includes unilateral, bilateral, and regional measures. Second, U.S. policy has become increasingly concerned with issues of fair trade. As national differences narrow and the intensity of competition increases, locational decisions become more sensitive to relatively small differences in domestic policies and practices. Paradoxically, the more similar countries are, the more significant their remaining differences become in determining trade and investment flows. This situation naturally creates pressures for harmonization of domestic rules and policies and increases calls for a level playing field.

Indeed, each of the major political forces in the United States has its version of this problem. For business it is "dumping"; domestic firms increasingly see the benefits that foreign firms derive from different national economic environments as unfair. For labor it is "social dumping"; domestic workers increasingly complain that foreigners observe more lenient labor and social standards. For environmentalists it is "ecodumping," the concern that foreigners who fail to observe strict standards will place pressures on domestic authorities to do likewise.

Increasingly, therefore, U.S. trade policy has been concerned with foreign domestic policies. Product standards, labor practices, intellectual property, environmental policies, technology policies, human rights, and competition policies, all once thought of as matters of purely domestic microeconomic concern, are coming under international scrutiny.

This shift from multilateral approaches that aim at removing border barriers toward a multitrack approach that aims at deeper integration is evident in numerous trade initiatives over the past decade. For example:

- *Unilateral Initiatives*: Over the 1980s, the United States has used Section 301 legislation to target foreign practices not covered under GATT. These included the failure to respect intellectual property, provide access to telecommunications markets, and other foreign regulatory practices deemed to discriminate against U.S. products and firms.

- *Bilateral Initiatives*: In the Structural Impediments Initiative (SII) negotiations between Japan and the United States, agreements covered behind-the-border concerns such as Japan's large retail store law, antitrust policies, infrastructure spending, and the behavior of corporate groups (*keiretsu*); and U.S. budgetary, credit-card, and education and training policies. In the New Economic Partnership Framework talks between Japan and the United States in 1993-94, issues included regulatory reform, economic harmonization, and detailed practices in Japanese sectors such as auto parts, glass products, telecommunications, and medical equipment procurement.

- *Regional Initiatives*: The United States signed the North American Free Trade Agreement (NAFTA) with Canada and Mexico, an agreement that not only removed border barriers to trade and investment but also established trinational panels to oversee national administrative trade actions and implementation of environmental policies and labor standards.

• *Multilateral Initiatives*: In the Uruguay Round that concluded in 1993, the United States sought and achieved trade liberalization in services and agriculture, and increased disciplines on standards and trade-related investment measures and rules on trade-related intellectual property rights.

EMERGING MARKETS

In addition to the pressures for and the tensions arising from the move toward deeper integration, a second key feature of the world economy forms an important backdrop for U.S. trade policy in the 1990s: the striking contrast between the economic prospects of the United States and other developed countries and that of the emerging markets of the developing and former communist countries. On the one hand, long-run potential growth rates in the developed economies have declined because of demographic factors (slow labor force growth) and slow productivity growth. In many developed countries there is profound pessimism about the future, a lack of confidence in government and leadership, and signs of growing pressures for protection. In the United States, in particular, because of slow productivity growth, average real wages are only 5 percent above their 1973 levels, as measured by the consumer price index, and there is growing inequality in wage earnings, with the less skilled and less well educated faring particularly poorly.

It is tempting to predict, therefore, that the United States will reduce its global role and retreat into a protectionist isolationism. But this would not solve the nation's problems. As noted, the U.S. economy has become increasingly globalized. America's influence over the world may have diminished, but its dependence on foreign markets, foreign technology, and foreign investment have been dramatically increased. As a large debtor nation, the United States must export to pay interest and dividends. The only lasting solution to the nation's domestic problems lies in investing in education, training, and technology and in successful competition in global markets.

By contrast with developments in the United States and other developed nations, a miraculous change is taking place in the developing and former communist countries. Throughout the world, emerging nations are now shifting toward the market system. The nations of the former Soviet Union, Eastern Europe, China, and the developing economies of Asia, Africa, and Latin American have turned away from statist, protectionist policies. Privatization and liberalization are the order of the day. Almost all are shifting toward outward-oriented policies and are increasing their dependence on the developed countries for markets. The contrast between the desire of these economies for integration into the global economy and the fears of those in developed countries is striking. Prosperity in the emerging nations should afford the developed world immense export opportunities. But to do so the global trading system must be kept open and credible trading rules must be maintained.

The successful absorption of these economies presents a win-win opportunity for both sides. The dynamic emerging markets offer firms in developed countries extraordinary export opportunities. Planned spending on sophisticated capital goods and infrastructure projects is immense.

But is the process of integration manageable? And even if, in the aggregate, the United States will be better off, will immense costs be imposed on the wage levels and employment opportunities of less skilled workers in the developed countries? Many suggest that already, over the past decade, the wages and employment prospects of unskilled workers in the developed countries have been seriously damaged.[1] Presidential candidate Ross Perot made considerable political capital with concerns about the "giant sucking sound" that would result as jobs left the United States because of NAFTA.

At the same time as the United States has officially pressed for more open foreign markets and increased its demands for changes in the policies of others, several quarters in the nation itself have expressed growing concerns about the intrusive effects of international agreements on America's ability to exercise its national sovereignty. Some making this argument, such as Pat Buchanan, are drawn from the right of the political spectrum; others, such as Ralph Nader, from the left; but, increasingly, these forces are raising questions about the desirability of agreements that constrain the autonomy of U.S. domestic policy and about international decision-making processes that do not have the transparency that is typical of the U.S. government.

In sum, the U.S. position in the world has changed; in response, U.S. trade policy, which is highly sensitive to domestic economic concerns, has done likewise. The United States has shifted away from an approach that relied almost exclusively on multilateralism and rules-based approaches to deal with border barriers. It has moved toward a multitrack approach that confronts issues of deeper economic integration, occasionally resorting to demands for export market shares. In reaction to these developments, however, there has been growing domestic political opposition to liberalization.

MULTILATERALISM

The Uruguay Round negotiations, launched in Punte-del-Este, Uruguay, in 1986 and concluded in 1993, were the most ambitious of the postwar multilateral liberalization efforts. There had been seven earlier major negotiations over the postwar period, but, with the exception of the codes of the Tokyo Round, these concentrated heavily on lowering tariff barriers to industrial products. The Uruguay Round agreement includes reductions in such tariffs—indeed it entirely eliminates tariffs in several sectors—but its scope is much more ambitious.

The United States had five major goals when the negotiations began: (1) improving market access for U.S. exports by reducing tariff and nontariff barriers; (2) adopting a more timely and effective dispute resolution mechanism; (3) reducing trade-distorting government subsidies and unfair practices; (4) extending GATT coverage to services; and (5) increasing protection against unauthorized use of patented and copyright products. Several of these initiatives—particularly extending the trading rules to agriculture, services, trade-related investment measures, and intellectual property rights—initially were met with considerable opposition from other countries.

Achievements

Despite this opposition, however, significant progress has been made on all these issues. For example, the agreement:

- Extends the trading rules to sectors such as agricultural products and services;

- Provides for new international disciplines on nontariff barriers such as trade-related investment measures, voluntary export restraints, technical barriers to trade, sanitary and phytosanitary measures, rules of origin, and government procurement;

- Clarifies the rules for unfair trade that deal with subsidies and dumping;

- Contains an international agreement on intellectual property rights that will afford U.S. high-technology producers with rights they have hitherto not enjoyed when their innovations have been copied without remuneration;

- Tightens the disciplines of the international system by establishing a new World Trade Organization (WTO) and a new and more binding system for settling international disputes;

- Provides for the elimination of the network of quotas—the Multifiber Arrangement—that currently protects the textile industries in developed countries, while retaining tariff protection for U.S. textile and apparel workers.

Objections

In the debate over the Uruguay Round, some voiced concern that the more binding dispute settlement procedures of the WTO will undermine U.S. sovereignty to an unacceptable degree. But the setting of international trade rules cannot be a one-way street. The cost of imposing greater discipline on America's trading partners is inevitably accepting these disciplines for the United States.

In addition, other opponents of the agreement raised objections that GATT inhibits the United States from undertaking measures to preserve the environment and the safety of workers and consumers. But it is simply not true that either GATT or the WTO prevents the United States from having higher product or worker standards than its trading partners. The only major inhibition is on standards that discriminate between U.S. products and foreign products.

It also should be emphasized that the United States remains sovereign over its domestic policies. Even with its strengthened dispute settlement mechanism, the WTO cannot force the United States to take actions against its will. If the WTO found U.S. policies in violation of the agreement and the United States did not wish to change these policies, Washington would have the option either of lowering its trade barriers in another area or of allowing other WTO members to raise theirs. Depending on their size and/or trading relations with the United States, many plaintiff countries will not lightly choose to raise their barriers against U.S. goods and services. In addition, the United States remains free to use its unilateral Section 301 measures in cases where other nations engage in practices not covered by the agreement.

The WTO, by its own terms, will continue to make decisions by consensus, as was the case under GATT. The agreement does, however, allow for members to be compelled to accept amendments that are supported by a three-fourths majority of the members or to withdraw from the agreement. Some have laid out a scenario in which other nations gang up on the United States to change the rules in a manner that is against U.S. interests. In the remote event that other nations actually try to tilt the rules of the WTO so that they no longer serve U.S. interests, the United States always could withdraw from the organization.

The Unfinished Agenda

The Uruguay Round ended without full agreement in key service sectors such as telecommunications, financial services, and transportation. In addition, the General Agreement on Trade in Services (GATS) remains full of exceptions. The trading system, therefore, remains far from the goal of free trade in services. There is also considerable scope for further liberalization in agriculture and civil aircraft. In addition, from the standpoint of many U.S. companies, the agreements on intellectual property rules give developing countries transitional adjustment periods that are too long.

Some believe, justifiably, that these issues should be dealt with before a new negotiating round is contemplated. After all, a telecommunications agreement was reached early in 1997, and a financial services deal was nailed down late in 1997. In addition, advocates of the issue-by-issue approach argue that the world should take its time and enjoy the success of having concluded an incredibly complex set of negotiations before thinking about what comes next. But thinking should begin now. Before the next negotiations can begin, it will be necessary to spend several years laying the conceptual groundwork. Indeed, the issues that were the

subject of agreement in the Uruguay Round in 1993, such as services and intellectual property rights, were prepared in the early
1980s.

What will be the central issues on the agenda for the next round?
It is clear that the negotiations are moving increasingly away
from the simple issues of lowering tariffs and removing border barriers, toward even more sensitive questions relating to domestic
economic policies. The Uruguay Round, for example, established
global rules for intellectual property, foreign investment, and
domestic subsidies. The U.S. government has proposed continuing this emphasis on domestic policy issues by suggesting that future
trade negotiations should include topics such as competition policies, the environment, labor standards, and investment.[2]

Investment

For international markets to function properly, foreign companies
must be provided with access and the ability to operate as easily
as their domestic competitors. When global markets are frag-
mented, nations are tempted to use their domestic policies to
exploit their monopoly. One antidote to such policies is to ensure
that domestic markets are competitive and open to foreign investment and trade.[3]

The agreement in the Uruguay Round on Trade-Related
Investment Measures (TRIMs), which prohibits trade-distorting
measures such as local content and export performance requirements, represents a minimal first step because it concentrates
only on measures that distort trade. It does not, however, guarantee rights of establishment and full national treatment. Similarly,
the GATS applies only to selected sectors and measures. To achieve
really open markets, it is necessary, by contrast, to promote
national treatment for all trade and investment, with no sectoral
exceptions.

The issues of free access and operation for foreign firms
require a comprehensive rather than a piecemeal approach. From
a public policy perspective, the principal goal should be to achieve
an international regime in which domestic markets are internationally
contestable. One necessary condition is to provide foreign firms
national treatment: the same rights to establish and operate as domestic firms. Important examples include access of foreign firms to private industry associations that have a regulatory role or provide
services necessary for operation in the domestic market. In some

cases, however, national treatment might not be sufficient to achieve open markets, as when regulatory mechanisms remain restrictive for both foreign and domestic firms. If the government monopolizes telecommunications services, for example, national treatment for a foreign telecommunications company means little. National treatment also may not suffice if there remain constraints or rules that have particularly adverse effects on the operation of multinational firms, such as local content requirements, rules of origin, and restrictions on international financial transfers.

To achieve contestable markets, therefore, a comprehensive approach is required. This approach should not be confined simply to rules for trade or investment. Instead it must encompass other fields, including competition policy, government regulation, technology policy, government procurement, corporate governance, and tax policies.

However, it is neither necessary nor desirable to harmonize policies in all these areas. Indeed, wherever possible, national diversity should be respected and permitted. Instead, a desirable approach is to decide on the requirements for transparency, minimum rules, and operating procedures. Beyond that point, "softer" mechanisms, such as mutual recognition agreements, should be permitted.

Competition Policies

Free trade produces efficient results when markets are competitive. When there are monopolies, however, the benefits from trade are less clear. The removal of border barriers may free foreign firms from the obligation to pay tariffs or the constraints of import quotas, but those firms may find their ability to compete severely impaired if domestic firms can fix prices, restrict output, fix market shares, or engage in practices such as "tying" and "exclusive dealing" that lock up domestic distributors. The failure to enforce competition policies by domestic authorities, therefore, is a matter of concern for those seeking free trade. Just as there is a case for international cooperation to achieve free trade, so too is there a case for international cooperation in competition policies.

National Rules, Global Competition

While markets and competition have become global, competition policies have not. National governments continue to exercise competition policies, for the most part, independently of one another. GATT, in particular, does not contain explicit agreements on competition policy, although it does have rules on antidumping and subsidies. These antidumping rules are sometimes justified as a form of competition policy governing predatory prices, but they favor domestic firms and actually are detrimental to competition. The rules applied to goods that cross borders are different from those that apply to domestic goods. Consequently, domestic firms often are able to sell at prices that would lead to sanctions against foreign firms even though they have exactly the same costs and prices.[4]

In addition, antidumping rules reflect the concerns of producers who compete with imports rather than the concerns of consumers. They deal with problems that arise when exported goods are priced too low but not when they are sold too high. While domestic competition laws do focus on providing consumers with competitively priced products, their ambit does not extend to consumers abroad. In most countries, domestic competition law actually exempts collusion by domestic firms for sales abroad. Exporters therefore can fix prices and divide up international markets using practices that would be illegal at home.

Moreover, governments may compel their exporters to adhere to so-called voluntary import restraints. For example, foreign firms selling in the United States that participate in cartels and voluntary export restraint arrangements under instructions from their home government can claim "sovereign compulsion" and thus receive immunity from U.S. antitrust rules. Countries also provide numerous exemptions to their domestic competition rules—a form of implicit subsidy that could enhance their competitiveness at the expense of foreigners. In most developed countries these exemptions apply to research and development ventures. In Japan exemptions also are granted to import, recession, and industry rationalization cartels.

Since competition is increasingly global, the decentralized application of competition policies through national bodies inevitably creates frictions. Many mergers and acquisitions involve firms from more than one country. Firms therefore may have to obtain permission in several jurisdictions before undertaking such mergers. This inhibits their ability to invest freely because jurisdictions require different sets of information, use different standards, and reach different conclusions. Increasingly some countries, most notably the United States, have tried to deal unilaterally with the absence of an international agreement in this area through extraterritorial means, giving rise to jurisdictional conflicts with other countries. In 1992 the Justice Department published new guidelines indicating that it would challenge foreign businesses that engaged in practices that harmed U.S. exports, if such practices would have violated U.S. antitrust laws had they occurred in the United States.[5] In the past, such U.S. efforts have been met by foreign actions that have sought to block the application of U.S. laws to their domestic industries.

Competition policy problems have been present in international markets for a long time. In the 1930s and 1940s, for example, international cartels were widespread. In response, the Havana Charter, which established a new International Trade Organization (ITO), contained a section that dealt with restrictive business practices. However, the charter was never ratified by the United States, and the ITO never came into being. In the 1960s and 1970s, developing countries expressed concerns in the United Nations about anticompetitive practices of multinationals. The result was voluntary codes of conduct for multinational corporations. While countries have increased their cooperative efforts bilaterally—the United States and the European Union now share information and the European Union has a single antitrust policy—the question is whether the United States should press for a multilateral international agreement and if so, what form it should take.

A single set of global competition policy rules would certainly provide more coherence than the current system. If effective, such rules would improve market access for foreign firms, allow for the elimination of the antidumping rules, and allow countries to avoid second-best industrial policies measures, such as Sematech in the United States and Airbus in Europe, which are motivated by the fear of vulnerability to foreign monopolies. However, achieving agreement on what the rules should be and how they should be enforced will not be easy.

Reflecting the consensus in economic theory about their effects, national rules are quite similar on issues relating to horizontal restraints of trade such as price fixing and cartels. (In the United States, the European Union, and Japan, price fixing and market sharing are illegal and predation is prohibited.) But partly because of the greater theoretical uncertainty, the legal treatment of vertical restraints—such as retail price maintenance, exclusive dealing, and territorial allotments—is much more varied. In addition, rules for dealing with mergers and defining dominant positions differ, as do the means for implementing policies. (The United States relies heavily on judicial action while the European Union and Japan place more emphasis on administrative action.)[6]

Options. Progress could be made internationally even in the absence of a comprehensive competition policy code that was enforced multilaterally. First, there is scope to improve cooperation and centralize data collection between national competition policy authorities. Second, there could be agreements providing for international oversight of domestic competition policy implementation rather than international rules. (In NAFTA, for example, trinational panels serve as appeal boards for the domestic application of trade rules.) Third, opportunities exist to undertake increased cooperation through bilateral and regional agreements when there are only modest differences in antitrust laws and there is some willingness to limit national sovereignty. Fourth, members of the WTO could simply agree not to use domestic courts to enforce international cartel agreements. (Like gambling debts in many jurisdictions, cartel agreements would be unenforceable.) This would be a minimal approach to the cartel question. The American Bar Association has recommended more boldly that countries repeal laws granting immunity to export cartels and prosecute cartel conduct both at home and in export markets. Fifth, an international agreement could be limited to the issues of price discrimination and predation. This would allow the eventual elimination of current antidumping statutes. In all these cases, international action would be taken only in large cases with international implications. In many markets, competition is a purely local concern, and there is no reason why an international body should get involved.

Finally, Harvard economist F. M. Scherer has suggested an even more ambitious approach.[7] He proposes creation of an International Competition Policy Office (ICPO) that initially would gather information, move on to investigate anticompetitive behavior, and then enforce penalties against such practices. Scherer emphasizes the importance of proceeding simultaneously with both cartel and merger policies. All cartels and companies with large shares of world export markets would register with the ICPO. Later all companies planning to merge also would have to register. Nations that think trade has been restrained would petition the

ICPO for redress. Initially the ICPO would cooperate with local authorities and recommend actions. Later it would be given power to intervene in cases with serious implications for global markets.

The ICPO would encourage domestic authorities to deal with most cases independently. It might, however, form international panels to arbitrate cases where parties claimed that others had violated internationally agreed norms or that domestic laws had not been enforced adequately.

Nonetheless, while these policies would provide considerable benefits to U.S. firms, from the viewpoint of American multinational firms concerned about market access, they would not be a panacea. Elimination of the antidumping rules would aid the many U.S. exporters who are now subject to foreign antidumping actions. However, the difficulties of obtaining international agreement on the appropriate scope of vertical restraints probably would limit the benefits from improved access. Even in the United States, "competition," not the opportunity for individual firms to enter the industry, is protected under U.S. antitrust law.[8] In the absence of evidence of restraints on competition, it may be impossible to win a case simply on the grounds that a new firm cannot gain entry. A multilateral competition policy initiative may, therefore, need to be accompanied by bilateral discussion of access issues, particularly with countries such as Japan, where there appear to be significant obstacles to access.

Environment

Some environmental problems, such as global warming and the depletion of the ozone layer, are obviously global matters that nations should solve collectively with a single set of rules. However, other environmental problems have a local character. In addition, nations place different values on a clean environment. There is a strong argument for not having these local issues decided internationally. Imposing developed-country standards on the environmental conditions of developing countries could be particularly damaging. It is noteworthy, in this regard, that NAFTA, for example, did *not* come up with uniform environmental standards. Instead, the side agreements to NAFTA allow each nation to determine its own environmental standards and deal primarily with the problem created by weak enforcement. Nonetheless, the need for global standards remains a controversial question, with many arguing for common environmental standards to prevent competition to attract foreign investment from placing downward pressure on environmental standards.

What role should the trade rules play in achieving international environmental standards? Article 20 of GATT allows contracting parties the explicit right to adopt measures that are necessary, among other goals, to protect the life or health of humans, animals, and plants and to conserve exhaustible resources. The preamble of the WTO recognizes the importance of environmental concerns. The WTO has established a Committee on Trade and the Environment to ensure the responsiveness of the multilateral trading system to environmental goals. Issues to be dealt with include questions such as the relationship of GATT rules to other international agreements; the denial of national treatment to like products on the basis of production methods used; the use of trade measures to protect the environment; and the scope for exceptions for environmental measures under Article 20 of GATT.

There is a case to be made for establishing a new World Environmental Organization (WEO) that would deal with international and global environmental issues.[9] There is also a case to be made that this organization should coordinate its activities with the WTO. Where the enforcement of international environmental agreements with large membership requires the use of trade sanctions, such as the ban on ivory trade or the international transportation of hazardous materials, waivers should be negotiated with the WTO. Such agreements establish a case that the regulations reflect genuine environmental concerns rather than efforts to restrict trade for protectionist reasons.

More heated debate concerns the discriminatory treatment of products on the basis of production methods. The WTO currently allows countries to exercise national sovereignty when dealing with domestic environmental questions. Controversy arises, however, when an importing country objects to production methods used by an exporting country. The most famous example occurred when the United States banned Mexican tuna that were caught with nets that were not in compliance with U.S. regulations designed to avoid the entrapment of dolphins. GATT found the U.S. actions in violation of GATT since they were applied not on the environmental impact of consuming products in the United States but to the environmental effects of the process by which they were "produced" outside the United States. Dan Esty of Yale University offers the interesting suggestion that countries should be able to take action when the production methods have an impact on its own environment, but not otherwise.[10]

A second major area of controversy arises from the principle that national environmental standards should be based on scientific evidence. The European Community banned the importation of U.S. beef that had been grown using supplementary growth hormones, despite the fact that, in the U.S. view, there was no scientific evidence that these hormones were damaging. To some the idea that standards should be based on scientific evidence seems unexceptionable. However, environmentalists point out that it can take considerable time for scientists to reach a consensus on environmental damage and other health hazards. They argue that a concerned, risk-averse nation should be allowed to pass environmental and other regulations even when an international scientific consensus does not exist. Obviously, there is a risk that nations could use such regulatory sovereignty for protectionist purposes.

Inevitably, those concerned about the environment will have to make trade-offs. The incorporation of environmental issues in the trade rules could increase their effectiveness. At the same time, there should be some discipline on these standards to ensure they do not unnecessarily restrict or distort trade or reduce legitimate national diversity. The NAFTA experience in the United States demonstrated that some environmental groups could indeed work cooperatively with trade officials to achieve their goals. On the other hand, it showed that others could not. As in all areas, achieving agreement in the WTO will require forging an international consensus that the measures proposed do enhance global welfare.

Labor Standards

In most developed countries, the government has an extensive role in the labor market. It commonly regulates work hours and the cost of overtime; mandates vacations and holidays and sick leave; sets minimum wages; restricts child and forced labor; ensures nondiscrimination; provides unemployment, disability, and retirement income insurance, and, in many countries, health insurance; and sets conditions for hiring and firing, unionization, and collective bargaining.

By and large, nations have taken these actions independently, although a voluntary set of international standards has been agreed to at the International Labor Organization (ILO); moreover

GATT does contain a fairly narrow prohibition on trade in goods made with forced labor.[11] Nonetheless, efforts to give these issues a higher profile in the international policy arena have been made by both the United States and the European Union. As early as 1953, the United States proposed adding a labor standards article to GATT, and it pushed unsuccessfully for the inclusion of labor standards in the Tokyo and Uruguay rounds. The United States also has tried to induce foreign compliance with worker rights in other aspects of its trade policy. Since the mid-1980s, the U.S. Congress has passed a series of laws that directly link preferential trade and investment benefits to respect for basic worker rights.[12] In Section 301 and Super 301 of the Omnibus Trade Act of 1988, the "systematic denial of internationally recognized worker rights" by foreign governments is defined as an "unreasonable trade practice" and made liable for U.S. countermeasures where "such denials cause a burden or restrictions on U.S. commerce." Labor standards were also an important issue in the recent NAFTA negotiations. While NAFTA itself did not include provisions on labor rights, one of the side agreements established an international enforcement regime for alleged violations of national minimum wage, child labor, and occupational health and safety regulations, and an oversight and evaluation mechanism (without enforcement powers) for other labor issues.[13]

At a multilateral level, there are now increasing calls for moving beyond the voluntary standards of the ILO and GATT's prohibition on forced labor.[14] The United States tried to ensure that discussions on labor standards would take place in the new WTO. French leaders have been vocal in calling for European action against other nations with lower standards of social protection. French Prime Minister Edouard Balladur once demanded that Europe be protected from "foreign traders with different values," and President François Mitterrand once called for trade sanctions against nations with "inadequate social protection."

Where nations effectively control their borders and prevent migration, most labor standards either will be confined to local effects or will operate through product market channels to affect international trade and investment flows. In fact, despite the widespread perception that labor policies have repercussions on trade and investment flows, in many cases government intervention in the labor market will have purely local impacts.

First, policies such as sick leave, maternity leave, and family leave usually are financed by payroll taxes. Often it is assumed that such taxes on labor raise employment costs, thereby affecting resource allocation. However, unless all elements of the compensation package, including wages, are subject to minimum standards, when standards involving sick leave and the like are imposed, employers can adjust other elements of the package to keep their total costs from rising substantially. Indeed, the evidence suggests that, in general, the supply of labor is fairly inelastic and that over the long run, most payroll taxes are borne by labor.[15] This fact implies that such taxes result in lower wages rather than higher compensation costs.[16]

Second, many labor measures actually reflect decisions that might have been taken in the marketplace anyway and are thus not binding constraints. Such could be the case with rules about work hours and vacation and minimum wages. Moreover, in many countries, compliance with binding measures is low and enforcement weak. Under some circumstances, evasion takes the form of employment in the informal sector.[17]

In practice, many labor market policies will not be perfectly neutral in their impact on different industries. However, if labor standards reflect the legitimate preferences of a particular nation, it is not obvious why other nations should be entitled to impose their views.

Two reasons for external pressure have been advanced. Some have tried to advocate tougher international labor standards on the grounds that they have positive economic effects. These include the alleged wage-raising effects of capital-labor substitution, productivity enhancement effects of workforce harmony brought about by increased worker participation, and the notion that a more equal distribution of income is necessary to stimulate consumer spending.[18] But these effects are controversial, and in any case, it is unclear why firms and/or nations should be forced to take actions that are in their own interest.

Instead, the more compelling assaults on complete national sovereignty are based on the notion that all people are entitled to basic human rights. But to what degree and under what circumstances should one country try to change the behavior of others through measures involving trade?

In some cases, the policies in poor countries that offend the sensibilities of those in rich nations actually result from different income levels rather than from different preferences or values. Thus those in extreme poverty may permit activities that under other circumstances they themselves would regard as abhorrent, such as child labor or a lack of pollution controls.

The long-run solution to these problems is clearly to raise incomes. Indeed, refusing to trade with such nations actually could retard rather than improve their abilities to provide worker rights. In the short run, however, some of these conflicts can be dealt with through explicit compensation schemes and subsidies. Where sufficient compensation is not forthcoming, however, externally imposed standards may damage economic growth. Moreover, there will remain cases in which divergent practices reflect divergent beliefs about the desirability of standards, so that compensation will not be possible.

Trade bans are of course not the only means of responding to labor measures found to be reprehensible in other nations. An alternative might be insistence on labeling such as "made with union workers" or "made using ecologically sound standards," which would allow private citizens to exercise their preferences.

In general, there is a strong case for allowing individual nations a wide scope for differentiation in applying labor standards, particularly when the costs and benefits of such standards are fully borne by the nation itself. Even where these standards do affect others through market forces, in principle, given diverse social preferences, the existence of diverse standards will raise global welfare. There is, however, a case for international standards where the failure to maintain certain standards offends fundamental human rights. One solution is to induce poor nations to comply by offering them compensation. A second is to use labeling and other forms of moral suasion. The denial of trading opportunities probably should come only as a last resort and only in the most egregious cases.

Governance and Transparency

The WTO is an organization of governments, but as it extends the scope of its activities, it needs to acknowledge the increasing importance of multinational firms and nongovernmental organizations in trade policy issues. The WTO should be reformed to improve the transparency of its deliberations and to provide nongovernmental organizations with opportunities to express their views on important policy issues. One mechanism might be formal hearings to which interested parties could be invited. A second would be standing groups of experts in both trade and other relevant fields who would be invited to provide counsel. In addition, the dispute settlement process could be opened up to allow interested parties to submit briefs to the panels and for the panels to publish all decisions, without parties to the dispute being able to prevent publication.

In sum, these issues all raise the potential for major conflicts between the desire for uniform standards—the so-called level playing field—and the desire for national diversity. The challenge in future negotiations will be finding an acceptable compromise between these two conflicting goals. The key will be to deal internationally only with the really global aspects of these issues while leaving purely domestic issues as local matters.

REGIONALISM: WHAT AFTER NAFTA?

In the late 1980s, the GATT negotiations were in trouble.[19] Europe was feared to be forming a protectionist "fortress Europe" with its Europe '92 initiative, and the United States and Canada had just signed a free trade agreement. It became conventional wisdom that the world was breaking up into three distinct trading blocks, centered in the United States, Europe, and Japan. Some feared the world was repeating the experience of the 1930s.

However, from the vantage point of the mid 1990s, these concerns appear misplaced. The Uruguay Round has now been completed successfully. Europe '92 did not raise external trade barriers, and both Europe and the United States are clearly engaged in initiatives to extend their regional arrangements to newcomers. In the case of the European Union, this has involved the accession of former European Free Trade Association (EFTA) nations Sweden, Finland, and Austria, and in the case of the United States, new initiatives have been launched to extend NAFTA to other Western Hemisphere nations and to achieve free trade in the Asia-Pacific region.

Indeed, the notion that the world would split into three distinct blocks was always unconvincing. In particular, such blocks do not accord with the U.S. national interest as a global trader. First, it is not in the U.S. interest to be confined to a relatively small region, such as the Western Hemisphere, which accounts for only a third of U.S. trade, while Japan is left to dominate the Asia-Pacific region. And second, as soon as it negotiates agreements with some of its trading partners, the United States inevitably feels pressures from others to extend similar benefits. President George Bush felt compelled to announce his Enterprise for the Americas Initiative, which called for a free trade area in the Western Hemisphere, at about the same time that he announced his negotiations with Mexico. Similarly, during his second campaign, Bush announced that he was prepared to negotiate such agreements with other nations outside the hemisphere.

There are some, notably those who were against NAFTA in the first place, who point to the financial problems experienced by Mexico as indicating that NAFTA was a failure. But trade agreements are not a panacea for all economic problems. NAFTA helped make Mexico creditworthy. Unfortunately, Mexico used this credit to maintain an overvalued exchange rate. Nonetheless, its ability to adjust to the peso crisis by selling goods in the U.S. market thanks to NAFTA considerably eased a difficult situation. NAFTA also helped ensure that Mexico will not try to adjust to its financial difficulties by using protectionist measures.

Having successfully achieved the passage of NAFTA, the Clinton administration has promoted two partly overlapping regional arrangements, the extension of NAFTA to other Western Hemisphere nations and the Asia Pacific Economic Cooperation (APEC) agreement.

Western Hemisphere

On December 9, 1994, in Miami, a hemispheric summit was held at which 34 leaders from throughout the Americas committed themselves to create a Free Trade Area of the Americas (FTAA) by 2005. In addition, President Clinton announced that the United States, together with its NAFTA partners Mexico and Canada, would initiate negotiations with Chile on accession to NAFTA.

The nations of Latin America have moved extensively to liberalize their markets. As was the case with NAFTA for Mexico, participating in an international free trade agreement with the United States will make their reforms more credible and permanent. For the United States, NAFTA extensions would help cement economic and foreign policy relations with important neighboring nations that are holding out hands of friendship. The United States would gain an opportunity to adjust to free trade with Latin America at a time when these economies are relatively small. The size of U.S. trade with all of the rest of Latin America is roughly equal to its trade with Mexico, about 7 percent of total U.S. imports. This implies, in the short run, relatively small adjustment costs—estimates of adjustment in the case of NAFTA typically ran to net employment gains or losses over a decade equal to about 250,000, about one month of U.S. employment growth in the recent economic expansion. Over the long run, however, as their populations indicate, these economies will be large. The United States therefore has an opportunity to take measures with considerable diplomatic payoff in the short run and considerable economic benefits over the long run.

One of the issues of concern in NAFTA was rules of origin and other measures that were adopted to win political support for NAFTA by providing competitive advantage to firms that could take advantage of the agreement. These measures distort investment decisions. There is a danger that if NAFTA is extended in a piecemeal fashion, such rules will proliferate. It would be far better, therefore, to negotiate any regional extension in a fairly comprehensive fashion. Ideally, latecomers would be allowed to join, provided they are prepared to adhere to some simple and clear "docking" provisions. By contrast, if the NAFTA extension occurs incrementally, there is a greater danger that the process will be captured by specific special interests that could use the detailed rules in a protectionist fashion.

In addition to broadening NAFTA, consideration also should be given to deepening it. In particular, Canada and Mexico sought free trade agreements to secure the access of their exports to the U.S. market. Their concern was not only about the effects of tariffs but also about administered trade policy actions aimed at dumping and subsidies. NAFTA dealt with these issues not by eliminating these measures but by providing international dispute settlement mechanisms. In the case of Canada and the United States, these have not worked in an entirely satisfactory manner, and they cannot do so as long as defective antidumping rules continue to be applied. NAFTA should follow the practice already used within the European Union, and between Australia and New Zealand, whereby agreement on common antitrust policies has allowed the elimination of antidumping rules.

APEC

In November 1994, in Bogor, Indonesia, the 18 nations of APEC committed themselves to achieve free trade and investment in the region by the year 2020 at the latest. Industrial countries in the region would proceed more rapidly and liberalize by 2010. Currently APEC members are at work preparing a blueprint to achieve these goals. According to the Council of Economic Advisors Economic Report of the President, negotiators will work to speed up implementation of the Uruguay Round agreements and to deal with issues not adequately covered that are of particular importance to APEC members.[20] These include investment, intellectual property, rules of origin, government procurement, competition policy, and infrastructure.

While this initiative is undoubtedly bold in its goals, important questions can be raised about it and its chances of success. The APEC process contains both risks and opportunities. The risks lie in creating an initiative that overpromises and thus leads to an erosion of credibility. The opportunity lies in achieving improved market access that moves beyond what is feasible through GATT. Indeed, even if the grand free trade vision for APEC is not realized, it could push WTO sectoral agreements, such as the Information Technology Agreement, that help enhance free trade and investment and make APEC markets, among others, more contestable.

The strength of APEC lies in its ability to bring together a large number of extremely diverse economies and to obtain agreement between them. These nations range from large and developed countries, such as the United States and Japan, to small countries, such as Brunei Darussalem, and developing countries, such as Mexico and the Philippines. The weakness lies in the problems of forging an agreement that is acceptable, credible, and binding, given the diversity and scope of the membership.

It was indeed significant that the members agreed on the goal of free trade. If nations in APEC believe that this goal actually will be attained, it will help allay concerns of nations on both sides of the Pacific about NAFTA and American intentions. For example, many Asian countries are concerned about being shut out of the NAFTA market, but since both Canada and Mexico are part of APEC, an APEC free trade area would prevent Asia from being excluded. Similarly, some Asian nations are concerned that the United States could lose interest in the Pacific region. But again, APEC's initiatives will help keep the United States engaged. At the same time, several nations, including the United States, Australia, and New Zealand, are concerned that an exclusionary

East Asian Economic Caucus could develop. Again the APEC arrangement allays such concerns.

Not all problems have been solved. If it were really to be put into place, an APEC arrangement would, of course, raise fears by nonmember countries in Europe and Africa that they were being excluded. While the agreement does make mention of ensuring access for nonmembers from developing countries, and while it is an article of faith among most APEC members that they should practice "open regionalism," these statements remain undefined. In the long run, it will be desirable for APEC to extend its free trade provisions to all countries that are prepared to reciprocate.

By contrast with APEC, other regional free trade agreements have been concluded between limited groups of countries. This allows members to soothe the political difficulties of removing barriers in all sectors by offering producers the prospects of preferential access. But simultaneous liberalization within all of APEC would not allow this opportunity, even on a temporary basis. Given the size of APEC and the presence of world-class competitors in almost every industry, firms would find that extremely tough foreign competitors are being provided with equal access to other APEC markets.

On the other hand, the virtue of the APEC approach is that it places considerable pressure on countries not to be left out. Indeed, the larger the market, the greater this pressure will be. It will be crucial that APEC indeed adhere to the principle of conditional access for new members.

Despite their proclamations in Indonesia, numerous nations in APEC are still not deeply convinced that free trade in the Pacific is an attractive option. Participating in such an agreement would of course be easy for economies such as Singapore and Hong Kong that currently have almost no trade barriers. But for developing nations such as Indonesia, Thailand, China, and Korea, the required adjustments are considerable. To them, opening trade to Japan and the United States is the equivalent of opening to the world. These nations are all enjoying considerable success implementing industrial policies that would be severely constrained in a free trade area. They are reluctant to agree to such changes unless they believe they have no alternative.

For its part, Japan also would prefer the current situation in which it is free to increase its economic ties with the Pacific through trade, aid, and investment rather than through formal free trade agreements.

In the United States, once it is taken seriously and goes beyond high-technology sectoral initiatives, APEC free trade will raise several concerns. Protectionists will not look kindly on the prospects of open competition with Asian nations such as China and Japan. In addition, as the debate about NAFTA made clear, many Americans will be reluctant to grant free trade access to non-democratic nations and those that do not respect human rights. Moreover, U.S. trade problems with several Asian countries relate not to barriers at the border, such as tariffs, that can be eliminated with a free trade agreement, but to domestic policies and regulations that close markets to outsiders. While it is possible to imagine U.S. agreement with the more open Asian economies such as Hong Kong or Singapore, the prospects for a free trade area patterned after NAFTA between the United States and Pacific nations such as Japan and Korea are much smaller.

The problems experienced by American (and other foreign) firms in selling in Japan are the "invisible barriers" presented by private sector practices that are allowed officially, rather than the formal rules that are the traditional subject matter of trade agreements. Accordingly, from an American standpoint, a free trade area with Japan would provide increased access for Japan to the U.S. market but would not necessarily provide reciprocal access for the United States. Only an agreement that included measures such as joint antitrust enforcement, mutual recognition of standards, and symmetrical market access for foreign investors would deal with the central problems perceived in U.S.-Japan relations.

In sum, while the United States might agree to deeper integration with Japan or Korea it is unlikely to seek a free trade agreement of the NAFTA variety. On the one hand, therefore, it is difficult to see how the United States would agree to free trade without changes in these domestic policies. And on the other hand, it is difficult to see how several APEC countries would agree to change the same policies. Indeed, the weakness of the nonbinding agreement on foreign investment that was concluded at the 1994 APEC meeting in Indonesia highlights these problems.

It is thus very important that, in addition to its large goals and visions, APEC also should make concrete progress with projects that build up a record of cooperation between the members. The leaders' declaration at Subic in 1996, endorsing the Information Technology Agreement, was a good example. In such ways, even if the grand schemes face insurmountable obstacles, at least the members will have something to show for their efforts.

Open Regionalism

The key goal for U.S. policy is that APEC markets should be made more contestable. Increasing the contestability of markets also would help achieve regionalism that is open in a different sense. If regional arrangements go beyond border barriers and reflect agreements on domestic practices that reinforce market forces, they will make entry for outsiders easier and create rather than divert external trade. For example, when Europe forms a market with a single standard or a single currency, it lowers the costs of entry into that market not simply for European firms but also for foreign companies. The key for outsiders is that the arrangements enhance market pressures and that they conform to the principles of transparency and openness. It is unlikely that APEC as a whole will emerge as a distinctive, deeply integrated arrangement patterned after the European Union. Nonetheless, there is scope for regional measures that would help open the Asian economies to each other and to the world. In several Asian countries, such as Japan and Korea, there is growing interest in deregulation. Some countries might find it easier to undertake these measures if they are part of an international agreement.

Pacific nations should, in addition to their free trade negotiations, work out functional market-oriented programs at the regional level. Doing so would include measures that improve the transparency and openness of regulatory practices; increase the speed with which nations move to adopt the intellectual property provisions in the Uruguay Round; provide foreign-owned firms with national treatment; increase foreign access to financial and other regulated sectors; enforce competition policies; and cut domestic agricultural subsidies.

The successful conclusion of agreements in these areas would provide benefits that accrue automatically both within and beyond the region. Concrete steps would go further to achieve open regionalism than an idealistic program that could stumble in the face of political opposition. In any case, such initiatives are essential complements to the removal of border barriers. If successful, they will dramatically increase the ability for the full APEC vision.

BILATERALISM AND DEEPER INTEGRATION: U.S.-JAPAN RELATIONS

There is considerable evidence that despite Japan's low tariffs and official policies of free trade and investment, foreign entry into that country remains extremely difficult. Indeed, Japan is distinguished by its low share of manufactured imports, low degree of intraindustry trade, low share of sales by foreign firms based in Japan, and high level of markups on foreign products which serve as the functional equivalent of high tariffs. The problems experienced by foreign firms and products relate to the "invisible barriers" presented by private sector practices such as *keiretsu* (Japanese corporate groups) and public policies such as the weak enforcement of antitrust policies. Any agreement with Japan that deals only with the formal border barriers will not ensure access for foreign firms and products.

The fundamental problem in U.S.-Japan relations, then, relates to access. Simply put, the U.S. market is relatively easy to enter, while the Japanese market is not. The most important goal of U.S. trade policy toward Japan should be to increase access for foreign products and investment in that country. Achieving this goal is not easy. It runs into a potent political obstacle: Japanese firms are only too happy to keep foreigners out, while Japanese consumers who would gain from access to cheaper foreign products are weak, passive, and often unwilling to rock the boat. Moreover, many of the barriers themselves are difficult to identify and remove. Some, such as the limits on rice imports, are transparent and reflect explicit government policies; but these are the exception. Many are more opaque and may stem from private market practices in a society in which close long-term relationships often outweigh the impact of market forces.

The Policy Focus

U.S. trade negotiators often have summarized U.S. complaints about Japan as "Japan's large trade surplus." This surplus sometimes is treated as if it proves that Japan's markets are closed and its trading practices are unfair. Yet anyone schooled in elementary economics knows that the level of a nation's trade balance tells us little about whether its markets are open or closed. Some countries with open markets—for example, Germany prior to unification—run large trade surpluses. Other countries with very closed markets—

for example, Mexico in the early 1980s—run large trade deficits. Indeed, Japan actually had much smaller trade surpluses as a share of gross national product in the 1950s and 1960s, when it was more closed, than it does today.

Trade balances reflect spending patterns rather than trade barriers. Japan has a large trade surplus today because it is spending less than its income—in particular, since it is in recession, its investment spending has plummeted. Suppose Japan increased its domestic spending and eliminated its trade surplus. Would that mean that its market was more open? The answer is no. Japan could balance its trade simply by consuming more of its exports at home. Moreover, even if its trade surplus was eliminated through an increased volume of imports, this could be the result of increased Japanese spending rather than an increased market share for foreign goods.

Therefore, U.S.-Japan negotiations should not confuse the issue by even discussing the size of the trade imbalance. This gives those who would like to argue that there is no problem an ideal opportunity to point to the analytical flaws in their opponents' case. The United States should focus only on the fact that Japan presents unusually large barriers to foreign goods and firms. Not surprisingly, many Japanese dispute these allegations. However, in recent years the Japanese government itself has begun to emphasize the need to deregulate the Japanese economy. It is therefore actually much easier now to reach agreement that more needs to be done to make Japanese domestic markets more competitive.

The Policy Approach

The United States should propose an agreement with Japan that (1) commits both countries to aim at establishing markets that are open to each other's firms and products; (2) establishes a set of interim "affirmative action" measures to make the Japanese market more accessible; and (3) lays out a long-term agenda for achieving deeper economic integration between the two nations through deregulation and enhanced use of competition policies. These policies should operate at both the sectoral and economy-wide levels.

Before negotiating the details of specific policies, it would be useful to determine the ultimate objectives. One problem with both the SII talks of the Bush administration—"the Super Impatient Initiative"—and the more recent Framework arrangement of the Clinton administration is that they jumped right into the details of specific policies without laying out a vision of where the relationship should be heading. By contrast, the Europe '92 program began with agreement on the goals of a single market and then laid out the steps that were required to achieve it.

Second, the debate over how to open the Japanese market resembles the debate about how to end racial discrimination in the United States. One aspect is deciding whether discrimination still exists. This involves heated argument. And the argument is not very productive because everyone agrees that there was racial discrimination in the past, just as everyone agrees that there was discrimination against foreign investment and products in Japan in the past. The more relevant question, therefore, is not whether discrimination still exists today but what to do about redressing the effects of previous discrimination.

In past American debates over trade with Japan, three positions have emerged. The first is equal opportunity. Those who advocate pure rules-based approaches want to change the rules, make discrimination illegal, and then sit back and see what happens. The second approach is managed trade. This camp argues for minimum market shares and short timetables. This position has become popular among many Americans, particularly given the success of the Semiconductor Agreement in securing more than a 20 percent market share for foreign firms in Japan. The third approach is affirmative action, which does not necessarily demand specific outcomes but does try to ensure that foreign products and firms receive adequate consideration.

Each of these approaches has well-known pitfalls. Equal opportunity measures do not bring speedy results, particularly when there is a long tradition of discrimination. Nonetheless, contrary to some revisionists' allegations, U.S. efforts to change the rules have paid off in numerous cases. For example, after 10 years of pressure, virtually all barriers to the importation of tobacco into Japan were removed. Similarly, the sectors that were the subject of the MOSS (market oriented sector specific) talks in the mid-1980s experienced particularly rapid growth in U.S. exports to Japan. In response to the SII talks, Japan has taken a number of measures to increase its antitrust enforcement, and it has reduced the number of exemptions granted from its antitrust laws (down from 1,079 in 1975 to 219 in 1992).[21]

Preset quotas or managed trade are more controversial. They may achieve the appearance of results, but they also can have counterproductive effects. Just as the implementation of a quota system in dealing with racial issues runs into the problem of using a racially based system in the name of ending racism, so the implementation of a quota system for market shares runs into the problem of using a managed trade mechanism in the name of ending managed trade. Managed trade agreements are deficient in that they may force the Japanese government to implement buying cartels, thereby reinforcing "Japan Inc." and the role of the public bureaucracy in the economy rather than reducing it. Just as questions arise over the merit of minority members who achieve high positions, so measures that actually force Japanese to buy foreign products can backfire when the products are not actually competitive. They also can encourage collusion between buyers and become ceilings as well as floors.

The United States has, in desperation, emphasized a managed trade approach on some Japanese trade issues. Examples include the U.S.-Japan semiconductor agreement, the agreement on automobiles negotiated by President Bush on his ill-starred trip to Japan, and the demands by the Clinton administration for explicit projections of U.S. auto parts purchases by Japanese automakers. By some interpretations, the United States also followed this approach in other agreements negotiated by the Clinton administration, although efforts were made by some U.S. negotiators to avoid specific market share undertakings while emphasizing the use of "objective indicators" to measure success. While the agreements negotiated in this vein may bring about increased market shares for foreign exporters, they also have proved costly for the United States.[22] First, they have allowed Japan to paint the United States as a managed trader and thus have impaired American credibility as the leader of a free trade system. Second, they place U.S. trade policy in the risky position of adopting the agendas of U.S. firms based on their political clout rather than their competitive merit. Third, they have raised concerns among the nation's trading partners who fear that U.S. gains in the Japanese market could come at their expense.

To be sure, affirmative action, the middle position, also has problems. It requires constant monitoring and pressure on those in charge of making the key decisions. Very good examples of affirmative action were features in the framework agreements that insisted not that Motorola be given a specific market share but that it be allowed to participate in the Japanese market for cellular telephone services.

This affirmative action works, however, only when those in

decision-making positions become convinced they need to reverse the effects of previous discrimination. It requires imaginative initiatives to ensure that foreign products and firms are given adequate opportunities to compete for government and private contracts. Such initiatives might include requirements that department stores devote a minimum floor space to imported products, that government-arranged mergers mandatorily provide foreign firms with an opportunity to bid, and so forth.

It is also necessary to conduct specific sectoral negotiations with Japan. However, as an operating procedure, the United States should emphasize rules-based approaches that are reinforced by affirmative action measures. Managed trade solutions should be used only as a very last resort.

These sectoral negotiations with Japan should be complemented by more general efforts to deal with issues such as antitrust policies, regulatory practices such as administrative guidance, intellectual property rights, high-technology policies, product standards and certification, corporate governance, and stockholders' rights. Fortunately, there is increasing recognition in Japan itself that actions in these areas are needed, not simply because they will improve foreign access but also because they are in the nation's own long-term interest.

When markets are deregulated, it is easier for newcomers to enter. This will be true both for newcomers who are foreign and those who are Japanese. Deregulation, therefore, is the key to increasing the participation of both foreign products and firms in Japan. If it vigorously supported deregulation, the United States would become more popular with Japanese consumers. By demanding deregulation, the United States might also help weaken those special interests and bureaucrats in Japan who oppose it.

Thus few issues are more important to the future of the Japanese economy than deregulation. It is clear in many recent Japanese government reports that microeconomic reform is one of the highest national policy priorities.[23] As a recent report to the Ministry of International Trade and Industry (MITI) makes clear, deregulation is vital to encourage investment, new entry, and growth in new industrial fields. Many sectors with growth potential in Japan—including construction, electric power, gas, water, finance, insurance, real estate, transportation, and communications— are highly regulated. In addition, more general issues relating to competition and regulatory policies include obsolete regulations that have reinforced business practices that restrict new entry, measures for corporate governance, and regulations of mergers and acquisitions.

Competition Policy

Japan has paid increasing attention to antitrust enforcement since the structural impediments initiative. Nonetheless, much stronger action would improve the contestability of its markets. The major problem is not the nature of Japanese rules but the weak manner in which they have been enforced. While a multilateral agreement on competition policy rules might make an important contribution in dealing with this issue, a more limited bilateral agreement could be extremely useful. Since enforcement is the issue, the idea would be to follow the NAFTA solution of adding an international (or binational) appeals panel to the antitrust process in both countries. Thus, for example, U.S. firms that faced cartel arrangements in Japan that Japanese authorities ignored would have the standing to appeal to the binational panel.

Reinforcing Measures

The successful conclusion of the Uruguay Round and the creation of a new World Trade Organization means there is now a much improved multilateral mechanism for settling trade disputes. Some of the issues that were part of the bilateral framework talks should be moved to the WTO so that they can be resolved using a multilateral body. Taking the Kodak-Fuji case to the WTO was a good initiative. Such moves help enlist support for the WTO in the United States and help make it clear that this country has no intention of undermining the multilateral trading system.

CONCLUSION

The United States has adopted a multitrack approach to trade policy. While it continues to pursue a multilateral approach at the WTO, the United States also has acted unilaterally through measures such as the Super 301; bilaterally, particularly in negotiations with Japan; and regionally, by negotiating NAFTA and proposals for free trade in the Western Hemisphere and APEC.

The key to a successful global system today lies in global partnership to achieve deeper integration. The United States will play a leading role in this partnership, but it can no longer dictate results to others. It has to adjust to its changed role as first among equals. Likewise, both Japan and Europe will have to take more responsibility for the world economic system.

Some may feel that as the largest single economy, the United States has an interest in a trading system dominated by power relationships, in which it uses domestic market muscle to penetrate foreign markets. But it also must be appreciated that as giant economies such as China, India, and Russia emerge on the world scene, U.S. interest is ultimately in a system based on rules rather than on power.

The traditional approach to trade policy under GATT aimed mainly at removing barriers at the borders, such as tariffs and quotas. GATT did not try to harmonize domestic practices, and, in particular, it imposed few disciplines on developing countries. But as globalization has increased, there is a growing recognition that the United States needs to move beyond border barriers and aim at much deeper integration.

It is difficult, however, to accomplish this at the global level. Thus regional and bilateral initiatives arrangements are viable complementary approaches. Contrary to the fears of many, regional trading arrangements could lead to more open economies. The measures taken to implement Europe '92 created a single market rather than a fortress. The adoption of single standards within Europe, for example, will make it easier for all who wish to sell there. Likewise, Mexico did not join the North American Free Trade Area in order to close its economy. Indeed, over the past six years it unilaterally opened its economy to imports and investment. If regional agreements in APEC can be concluded that allow market forces to operate more freely within Asia, they likewise would confer benefits on firms outside the region.

The key to ensuring that regional trading systems remain open, however, is strong multilateral discipline from the WTO. Regional trading arrangements can complement but they can never substitute for a single system of international rules. Indeed, now that the Uruguay Round is completed, global rules are likely to be extended to areas such as competition policy, investment, and perhaps environment, labor standards, and improved governance. Undoubtedly the road will not be smooth, and countries will continue to adopt unilateral and managed trade solutions. However, achieving open, contestable international markets is a vital ingredient for global prosperity.

NOTES

1. My research calls these views into question. It suggests the major source of the problems facing workers in the developed countries is changes in technology, in particular labor-substituting technical change rather than trade. See Robert Z. Lawrence, *Trade Multinationals and Labor,* National Bureau of Economic Research Working Paper, 1994, and *Single World, Divided Nations?* (Washington, DC: OECD Development Centre and the Brookings Institution, 1996).

2. These proposals are not necessarily supported, however, by a majority of Americans. In particular, the newly elected Republican Congress has been reluctant to give the president international negotiating authority on environmental and labor-standards issues.

3. It is beyond the scope of this chapter to describe a full set of policy prescriptions for the post-Uruguay agenda. For such an attempt, see Robert Z. Lawrence, Albert Bressand, and Takatoshi Ito, *A Vision for the World Economy: Openness, Diversity, and Cohesion* (Washington, DC: Brookings Institution, 1996).

4. Companies that charge prices abroad lower than their domestic prices or that set prices below average cost are guilty of dumping under GATT rules. If either form of pricing causes injury, an offsetting duty may be assessed on foreign sales. But what is the "unfairness" these rules are designed to offset? One answer might be the implicit subsidy a monopoly position at home provides for sales abroad. However, the solution actually applied—a compensating duty—does not deal with the source of the problem: the closed foreign market that allows the foreign company to maintain its domestic monopoly. An alternative answer is that the foreign company is behaving in a predatory fashion. But the country imposing the penalty need not show predation. Selling below *marginal* cost might constitute evidence of predation. However, dumping is defined as selling below *average* cost, although such behavior may be appropriate business strategy, particularly when a company has excess capacity or enters a new market. In addition, companies rationally may let profit margins fall, rather than raise prices, in the face of currency fluctuations or other changes in market conditions thought to be temporary.

5. Previously U.S. policy has been understood to prevent challenges to anti-competitive practices in foreign markets unless there was direct harm to U.S. consumers.

6. Edward M. Graham and J. David Richardson argue that the clearest economic cases can be made for issues relating to cartelization and mergers and acquisitions. They believe convergence on monopoly, or other horizontal restraints, and price fixing rules are also possible. They are more skeptical about the opportunities in the area of vertical restraints. See "Summary of Project on International Competition Policy," paper submitted to the Joint Roundtable of the Competition Law and Policy and the Trade Committee, OECD, Paris, 1994.

7. F. M. Scherer, *Competition Policies for an Integrated World Economy* (Washington, DC: Brookings Institution, 1994).

8. U.S. Council of Economic Advisers, *Economic Report of the President* (Washington, DC: Government Printing Office, 1994), p. 246.

9. See Daniel C. Esty, *Greening the GATT: Trade Environment and the Future* (Washington, DC: Institute for international Economics, 1994); and Ford Runge, *Freer Trade, Protected Environment* (New York: Council on Foreign Relations Press, 1994).

10. Esty, *Greening the GATT*, p. 234. This suggestion leads to the controversy over so-called psychological spillovers. These occur when one country has more lenient standards that offend the citizens in another country, but the environmental impact of these standards is locally confined. See Richard N. Cooper, *Environment and Resource Policies for the World Economy* (Washington, DC: Brookings Institution, 1994). In my opinion, efforts to address psychological spillovers should be taken within multilateral agreements rather than through unilateral measures. When countries use unilateral measures, they should pay compensation through lowering other tariffs if they inhibit entry of such products.

11. The original charter of the ITO in 1948 contained a section on labor rights, although it was never ratified by the U.S. Congress for other reasons.

12. Eligibility under the Caribbean Basin Economic Recovery Act of 1983, the GSP (Generalized System of Preferences) in 1984, the Overseas Private Investment Corporation (OPIC) in 1985, and 1987 U.S. participation in the Multilateral Investment Guarantee Agency all have been conditioned on adherence to ILO standards on worker rights, which include the rights to associate and bargain collectively, the banning of forced or compulsory or child labor, the provision of reasonable conditions for worker health and safety, and the existence of a national mechanism for determining a generally applicable minimum wage.

13. Conspicuous by its absence, and an important reason for the opposition of organized U.S. labor to NAFTA, were rights of association, organizing, and bargaining.

14. See Terry J. Collingsworth, William Goald, and Pharis J. Harvey, "Time for a New Global Deal," *Foreign Affairs* (January/February 1994).

15. *OECD Employment Outlook, 1993,* (Paris: Organization for Economic Cooperation and Development, 1993).

16. Actually, some labor standards may increase the supply of labor and enhance productivity. Thus a safer workplace may reduce sick leave time; likewise increased unionization and worker participation in decision-making could increase productivity.

17. Ronald Ehrenberg notes that the substantial differences in benefit levels prevailing across the United States indicate that even within an integrated market, there is considerable scope for exercising local preferences. Maximum weekly unemployment insurance varies from $154 in Nebraska to $468 in Massachusetts. Ronald G. Ehrenberg, *Labor Markets and Integrating National Economies* (Washington, DC: Brookings Institution, 1994).

18. Collinsworth, Goald, and Harvey, "Time for a New Global Deal."

19. For a more complete discussion of regionalism see Robert Z. Lawrence,

Regionalism, Multilateralism, and Deeper Integration (Washington, DC: Brookings Institution, 1996).

20. U.S. Council of Economic Advisers, *Economic Report of the President* (Washington, DC: Government Printing Office, 1995), p. 220.

21. Arvind Subramanian, "The International Dimension of Competition Policies," in *International Trade Policies: The Uruguay Round and Beyond. Volume II. Background Papers* (Washington, DC: International Monetary Fund, 1994), p. 69.

22. In August 1994, agreements were reached on intellectual property protection, in government procurement in telecommunications equipment and services covering purchases by the government and by Nippon Telegraph and Telephone (NTT), and in medical technology. These agreements call for more complete information about procurement to be made available, full consideration of international standards for equipment, and the use of overall best value to judge competing bids.

    In insurance, the agreements ease restrictions on the introduction of new products, ease rate restrictions on policies to large customers, and deregulate in a way that does not prejudice foreigners already in the market. In January 1995 the Japanese government opened its public pension fund to foreign investment advisory services, relaxed conditions for issuing corporate debt, and agreed to introduce a domestic derivatives market. The agreement in flat glass committed Japanese distributors to carry imported glass and required the Japanese government to consider foreign glass in public procurement.

23. See, for example, *The Subcommittee for Long-Range Issues of the Industrial Structure Council Interim Recommendations to Ministry of International Trade and Industry* (mimeo, February 1994).

Chapter 18

Goals and Challenges for
U.S. Trade Policy

Alan Wm. Wolff

The interests of the United States lie with open markets. Market forces must determine competitive outcomes both at home and abroad if the nation's economic self-interest is to be served.

U.S. trade policy has evolved and been tested in a very large domestic common market of 50 states in which vigorous competition is the rule and in which, for most commerce, borders do not exist. Its outlook also has been formed during a period of increasing openness to the goods, services, and investments of other countries, particularly over the last few decades. U.S. tariffs have become negligible, and protection in the form of escape clause actions and voluntary restraint agreements has moved toward the vanishing point. The firmly held mainstream view of the two American political parties is that this great experiment has worked. The United States and its industries on the whole are stronger for having been tested in the unforgiving fire of international competition, often with an overvalued dollar. The country's commercial interests rest with full access to foreign markets and in reciprocating with open access to its own market.

U.S. trade philosophy is, of necessity, evangelical. It is not enough that its borders remain open for both exports and imports. The international trading system must provide a global regime that is equally open—for no good, service, or investment can cross the U.S. border unimpeded without there being another market sufficiently open to allow that transaction to take place. The United States has, in general, been the principal champion of the General Agreement on Tariffs and Trade (GATT), and its negotiators were instrumental in designing the World Trade Organization (WTO). The WTO and GATT systems were painstakingly constructed to assure that borders are open. But this is not sufficient. The heart of what the nation seeks is that foreign economies be at least as open as its own. Markets must not only be open at the border but contestable. For this to occur, all actors—buyers, sellers, and investors—must be motivated solely by commercial considerations (thus U.S. support for privatization), and market factors—neither bribes or cartels nor government edicts or guidance—must determine competitive outcomes.

Are there exceptions and qualifications to this picture? Of course there are. It has taken a long time for the United States to adopt this view of trade policy. Other nations have their own vision of where self-interest lies as well as their own criticisms of America's actions and policies. Other countries do not all share the American enthusiasm for domestic antitrust enforcement. They are not all equally offended by collusive or corrupt business behavior. They have not all organized their economies with an eye to maximizing consumer welfare. They do not all share the U.S. view that dumping is to be condemned and offset. None of them welcomes the use by the United States of its trade leverage to pry open a foreign market or to advance foreign policy goals.

Few, if any, trading partners would concede to the United States a moral superiority in trade matters. But the purpose of this chapter is not to defend past policies or actions or to define morality but to outline the essentials of a recommended course to be set by the nation's trade policymakers in furtherance of the interests of this country.

The United States faces formidable challenges in the next few years—the conduct of trade and other economic relations with China, Russia, Japan, and the European Union; continuing progress toward global trade liberalization primarily through the WTO; the integration of trade, finance, and monetary policies within the U.S. government; maintaining a domestic political base to support an open trade policy; and creating an optimal domestic economic environment for the growth and maintenance of the nation's international competitiveness.

THE CHALLENGE OF CHINA

A principal objective of American trade policy must be to integrate China more fully into the global system of trade and investment, and that means bringing China into the WTO, fully subject to its rules and obligations and accelerating China's transformation into a market economy. The global economy must be driven largely by market forces, or the obligations of WTO membership have little meaning. China is too large, both as a producer and as a market, to give it exceptional treatment. The existence of China as an outlier would deprive the WTO of the right to use, without further qualification, the word "World" in its name. The challenge is to negotiate terms of accession to the WTO and a bilateral agreement with China to deal with state ownership, investment, and trading that will most closely yield results similar to those expected from the operation of market forces—no small task.

Current WTO members must exercise particular care that the manner of China's accession to the WTO not result in the loss of appropriate leverage to help assure continuing liberalization of that nation's economy. The importance of retaining leverage has been masked by several factors that make Chinese trade appear to be less problematic, or more liberal, than China's policies would suggest. First, economic controls of state planning agencies are not given universal application throughout China. Second, China has experienced extraordinary economic growth for more than a decade, providing remarkably attractive opportunities for foreign firms. And finally, the product lines in which Chinese exports have been concentrated have been somewhat limited from the U.S. perspective—not, for example, autos, advanced electronics, or civil aircraft. Chinese exports have caused major adjustments in other countries that export to the United States and with which China competes. There is no public perception that trade with China has caused major dislocations in the United States.

Regularization of U.S.-Chinese trading relations must take place in parallel with China's movement to a seat in the WTO. Trade sanctions have a long history of ineffectiveness as a means of changing political conduct. Trade policy will not successfully bear the burden of shaping Beijing's policies regarding, for example, nuclear nonproliferation or other political questions. Some of these issues may have even greater importance to the United States than trade concerns, particularly in the near term, but it has been demonstrated time and again that trade sanctions rarely bring about constructive changes in foreign policies. Trade sanctions should, accordingly, be reserved for use where they can be effective—for dealing with trade offenses.

A trade policy designed to move China toward economic liberalization may, however, also serve U.S. foreign policy goals. Michael Novak has argued in his book *Democratic Capitalism* that market liberalization and political freedom are necessary each to the other, and the presence of one gives rise to the other. The future security of the United States would be well served if China moved toward democracy. Economic freedom will enhance the chances that political freedom will follow. It may be that Western-style democracy will not emerge soon in a country with China's history, but it also would be contradictory for complete state control and autocracy—which are essential to totalitarianism—to exist in a functioning market economy.

One recent example illustrates the linkages. It is the strongly enunciated policy of the World Bank that access to the Internet must remain unimpeded in China so that investors may have access to necessary information. Free commerce requires free communication.

In many ways, China is America's most profound trade policy challenge. The conditions for investment and trade in China are chaotic. The rewards of both trade and investment can be unrivaled. At the same time, there can be uncontrolled piracy of intellectual property and sometimes of goods. Part of this and other problems can be traced to a lack of enforcement, but there are other explanations as well, such as the absence of full central control. Local authorities often permit relatively free trade with few regulations. Some observers are concerned that the central government would, were it able to do so, impose a mercantilist regime of high tariffs, restrictive trading rights, and investment performance requirements.

The Sino-American trade relationship is characterized by no-holds-barred bargaining, with threats and counterthreats. This is trade policy conducted in a state of nature. U.S. leverage is not yet hindered by WTO dispute settlement rules, nor are China's policies and practices. It is not yet clear what model China will follow if the center gains control. If China can reap the benefits of an open trading system while remaining illiberal compared with the West, it may well be tempted to do so. The terms of China's accession to the WTO, and the freedom for response retained by the United States and China's other trading partners, will be key to whether existing members of the WTO retain the leverage to deal with the trading problems that are unavoidable with a nation the size and with the characteristics of China.

In many ways, China is the *aqua regia* for the WTO—the one acid that can test the organization's value. China is so large and its heritage so at odds with the assumptions of the WTO trading system that each WTO rule and institution must be reexamined as to its effectiveness in this new context. Examples are whether the code on Trade Related Investment Measures (TRIMs) reaches forced technology transfer, whether the rules on state trading reach the potential trade distortions of state ownership, investment, and the procurement practices of newly privatized companies, and whether dispute settlement can be effective where a large number of cases may be brought and where the trading practices objected to are largely opaque and evidence is hard to accumulate.

But it is far from a bad thing for assumptions regarding the effectiveness of the WTO regime to be tested and improvements proposed.

THE CHALLENGE OF RUSSIA

At its most fundamental level, the conduct of a successful trade policy requires having trade partners. Were the world economy dominated by state-trading nonmarket economies, the level of world trade would be a small fraction of what it is today. The prospects for global economic growth would be minimal.

A relatively few years ago, the world was characterized by two superpowers offering sharply divergent economic visions: market economies for the West; central planning, barter, and command economies for the East. The single most outstanding event of this century may well be the movement of nearly the entire globe toward the first of these models.

For reasons of trade policy as well as of national security, this generation will be judged by the apparent success or failure of its policies toward Russia. The West must exercise all reasonable measures to prevent Russia and the other former Soviet-dominated territories from slipping back into the economic and political abyss of state-run economies and authoritarian regimes. Is the West doing everything in its power to ensure that the Yeltsin presidency does not become the modern equivalent of the evanescent Kerensky regime or the Weimar Republic? Is the policy machinery of the West sufficiently engaged to avoid a catastrophe of this magnitude?

The United States invested trillions of dollars on military preparations for the Cold War and risked nuclear winter as a result of the constant potential for conflict with the Soviet Union over the 45 years following World War II. The United States conceived the Marshall Plan so that its allies and former enemies would not fall prey to forces that would bring about another convulsion of nations. Nothing remotely equivalent in level of effort or attention has been undertaken to consolidate the gains for democracy and the market system made possible by the collapse of the Soviet empire.

Large infusions of public funds, however, are not available; nor would they be the best means of solving the problems of the former Soviet states. What is needed, instead, are multilateral guarantees or equivalent measures that would increase the flow of private capital into the former Soviet Union, together with a major technical assistance program to improve the legal and market institution infrastructure. Existing multilateral institutions must address this task or a new institution should be formed for this purpose. The United States cannot pretend that this is not in part an American problem.

A timid or reluctant approach to the Russian challenge will cost the West dearly, even if a failure of policy does not take the form of immediate conflict with Russia. Regional conflicts, such as the Persian Gulf War, which required deployment of 540,000 troops, if sponsored by a hostile Russian regime, whether of the extreme right or left, would make Western investments in Russia pale by comparison. It is not enough to say that something should have been done six or seven years ago; the time to act is now.

THE CHALLENGE OF JAPAN

The U.S.-Japan bilateral trading relationship easily qualifies as one of the most troubled in the world. Japan historically has resisted calls for trade liberalization with respect to any product or service that has benefited from a scheme of Japanese government-supported protection. In Japan, a policy of industrial targeting was practiced for decades in many industrial sectors, with sophisticated protectionism included as a central element. Japan's protection was constructed as a defense in depth with only the surface aspects visible.

Most of the attention to the market access problem in Japan has come from the United States. Japan's negotiating style was first to refuse to admit to the existence of a problem and then to yield ground only very slowly. Ultimately, Japan was pragmatic—agreeing to painstaking negotiations initiated by its trading partners. These talks generally were allowed to result in very slow, but discernible, progress in bringing about some trade liberalization.

Through cycles of conflict and compromise, a relative equilibrium was reached in U.S.-Japanese trade relations. The United States would make its claim, and Japan would resist. Then, with more heat than light generated, a resolution would be reached that resulted in greater two-way trade, not less. The trade relationship might have continued for some time along this uncomfortable but acceptable path if the Cold War had not ended unexpectedly. This event coincided with a resurgence of Japanese nationalism. Pragmatic bilateral trade negotiations, formerly conducted with grimaces and grudging acquiescence, have in some cases recently been supplanted by a Japanese rejection of *gaiatsu* (foreign pressure). Requests for consultations or negotiation on trade barriers have been treated as affronts to Japanese sovereignty. In other cases, such as insurance, the prior cyclical pattern of resistance, *gaiatsu*, and compromise has been maintained.

The policy of rejection was articulated most prominently by Shintaro Ishihara in his book *The Japan That Can Say "No"!* Its realization has been sought by Prime Minister Ryutaro Hashimoto and a school of hard-line Ministry of International Trade and Industry (MITI) bureaucrats. The bureaucrats have stated that it is both inappropriate and unnecessary to respond positively to American requests or demands for further access to the Japanese market. For U.S. trade policy and the fledgling WTO, this stance poses a serious challenge.

The WTO system is based on each member, most particularly large members, reciprocating benefits received with meaningful trade concessions, implicitly but most definitely based on each possessing a functioning domestic market in which to do business. If there is a basis for believing that a large member is not meeting this threshold requirement, and there is no ready means to rectify the deficiency, not only are the seeds of a major conflict sown, but the basis for the WTO compact itself is called into question.

Is this conflict one that the United States should avoid? There has been a debate in academic circles, and at times between U.S. government agencies, as to whether the trade battle of the moment needed to be fought. After all, wasn't the friction detrimental to the bilateral relationship? However, the United States has no acceptable alternative but to fight each sectoral trade battle for increased market access as each problem emerges. There are three basic policy options for dealing with Japan: (1) to declare, as some academic economists have, that Japan's mercantilism does not matter (or does not exist)—but this course is contrary to U.S. commercial interests and reality, and could not be sustained politically; (2) to meet protection with countervailing protection and simply trade less with Japan—but this runs counter to fundamental U.S. goals and the interests of both American consumers and industrial users of Japanese goods; or (3) to engage in constant efforts to win market access, product sector by product sector, however difficult and contentious the effort may be.

Japan's newly articulated basis for intransigence over trade issues—what it calls "an end to the era of bilateralism"—is not the only cause for concern. There is also evidence that a number of Japanese policymakers have rejected the direction of economic liberalism that has characterized post–World War II U.S. global leadership. In 1996, it was reported that Japan's Official Development Agency (ODA) was preaching a new policy line for adoption by the developing countries of Asia. The ODA reportedly proposed the following prescription: "You are at 50 percent liberalization, we are at 80 percent. Do not follow the Western model of 100 percent liberalization. Follow Japan, at 80 percent." This direction also was articulated by some MITI bureaucrats who envision a new mission for the ministry: ostensibly no longer the promotion of Japanese industry nor the management of trade relations with the United States, but instead the provision of technical assistance to the developing countries of Asia to show them how to make trade policy support neomercantilist industrial policies. A cynical observer might see this less as a new philosophy than as an attempt to give Japanese plants in Southeast Asia protection against "foreign" (read U.S. and European) competition. MITI would be continuing its historic role of protecting Japanese manufacturing but on a larger stage of a Greater Japan.

If it fully materializes, this second Japanese challenge to the United States—to the direction of its leadership—is as serious as greater resistance to American pressure to unwind Japan's protectionist measures. The capacity for Japan to be an equal partner for leadership in the world trading system would be called into question if it turns out that Japan is not working toward global trade liberalization. Fortunately, at least some Japanese voices favor economic liberalism, in the name of "deregulation," as being in the country's national commercial interest by fostering the international competitiveness of its industry. Even if the chances for early sweeping reforms are nonexistent, there may be further movement in the right direction in Japan in the future.

What then should be the optimal U.S. trade policy with respect to Japan? For the United States, the only course is to seek full market access, no matter how difficult or tortuous the pursuit of that objective might be. America's evangelical free trade mission cannot avoid confronting this, perhaps the most serious, challenge to its credo. The Japan problem is serious enough to merit greater policy attention, resources, and the development of a more effective, systematic approach by its major trading partners.

U.S. and European policy toward Japan requires three elements: knowledge, leverage, and the right objectives. First, there is no substitute for assembling the necessary analytical resources and understanding the nature of market closure in Japan in any particular product or service sector. The second requirement is leverage. The newest element in the leverage equation—the WTO dispute settlement process—holds out the promise of Japan being held accountable for its protectionist measures. The effectiveness of this process will be tested shortly. Other forms of leverage are far more sophisticated, such as gaining support within Japan from allied commercial interests and from public opinion makers in the press, academe, or politics, who see that nation's interests as lying somewhere beyond mercantilism. There is also leverage to be gained in bringing other countries into previously bilateral negotiations over any given issue, for their own commercial gain or to serve their broader policy objectives.

If the hurdles of first understanding the Japan market access problem and then bringing to bear the requisite leverage to obtain a solution are cleared, there remains the last hurdle of seeking the right objectives. In the case of a tariff, this problem is close to nonexistent—the solution is to phase it down or eliminate it. In the case of a complex protectionist scheme achieved through blocking access to distribution, stifling price competition at the retail level, and curbing expansion of access to the end-consumer, the solutions negotiated will have to be at least as sophisticated as the schemes of protection. The tangle of obstacles and measures have to be unwound. For this course of action to be successful, the Japanese government must take proactive measures to assure the working of the domestic market. In the final analysis, the Japan problem demands a Japan solution. The question, as always, is the pace of progress. This is a greater challenge for policymakers in Tokyo than it is for their counterparts in Washington, Beijing, or Brussels. Japan's future competitiveness and its relations with its trading partners depend on it identifying and implementing the right remedial measures.

THE U.S.-EUROPEAN PARTNERSHIP

Despite repeated bouts of petulance on both sides of the Atlantic over shortsighted trade measures, a U.S.-European alliance over global trade policy does exist. This alliance is visible when it is most needed—to conclude successful major rounds of multilateral trade negotiations, to strengthen the structure of the international trading system, and to reach new levels of economic integration. The challenge for the United States and Europe alike has been to join together to manage the system in between the launching and winding-up of major rounds. At a number of levels, this is beginning to occur. The two regions led the way to conclude a broad Information Technology Agreement (ITA) and a Telecom Services Agreement. They are encouraging their private sectors to cooperate in crafting mutual recognition accords, which will lead to harmonization of their respective domestic regulatory regimes— all to be more open to the goods and services of the other.

It is worth investing time and effort to forge a closer working relationship with Europe, regardless of the periodic difficulties, however incendiary these may be. (The confrontation over the Helms-Burton legislation or the Boeing/Airbus dispute are examples.) The United States and the European Union also share a number of common interests with respect to China, Russia, and Japan and in their bilateral trading relationship. A working, bilateral international trade policy coordination mechanism should be established.

This cannot occur solely at the ministerial level. Consultation needs to be achieved (and is beginning) on a broad range of subjects at the working levels of officialdom as well. Perhaps as valuable as any other means of cementing the partnership would be sharing information and conducting joint analyses of barriers and market failures that impede the flow of international trade in third-country markets. The most valuable benefit that could be obtained from the proposed transatlantic free trade discussions would be a working policy coordination mechanism that leads to a real partnership in management of the world economic system.

TRADE AGREEMENTS AND UNILATERAL ACTS

The foremost tool of post–World War II U.S. trade policy has been and must remain the GATT (now WTO) system. There is no substitute. Given the openness of the U.S. economy and a trading system based on the most-favored-nation (MFN) principle, there is no other practical way to spread as far as possible the area of reciprocal openness. Given that U.S. well-being lies with maximum openness reciprocated by others abroad, a multilateral trading system of great breadth and scope is essential to the success of U.S. trade policy.

This having been said, it still makes sense to promote regional integration. For the United States, this primarily means the North American Free Trade Agreement (NAFTA) and the Free Trade Area of the Americas. For Europe, this regional impulse has meant periodic European Union enlargement. There are benefits both to the region and to nonparticipants. This is both accepted as GATT theory and valid in reality. Both by showing the way to deeper integration and more rapid liberalization and in causing nonparticipants to worry about being left out, regional economic integration has been a driver of progress in multilateral trade agreements. Since the beginning of the Kennedy Round of Multilateral Trade Negotiations, which concluded on June 30, 1967, a major motivation for multilateral talks has been the prospect that without global negotiations the dominant trade instruments would be regional deals that might work to the disadvantage of nonparticipants. Europe must watch with some concern as the Pacific nations work on the Asia Pacific Economic Cooperation forum; Japan must be vigilant in protecting its interests as a Free Trade Area of the Americas extends south; and both Japan and the United States must look carefully at the expansion of Europe's special trade arrangements.

Aside from regional economic integration, there are valid reasons for trade negotiations on less than a multilateral basis. Countries often have specific commercial interests with other countries that require bilateral consultation and negotiation. The creation of a WTO dispute settlement mechanism did not constitute a decision by trading nations that all future issues between countries would be litigated immediately. Litigation always should be a next-to-last resort. Most trade problems that the United States or any country has with its major trading partners ought to be handled in bilateral negotiations, if at all possible. In many cases, for example, the WTO's substantive rules may not yet extend to a particular trade dispute, and thus a litigative approach will not be available. Of course, if a bilateral deal is struck, the benefits ought to be available to all on a nondiscriminatory basis.

As a last resort, unilateral action in trade cases may be unavoidable. At one end of the policy spectrum, such action can take the form of matching foreign subsidies with one's own domestic subsidies. At the other end, it can mean taking retaliatory trade measures. Although multilateral condemnation may bring about solutions in almost every instance, ultimately the ability of the WTO's dispute settlement mechanism to resolve disputes will depend in some cases on the belief that unilateral action exists as a real possibility, if the multilateral panel process is unable to yield results. For the United States to maintain its leverage, new tools will have to be considered—including, for example, the imposition of fines on companies engaging in anticompetitive behavior that results in market closure. It must be concluded that the costs of using the existing tools, such as Section 301 of the 1974 Trade Act, have been raised to the point where they have diminishing credibility for all but the largest or most egregious cases.

PREPARING FOR A "NEW ROUND" OF WTO NEGOTIATIONS

It is in America's interest to extend the coverage of the substantive rules of the WTO to open the world's markets further.

Whether this is accomplished in a major round of multilateral trade negotiations or piecemeal is always the subject of debate after major trade talks have been concluded. In this debate the never-again school gradually yields to the there-is-no-other-way-to-get-there-from-here school. However the negotiations are structured, a variety of issues, both new and unfinished business, must be addressed.

Listed roughly in their order of proposed priority, the subjects include but would not be limited to:

- *Private anticompetitive practices.* Private restraints of trade are the single largest remaining distortion of world trade. There exists no greater rule-making challenge for the current generation of trade policymakers. Commitments to market access depend on the existence of functioning internal markets. It is imperative to identify these remaining barriers to international trade and then make denial of market access—no matter what the cause—fully actionable.

- *Open dispute settlement procedures.* The essence of the WTO is its new dispute settlement process. It is very important that it be effective and that it generally be viewed as accomplishing what it has been created to do—to render judgments fairly and impartially. Confidence in the new system would be greatly enhanced if the international process were as open as domestic U.S. judicial proceedings. Briefs and proceedings should be open to the public. These are not negotiating or mediation sessions, but adjudications, and *in camera* proceedings are not warranted. National delegations should include knowledgeable private parties at interest or experts whenever a participating country deems it appropriate. If not, the presentation of cases against protectionist schemes will always will be imbalanced in favor of the defendant country, whose officials have greater knowledge of the facts surrounding their own measures.

- *Trade barrier elimination for information technology goods and services.* There is no economic rationale for any country to reduce its own competitiveness in this sector by impeding inputs of goods that spur innovation. An ITA-II should be negotiated to remove remaining impediments to international trade in information technology goods and services.

- *Tighter subsidy disciplines.* The practice of allowing certain sub-sidies to go unchallenged without the possibility of response because of their supposed nobility of purpose—protection of the environment, regional aid, support of research and develop-ment, or worker dislocation payments—should be ended. This "greenlighting" of state aids should be repealed. Money is fun-gible. Whenever a government bears a cost that otherwise would be borne by private producers, the subsidy should be subject to being offset if it causes harm to the trade of others. The effects of past subsidies are not eliminated by the privatization of com-panies or by a nation ceasing to be a nonmarket economy. Strong enforcement of antisubsidy rules and laws, along with bud-getary constraints currently affecting most governments, should reduce the incidence of subsidies as a major cause of trade dis-tortion.

- *Liberalization of government procurement.* The remaining pro-tection of domestic firms should be converted to tariff protection, bound at a fixed margin of preference and phased out over an agreed period.

This is not an exclusive list of issues worthy to be subject for new negotiations, but it provides a good series of starting points.

A number of new domestic trade laws need to be enacted before the United States should participate in new multilateral talks. As part of new "Fast Track Trade Agreement Authority," Congress should create an American review panel for WTO decisions. This WTO Dispute Settlement Commission would be composed of judges who would examine each decision, rendering an opinion as to whether the panel had acted within its judicial mandate. The effect of the commission would be to provide independent domestic review that would tend to add credibility at home to the international process, increasing accountability and countering any unwarranted chal-lenge or complaint when a decision adverse to U.S. interests is ren-dered.

In addition, Congress should establish goals for future trade negotiations. Care is needed to ensure that Congress, which has been given the commerce power under the U.S. Constitution, become more engaged in trade policy. There is a high risk that its failure to do so will result in its withholding approval of agree-ments entered into by the executive branch.

ECONOMIC POLICY INTEGRATION

Very often, trade, finance, and monetary policies are conducted as if they are unrelated, although international financial and monetary policies exist in large part so that trade can take place. However, trade policy discussions rarely intrude on the world of finance and international monetary policy, except at the margins—such as past efforts to curb the export credit race either generally or with respect to large commercial aircraft.

Any survey of trade policy would be remiss if it did not include at least a few words of warning on these rarefied policy matters. Trade policy is discredited by a 45 percent swing in the yen/dollar relationship over a relatively short period or a 50 percent devaluation of the Mexican peso overnight. The relationship of the Chinese yuan or the new euro to the dollar are fit subjects for concern by trade policymakers. Some hard questions have to be asked early in the process about the monetary relationships that underlie any given bilateral trading relationship. The answers vis-à-vis the yen/dollar relationship may lie in large part in U.S. fiscal and monetary policy, but not solely. In the case of Mexico, the collapse of the Mexican economy so undermined NAFTA, which was the right trade policy, that neither candidate in the 1996 U.S. presidential race would readily mention his support for the agreement.

The relationship of investment and trade has received insufficient attention. Freedom to invest clearly plays a major role in the difference in trading patterns and the tenor of the bilateral relationship between Europe and the United States, on the one hand, and the U.S.-Japan relationship, on the other. Investment is one of the largest categories of issues on America's agenda with China. The liberal international trading system lacks a multilateral investment code. Clearly, also, as in most trade policy questions, there is a dearth of good data and analysis on which to base policy decisions.

A variety of coordinating policy mechanisms have been established in the executive branch, from the Council on International Economic Policy during the Nixon administration to the current National Economic Council, to consider in a holistic fashion America's international economic policy. The task of coordination of disparate policies has not become any easier with the passage of two and a half decades. The need for international economic policy coordination has become even more important given the openness of the U.S. economy in a post–Cold War environment in which economic and commercial interests have gained in relative importance.

The mechanisms exist for effective coordination. They should be utilized.

MAINTAINING THE DOMESTIC POLITICAL BASE

None of the hoped-for results of a liberal trade policy can be achieved if the necessary domestic political base is not preserved. The idea of trade liberalization is being challenged in the United States today as it has not been since 1970, when the House of Representatives passed import quota legislation. In the primaries leading up to the most recent U.S. presidential election, two candidates, Ross Perot and Patrick Buchanan, declared that the most prominent of American trade agreements are contrary to the nation's best interests. It is not clear whether the junior half of the U.S. House of Representatives shares the passion for trade liberalization that their Republican leaders feel.

We may have passed through the era when public opinion held that real incomes have fallen or have stagnated for years (although there is a debate about the facts), where downsizing by large corporations created a level of uncertainty and concern unmatched by the unemployment statistics themselves, and where the promised gains from trade, such as NAFTA, appeared to have been empty. Nevertheless, it is significant that trade liberalization—which has been condemned by labor interests for years—is now also criticized by a number of environmental groups and others concerned over cession of America's sovereignty. In short, trade liberalization is questioned by those on both the left and the right of the American political spectrum.

Congress is no longer organized to maintain a strong interest at the member level in trade policy issues—other than the more politically charged political issues such as the link between Chinese trade and human rights, trade sanctions for investing in Cuba, or the NAFTA-linked issues of labor and the environment. Committee oversight of trade has diminished as tariffs have been lowered, and, with the adoption of fast-track procedures, the real action has been passed to the executive branch. Congressional participation has diminished to a general blocking power rather than an active role.

Despite the complexity of the tasks at hand, staffing of the negotiating function has not grown. In fact, the resources given to trade law administration have been cut. Staffing, for example, has not been increased sufficiently in response to the growing burden the new dispute settlement mechanism puts on the government.

The WTO dispute settlement mechanism itself is not transparent, which could lead to criticism of U.S. participation in the WTO. There is a serious issue of whether the NAFTA dispute settlement mechanism, in its delegation of U.S. judicial functions, oversteps what is permitted under the U.S. Constitution. Noted judicial authorities have charged that judicial process was more violated than adhered to in a major U.S.-Canadian dispute settlement case, both at the panel and at the appellate levels. The erosion of Americans' confidence in international dispute settlement following a major loss by the United States in a badly decided WTO case is inevitable. Reactions could be very harsh.

The original balance struck in trade law and international trade agreements—that there would be trade liberalization, but if there was unfair or otherwise injurious trade, it would be offset or in some way remedied—has been forgotten. The import relief clause, originally designed to give temporary relief if lowering the tariff wall gave rise to injury, apparently has become a dead letter. Indeed, some quarters now seek to curb actions against imports that benefit from government subsidies or the advantages of a closed home market and are sold below the production cost, to the injury of an American industry.

Care must be taken to nurture the domestic political base to avoid its being seriously eroded. This is not an impossible task. Demonstrable progress is needed in removing foreign trade barriers and eliminating trade-distorting practices.

THE CREATION OF AN OPTIMAL DOMESTIC ENVIRONMENT

America's policies at home must be designed to complement its trade policy—the maintenance and expansion of open markets. Ultimately, it is U.S. competitiveness that allows the United States to benefit from open world markets. In a virtuous circle, U.S. business competitiveness is further enhanced by competing in all markets.

A strategy to ensure continued U.S. international competitiveness consists of a variety of key components:

• The American workforce at all levels should receive training second to none. For those directly involved in commercial diplomacy, this means training in foreign languages and in the skills of negotiation and representation of commercial and trade interests.

• The cost of capital must remain competitive. Sound macroeconomic policy is an imperative component of competitiveness, both to ensure an adequate rate of investment and an exchange rate at which trade—both imports and exports—can take place.

• The attractiveness of the United States as one of the best places in which to invest, conduct research and development, and design products must be maintained. A wide variety of factors make a country an optimal place in which both citizens and foreign entities wish to conduct their most productive activities. One element is a strong university system. On this point, the United States can be proud. There is less to be said in favor of our secondary and primary school systems, although these are certainly not beyond remedy.

• The executive branch and Congress both should resist the temptation to regulate trade for purposes unrelated to enhancing trade liberalization. Trade holds an almost fatal attraction to some as a means of exercising leverage over other countries for foreign policy or other non–trade-related purposes. In the main, this temptation must be vigorously resisted in order to promote the economic well-being of the United States as well as to preserve the strength of its bilateral relationships and of the multilateral trading system. Departures from this standard should be undertaken only after very serious debate and for reasons of overriding national interest.

• There will be differences as to what policies best strengthen U.S.-based competitors engaging in world trade. Some measures have a slightly greater degree of government involvement than others. Many in government (in both political parties) and in industry would say that the experiment in joint precompetitive research in semiconductor manufacturing (SEMATECH) was a successful case of cooperation within an industry, with government acting as a catalyst and a limited investor.

Whatever the state of the debate about the appropriate level of government involvement in assisting the international competitiveness of U.S. firms, a core group of public policies can be adopted that will promote American competitiveness.

REQUIREMENTS FOR SUCCESSFUL TRADE POLICY IMPLEMENTATION

The successful pursuit of America's trade objectives requires three elements: a sound analytical base, adequate resources, and leverage.

America's information for major trade negotiations is perhaps second to none. The creation of the private sector advisory mechanism more than 20 years ago is a resource unmatched abroad. Outside of major negotiating rounds, however, the information available to policymakers quickly becomes very uneven.

Enhancing the information available requires better organization of existing resources and, where necessary, their supplementation. As among competing budgetary priorities, a simple calculation must be performed: How important is international trade to the United States? How important are obtaining and maintaining open markets abroad? If the rewards and the return on investment are sufficient, then both the government and the private sector can and will make the necessary investment in analysts, negotiators, and staff for international dispute settlement.

Last, there is the question of leverage. Sufficient leverage needs to be available to U.S. trade negotiators when the organization of a foreign economy or its industrial, agricultural, or service sectors depart from the WTO's unspoken assumption that all members have laissez-faire economies. If major players play by different rules from those of the WTO or if they prevent market forces from determining competitive outcomes to the detriment of imports, the basis for the WTO is undermined.

The WTO's dispute mechanism is available as possible leverage. But its effectiveness will depend on the degree to which substantive rules apply to the market restrictions encountered. WTO panels cannot reach private restrictive business practices or their subspecies, corrupt business practices. Without further negotiation and agreement, WTO litigation is not likely to provide any satisfactory answer.

There may be some debate in academic circles and in some think tanks as to whether foreign restrictions should be troubling. Some will opine that if foreign countries choose a protectionist, mercantilist path, they alone will bear the costs. This philosophic acceptance of the fact that American openness to foreign goods and services will, on ocassion, go unrequited is, however, self-defeating. It will erode the remaining public support for maintenance of a liberal world trading system. This state of affairs is, therefore, unacceptable. Protectionist measures adopted as expressions of economic nationalism abroad are contrary to America's national commercial interests. Maintenance of leverage, therefore, will be an essential component of the conduct of U.S. trade policy.

The United States stands today on the bright, broad uplands of a trading world free of most of the barriers its negotiators long sought to eliminate. Economic integration is being achieved that is deeper and broader than anything envisaged by the pioneers of trade liberalization who led the way to creation of GATT half a century ago. Momentum exists for going forward. U.S. leadership will be essential, but partnership with others is a ripe possibility. There is no shortage of challenges, but the potential for success has never been greater.

Index

180–86; and labor markets, 109; and multilateral rounds, 130, 131, 135; and public perceptions of unfairness, 70; and regionalism, 337, 343; and regulatory reform, 246; security relationship with, 172–73; and TAFTA, 155, 159–60; workforce training in, 87–88; and the WTO, 311
JFTC (Japanese Fair Trade Commission), 216
Jobs, 61–69, 89–91, 108–12. *See also* Labor
Johnson, Lyndon B., 128
JTPA (Job Training Partnership Act), 89–91
Justice Department, 329

K
Kantor, Mickey, 35, 68, 70, 126
Keiretsu model, 167, 320, 344
Kenen, Peter, 99–100
Kennedy Round, 92, 127, 129, 136, 364
Kodak, 134, 136, 179, 205, 349
Korea, 50–51, 137, 174, 225, 341, 343
Krueger, Anne, 271

L
Labor, 12–13, 73, 170, 209, 259–83, 333–36. *See also* Jobs
Labor Department, 271
Large Scale Retail Store Law, 185
Latin America, 28, 32, 50–51, 137, 146, 151–52, 155; and anticorruption efforts, 228; and balance-of-power issues, 167–68
Libya, 72
Liemt, Gijsbert van, 270
Living-standard indicators, 51–59
Louvre Agreement, 105

M
Maastricht Treaty, 254
Macroeconomic policies, 102–5
MAI (Multilateral Agreement on Investment), 136

Majoritarian problem, 60
Malawi, 233
Malaysia, 137, 214–15, 233
Marshall, Ray, 271
McKinsey Global Institute, 119
MEAs (multilateral environmental agreements), 286, 287–91, 297
Medicare, 106, 165
MERCOSUR, 129, 133, 168
Mexico, 47, 49–51, 225, 300, 302; and anticorruption efforts, 234; and multilateral rounds, 133, 138, 148; peso crisis in (1994), 23, 133, 166, 368; and regulatory reform, 245. *See also* NAFTA (North American Free Trade Agreement)
MFN (most-favored-nation) status, 14, 16, 20, 29, 143–44, 146, 149, 154–56, 192–95, 199, 240, 364
Ministry of Finance, 246
Ministry of International Trade and Industry (MITI), 348, 360, 361
Mitterand, François, 334
Mohammed, Mahatir, 215
Montedison Company, 239
Montreal Protocols, 249, 286
Moral purpose, 72–73, 76
MOSS (Market Oriented Sector Specific) talks, 346
Motion Picture Association, 79
Motorola, 347
MOUs (Memorandums of Understanding), 189, 191
MRAs (mutual recognition agreements), 251, 254–58
Multifiber Agreement, 324
Multitrack strategy, 13–17
Mun, Thomas, 126

N
Nader, Ralph, 322
NAFTA (North American Free Trade Agreement), 13, 18–19, 29, 32–33, 65, 107, 127, 129, 132–34, 136, 148, 150, 153, 155, 159, 168, 171, 213, 313–16, 320–22, 330–31, 333, 337–40, 342, 349–50, 364, 368–69, 370; and anticorruption

ABOUT THE AUTHORS

CLAUDE BARFIELD is Resident Scholar and Coordinator of Trade Policy Studies at the American Enterprise Institute. His latest publication in the trade policy area is *Expanding U.S.-Asian Trade and Investment: New Challenges and Policy Options.*

GEZA FEKETEKUTY is Director of the Center for Trade and Commercial Diplomacy, Monterey Institute of International Studies. Previously he served in various senior positions in the Office of the U.S. Trade Representative and was Chairman of the OECD Trade Committee. He has written widely on trade policy issues.

ELLEN L. FROST, Senior Fellow at the Institute for International Economics, served as Counselor to the U.S. Trade Representative from 1993 to 1995. She is the author of *Transatlantic Trade: A Strategic Agenda* and *For Richer, For Poorer: The New U.S.-Japan Relationship.*

R. MICHAEL GADBAW is currently Vice President and Senior Council for International Law and Policy at General Electric Company. Previously he served in the U.S. government as a legal adviser in the Treasury Department and Deputy General Counsel in the Office of the U.S. Trade Representative. He also practiced law as a partner in the Washington office of Dewey Ballantine.

EDWARD M. GRAHAM is Senior Fellow at the Institute for International Economics. He is the author or coauthor of several books, including *Foreign Direct Investment in the United States* (with Paul Krugman) and *Global Corporations and National Governments,* as well as more than 70 published articles. His most recent book, *Global Competition Policies* (with J. David Richardson), was published in late 1997.

MICHAEL HART is Professor of International Affairs at Carleton University in Ottawa, Canada, and Senior Associate of its Centre for Trade Policy and Law. During the winter months he is a Visiting Professor at the Center for Trade and Commercial Diplomacy, Monterey Institute of International Studies. Previously he was a senior trade official with the government of Canada. He is widely published in the trade policy area.

THOMAS R. HOWELL is a Partner in the Washington law firm of Dewey Ballantine, where he specializes in international trade matters. He has represented domestic clients in U.S.-Japan disputes in semiconductors, telecommunications equipment, photographic film and paper, and soda ash. He has litigated cases on behalf of U.S. flat-rolled steel producers involving various countries in Europe, Latin America, and the Far East.

GARY C. HUFBAUER, a scholar on international trade, tax, and finance questions, is Director of Studies and the Maurice R. Greenberg Chair at the Council on Foreign Relations. Previously he was the Reginald Jones Senior Fellow at the Institute for International Economics.

MERIT E. JANOW is a Professor in the Practice of International Trade at Columbia University's School of International and Public Affairs. She is also Co-Director of Columbia's APEC Study Center. From 1990 to 1993, Ms. Janow was Deputy Assistant U.S. Trade Representative for Japan and China at the Office of the U.S. Trade Representative. Before joining USTR, she practiced corporate law in New York, and she lived in Tokyo for more than 10 years.

JIM KOLBE (R-Ariz.) is a senior Member of the U.S. House of Representatives Appropriations Committee. He currently chairs the Subcommittee on Treasury, Postal Service, and General Government. An ardent free trade proponent, Mr. Kolbe is known for his leadership in securing passage of the North American Free Trade Agreement and the Uruguay Round Trade Agreement.

ROBERT Z. LAWRENCE is the Albert L. Williams Professor at the John F. Kennedy School of Government, Harvard University, and the New Century Senior Fellow at the Brookings Institution.

ROBERT MATSUI (D-Calif.) is a senior Member of the U.S. House of Representatives Ways and Means Committee. He currently serves as ranking Member on the House's Trade Subcommittee and is widely recognized as a national leader on trade policy issues.

ROBERT J. MORRIS was a career officer in the U.S. Foreign Service. In 1985 he retired after 25 years service to become Senior Vice President, Washington, of the U.S. Council for International Business, representing American business in international organizations such as the OECD, ILO, and the International Chamber of Commerce.

ERNEST H. PREEG holds the William M. Scholl Chair in International Business at the Center for Strategic and International Studies. He participated in trade negotiations from the Kennedy Round in the 1960s to the Uruguay Round in the 1980s and is the author of *Traders and Diplomats, Traders in a Brave New World,* and a forthcoming volume, *From Here to Free Trade.*

TIMOTHY J. RICHARDS is a Senior Manager for International Trade and Investment with General Electric Company. From 1988 to 1996 he served in the Office of the United States Trade Representative as Director for Information Industry Trade Policy, the Trade Policy Attaché at the U.S. Mission to the European Communities, and the Deputy Assistant U.S. Trade Representative for Western Europe and the Middle East.

J. DAVID RICHARDSON is Professor of Economics and International Relations in the Maxwell School of Citizenship and Public Affairs at Syracuse University. He is a Research Associate of the National Bureau of Economic Research, Cambridge, Massachusetts, and spends two days each week as a Visiting Fellow at the Institute for International Economics.

A. E. RODRIGUEZ is Senior Manager with Price Waterhouse's litigation support group and Senior Fellow at the Center for Trade and Commercial Diplomacy, Monterey Institute of International Studies. Previously he was a Senior Economist at the U.S. Federal Trade Commission.

HOWARD ROSEN is the Minority Staff Director of the Joint Economic Committee of the U.S. Congress. Previously he was the Executive Director of the Competitiveness Policy Council and Assistant Director of the Institute for International Economics. He has also served as an Economist with the U.S. Department of Labor and the Bank of Israel in Jerusalem, Israel.

JEFFREY J. SCHOTT is a Senior Fellow at the Institute for International Economics. He is the author or editor of several books on the world trading system, including *The Uruguay Round: An Assessment* and *The World Trading System: Challenges Ahead.*

BRUCE STOKES is a Senior Fellow at the Council on Foreign Relations, where he directs the Council's trade programs. He is also a columnist on international economics for the *National Journal.* He edited the Council book *Open for Business: Creating a Transatlantic Marketplace.*

MARINA V. N. WHITMAN is Professor of Business Administration and Public Policy at the University of Michigan and is a Director of ALCOA, Browning-Ferris Industries, Chase Manhattan Banking Corporation, Procter & Gamble, and UNOCAL. Previously she served as a Vice President of the General Motors Corporation and as a member of the President's Council of Economic Advisers. She serves or has served on numerous national boards and committees dealing with economic and governmental issues.

ALAN WM. WOLFF is Managing Partner of Dewey Ballantine's Washington, D.C., office and chairs the firm's International Trade Practice Group. The firm is active in advising major corporations engaged in international trade and investment. Mr. Wolff previously served as U.S. Deputy Trade Representative and has written and spoken widely on international trade topics.

CHI ZHANG is a Research Professor at the Center for Trade and Commercial Diplomacy, Monterey Institute of International Studies. Previously he worked at the Institute for International Economics.